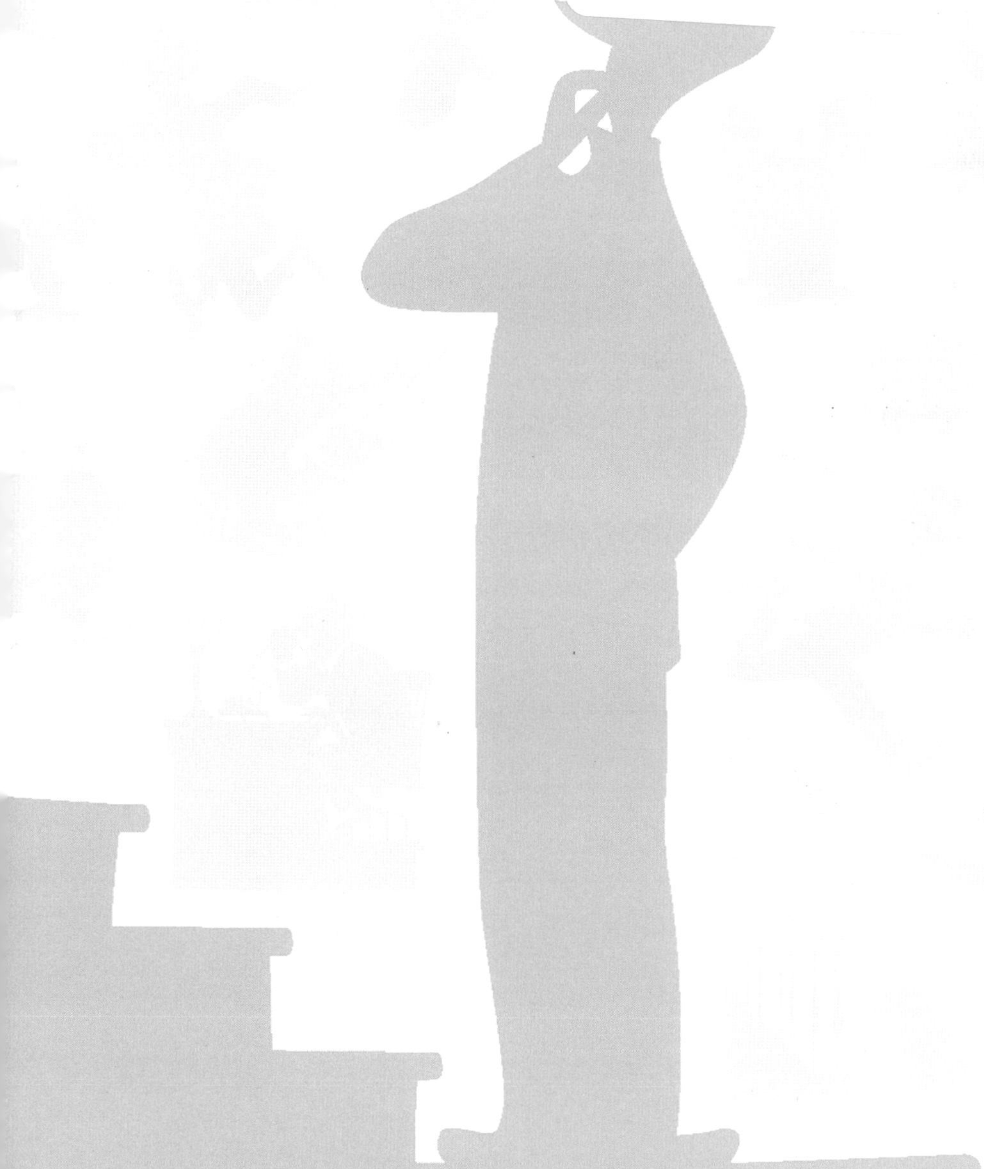

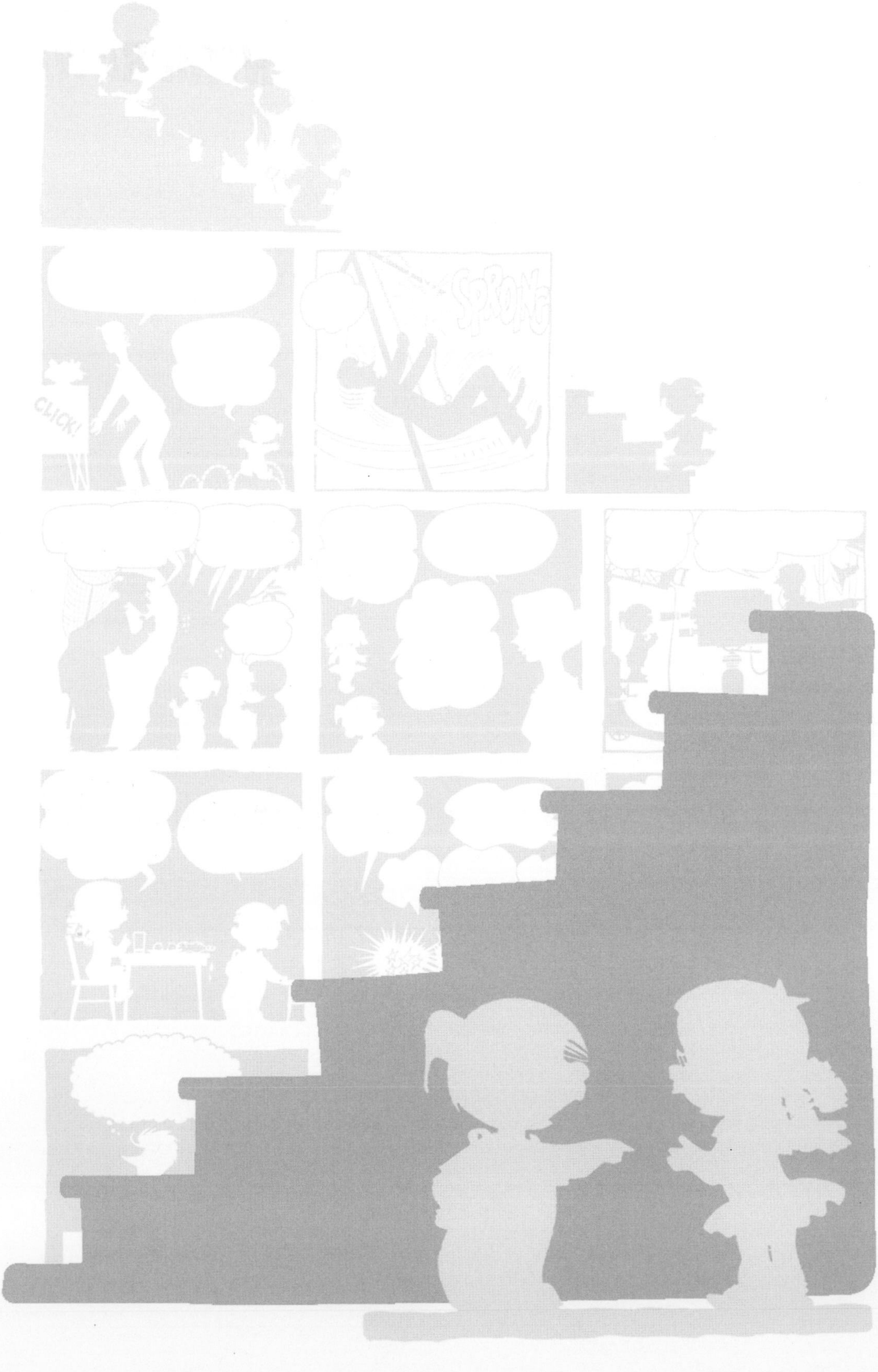
CLICK!
SPRONG

Hank Ketcham's

Dennis the Menace®

The Cult-Classic Comicbooks

by Al Wiseman
& Fred Toole

COMICS
COMICS 10¢
COMICS
10¢
Comics
10¢ Comics

PAPERCUTZ

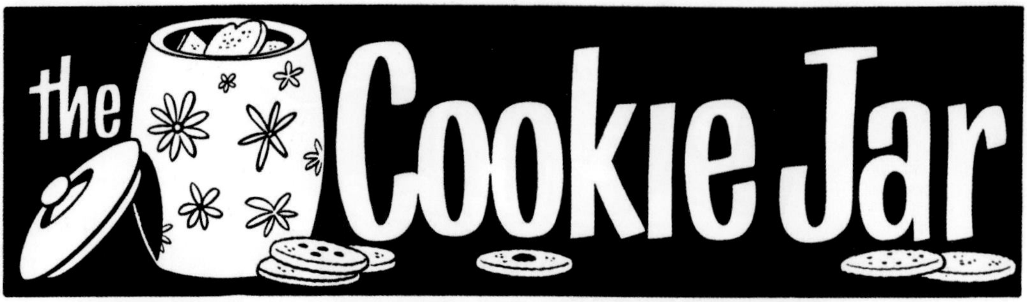
the Cookie Jar

INSIDE STORIES OF DENNIS THE MENACE

HERE IS YOUR COMIC BOOK "TEAM"

IF YOU had been passing the door of the Fred Toole Advertising Agency back in 1953, you would have heard some talk that would seem very strange in the advertising business:—

"We should have him ring the alarm bell, but he doesn't know what it is—he's just a little boy—he thinks it's the elevator button!"

"Right! He rings the alarm and the cops come to the bank, thinking it's another holdup. Then..."

Talking were advertising man Fred Toole and cartoonist Al Wiseman. Together they were dreaming up the very first "Dennis the Menace" comic book.

Both were friends of Hank Ketcham, who two years before had started "Dennis" as a newspaper cartoon feature. Hank thought "Dennis" would be a "natural" as a comic book. And both men were experienced in the cartoon field—Fred as a gag writer, Al as a cartoonist whose work had appeared in most of the top magazines.

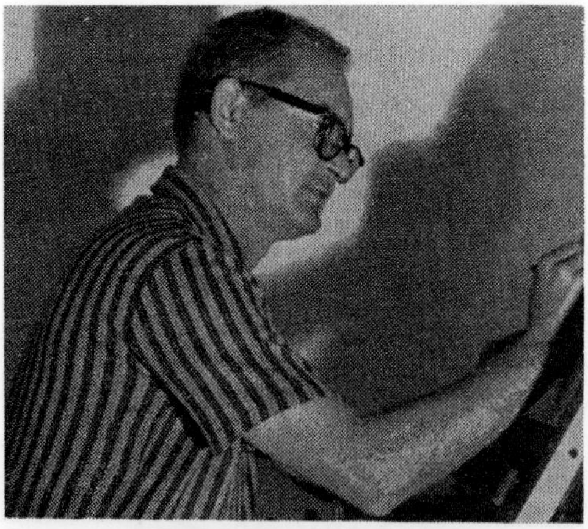

Al Wiseman, cartoonist

Their first book was okayed by Hank, and proceeded to make comic book history. While most comic books sell 50% or 60% of the copies printed, that first "Dennis" book sold almost 100%—something unheard of in comic book publishing. Fred and Al immediately quit the advertising business to work full time on the dozens of "Dennis" books they have produced since that day in 1953.

Asked how he gets all his ideas, Fred grins: "Oh, I just scratch my head until something comes out." Actually, he is always watching for situations wherever he goes, thinking: "Now, what would a mischievous little boy do here?" He has

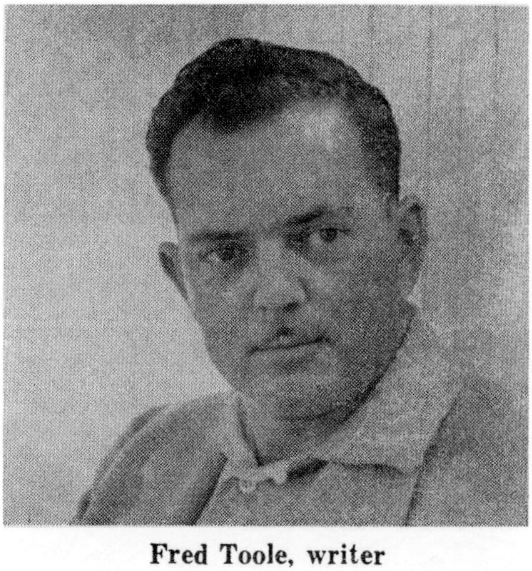

Fred Toole, writer

taken "Dennis" many places — to the circus, aboard a battleship, an Army camp — even to Hawaii.

Sometimes Al protests: "Don't make the stories so *complicated,* Fred!" But whatever Fred describes in the script, Al tries to draw faithfully. Al is one of the most painstaking cartoonists in the country. He draws every object from real life or from photographs, and whether he draws a stagecoach or an Army tank, you may be sure that it is accurate and educational.

The Dennis comics have been so successful that recently two additional artists have been added to the staff: Bruce Ariss, former TV, motion picture, and ad agency art director, and new "girl Friday" Tuesday Smith, former Milwaukee commercial artist and children's librarian.

That's your comic book team—and they hope you'll continue to enjoy their efforts for many books to come!

Above: "The Cookie Jar" from DENNIS THE MENACE #42 (May 1960)

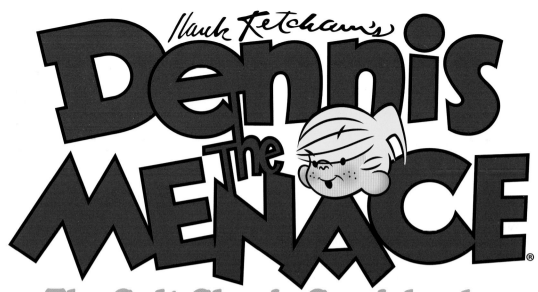

Hank Ketcham's Dennis the Menace

The Cult-Classic Comicbooks
by Al Wiseman & Fred Toole

Introduction by Fred Hembeck
Afterword by Bill Wray
Story selections and Foreword by
Jim Wiseman
Edited by Bill Alger

PAPERCUTZ
New York

AL WISEMAN

Al Wiseman has got to be one of the most prolific cartoonists in the business.

Besides drawing 'Dennis the Menace' for Hank Ketchum and the Hall Syndicate for more than 13 years, Al has sold cartoons to all magazine markets, major and minor, art directed motion pictures for the Boeing Co., drew 'Belvedere' for George Crenshaw, illustrated books for Prentice Hall, Inc., Alaska Magazine, Altair Industries, Celestial Arts, and Sullivan Behavioral Books, and coloring books for Physician's Art Service.

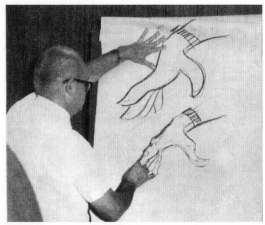

Above: From CARTOONEWS #1, April 1975

This book is dedicated to these members of Al Wiseman's wonderful family who have always been patient with my endless barrage of questions about Al's life and career: Vadis Davis, Jan Wiseman Pisciotta, Merrily Wiseman Russo and Sue Dewer. Thanks also to Fred Toole's widow Molly, who couldn't have been kinder when I spoke with her on the phone many years ago.

Special Thanks to Jim & Teresa Wiseman for all their help in putting this book together (including supplying rare Wiseman family photos and also scanning piles and piles of DENNIS comics.)

-Bill Alger, Editor

Dan Berlin
Dani Breckenridge – Editorial Interns
Bill Alger – Design/Production
Jeff Whitman – Production Coordinator
Bethany Bryan – Associate Editor
Jim Salicrup – Editor-in-Chief

ISBN: 978-1-62991-281-3

Papercutz books may be purchased for business or promotional use. For information on bulk purchases please contact Macmillan Corporate and Premium Sales Department at (800) 221-7945 x5442.

Printed in China through Four Colour Printing Group
Shenzhen Caimei Printing Co., Ltd.
Caimei Printing Building, Guangyayuan, Bantian, Longgang
Shenzhen 518 129
China

Distributed by Macmillan

First Printing

TABLE OF CONTENTS

FOREWORD

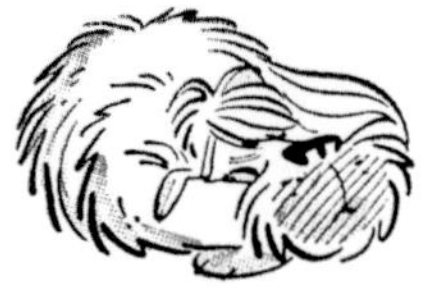

by Jim Wiseman

Asking me to choose my favorite stories from all the DENNIS THE MENACE comicbooks that my dad drew was a task that created a lot of old memories. My first reaction was "all of them" for each generated a special memory - some memories surrounding what was going on during the time he drew some of those stories, some memories were revived by reading them all again after so many years. Al managed to include a lot of personality into those drawings - slipping in the names of friends and acquaintances, borrowing the names of local businesses and incorporating them into his drawings. And not to mention that Ruff was fashioned after our beloved family dog Ruff.

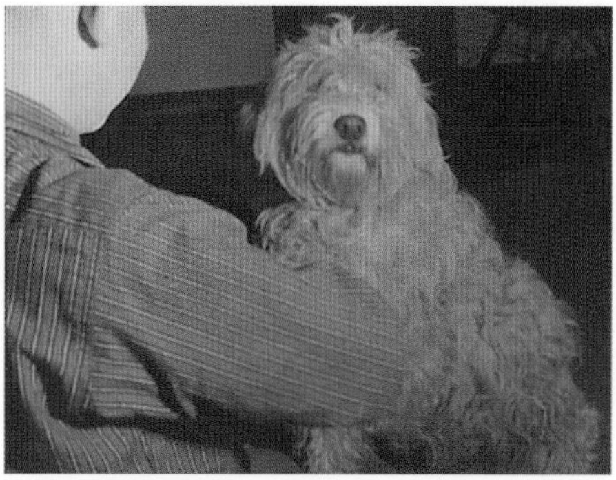

Above: Jim with the Wiseman family dog, Ruff.

Our family was, of course, close to Fred and Mollie Toole, real-life Mr. and Mrs. Wilson, Fred authoring most of the comicbook stories. In looking at these stories there are some I've chosen for the storyline, some of I've chosen just because I like them, and some because of my dad's artwork. The *Dennis The Menace Goes to Mexico* has particular sentimental value as I went with my dad to Mexico while he did the research - not to mention that was my wife's favorite comicbook as a child.

I am continually amazed when I look at my dad's technique and detail - he was the master at using silhouette as a strong technique of conveying a moment, his text was clean and precise and managed to really make you hear a sound or a yell or a bellow just by seeing the way he positioned the word. His attention to detail was always incredible to see - particularly the original ink work. One only has to look at the detail in the *Dennis Goes to Mexico* book to appreciate his line work. We are lucky to have the original mask that was portrayed in one story.

I think it was difficult for my dad, as it would be for any true artist, to be a ghost. His work and creativity is, after all these years, still recognizable while millions never knew that he was the one responsible for the artwork of those great comicbooks.

I hope you enjoy these as much as I enjoyed revisiting them myself.

-Jim Wiseman

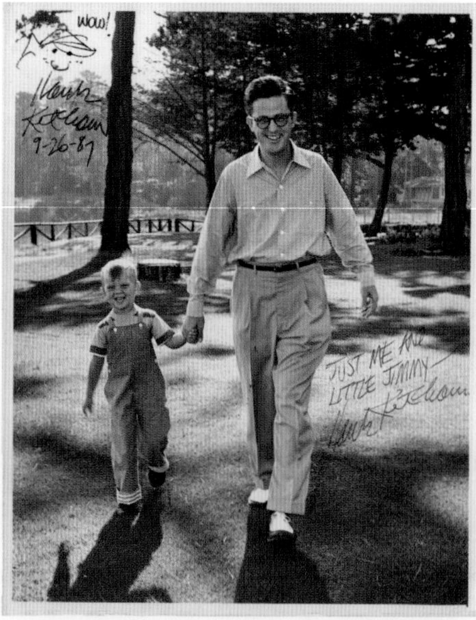
WOW!
9-26-87
JUST ME AND LITTLE JIMMY

Above: Young Jim Wiseman (circa 1953) looked so much like the character Dennis, that Jim portrayed him during a promotional photo shoot with Dennis creator Hank Ketcham.

INTRODUCTION

"Hembeck on Wiseman" by Fred Hembeck

What follows is a slightly edited piece I wrote on the Internet for my then-new blog, *Fred Sez*, back on December 21st, 2003. One of the fun things about having a blog is being able to write about anything that you want, and one thing I had always wanted to write about was my absolute love and devotion for the work of Fred Toole and Al Wiseman on the classic DENNIS THE MENACE comicbooks. While using the holiday season as a springboard, it's really year-round praise I'm affording the pair, and I'm delighted that the folks at Papercutz asked permission to include it within the pages of this outstanding, long-overdue volume! So, cue up Bing Crosby crooning "White Christmas" and read on, friends....

Generally, this is the time of year when we all once again hear the familiar tale of the Three Wise Men. Well, no disrespect meant, but you won't be hearing their story from me here today. Instead, as part of my own modest celebration of the season, I'd like to instead share a little with you about another, unfairly neglected wise man—namely, master cartoonist, Al Wiseman!

You've all heard of DENNIS THE MENACE, right? When Hank Ketcham's syndicated gag panel debuted in the nation's newspapers back in 1951, it was the very definition of an overnight success story. The mischievous— and perennial— five-year-old's immense popularity soon demanded that a comicbook series be developed, so to produce the words and pictures for this new enterprise, Ketcham enlisted the aid of writer Fred Toole and artist Al Wiseman, luring both old friends away from lucrative jobs in the advertising field. When, as legend has it (as well as the text feature found on the inside back cover of the May, 1960 issue of DENNIS THE MENACE—number 42—that's my primary source for this information), at a time when top titles sold somewhere between 50 and 60 percent of their total copies printed, the very first DENNIS comic in 1953 sold out almost its entire print run! Yup, you read that right—an almost astonishing 100 percent sell-through! No wonder Fred and Al left their jobs at the agency soon after the sales figures came in, and devoted most of the following decade towards making the regular DENNIS THE MENACE title—and it's various spin-offs—among the very best comicbooks ever produced, bar none!

That's me talking now, not a paraphrase of the rosy-colored picture painted by that undoubtedly biased promo page from 1960. I've long felt Toole and Wiseman's long tenure on the popular title measures up to just about anything else produced in the comicbook field's first quarter century. But while John Stanley and Irving Tripp's LITTLE LULU has long had a vocal core of influential admirers—and I wholeheartedly count myself in that thriving number, except for maybe the "influential" part—and the reputation of another of my all-time favorites, Bob Bolling's LITTLE ARCHIE, is gaining momentum with critics every day—the equally wonderful, but subtlety different, work of the DENNIS THE MENACE team continues to be mostly overlooked. Why is this?

Well, perhaps in the case of LULU, I'd venture it has something to do with the long, long ago cessation of the gag panel produced by creator Marge Henderson Buell, and as that inexorably faded from the culture's collective memory, the superior—and more accessible—comicbook stuck in the public's mind in its stead. As for LITTLE ARCHIE —a concept that, ironically, owes it's very existence to DENNIS's initial massive success —I believe it was Bolling's uniquely idiosyncratic take on the almost generic Archie cast of characters that has made his fine work worthy of remembering some six decades after the fact.

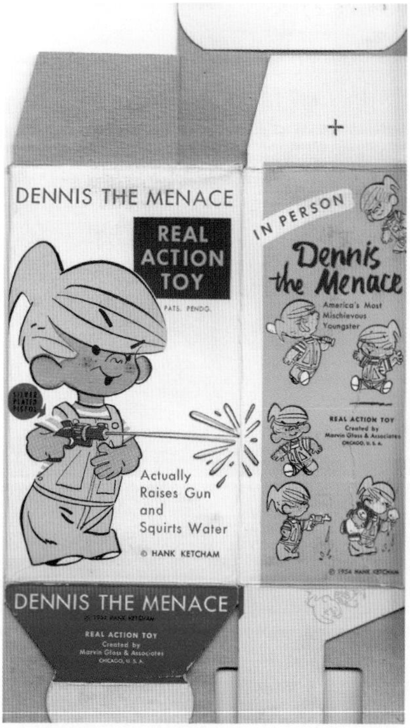
DENNIS THE MENACE
REAL ACTION TOY
Actually Raises Gun and Squirts Water
© HANK KETCHAM
IN PERSON
Dennis the Menace
America's Most Mischievous Youngster
REAL ACTION TOY
DENNIS THE MENACE
REAL ACTION TOY

But Toole and Wiseman's DENNIS? Unlike the other two great kid strips mentioned above, the core character's creator didn't quietly fade into the background as the years wore on. In fact, if anything, Hank Ketcham seemed to gleefully court the celebrity his pint-sized pest bestowed upon him, as he skillfully guided his brainchild through various media configurations— television, cartoons, live-action films, books, all sorts of merchandise—while still maintaining a noteworthy presence in the comics pages of an impressive number of the nation's newspapers. To the public, then, Hank Ketcham IS DENNIS THE MENACE—even now, several decades after his death. And it's my additional theory that, with such a glut of DENNIS product spewing out over the past six decades, the comics cognoscenti have deemed any property that successful— especially one dealing with kids and clearly aimed at the middle class—to be unworthy of their elite attention, and have given scant consideration to the comics, now long gone, wrongfully assuming them to be just another small piece of a past marketing phenomenon. But they'd be wrong, because these really are brilliantly produced comics...

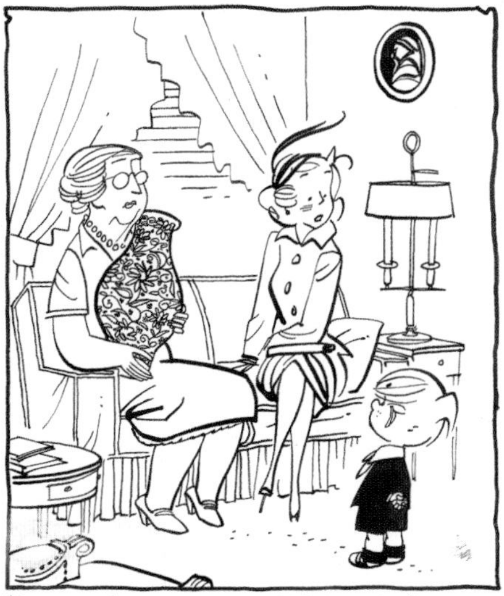

"BECAUSE SHE'S AFRAID YOU MIGHT BREAK IT, DEAR."

I trust you're all familiar with the basic premise— a five-year-old's innocent yet non-stop rambunctious behavior makes life for his harried parents one never-ending bout of embarrassment, alternating with exhaustion. Works beautifully for a single panel gag, but just try hanging story after story on that concept and making it work. Well, Toole and Wiseman did—and repeatedly. As with all good comics, the exemplary art—which we'll get to later—had tremendously strong underpinnings provided by Fred Toole's farcical yet still realistic scripts. While the writing started out in a rather broad manner in the earliest issues, as time went on, it quickly came to adhere to a far more recognizable reality than any other found contemporaneously in the field. Unlike both *Tubby* and *Little Archie*, there were no friendly Martians visiting Dennis and his young pals. Everything that happened in a Dennis story could actually happen to the reader. Oh, sure, any number of unlikely coincidences would have to occur to bring certain more outlandish tales to fruition in a real-life setting, but Toole made certain that Dennis's exploits were never completely out of the realm of possibility!

And while the primary focus was always on the tiny tornado, parents Henry and Alice Mitchell were never simply portrayed as cardboard foils for the stars lovable antics. Father Henry in particular was oft-times effectively used as a top-notch straight man for the little tyke, finding himself in jams that were every bit as laugh-provoking as anything found throughout the entire run of the series! And Henry, try as he might, found himself constantly exasperated by his progeny's well-intentioned—but usually disastrous—escapades. He was always justthisclose to losing his temper big time—and more than once, folks, he actually did! Reading these tales as a child, I saw Dennis's dad as a purely comic presence—now, after 25 years with my girl Julie, I see him as one of the great sympathetic figures in the history of comics. That poor, poor man—what he had to endure...

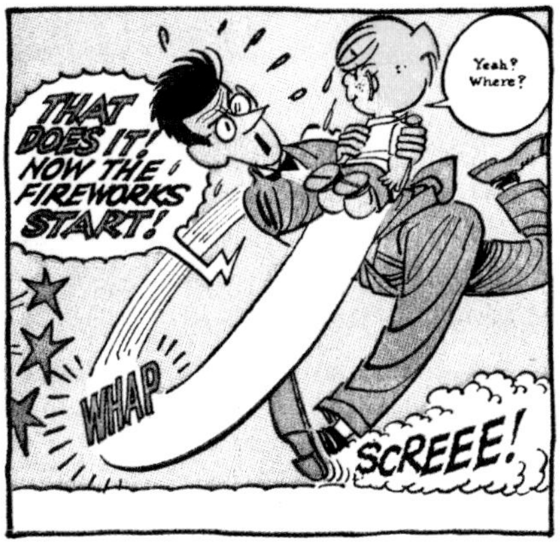
THAT DOES IT! NOW THE FIREWORKS START!
Yeah? Where?
WHAP
SCREEE!

All this and more came through in Toole's witty and inventive scripting. He could take the smallest, the slightest, the most incredibly mundane of concepts to hang a plot on, and still make it sing. I'll give you an example from one of the Christmas specials that I'm planning to eventually get around to discussing (Yay! We're almost there!). Coming up with fresh ideas, year after year, to fill up nearly a hundred pages with tales revolving around a single theme couldn't have been easy, but this underrated scribe somehow managed. By 1964, you'd have thought all possible angles would've been exhausted, but not if you read a nine-page gem entitled "Window Wonderland"...

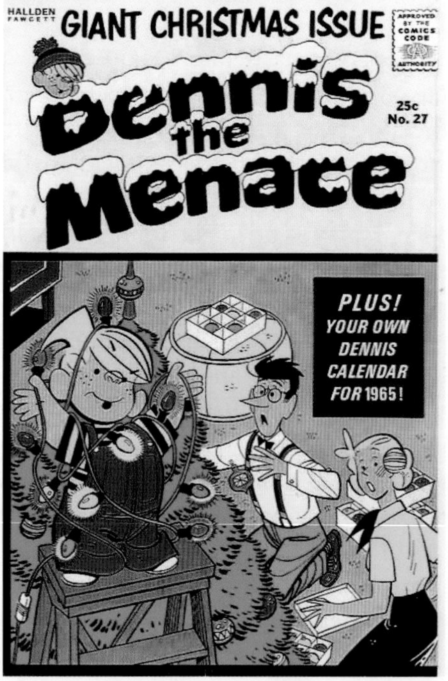
HALLDEN FAWCETT
GIANT CHRISTMAS ISSUE
APPROVED BY THE COMICS CODE AUTHORITY
Dennis the Menace
25c No. 27
PLUS! YOUR OWN DENNIS CALENDAR FOR 1965!

Henry comes home from the office with a specially drawn design done for him by an associate, a design that spells out the word "Noel" in fancy Olde English-like lettering. Alice has to clear out, but Dennis eagerly jumps in to help his dad as Henry carefully endeavors to cut out each letter in a different colored piece of bright cellophane, with the plan thereafter being to adhere each letter to the window with black tape (in reverse), finally spraying some artificial snow around it as a finishing touch. Now, this sounds incredibly dry, but the amazing thing is, the story not only works as a sufficiently detailed set of step-by-step how-to instructions (aided, of course, by Wiseman's expertly drawn pictures), but he also manages to wring more than a modicum of truth-based humor out of that simple scenario...

After all, what parent at one time or another hasn't sat down with their small child, intent on doing a mildly complicated craft project together, only to soon regret the notion when it becomes crystal clear that their potential helper hasn't nearly the patience necessary to complete the deal, instead continuously getting recklessly ahead of things, much to the everlasting chagrin of the adult? Well, that's this story in a nutshell, but it's the manner in which Toole fills his pages with gag after gag that makes such a slight premise so richly entertaining.

Of course, aided by anything less than stellar art, these scripts would lose a fair amount of their impact, but with Al Wiseman as his creative partner, Fred Toole most assuredly didn't have to worry about that. Their combined talents caught the essence of the "modern" fifties far better than any other series published during that transitional era, and compared favorably with the very best of the family-oriented sitcoms broadcast during television's first decades. The meticulously precise line work of Wiseman was responsible for a large portion of this success. While naturally attempting to match Ketcham's stylistic nuances, as the years wore on, more and more of Wiseman's individuality crept through. Comparing a story from 1953 to one drawn a decade later easily proves this point—the art is still identifiable as the work of the same person, but one whose natural inclination towards a more controlled line has gradually eased out the more fluid strokes associated with the strip's originator.

This is by no means a bad thing, mind you, because, despite a more exacting style, Wiseman always manages to imbue his characters with a zestful animation that gracefully sells each and every one of Toole's cleverly conceived comedic conceits. And as much as he may have excelled at bringing the central cast to life on the page, his unparalleled ability to create a thoroughly believable environment for them to frantically frolic in should in no way be overlooked. According to the aforementioned 1960 promo page, Wiseman drew everything from life (or failing that, a really good reference photograph). Every last detail in a DENNIS story looked exactly right, and I daresay, no one in the world of post-Code comics drew incidental background material with the convincing authority Wiseman did. Quite a few DENNIS stories took place inside their typically furnished suburban home, and every item —kitchen appliances, couches, chairs, even TV sets—accurately reflected those currently being used in actual homes all across the land.

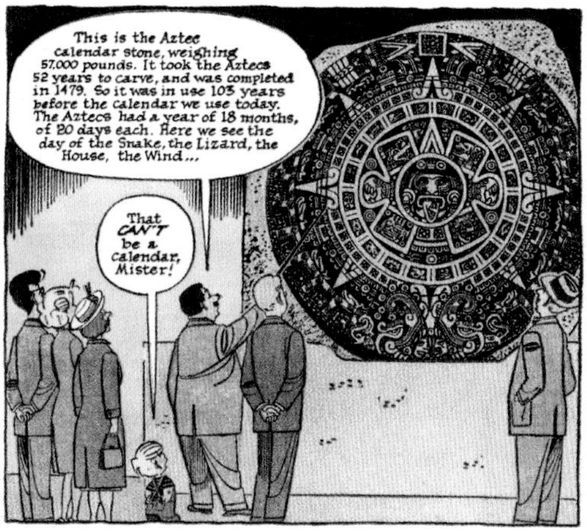
This is the Aztec calendar stone, weighing 57,000 pounds. It took the Aztecs 52 years to carve, and was completed in 1479. So it was in use 103 years before the calendar we use today. The Aztecs had a year of 18 months, of 20 days each. Here we see the day of the Snake, the Lizard, the House, the Wind...
That CAN'T be a calendar, Mister!

And when Wiseman was called upon to illustrate the Mitchell clans' periodic vacation treks—to Mexico, Washington D.C., Hollywood, and Hawaii—he outdid even himself and produced some of the most authentically gorgeous art ever—yes, you read that right! I said "ever"—to find its way into a "lowly" comicbook. For these giant specials alone, Toole and Wiseman should be enshrined in some Funnybook Hall of Fame, as their stories wonderfully realized sense of place is unequaled in comics history.

Which brings us to these Christmas specials. Each one a treasure, they all featured a loosely connected series of sequentially arranged short stories, always culminating with the final episode focusing on Dennis enthusiastically awakening early—usually, very early—on Christmas morning. Despite the necessarily formulaic nature of this arrangement, Toole and Wiseman never repeat themselves. Certainly, there are variations on favorite themes—shopping, too many Santas, tree decorating, hiding gifts—but somehow, a fresh angle is always unearthed by this talented pair to make each and every Christmas special, well, special!

And in keeping with the realistic slant favored by the creators, Santa, despite making numerous appearances over the years, is never even hinted at as being genuine —not even in that corny, "end of story, wink-wink, nudge-nudge, is he or isn't he really the one" manner so familiar to anybody who's ever seen a very special Christmas episode of some generic sitcom over the years. Nope, Santa is always either Dad, a relative, a store employee, a rich fellow with a beard, Mr. Wilson, or maybe even a cop! This is not to say any of the adults ever come right out and dash the dreams of small children all across the world by stating definitively that there is indeed no Santa (and to any small children reading this right now—what are the odds?—please understand, I'm not saying that either. Honest!), but clearly, the knowledge that ol' St. Nick has a passel of red-suited stand-ins was understood by all save the youngest members of the cast. That, in addition to the occasional nod towards the generally avoided (at least, in comics) religious aspect of this widely celebrated holiday, separated the DENNIS Christmas specials from the rest of the pack. (And you might even find our star going off to the little boys room from time to time, another function of day-to-day existence generally avoided by, oh, I'd say a good 99.99 percent of the remainder of the comics on the stands, if not more...)

For years and years, I'd contentedly read and reread these delightful collections during the waning weeks of December, with the likes of the great Nat King Cole crooning "The Christmas Song," blissfully providing appropriate background music. But unlike the similarly treasured LITTLE LULU HALLOWEEN GIANTS I enthused about in a previous blog post, I did not actually own any of the DENNIS holiday specials while I was growing up. Sure, I had plenty of the other DENNIS specials released during the early sixties in my possession—the aforementioned vacation issues, whole books co-starring Joey, Margaret, Ruff, and Mr. Wilson, several based on the Jay North *Dennis the Menace* television series—but the only Christmas special I ever owned back in the sixties was one drawn by Owen Fitzgerald.

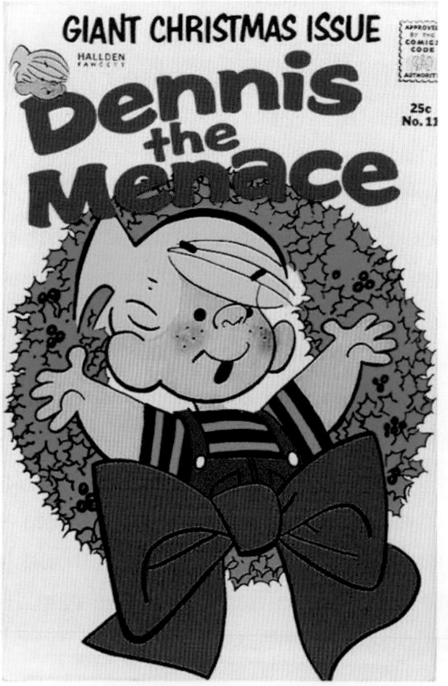
GIANT CHRISTMAS ISSUE
HALLDEN
Dennis the Menace

Time for a digression, within a digression. My earliest copies of DENNIS THE MENACE were supplied in the legendary gratis box of kiddie comics passed on to my dad by a coworker, undoubtedly the most significant offhand gift bestowed upon me in my entire misbegotten life, a story I've told time and again, even once in illustrated form. Several issues containing Wiseman art were included—such as the winter-themed number 41—and once I soon after started buying my own comics, I made sure to include every available DENNIS publication in amongst my, ahem, "more mature" super-hero-type purchases. But with so many triple-sized editions being released as the success of the TV show apparently upped the demand for DENNIS product to an all-time high, something had to give, and that something was, sadly, Al Wiseman's exclusive and total reign over the DENNIS comics. Happily, he continued to handle the majority of the evermore frequently issued giants, but suddenly, the regular DENNIS title was being drawn by— and pardon me for saying this—a terrible artist! Arrgh!

Ranking right up there—or should I say, down there? —with Ross Andru taking over for Carmine Infantino on THE FLASH and John Romita stepping in for Steve Ditko on AMAZING SPIDER-MAN, I was similarly aghast at this radically new artistic approach. Whereas Wiseman was precise and controlled, this new guy's drawings seemed sloppy and dashed off with little thought as to the very quality of the line work. It was only the still-enjoyable writing of Toole, as well an ingrained fondness for the characters, that kept me coming back. I somehow missed the handful of Wiseman CHRISTMAS GIANTS issued during the mid-sixties, winding up with only a single one drawn by this scourge with a fast and loose brush. At the time, it was like a getting a piece of coal in my stocking...

For years and years, I had absolutely no idea

who the perpetrator was who had come in and all but ruined DENNIS for me. It wasn't until I read something somewhere by the estimable Mark Evanier, championing the work of a long-time cartoonist named Owen Fitzgerald, including the DENNIS assignment on a long, impressive list of accomplishments, that I suddenly came to realize just whose work I'd vilified in the remote recesses of my mind for all those years. Subsequently, getting an opportunity to more closely examine a lot of the work he did during the fifties for other publishers, particularly on DC titles such as BOB HOPE and other girlie-centric titles, I finally began to appreciate his not-insubstantial talents. Just as I eventually came around to Romita on Spidey, and Andru on most everything else, I came to realize I'd judged Fitzgerald unfairly. He was not a terrible artist—anything but. But was he the ideal choice to fill in and provide some breathing room for Wiseman? I still don't think so, as their stylistic approaches were just too far apart to be anything but jarring when seen in quick succession. But I did form a new appreciation for his Alice Mitchell —rorwff!...

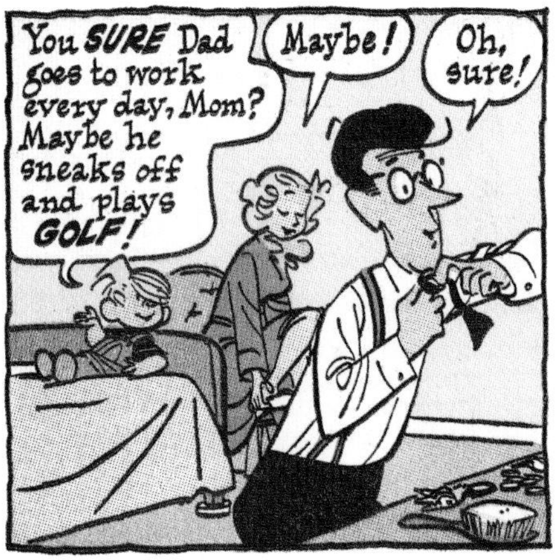
You SURE Dad goes to work every day, Mom? Maybe he sneaks off and plays GOLF!
Maybe!
Oh, sure!

It was while perusing the colorful-yet-slowly-decaying wares found in the dealer's room at a mid-seventies New York City Comicon that I accidentally stumbled across these five holiday specials. In fact, there was also a handful of other GIANT editions I'd never seen before—including several generic vacation issues that predated the wildly successful single destination tomes of later years—as well as a healthy run of the standard sized DENNIS title too. And they were all reasonably priced! Well, never one to spend overmuch for back issues, I was reluctant to commit all my available cash to the whole kit and caboodle, ultimately choosing instead to buy just the dozen or so GIANTs that I'd never encountered before, leaving the rest in their sales boxes. It's a decision that, yes, has haunted me for many years—but hey, I was just out of college, okay, and didn't have the ready finances, dig? Still, I shoulda grabbed 'em all—y'see, reading my brand-new purchases renewed my then-latent enthusiasm for the work of Toole and Wiseman, and I wound up spending the next several years relentlessly poring over tiny ads in CBG (*The Comics Buyer's Guide*), searching out as many of the early DENNIS issues as I could find at fairly cheap prices (including number 30 from 1958, featuring a story where Dennis, in a manner of speaking, meets his maker(s)). I never did quite complete my collection, but I probably wound up with at least two-thirds of the Wiseman illustrated issues (and there's at least one other Christmas book drawn by Al that I don't own, though my good friend and fellow Wiseman fan, Terry Austin, once lent me his copy to read, which brightened that particular holiday season immensely, believe you me!...)

The funny thing is, I was deep into my twenties when I picked up these books, already hooked up with my dear wife-to-be Lynn, and yet I'm as fond of these five publications as I am of anything I read at the impressionable age of eight. Now, that either says a lot about the power of the material contained therein—or about my blatantly stunted maturity?! Hey, maybe it's a little of both, y'know? But as I casually indicated above, I'm hardly alone in my appreciation of the DENNIS THE MENACE comics team. Besides Terry, I know for

a fact such top-notch artists and creators as Bret Blevins, Bill Alger, Walt Simonson, Jim Shooter, Bill Wray, and the Hernandez Brothers hold this work in the highest of esteem as well. And, hey, let's add my old pal Rocco Nigro to that list while we're at it, too...
I believe the only thing that's keeping this series from getting the sort of respect it so richly deserves is a vocal and unrelenting champion. I'm not saying I'm that person, but if this heartfelt tribute does anything to nudge things in that direction, I'd be extremely pleased. Too often, aficionados, overly steeped in the fantasy aspect of comics, indiscriminately turn their noses up at material aimed at a younger audience as being essentially worthless, but I'd happily match the Toole/Wiseman material up against the more famous adventure-oriented titles of the period, and save for a few isolated stories here and there, feel confident DENNIS would triumph if handed to a non-biased third party to examine. Because, friends, the books really were that good!...

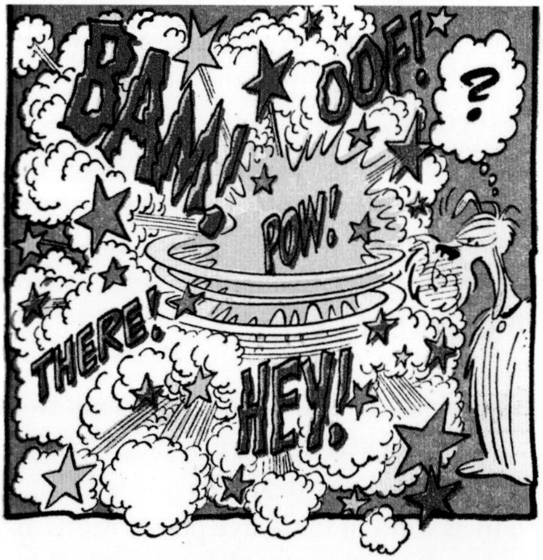
BAM!
OOF!
?
POW!
THERE!
HEY!

A few words about the lettering. It's perhaps the most expressive ever seen in a comicbook. Period. Al Wiseman proved to be as superb a calligrapher as he was a cartoonist. The imaginative use of upper case, lower case, and brightly colored display lettering, all within the context of a character's single word balloon, allows for us to "hear" the dialog far more effectively than is possible when merely utilizing a standard approach. The comedy is only intensified when one gets a truer sense of a gags proper line-reading, and the exasperation that comes through when poor put-upon Henry's words blurt out in large, red letters—contained in a suitably jagged word balloon—can be palpable, and thus, truly hilarious. To paraphrase my soul-mate on "The Simpsons," best lettering ever...

A final note. One of the thrills of putting yourself out on the Internet is that you just don't know from day to day who might turn up. Well, several days ago, while periodically checking for any fresh entries in my Guest Book, I was surprised—and extremely excited—to see that, of all people, the late Al Wiseman's son, Jim, had checked in! He had a few gracious words to say about "Petey," my meager—yet personally extremely satisfying—attempt to blend Lee and Ditko's pre-Spider-Man Peter Parker with the vastly attractive style employed by his father on the DENNIS comics. As I informed him in a return note—in addition to thanking him for his good wishes—I had just the day before dug out his dad's Christmas classics with the full intention of doing this particular write-up. So, I went on, wait just a bit —I'll tell you exactly what your father's art meant to me over on my web-site! And I'm gonna let everybody else know, too! Well, here it is, Jim. I think by now you can clearly gather that your dad's work meant a whole heckuva lot to me, and I hope I've done him a small measure of justice in my muddled attempts to explain his lasting appeal to those out there who weren't lucky enough to grow up like I did, reading comics featuring his expressive drawings, rendered with that impeccable steady line of his!

So, to end things with the words Dennis repeated on the last page of several of these Christmas extravaganzas (mirroring a particularly famous Ketcham cartoon) as he sits among a massive pile of presents, now bereft of their hastily torn off gift-wrapping:

"Is this ALL?"

Yup! At least for now...
Merry Christmas everyone!

Fred Hembeck *has been drawing his quirky, corny, and occasionally incisive cartoons for many years now, nearly as long as he's been reading the comicbooks that inspired him to do so in the first place! Working for many, many publishers over the past few decades, 2015 saw the release of HOUSE OF HEM, a collection of some of his most notable past material produced for Marvel Comics. His Wiseman inspired series, "Petey: The Adventures of Peter Parker LOOOONG Before He Became Spider-Man" sadly did not make the cut, but hey, that's what a Volume Two is for, right?...*

http://www.hembeck.com/FredSez/FredSezDecember2003.htm

Access to the original piece in the link above, should you want to compare...

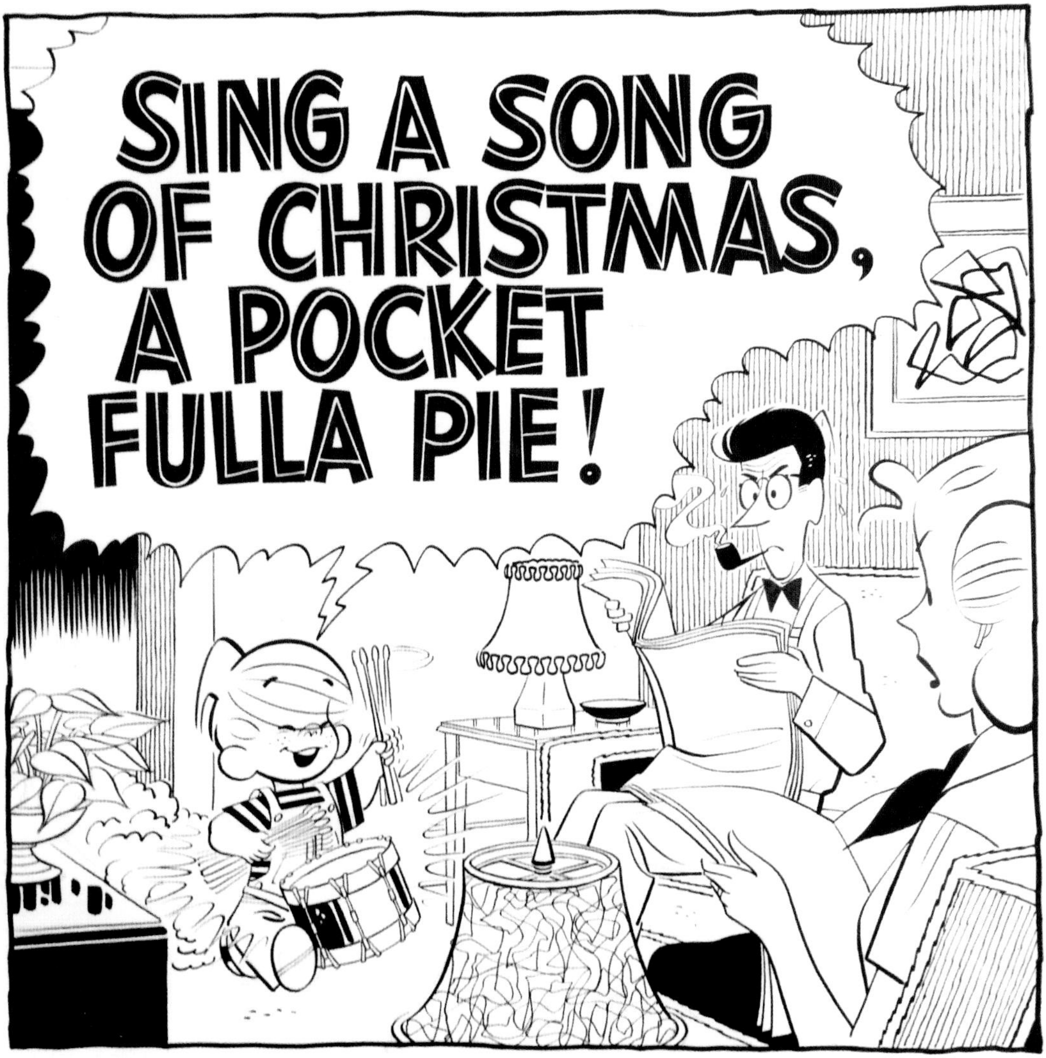
SING A SONG OF CHRISTMAS, A POCKET FULLA PIE!

Hank Ketcham's Dennis the Menace

WHO'S WHO

A brief description of Dennis's family & friends

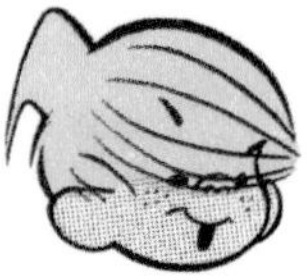

Dennis Mitchell

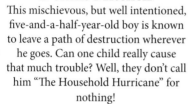

This mischievous, but well intentioned, five-and-a-half-year-old boy is known to leave a path of destruction wherever he goes. Can one child really cause that much trouble? Well, they don't call him "The Household Hurricane" for nothing!

Henry Mitchell

Dennis's long suffering dad is constantly engaged in a valiant inner struggle to avoid losing his temper with his misbehaving son. What are the chances that Henry will finally succeed and find true peace of mind? Well, with Dennis around, not very good.

Alice Mitchell

Dennis' mom is a calming figure in the Mitchell family. She often serves as an informal referee to sooth tensions between Dennis and his dad. But sometimes, even kindly Alice can't hide her frustration with Dennis's unruly behavior.

Ruff Mitchell

What can you say about Dennis's lovable pal Ruff? Well, he's a big, rambunctious, faithful Airedale mix. And just might be the best darn dog in the whole wide world!

Mr. Wilson (George Everett Wilson Sr.)

Would George Wilson really enjoy life so much more if he didn't have to deal with Dennis, that annoying kid next-door? That's what he'd have everyone believe. But deep down inside, Mr. Wilson truly enjoys the daily visits from Dennis, even if it does drive him a bit batty.

Margaret Wade

Easily identified by her red hair (except in her first story, where it was blonde) and freckles, Margaret gives off an air of superior self-important bossiness. Studious and ambitious, she's the exact opposite of Dennis, yet she finds herself attracted to him. Dennis, meanwhile usually just wants to get far, far away from her.

Joey McDonald

He's a bit shy and not-too-bright, but good-natured Joey is unfailingly loyal to his older mentor, Dennis. As time goes on, Joey becomes Dennis's constant sidekick and best friend.

Gina Gillotti

Strong-willed and independent, Italian-American Gina is also a whole lot of fun to hang out with. Dennis prefers her to Margaret, and really, who wouldn't?

Tommy Anderson

Dennis' best bud at school can be duly counted on to join Dennis on his various misadventures. "What's Tommy's personality?" you might ask. Well... he doesn't really have one. Tommy's pretty much just a generic friend who gives Dennis someone to talk to during a story. But sometimes, just being someone's friend is enough.

Punky Davis

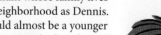

Punky is an infant whose family lives in the same neighborhood as Dennis. In fact, he could almost be a younger version of Dennis. Similar hair, but red. Similar adventures, but more fantastical. Unlike Dennis, however, Punky is never aware of the consequenses of his actions because he only speaks "baby talk."

THE INSIDE STORY
HEY, MOM! GUESS WHAT!
I KNOW what!
GUESS WHAT, DAD!
I KNOW what!
Yeah? What?
PICK UP THOSE COMIC BOOKS!

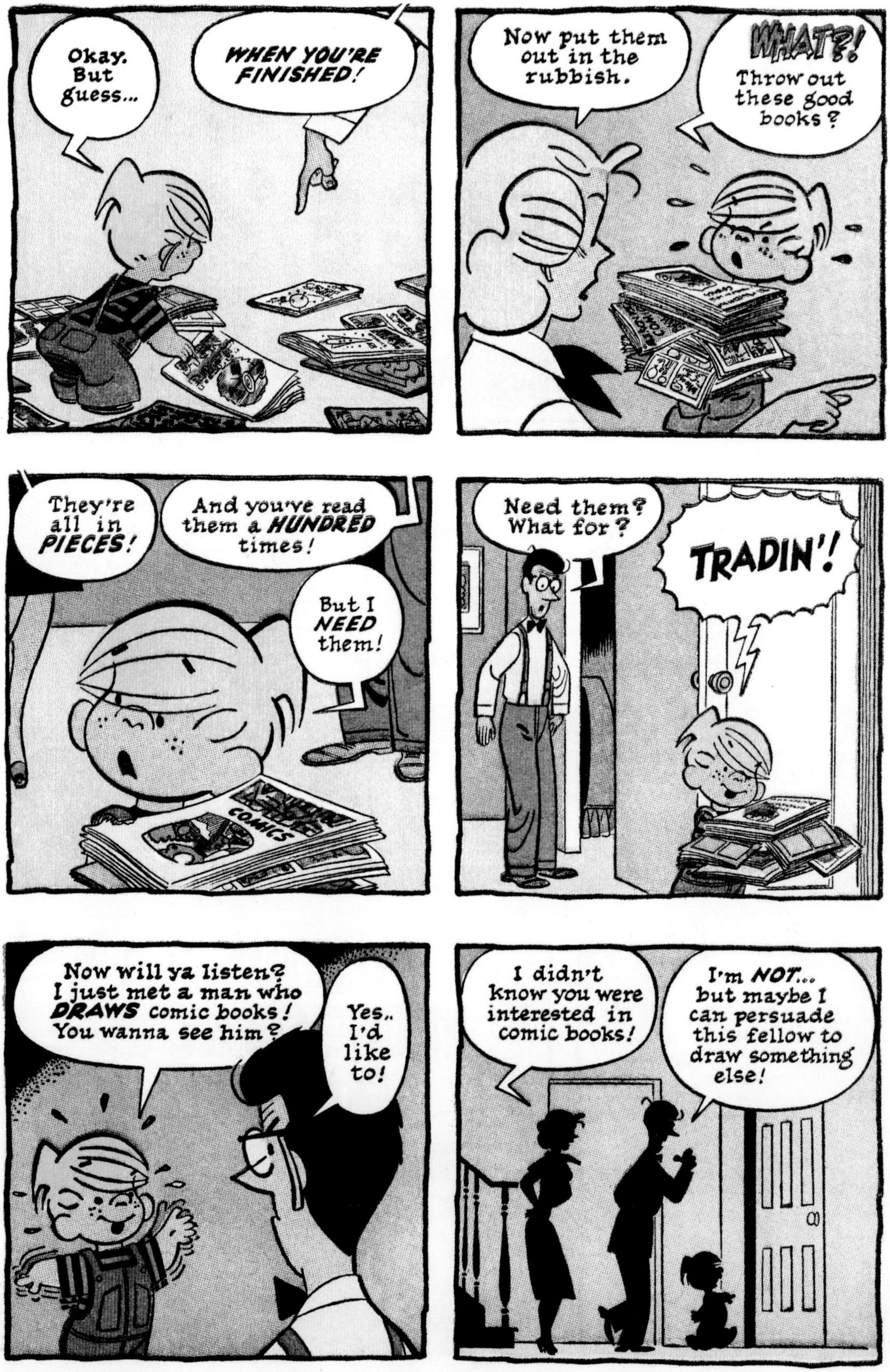
Okay. But guess...
WHEN YOU'RE FINISHED!
Now put them out in the rubbish.
WHAT?!
Throw out these good books?
They're all in PIECES!
And you've read them a HUNDRED times!
But I NEED them!
COMICS
Need them? What for?
TRADIN'!
Now will ya listen? I just met a man who DRAWS comic books! You wanna see him?
Yes.. I'd like to!
I didn't know you were interested in comic books!
I'm NOT... but maybe I can persuade this fellow to draw something else!

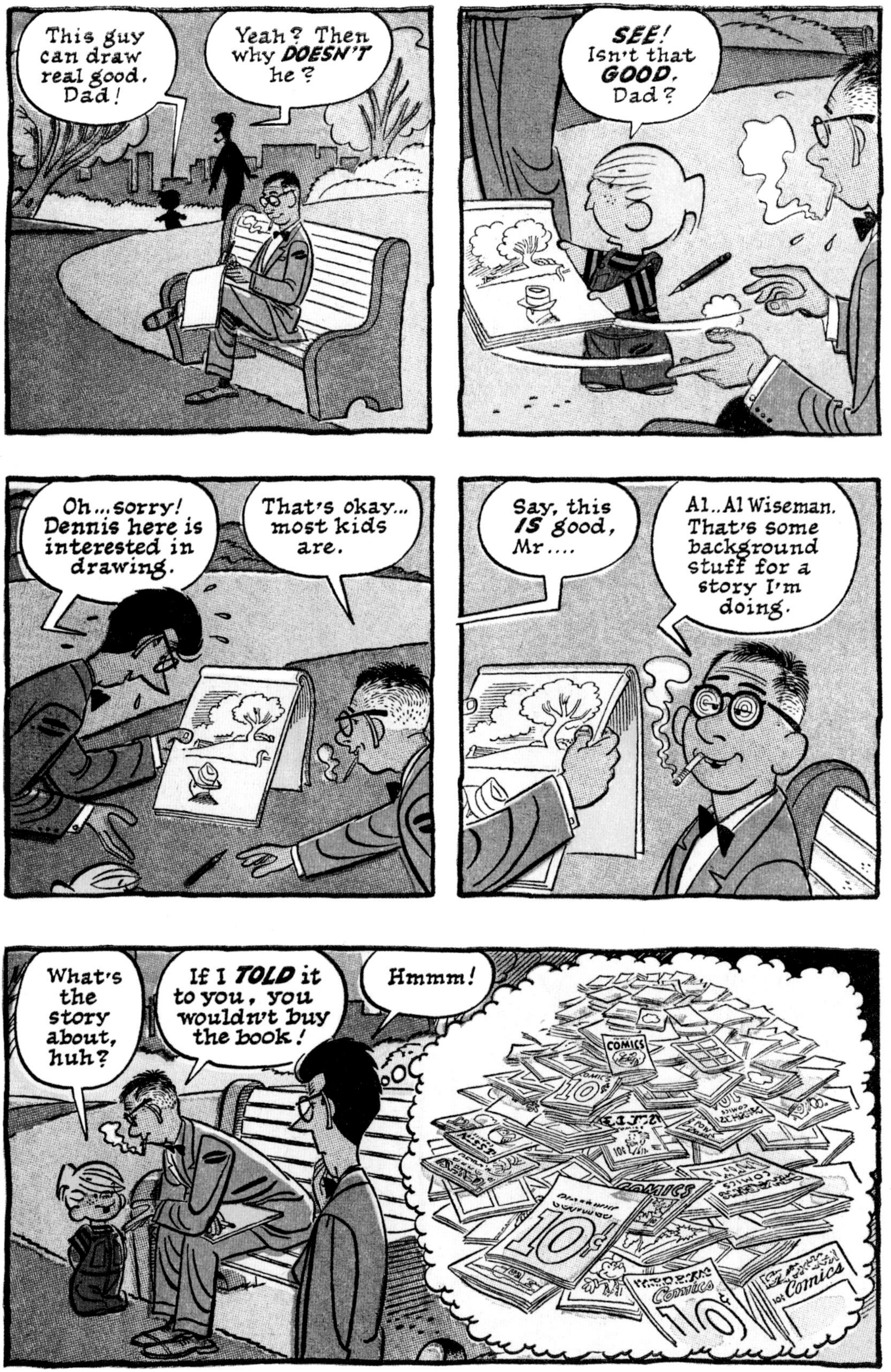
This guy can draw real good, Dad!
Yeah? Then why DOESN'T he?
SEE! Isn't that GOOD, Dad?
Oh...sorry! Dennis here is interested in drawing.
That's okay... most kids are.
Say, this IS good, Mr....
Al..Al Wiseman. That's some background stuff for a story I'm doing.
What's the story about, huh?
If I TOLD it to you, you wouldn't buy the book!
Hmmm!

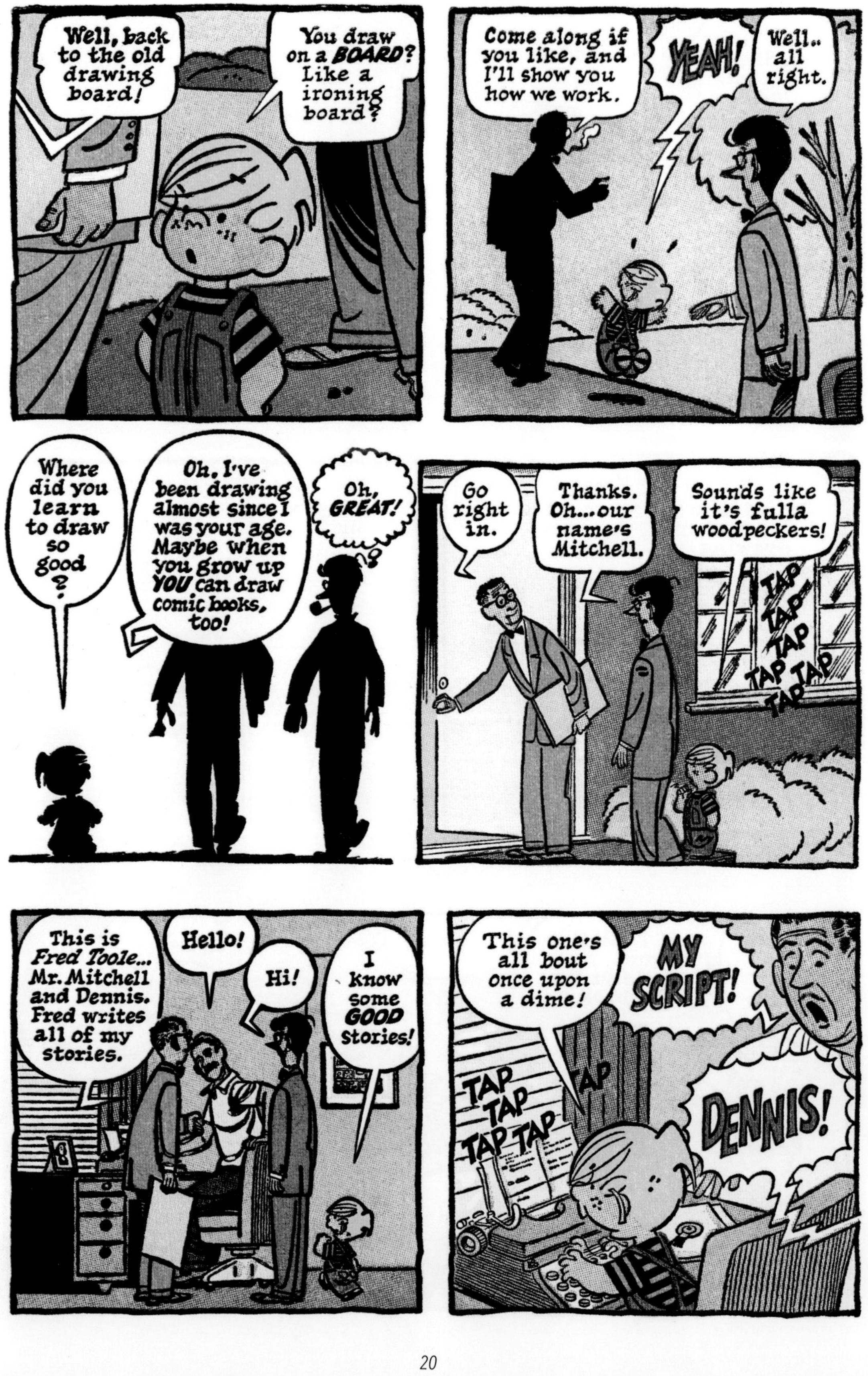
Well, back to the old drawing board!
You draw on a BOARD? Like a ironing board?
Come along if you like, and I'll show you how we work.
YEAH!
Well.. all right.
Where did you learn to draw so good?
Oh, I've been drawing almost since I was your age. Maybe when you grow up YOU can draw comic books, too!
Oh, GREAT!
Go right in.
Thanks. Oh...our name's Mitchell.
Sounds like it's fulla woodpeckers!
TAP TAP TAP TAP TAP TAP
This is Fred Toole... Mr. Mitchell and Dennis. Fred writes all of my stories.
Hello!
Hi!
I know some GOOD stories!
This one's all bout once upon a dime!
MY SCRIPT!
TAP TAP TAP TAP TAP
DENNIS!

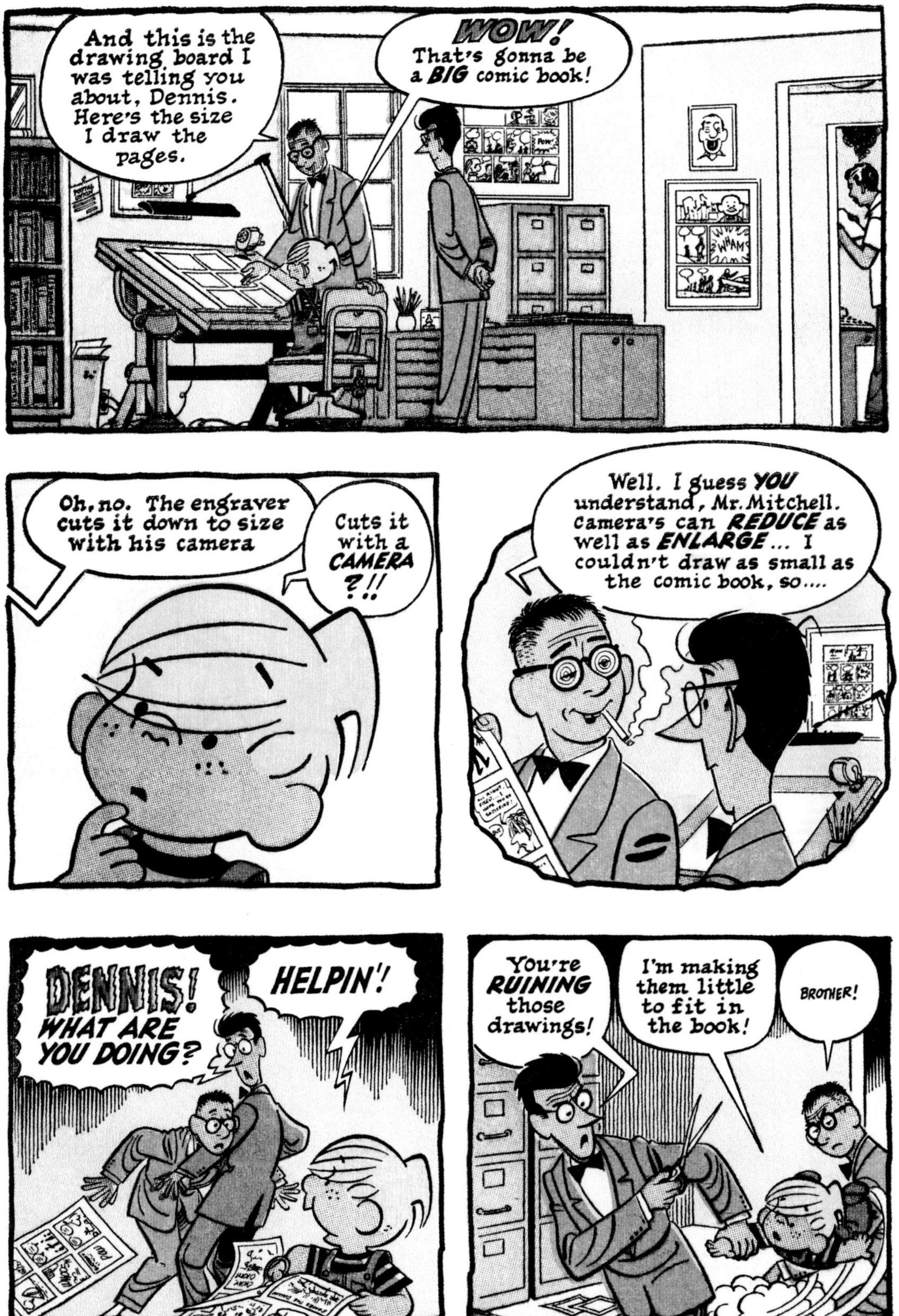
And this is the drawing board I was telling you about, Dennis. Here's the size I draw the pages.
WOW! That's gonna be a BIG comic book!
Oh, no. The engraver cuts it down to size with his camera
Cuts it with a CAMERA ?!!
Well. I guess YOU understand, Mr. Mitchell. Camera's can REDUCE as well as ENLARGE... I couldn't draw as small as the comic book, so....
DENNIS! WHAT ARE YOU DOING?
HELPIN'!
You're RUINING those drawings!
I'm making them little to fit in the book!
BROTHER!

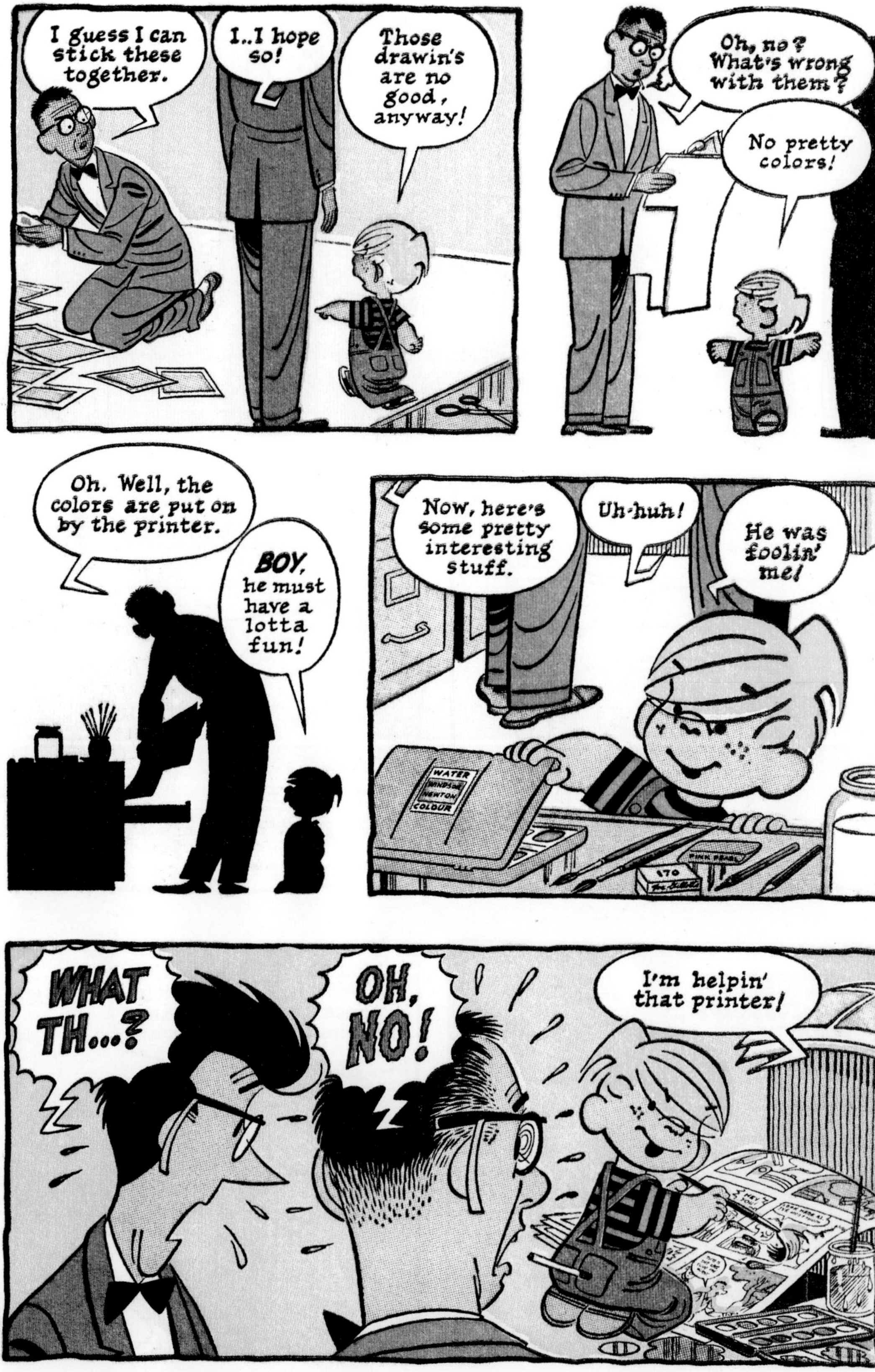
I guess I can stick these together.
I..I hope so!
Those drawin's are no good, anyway!
Oh, no? What's wrong with them?
No pretty colors!
Oh. Well, the colors are put on by the printer.
BOY, he must have a lotta fun!
Now, here's some pretty interesting stuff.
Uh-huh!
He was foolin' me!
WATER
WINDSOR
NEWTON
COLOUR
WHAT TH...?
OH, NO!
I'm helpin' that printer!

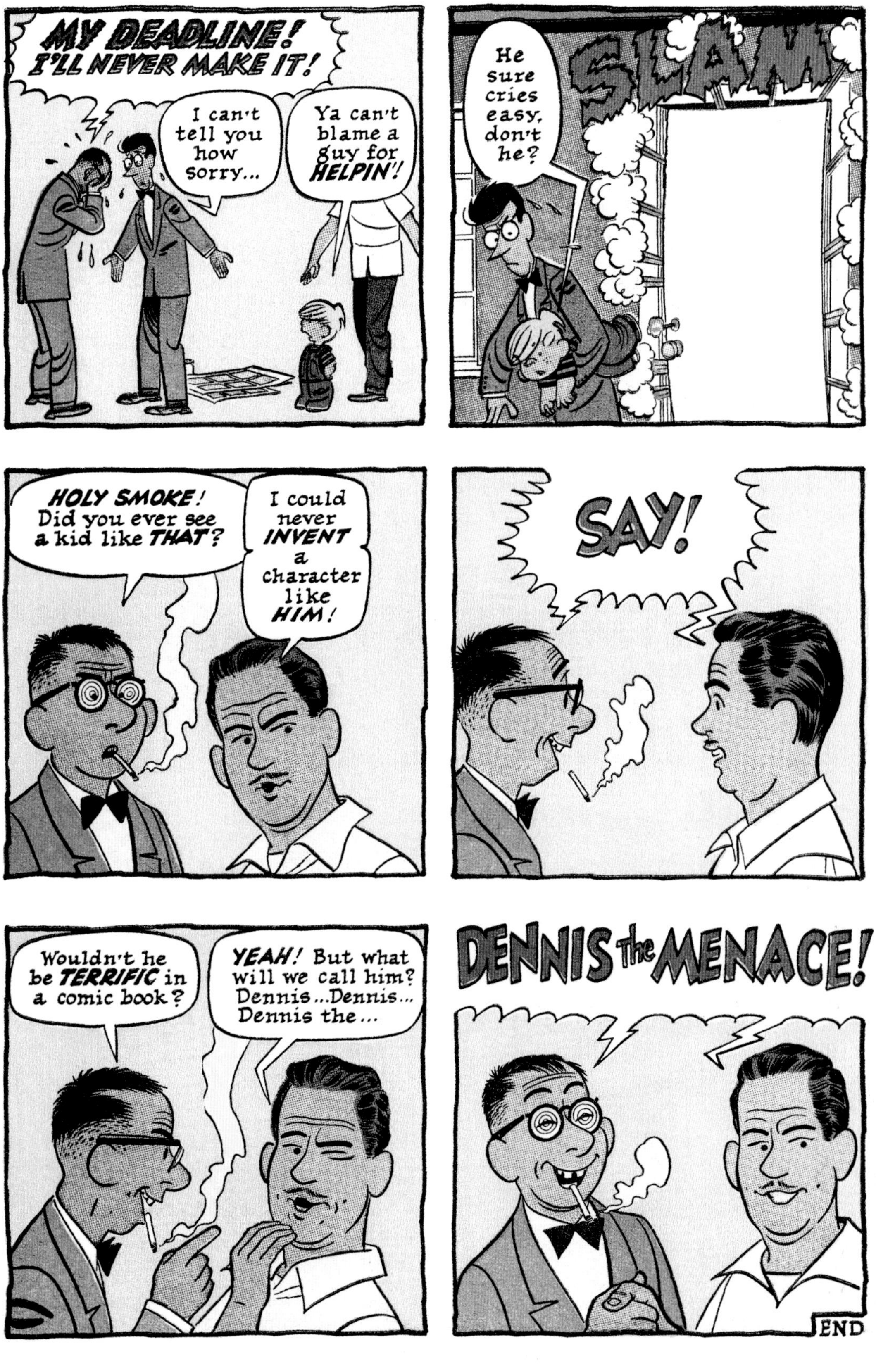
MY DEADLINE! I'LL NEVER MAKE IT!
I can't tell you how sorry...
Ya can't blame a guy for HELPIN'!
He sure cries easy, don't he?
SLAM
HOLY SMOKE! Did you ever see a kid like THAT?
I could never INVENT a character like HIM!
SAY!
Wouldn't he be TERRIFIC in a comic book?
YEAH! But what will we call him? Dennis...Dennis... Dennis the...
DENNIS the MENACE!
END

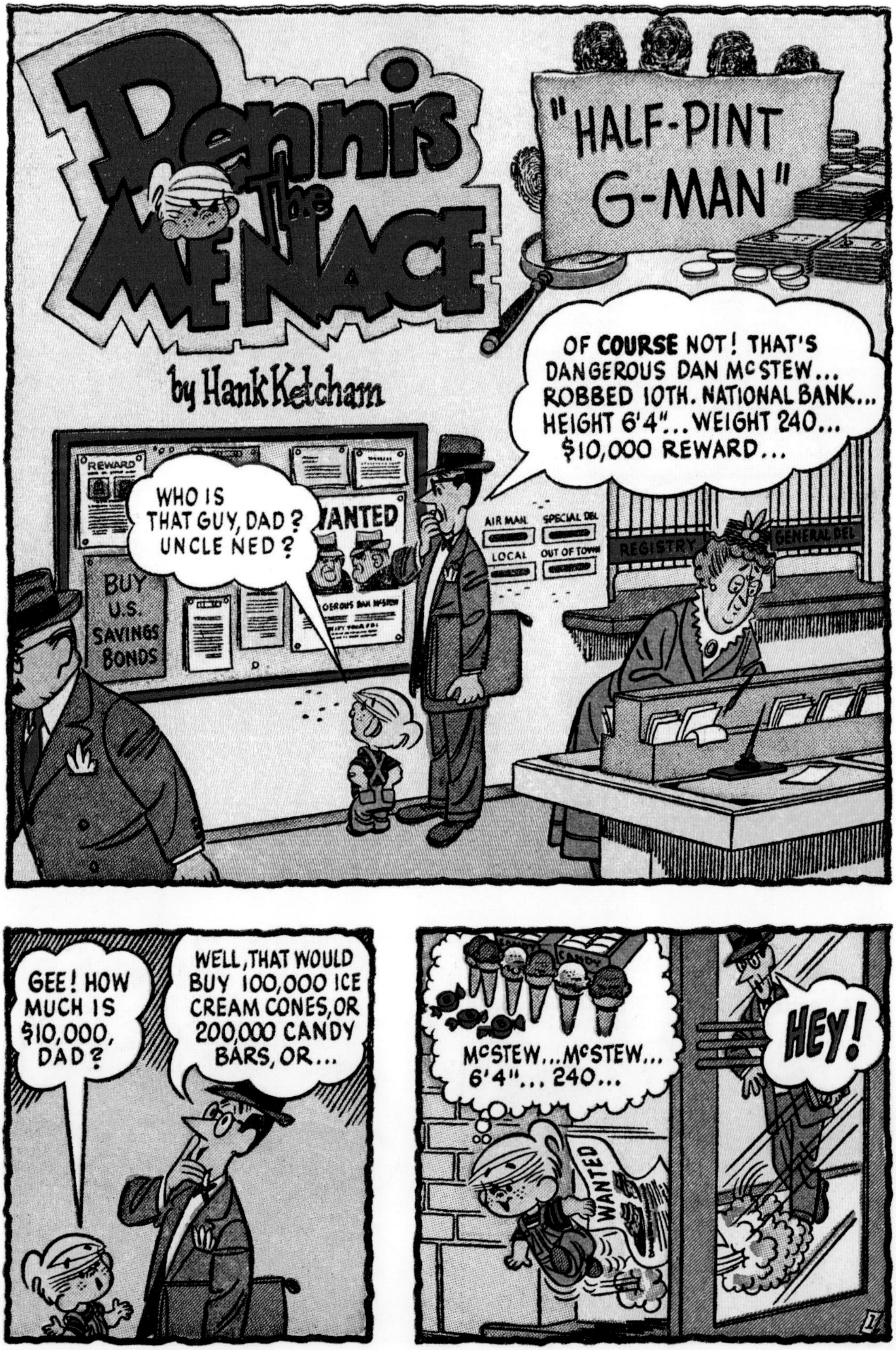

Dennis the Menace
by Hank Ketcham
"HALF-PINT G-MAN"
REWARD
WANTED
BUY U.S. SAVINGS BONDS
AIR MAIL
SPECIAL DEL
LOCAL
OUT OF TOWN
REGISTRY
GENERAL DEL
WHO IS THAT GUY, DAD? UNCLE NED?
OF COURSE NOT! THAT'S DANGEROUS DAN McSTEW... ROBBED 10TH. NATIONAL BANK... HEIGHT 6'4"... WEIGHT 240... $10,000 REWARD...
GEE! HOW MUCH IS $10,000, DAD?
WELL, THAT WOULD BUY 100,000 ICE CREAM CONES, OR 200,000 CANDY BARS, OR...
CANDY
McSTEW...McSTEW... 6'4"... 240...
WANTED
HEY!

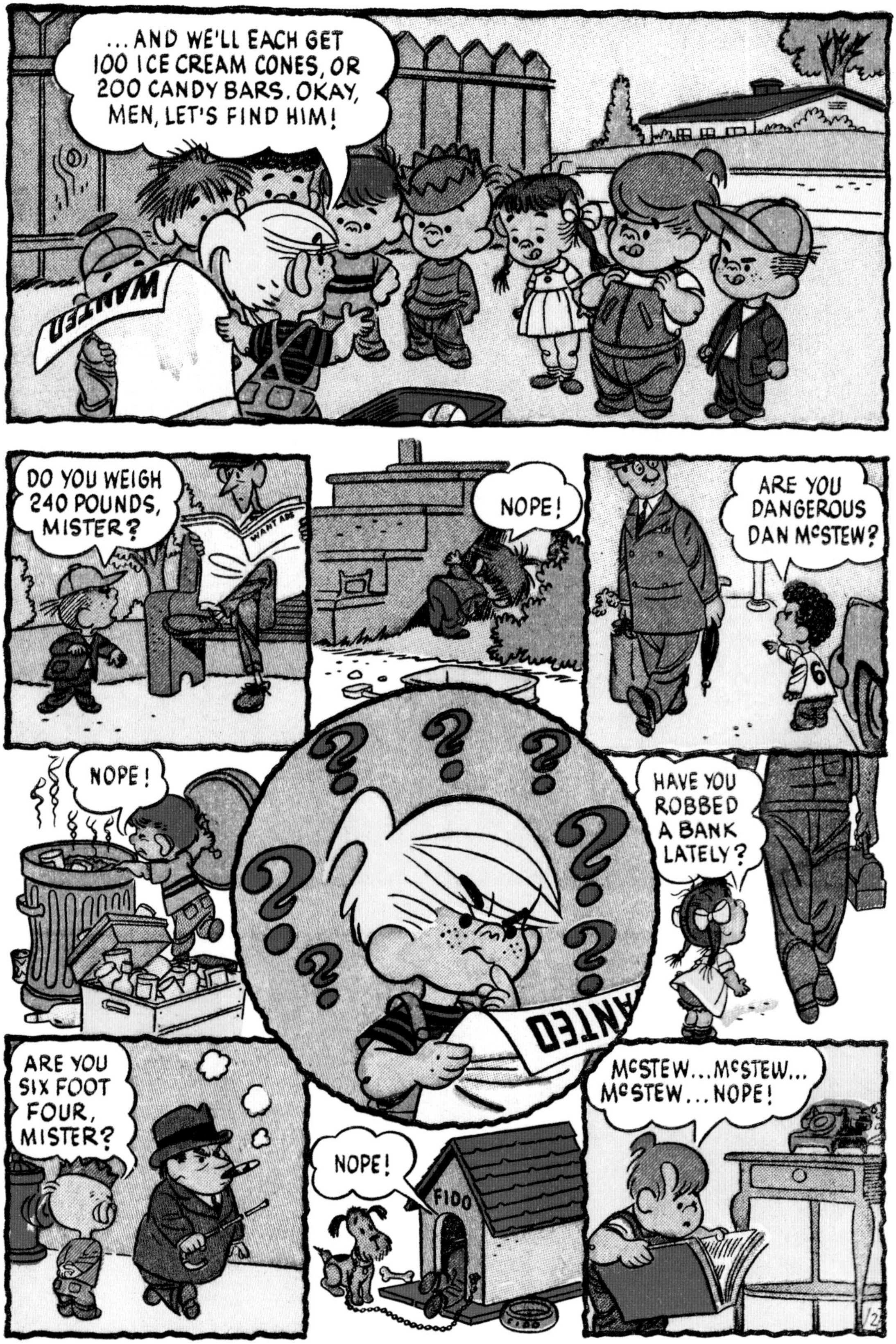

... AND WE'LL EACH GET 100 ICE CREAM CONES, OR 200 CANDY BARS. OKAY, MEN, LET'S FIND HIM!
WANTED
DO YOU WEIGH 240 POUNDS, MISTER?
WANT ADS
NOPE!
ARE YOU DANGEROUS DAN McSTEW?
NOPE!
HAVE YOU ROBBED A BANK LATELY?
ARE YOU SIX FOOT FOUR, MISTER?
NOPE!
FIDO
McSTEW... McSTEW... McSTEW... NOPE!

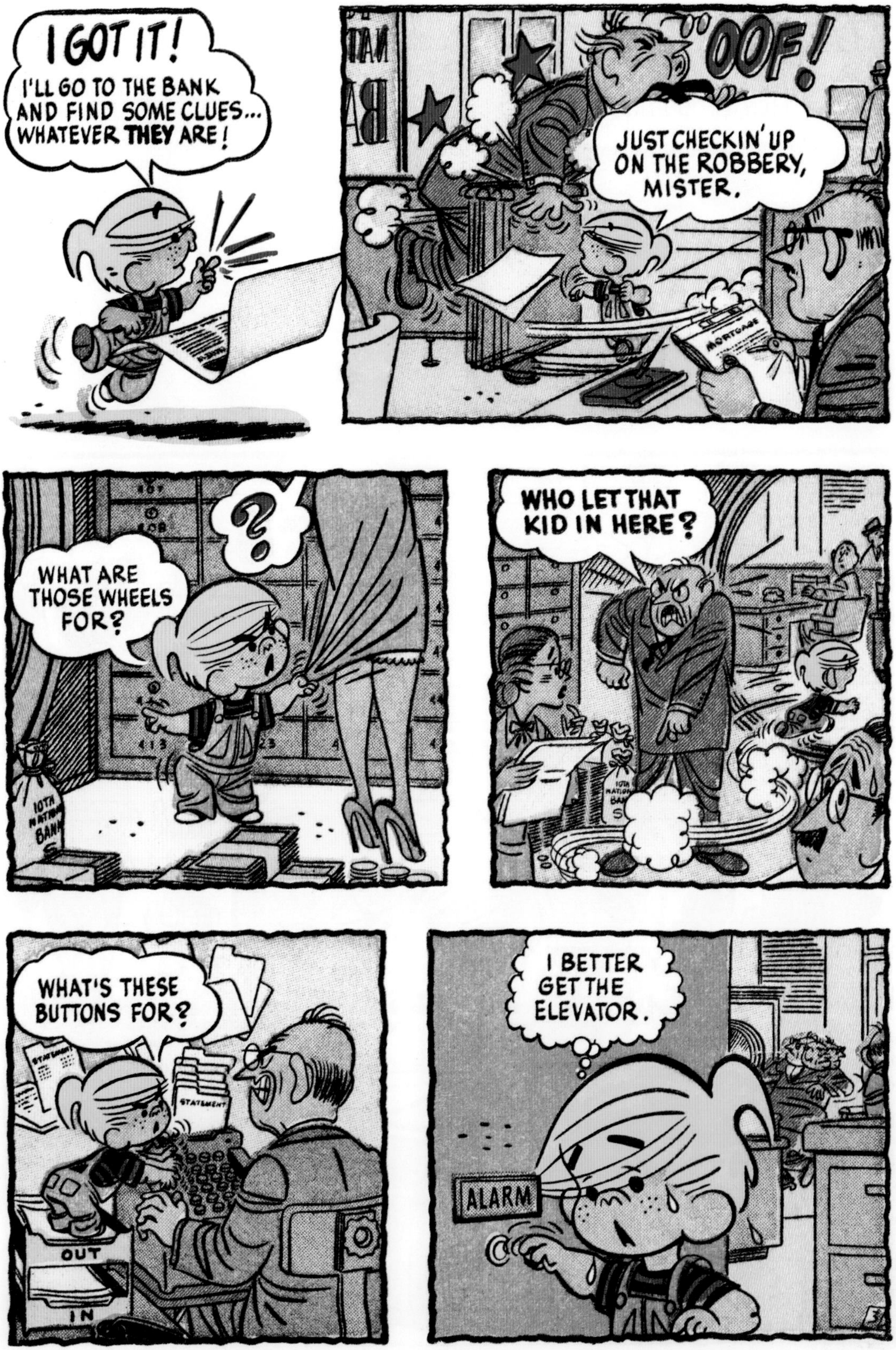
I GOT IT!
I'LL GO TO THE BANK AND FIND SOME CLUES... WHATEVER **THEY** ARE!
OOF!
JUST CHECKIN' UP ON THE ROBBERY, MISTER.
MORTGAGE
WHAT ARE THOSE WHEELS FOR?
?
WHO LET THAT KID IN HERE?
WHAT'S THESE BUTTONS FOR?
STATEMENT
OUT
IN
I BETTER GET THE ELEVATOR.
ALARM

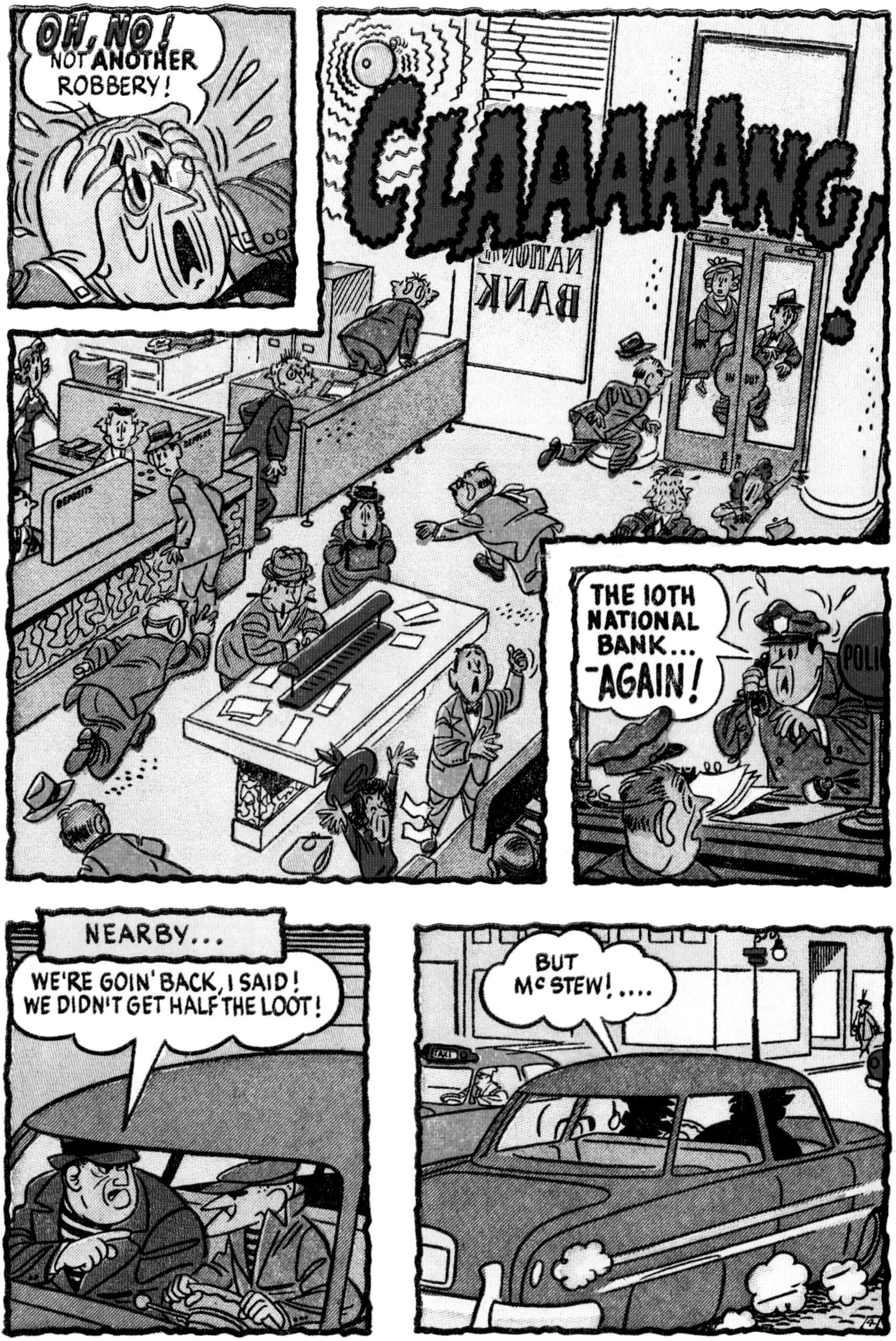
OH, NO! NOT ANOTHER ROBBERY!
CLAAAAANG!
THE 10TH NATIONAL BANK... —AGAIN!
NEARBY...
WE'RE GOIN' BACK, I SAID! WE DIDN'T GET HALF THE LOOT!
BUT McSTEW! ....

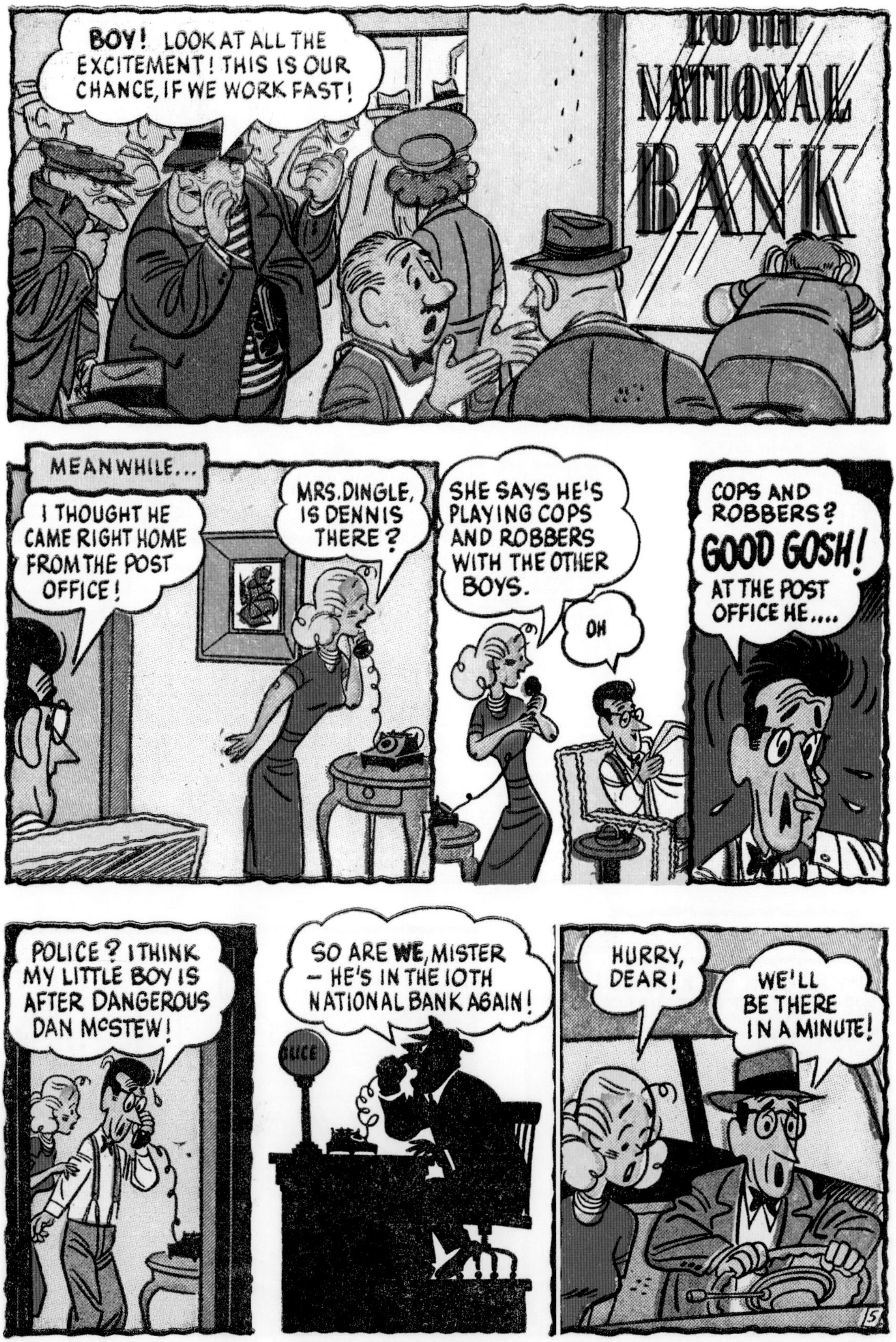
BOY! LOOK AT ALL THE EXCITEMENT! THIS IS OUR CHANCE, IF WE WORK FAST!
NATIONAL BANK
MEANWHILE...
I THOUGHT HE CAME RIGHT HOME FROM THE POST OFFICE!
MRS. DINGLE, IS DENNIS THERE?
SHE SAYS HE'S PLAYING COPS AND ROBBERS WITH THE OTHER BOYS.
OH
COPS AND ROBBERS? GOOD GOSH! AT THE POST OFFICE HE....
POLICE? I THINK MY LITTLE BOY IS AFTER DANGEROUS DAN McSTEW!
SO ARE WE, MISTER – HE'S IN THE 10TH NATIONAL BANK AGAIN!
HURRY, DEAR!
WE'LL BE THERE IN A MINUTE!
5

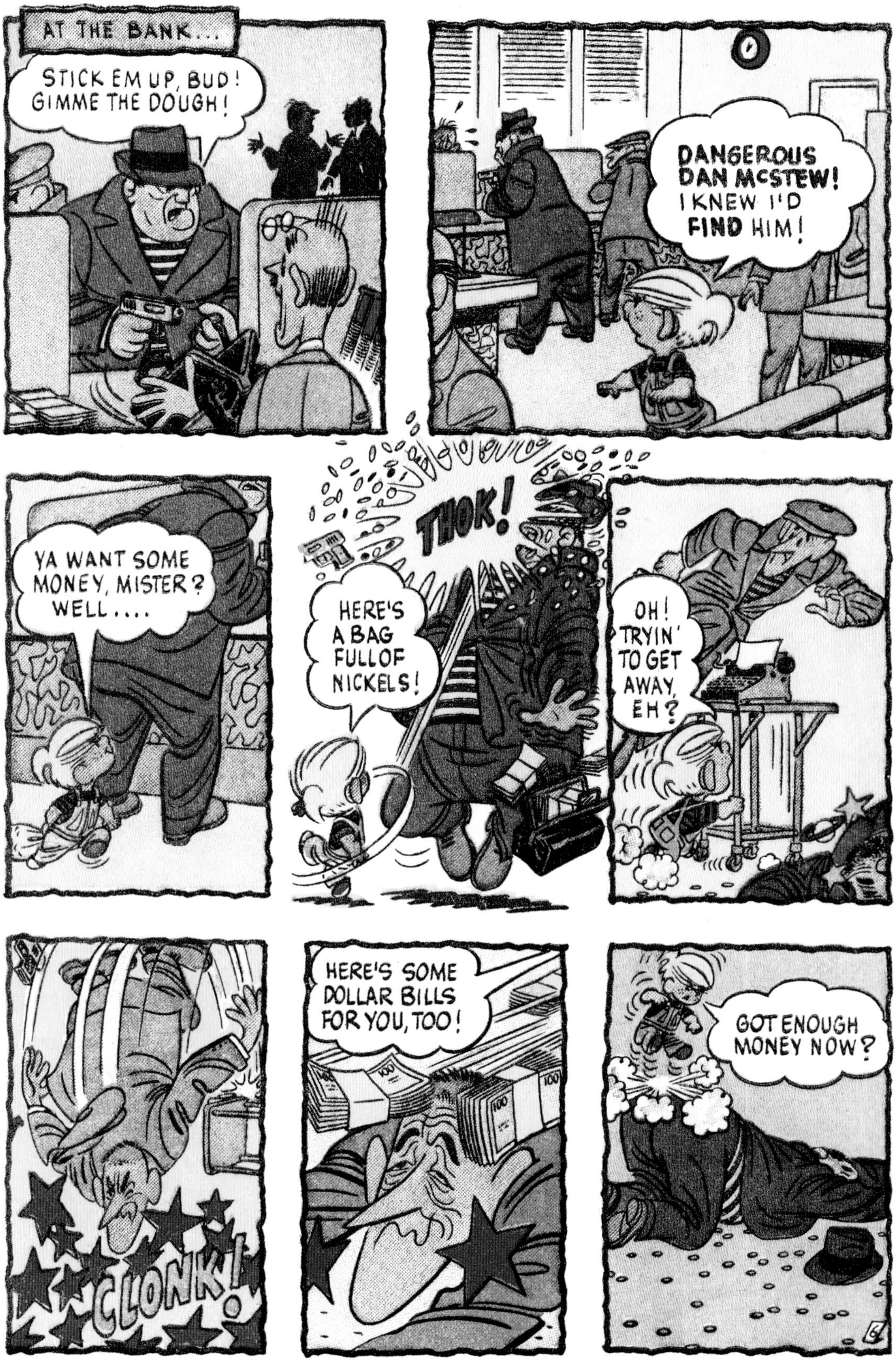
AT THE BANK...
STICK EM UP, BUD! GIMME THE DOUGH!
DANGEROUS DAN McSTEW! I KNEW I'D FIND HIM!
YA WANT SOME MONEY, MISTER? WELL....
THOK!
HERE'S A BAG FULL OF NICKELS!
OH! TRYIN' TO GET AWAY, EH?
CLONK!
HERE'S SOME DOLLAR BILLS FOR YOU, TOO!
GOT ENOUGH MONEY NOW?

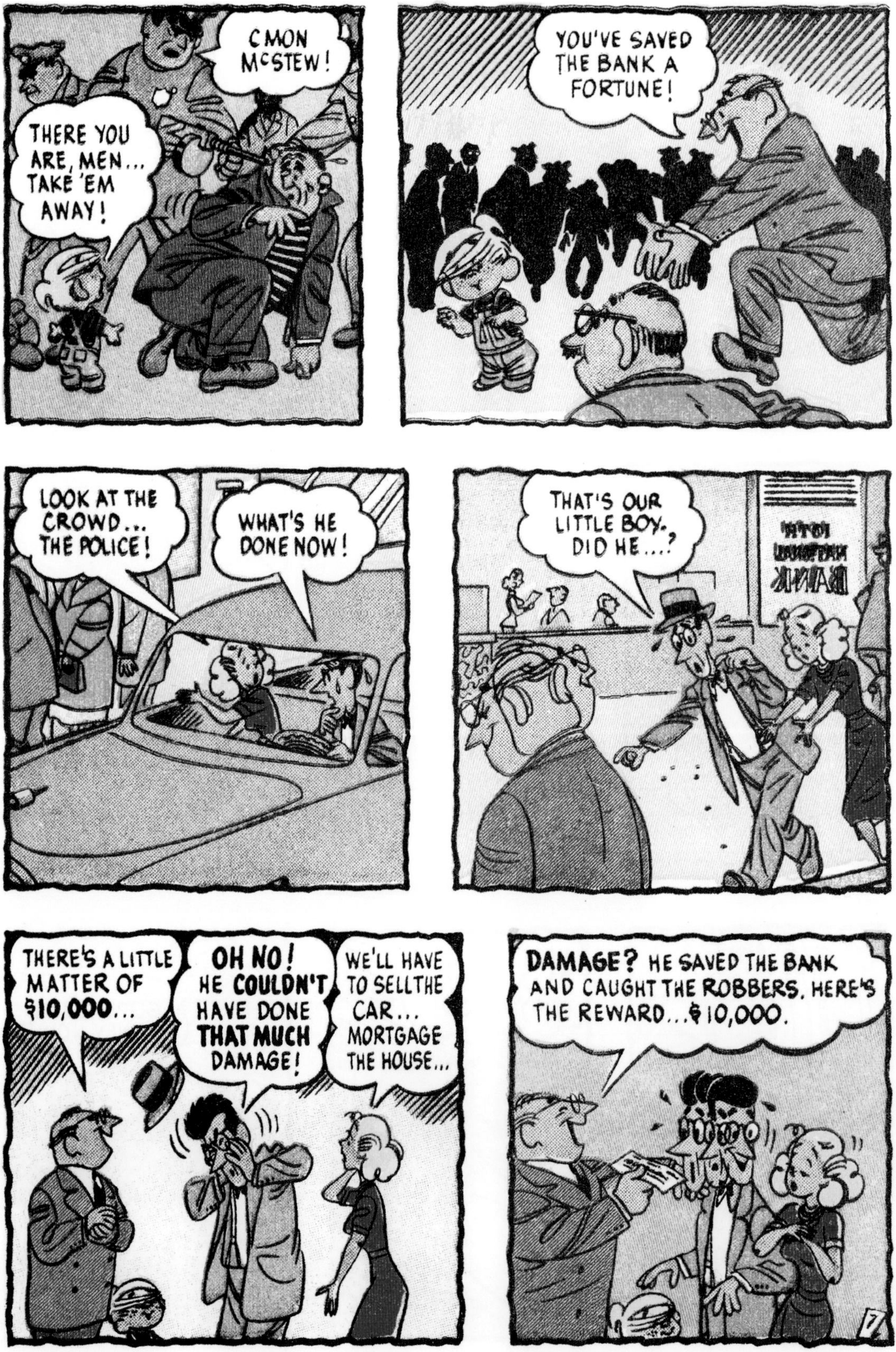
C'MON McSTEW!
THERE YOU ARE, MEN... TAKE 'EM AWAY!
YOU'VE SAVED THE BANK A FORTUNE!
LOOK AT THE CROWD... THE POLICE!
WHAT'S HE DONE NOW!
THAT'S OUR LITTLE BOY. DID HE...?
THERE'S A LITTLE MATTER OF $10,000...
OH NO! HE COULDN'T HAVE DONE THAT MUCH DAMAGE!
WE'LL HAVE TO SELL THE CAR... MORTGAGE THE HOUSE...
DAMAGE? HE SAVED THE BANK AND CAUGHT THE ROBBERS. HERE'S THE REWARD...$10,000.

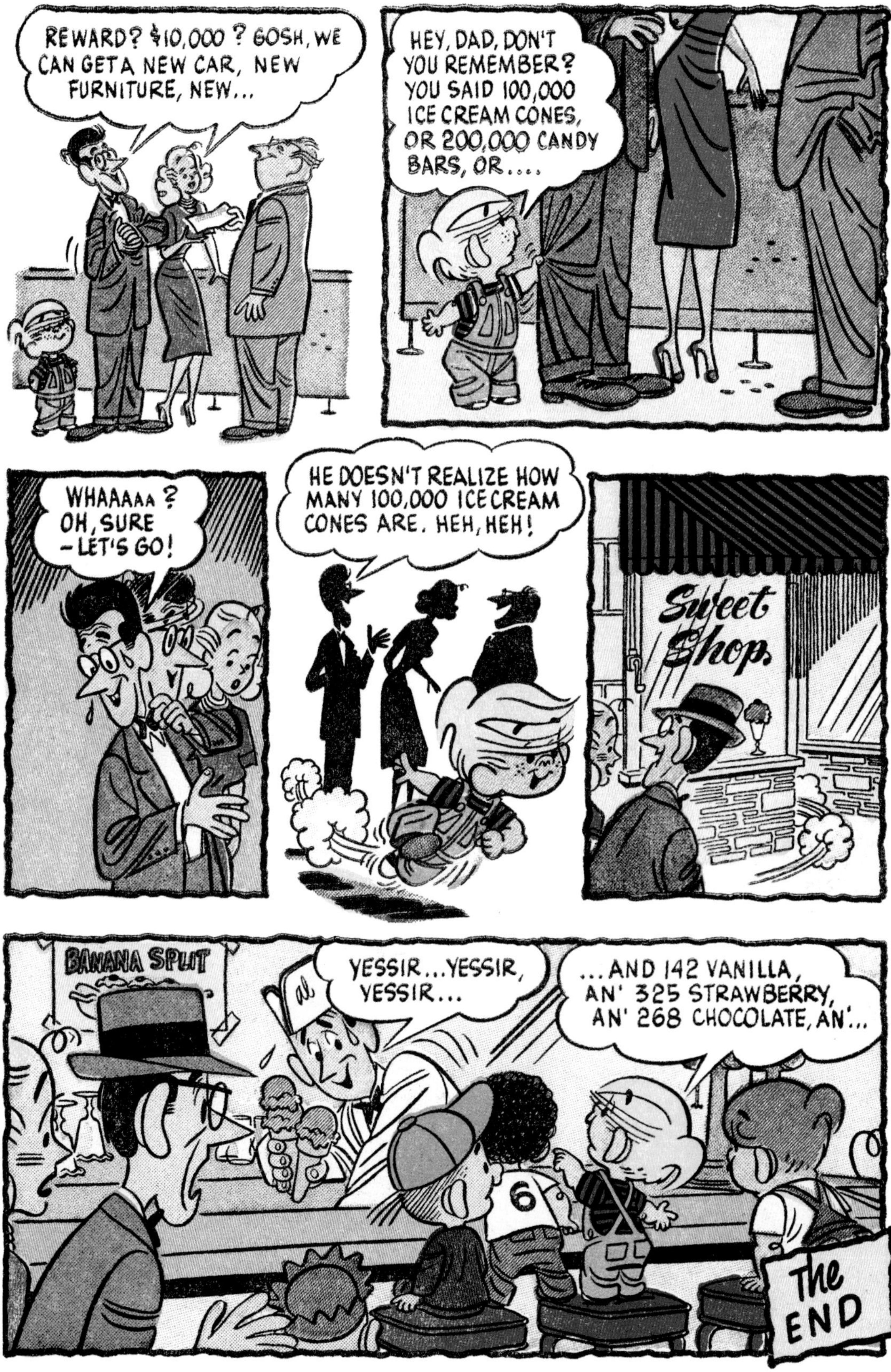
REWARD? $10,000 ? GOSH, WE CAN GET A NEW CAR, NEW FURNITURE, NEW...
HEY, DAD, DON'T YOU REMEMBER? YOU SAID 100,000 ICE CREAM CONES, OR 200,000 CANDY BARS, OR....
WHAAAAA ? OH, SURE -LET'S GO!
HE DOESN'T REALIZE HOW MANY 100,000 ICE CREAM CONES ARE. HEH, HEH!
Sweet Shop
BANANA SPLIT
YESSIR...YESSIR, YESSIR...
...AND 142 VANILLA, AN' 325 STRAWBERRY, AN' 268 CHOCOLATE, AN'...
6
The END

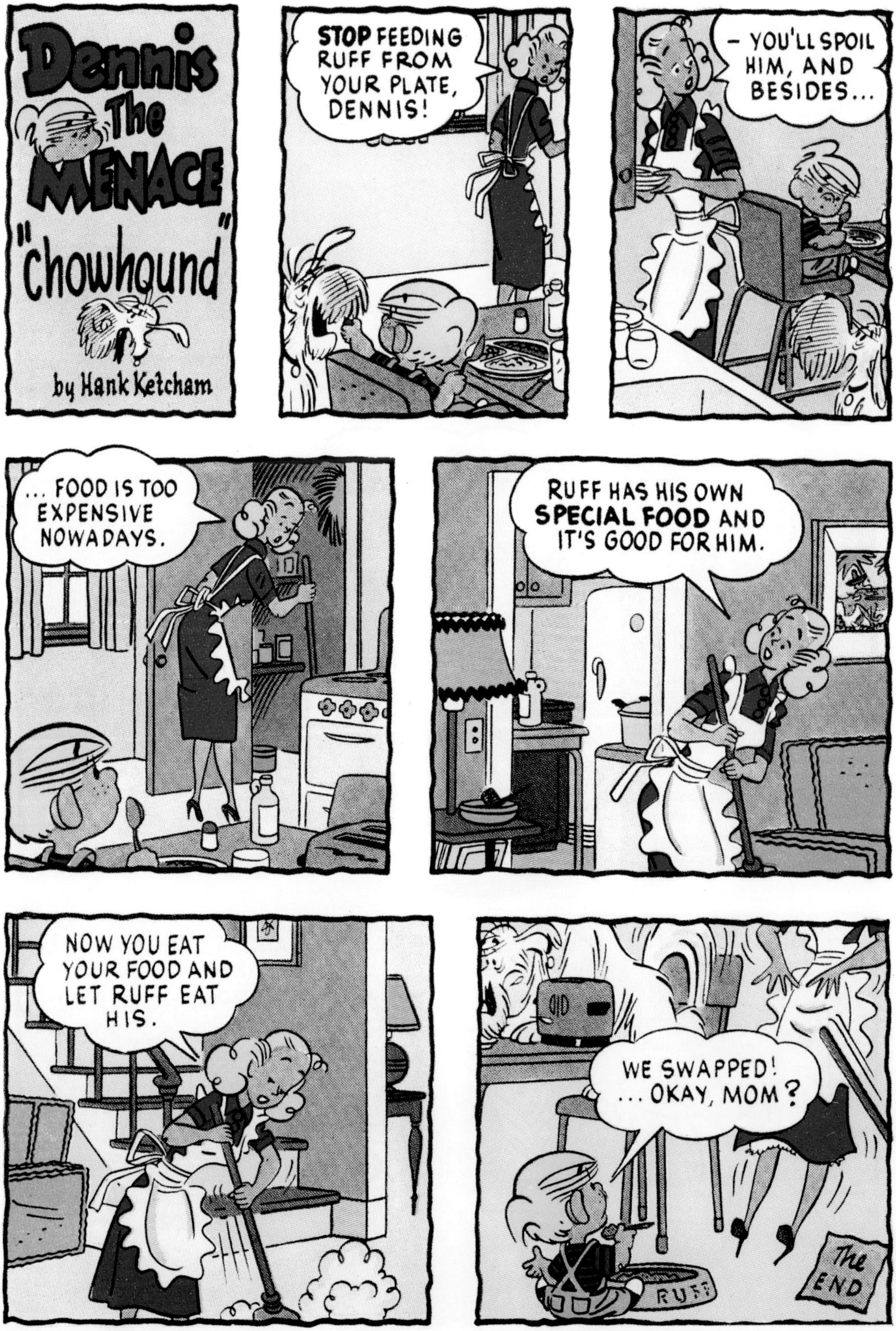
Dennis The MENACE
"Chowhound"
by Hank Ketcham
STOP FEEDING RUFF FROM YOUR PLATE, DENNIS!
– YOU'LL SPOIL HIM, AND BESIDES...
... FOOD IS TOO EXPENSIVE NOWADAYS.
RUFF HAS HIS OWN SPECIAL FOOD AND IT'S GOOD FOR HIM.
NOW YOU EAT YOUR FOOD AND LET RUFF EAT HIS.
WE SWAPPED! ... OKAY, MOM?
RUFF
The END

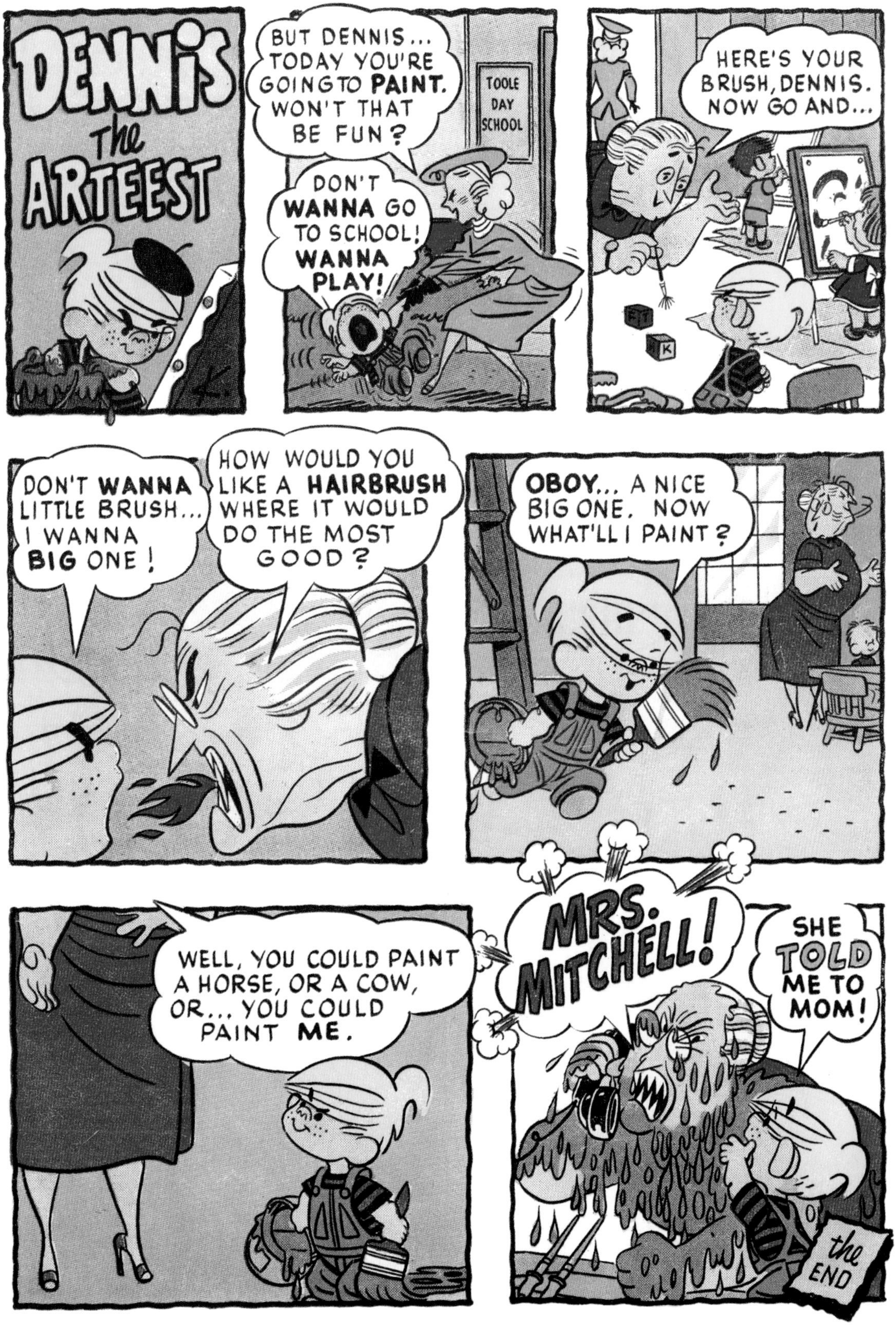
DENNIS the ARTEEST
BUT DENNIS... TODAY YOU'RE GOING TO PAINT. WON'T THAT BE FUN?
TOOLE DAY SCHOOL
DON'T WANNA GO TO SCHOOL! WANNA PLAY!
HERE'S YOUR BRUSH, DENNIS. NOW GO AND...
DON'T WANNA LITTLE BRUSH... I WANNA BIG ONE!
HOW WOULD YOU LIKE A HAIRBRUSH WHERE IT WOULD DO THE MOST GOOD?
OBOY... A NICE BIG ONE. NOW WHAT'LL I PAINT?
WELL, YOU COULD PAINT A HORSE, OR A COW, OR... YOU COULD PAINT ME.
MRS. MITCHELL!
SHE TOLD ME TO MOM!
the END

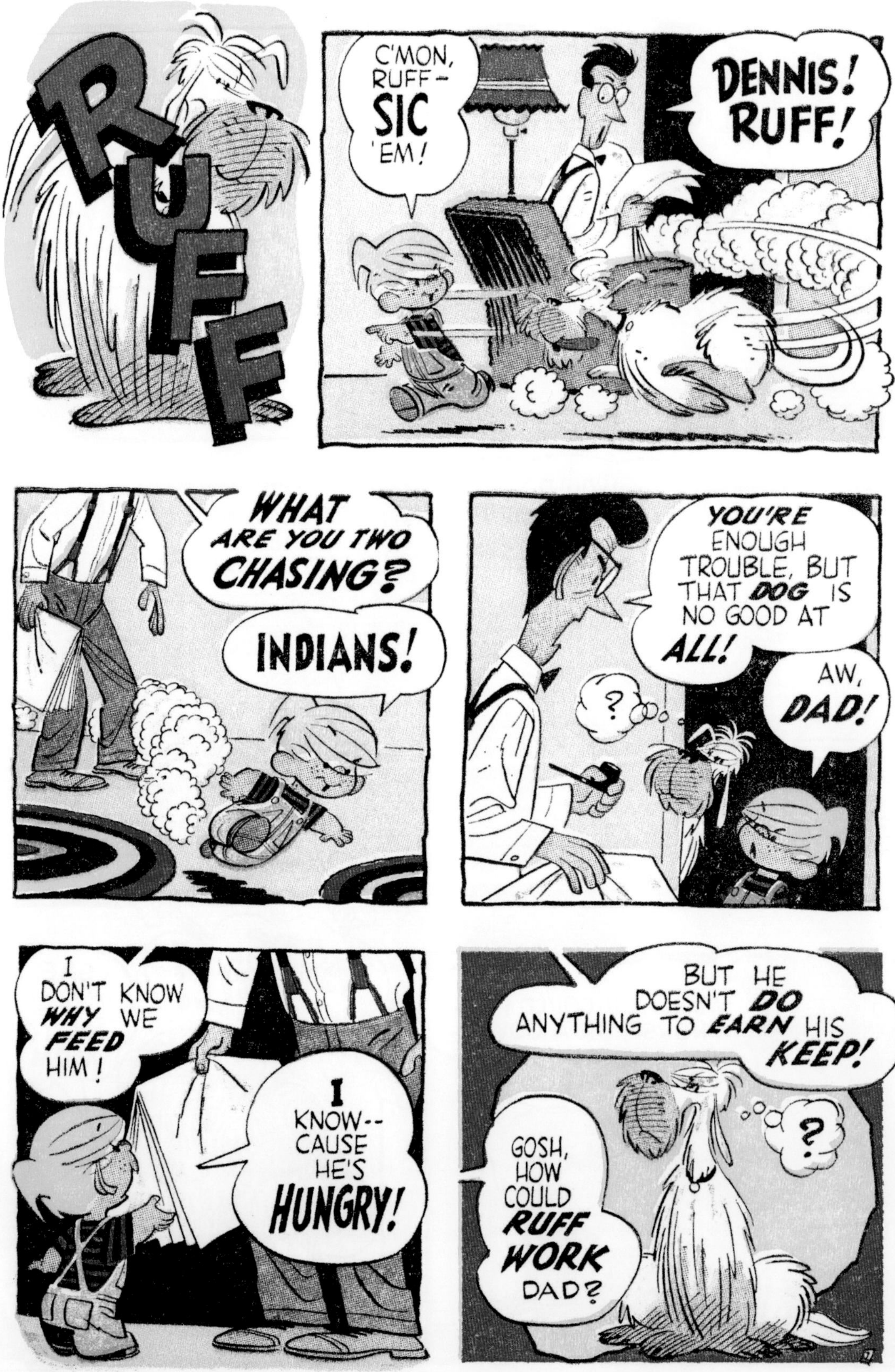
RUFF
C'MON, RUFF— SIC 'EM!
DENNIS! RUFF!
WHAT ARE YOU TWO CHASING?
INDIANS!
YOU'RE ENOUGH TROUBLE, BUT THAT DOG IS NO GOOD AT ALL!
?
AW, DAD!
I DON'T KNOW WHY WE FEED HIM!
I KNOW-- CAUSE HE'S HUNGRY!
BUT HE DOESN'T DO ANYTHING TO EARN HIS KEEP!
?
GOSH, HOW COULD RUFF WORK DAD?

LOTS OF DOGS WORK.. ESKIMO DOGS PULL SLEDS!
SOME DOGS ARE GOOD FOR HUNTING!
?
BOP!
BUT RUFF ISN'T EVEN A GOOD WATCH DOG!

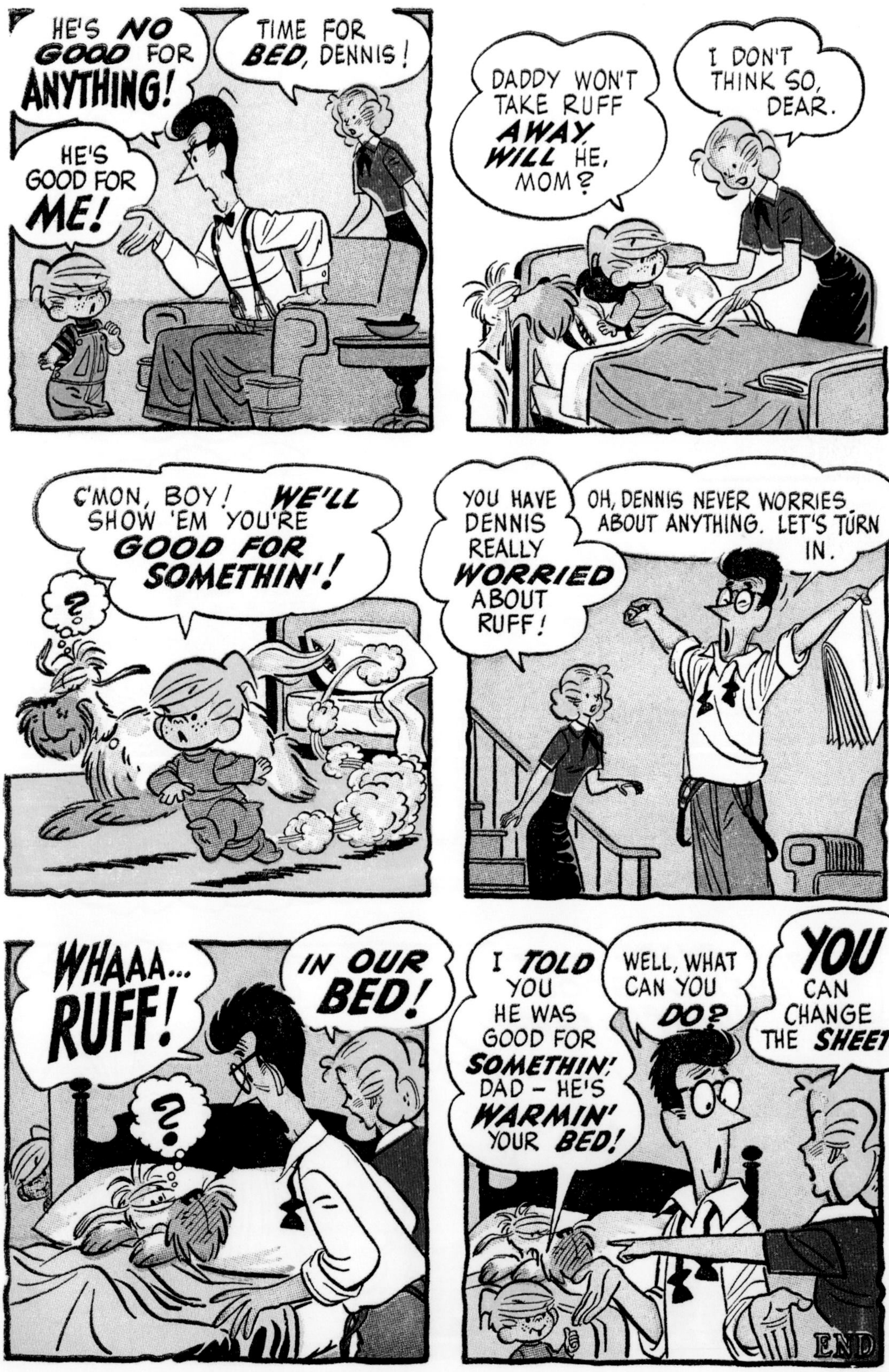

HE'S NO GOOD FOR ANYTHING!
TIME FOR BED, DENNIS!
HE'S GOOD FOR ME!
DADDY WON'T TAKE RUFF AWAY, WILL HE, MOM?
I DON'T THINK SO, DEAR.
C'MON, BOY! WE'LL SHOW 'EM YOU'RE GOOD FOR SOMETHIN'!
?
YOU HAVE DENNIS REALLY WORRIED ABOUT RUFF!
OH, DENNIS NEVER WORRIES ABOUT ANYTHING. LET'S TURN IN.
WHAAA... RUFF!
IN OUR BED!
?
I TOLD YOU HE WAS GOOD FOR SOMETHIN'! DAD – HE'S WARMIN' YOUR BED!
WELL, WHAT CAN YOU DO?
YOU CAN CHANGE THE SHEETS!
END

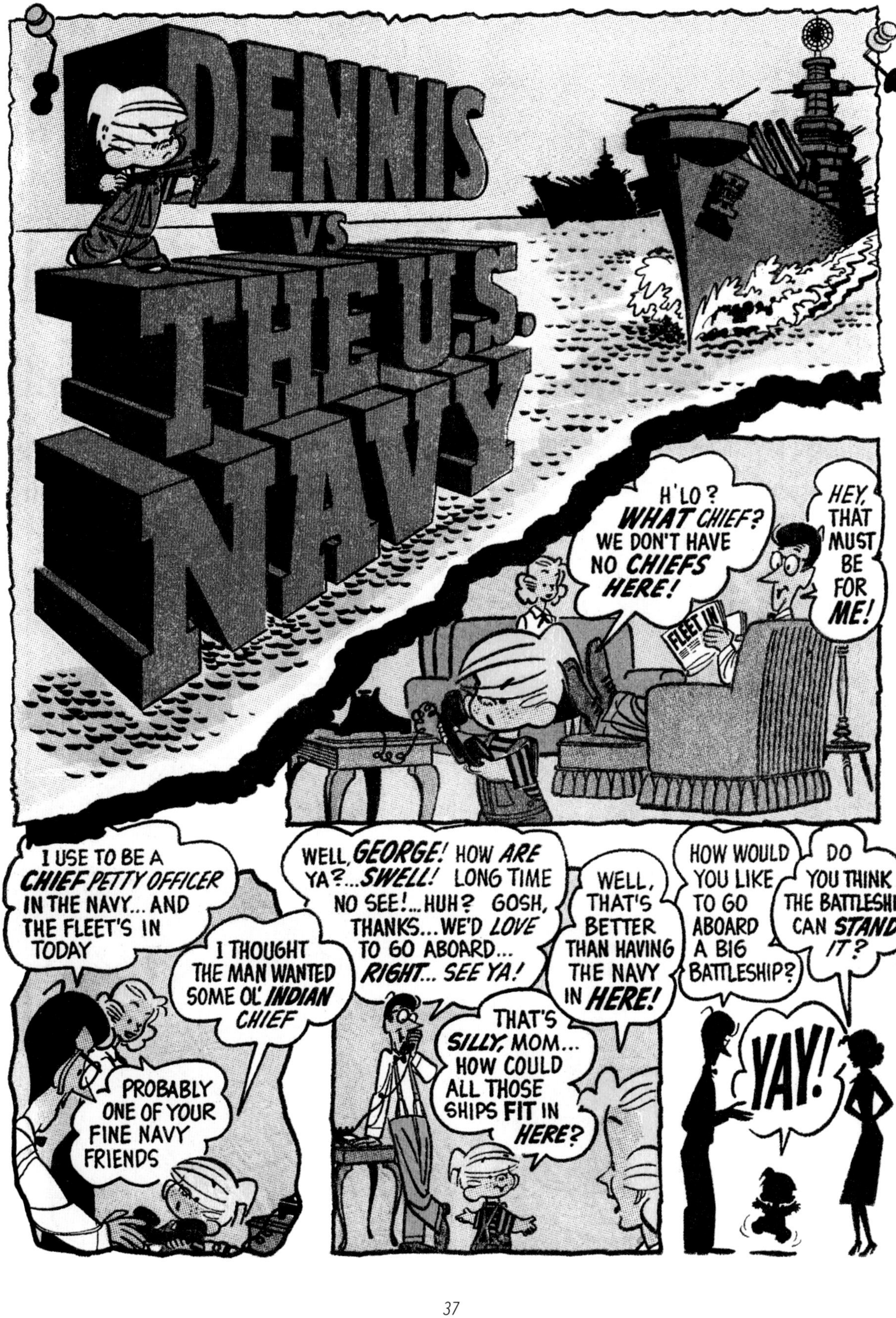
DENNIS VS THE U.S. NAVY
FLEET IN
H'LO? WHAT CHIEF? WE DON'T HAVE NO CHIEFS HERE!
HEY, THAT MUST BE FOR ME!
I USE TO BE A CHIEF PETTY OFFICER IN THE NAVY... AND THE FLEET'S IN TODAY
I THOUGHT THE MAN WANTED SOME OL' INDIAN CHIEF
PROBABLY ONE OF YOUR FINE NAVY FRIENDS
WELL, GEORGE! HOW ARE YA?...SWELL! LONG TIME NO SEE!...HUH? GOSH, THANKS...WE'D LOVE TO GO ABOARD... RIGHT... SEE YA!
WELL, THAT'S BETTER THAN HAVING THE NAVY IN HERE!
THAT'S SILLY, MOM... HOW COULD ALL THOSE SHIPS FIT IN HERE?
HOW WOULD YOU LIKE TO GO ABOARD A BIG BATTLESHIP?
DO YOU THINK THE BATTLESHIP CAN STAND IT?
YAY!

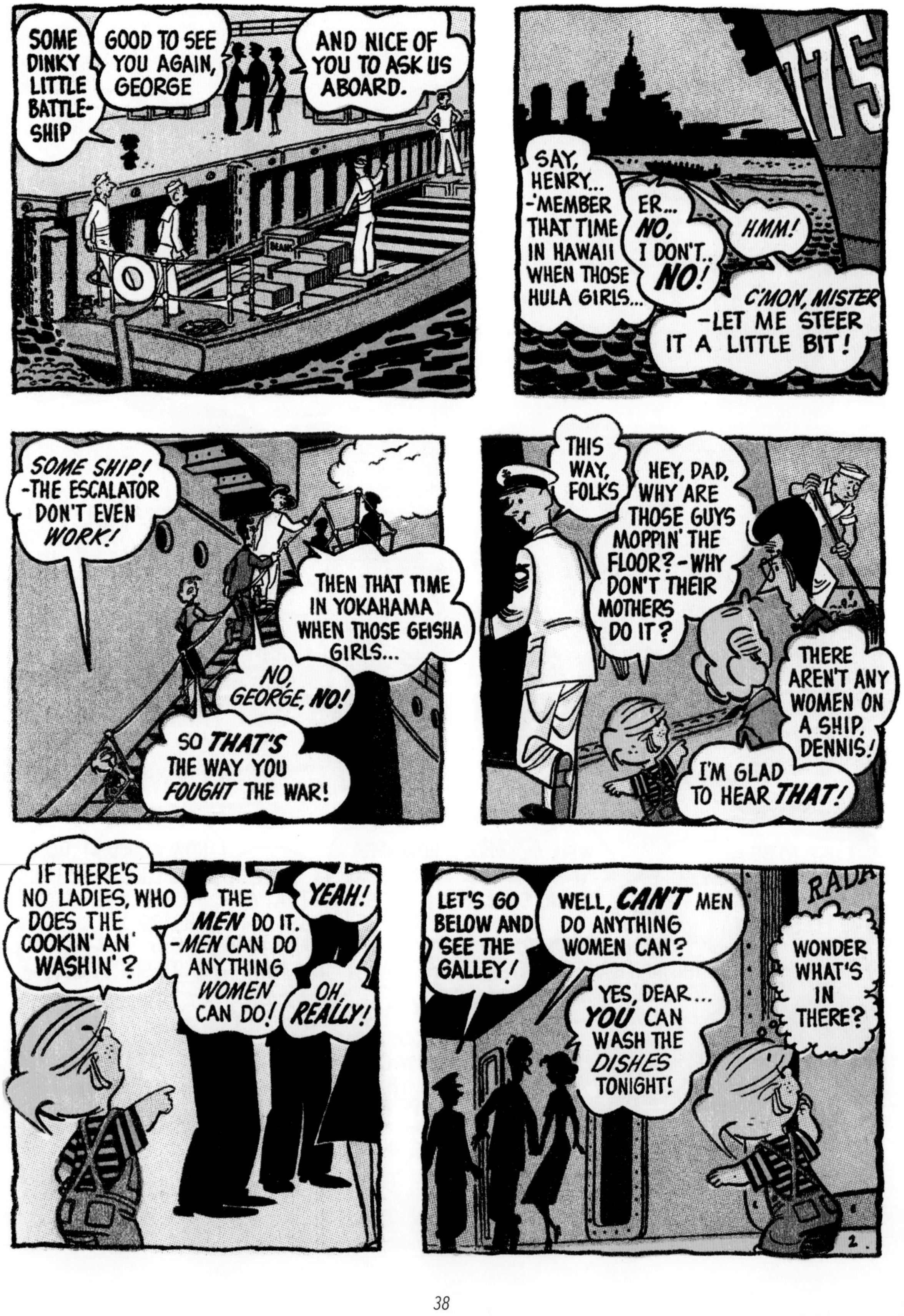
SOME DINKY LITTLE BATTLE-SHIP
GOOD TO SEE YOU AGAIN, GEORGE
AND NICE OF YOU TO ASK US ABOARD.
775
SAY, HENRY... -'MEMBER THAT TIME IN HAWAII WHEN THOSE HULA GIRLS...
ER... NO, I DON'T.. NO!
HMM!
C'MON, MISTER -LET ME STEER IT A LITTLE BIT!
SOME SHIP! -THE ESCALATOR DON'T EVEN WORK!
THEN THAT TIME IN YOKAHAMA WHEN THOSE GEISHA GIRLS...
NO, GEORGE, NO!
SO THAT'S THE WAY YOU FOUGHT THE WAR!
THIS WAY, FOLKS
HEY, DAD, WHY ARE THOSE GUYS MOPPIN' THE FLOOR?-WHY DON'T THEIR MOTHERS DO IT?
THERE AREN'T ANY WOMEN ON A SHIP, DENNIS!
I'M GLAD TO HEAR THAT!
IF THERE'S NO LADIES, WHO DOES THE COOKIN' AN' WASHIN'?
THE MEN DO IT. -MEN CAN DO ANYTHING WOMEN CAN DO!
YEAH!
OH, REALLY!
LET'S GO BELOW AND SEE THE GALLEY!
WELL, CAN'T MEN DO ANYTHING WOMEN CAN?
YES, DEAR... YOU CAN WASH THE DISHES TONIGHT!
RADA
WONDER WHAT'S IN THERE?
2.

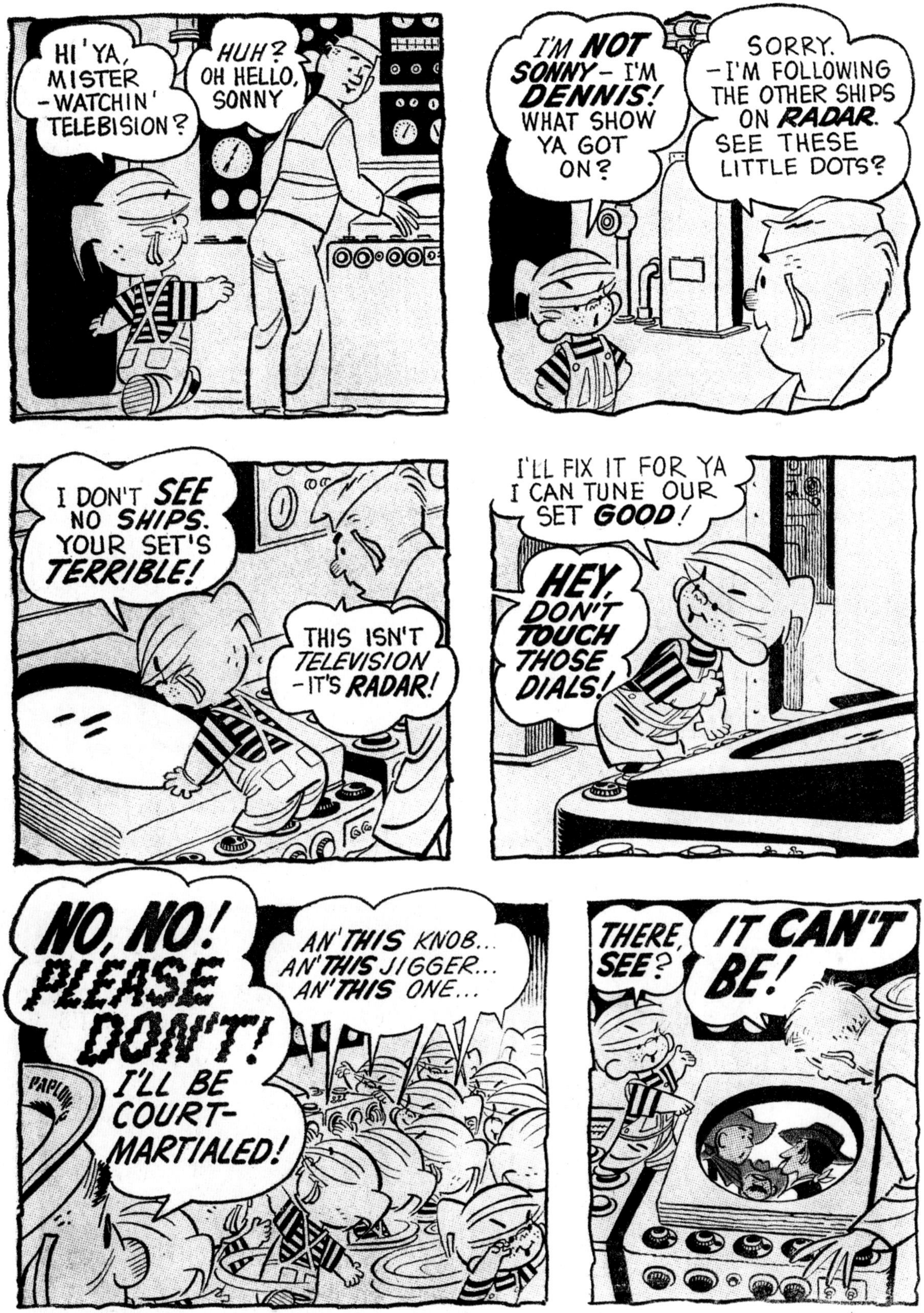
HI 'YA, MISTER -WATCHIN' TELEBISION?
HUH? OH HELLO, SONNY
I'M NOT SONNY- I'M DENNIS! WHAT SHOW YA GOT ON?
SORRY. -I'M FOLLOWING THE OTHER SHIPS ON RADAR. SEE THESE LITTLE DOTS?
I DON'T SEE NO SHIPS. YOUR SET'S TERRIBLE!
THIS ISN'T TELEVISION -IT'S RADAR!
I'LL FIX IT FOR YA I CAN TUNE OUR SET GOOD!
HEY, DON'T TOUCH THOSE DIALS!
NO, NO! PLEASE DON'T! I'LL BE COURT-MARTIALED!
AN' THIS KNOB... AN' THIS JIGGER... AN' THIS ONE...
THERE, SEE?
IT CAN'T BE!

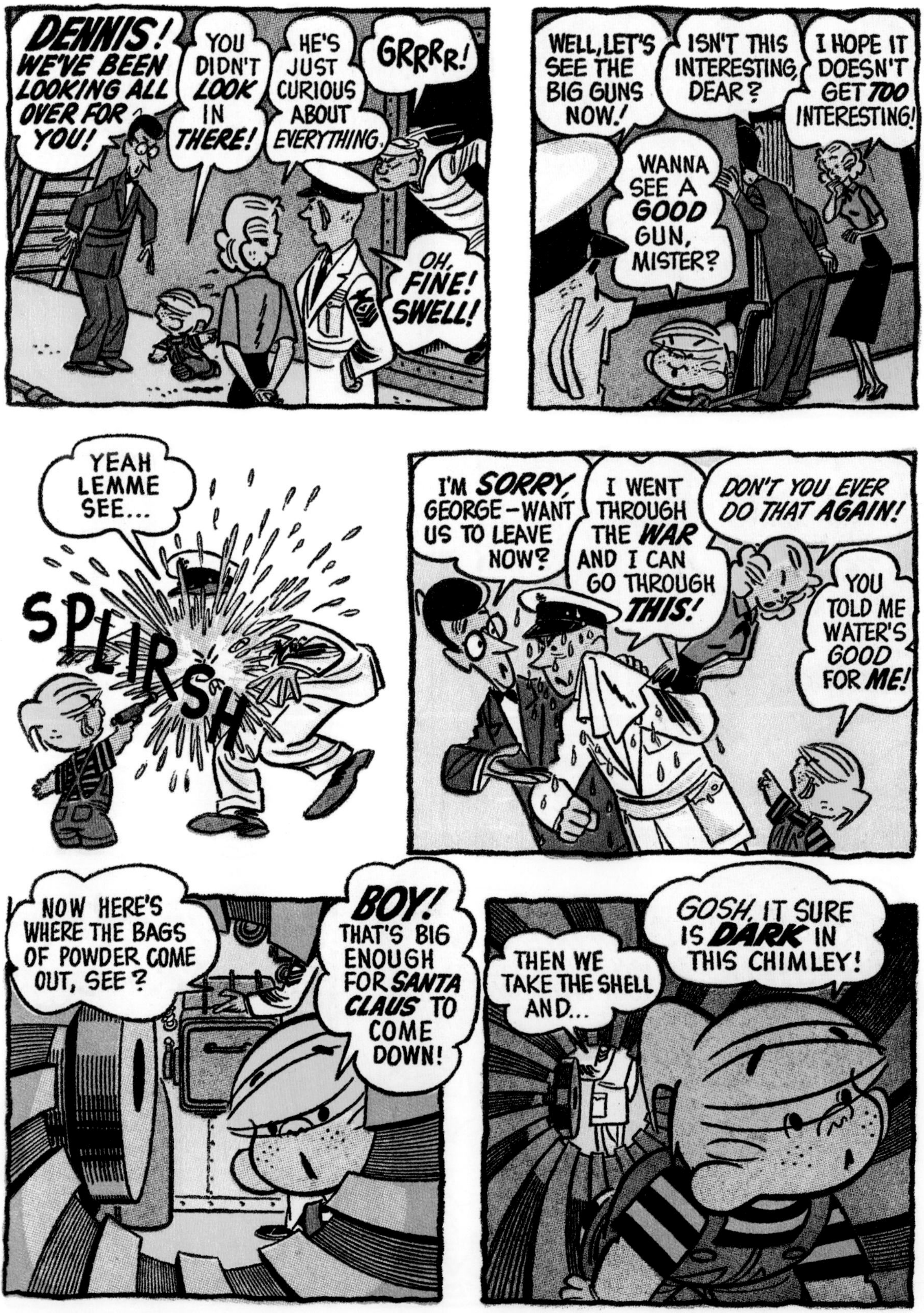
DENNIS! WE'VE BEEN LOOKING ALL OVER FOR YOU!
YOU DIDN'T LOOK IN THERE!
HE'S JUST CURIOUS ABOUT EVERYTHING.
GRRRR!
OH, FINE! SWELL!
WELL, LET'S SEE THE BIG GUNS NOW!
ISN'T THIS INTERESTING, DEAR?
I HOPE IT DOESN'T GET TOO INTERESTING!
WANNA SEE A GOOD GUN, MISTER?
YEAH LEMME SEE...
SPLIRSH
I'M SORRY, GEORGE—WANT US TO LEAVE NOW?
I WENT THROUGH THE WAR AND I CAN GO THROUGH THIS!
DON'T YOU EVER DO THAT AGAIN!
YOU TOLD ME WATER'S GOOD FOR ME!
NOW HERE'S WHERE THE BAGS OF POWDER COME OUT, SEE?
BOY! THAT'S BIG ENOUGH FOR SANTA CLAUS TO COME DOWN!
THEN WE TAKE THE SHELL AND...
GOSH, IT SURE IS DARK IN THIS CHIMLEY!

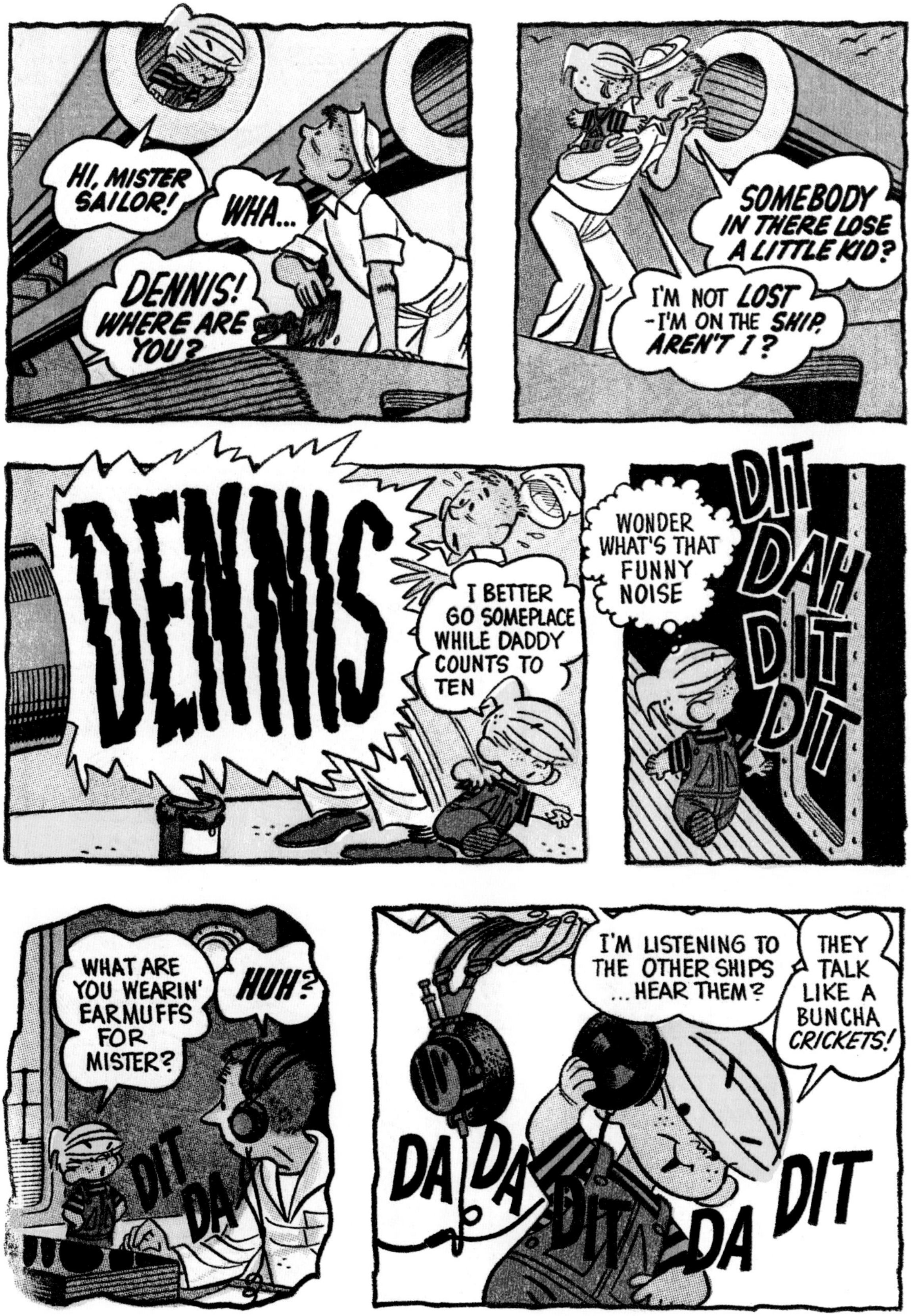

HI, MISTER SAILOR!
WHA...
DENNIS! WHERE ARE YOU?
SOMEBODY IN THERE LOSE A LITTLE KID?
I'M NOT LOST -I'M ON THE SHIP, AREN'T I?
DENNIS
I BETTER GO SOMEPLACE WHILE DADDY COUNTS TO TEN
WONDER WHAT'S THAT FUNNY NOISE
DIT DAH DIT DIT DIT
WHAT ARE YOU WEARIN' EARMUFFS FOR MISTER?
HUH?
DIT DA
I'M LISTENING TO THE OTHER SHIPS ... HEAR THEM?
THEY TALK LIKE A BUNCHA CRICKETS!
DA DA DIT DA DIT

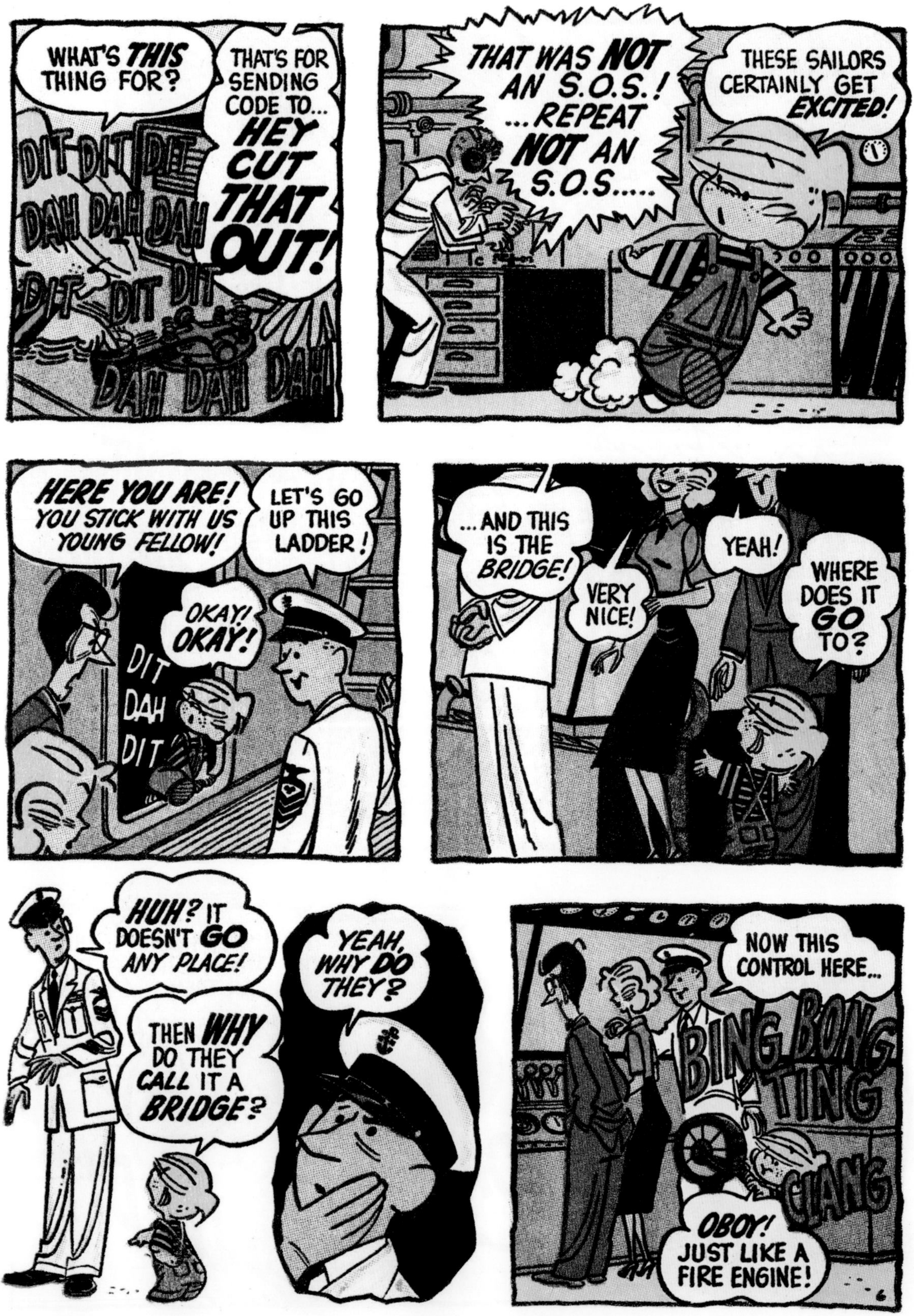
WHAT'S THIS THING FOR?
THAT'S FOR SENDING CODE TO... HEY CUT THAT OUT!
DIT DIT DIT
DAH DAH DAH
DIT DIT DIT
DAH DAH DAH!
THAT WAS NOT AN S.O.S.! ...REPEAT NOT AN S.O.S.....
THESE SAILORS CERTAINLY GET EXCITED!
HERE YOU ARE! YOU STICK WITH US YOUNG FELLOW!
LET'S GO UP THIS LADDER!
OKAY! OKAY!
DIT DAH DIT
...AND THIS IS THE BRIDGE!
VERY NICE!
YEAH!
WHERE DOES IT GO TO?
HUH? IT DOESN'T GO ANY PLACE!
THEN WHY DO THEY CALL IT A BRIDGE?
YEAH, WHY DO THEY?
NOW THIS CONTROL HERE...
BING BONG TING
CLANG
OBOY! JUST LIKE A FIRE ENGINE!

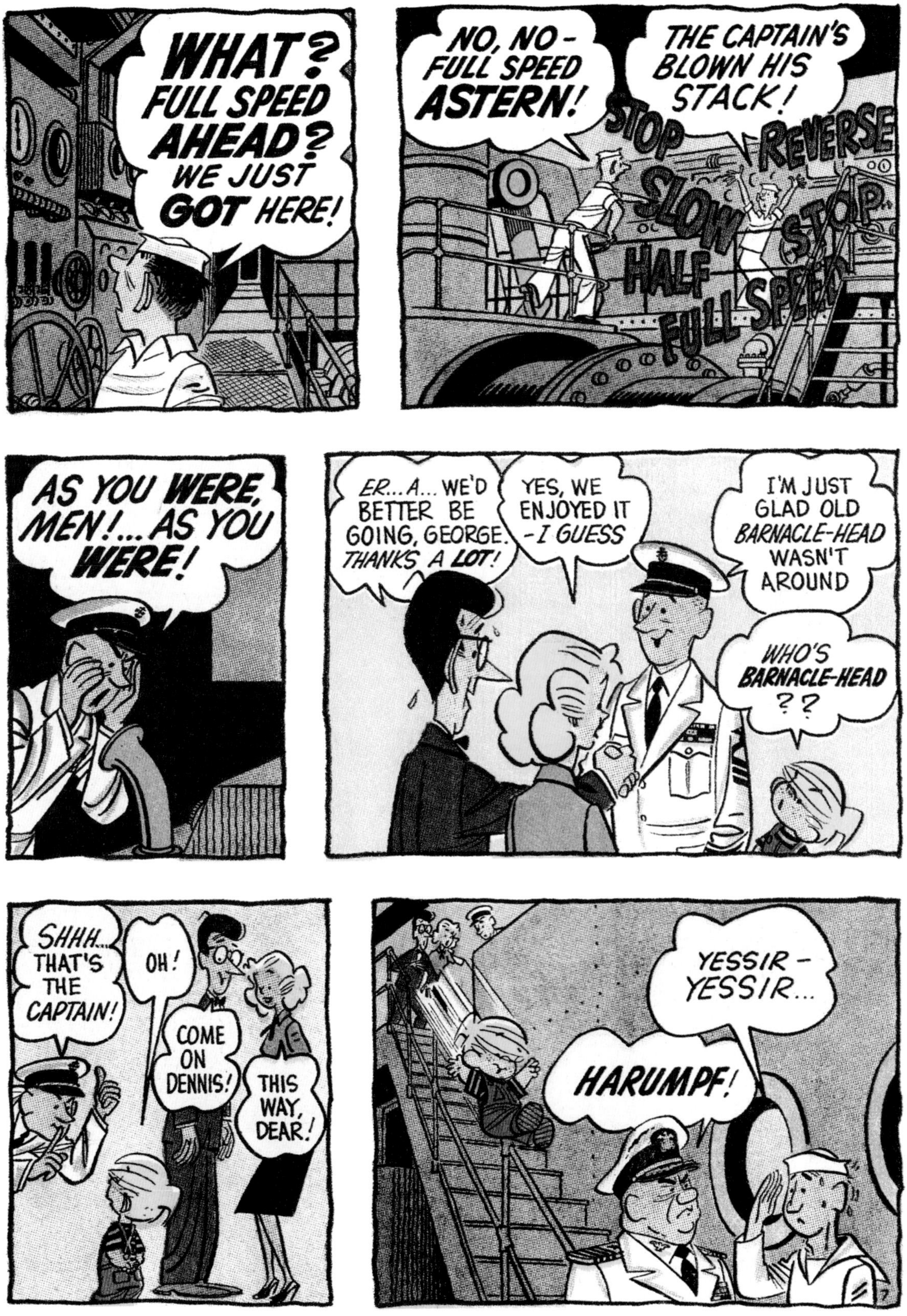
WHAT? FULL SPEED AHEAD? WE JUST GOT HERE!
NO, NO - FULL SPEED ASTERN!
THE CAPTAIN'S BLOWN HIS STACK!
STOP
REVERSE
SLOW
STOP
HALF
FULL SPEED
AS YOU WERE, MEN!... AS YOU WERE!
ER...A... WE'D BETTER BE GOING, GEORGE. THANKS A LOT!
YES, WE ENJOYED IT -I GUESS
I'M JUST GLAD OLD BARNACLE-HEAD WASN'T AROUND
WHO'S BARNACLE-HEAD ??
SHHH... THAT'S THE CAPTAIN!
OH!
COME ON DENNIS!
THIS WAY, DEAR!
YESSIR - YESSIR...
HARUMPF!

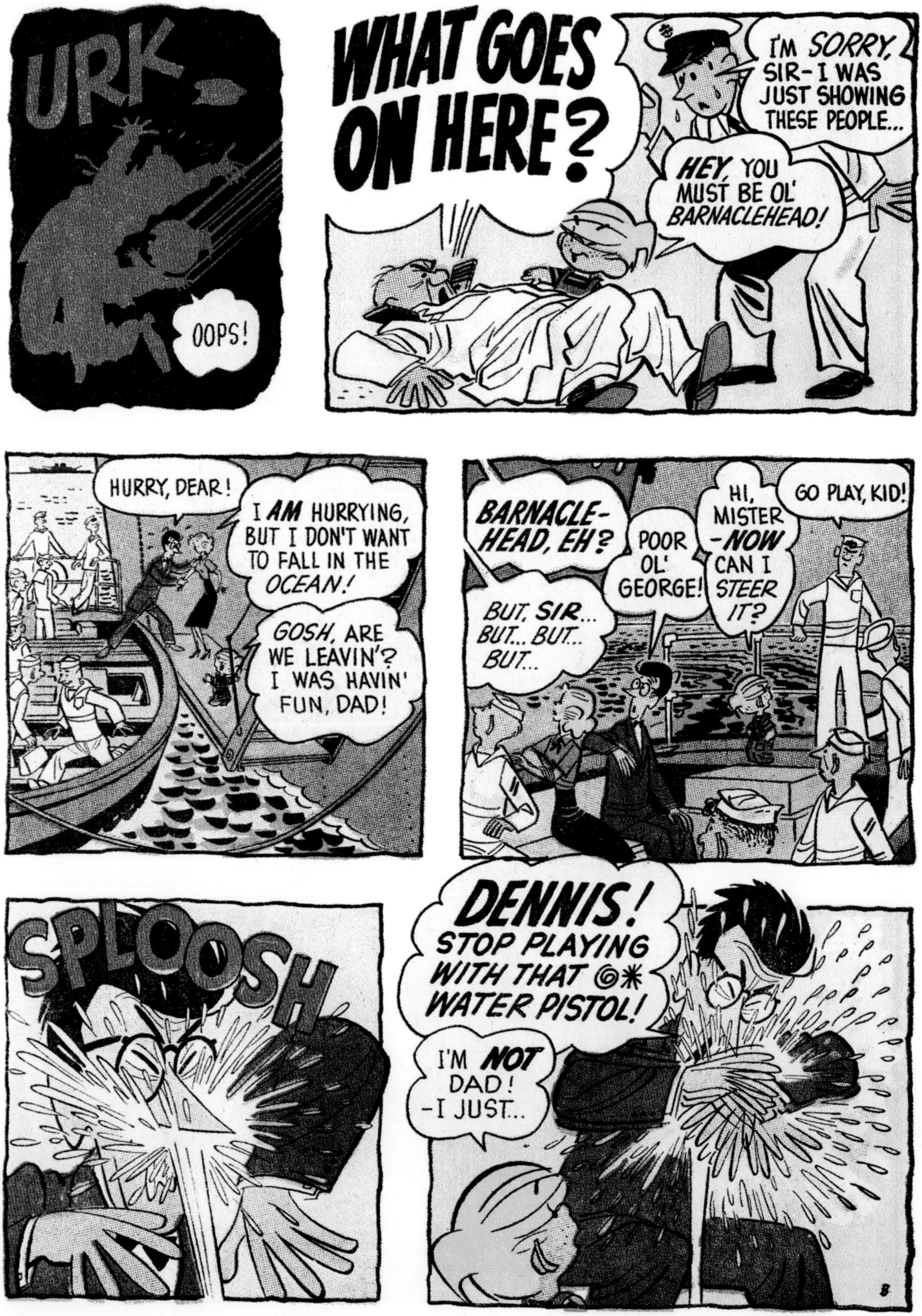
URK
OOPS!
WHAT GOES ON HERE?
I'M SORRY, SIR- I WAS JUST SHOWING THESE PEOPLE...
HEY, YOU MUST BE OL' BARNACLEHEAD!
HURRY, DEAR!
I AM HURRYING, BUT I DON'T WANT TO FALL IN THE OCEAN!
GOSH, ARE WE LEAVIN'? I WAS HAVIN' FUN, DAD!
BARNACLE-HEAD, EH?
BUT, SIR... BUT... BUT... BUT...
POOR OL' GEORGE!
HI, MISTER -NOW CAN I STEER IT?
GO PLAY, KID!
SPLOOSH
DENNIS! STOP PLAYING WITH THAT @* WATER PISTOL!
I'M NOT DAD! -I JUST...
8

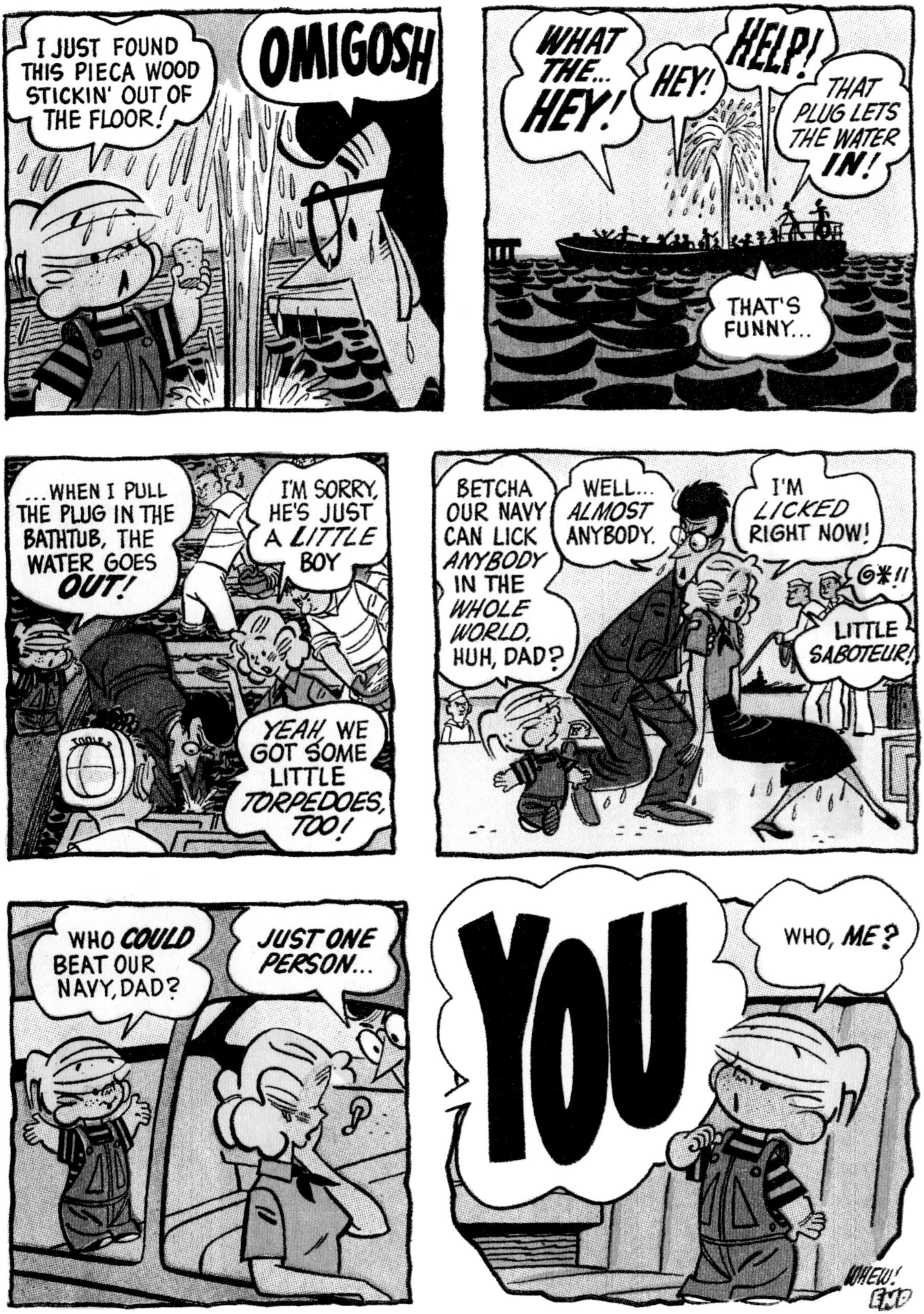
I JUST FOUND THIS PIECA WOOD STICKIN' OUT OF THE FLOOR!
OMIGOSH
WHAT THE... HEY!
HEY!
HELP!
THAT PLUG LETS THE WATER IN!
THAT'S FUNNY...
...WHEN I PULL THE PLUG IN THE BATHTUB, THE WATER GOES OUT!
I'M SORRY, HE'S JUST A LITTLE BOY
YEAH, WE GOT SOME LITTLE TORPEDOES, TOO!
BETCHA OUR NAVY CAN LICK ANYBODY IN THE WHOLE WORLD, HUH, DAD?
WELL... ALMOST ANYBODY.
I'M LICKED RIGHT NOW!
@*!!
LITTLE SABOTEUR!
WHO COULD BEAT OUR NAVY, DAD?
JUST ONE PERSON...
YOU
WHO, ME?
WHEW!
END

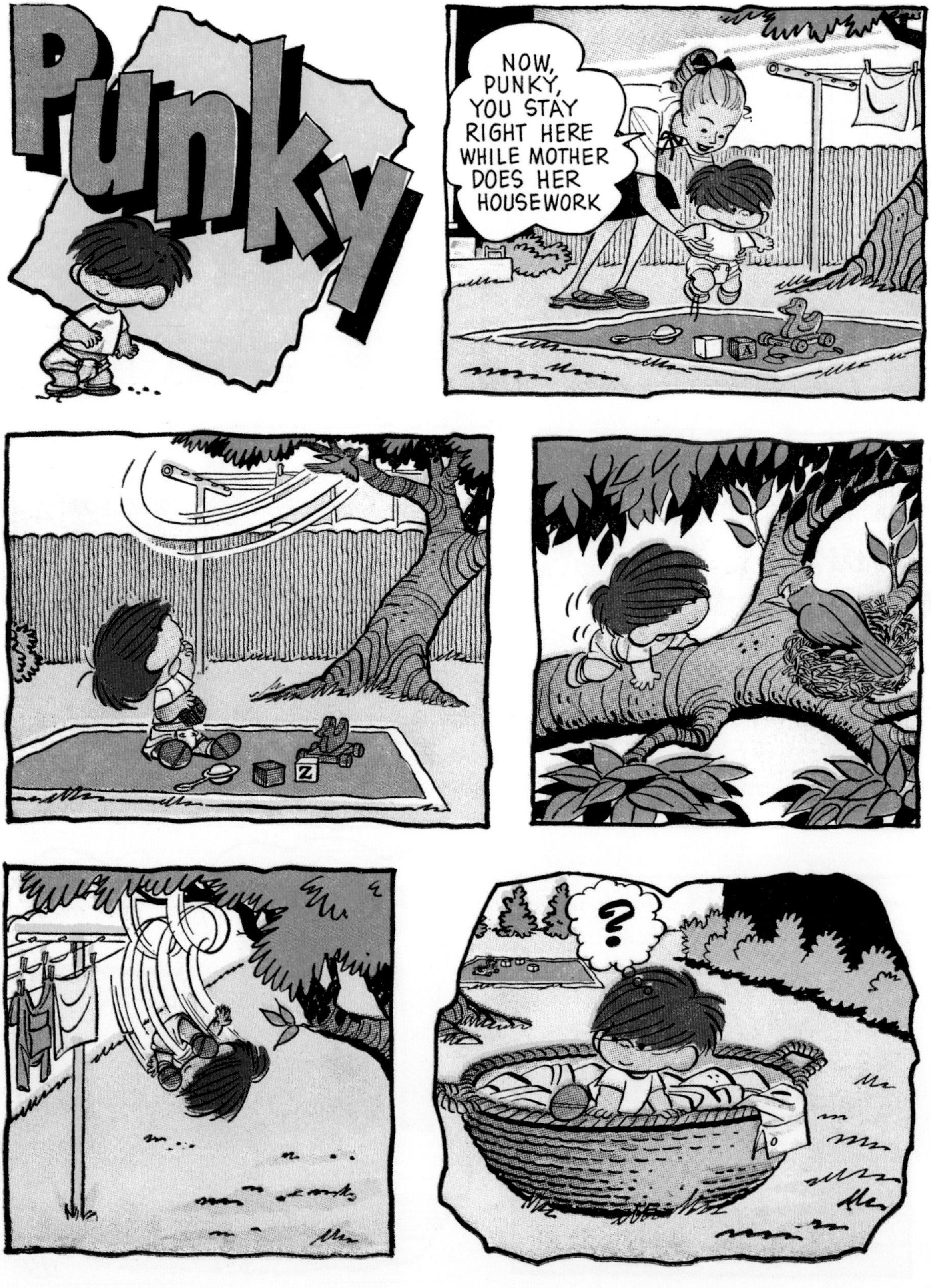
Punky
NOW, PUNKY, YOU STAY RIGHT HERE WHILE MOTHER DOES HER HOUSEWORK
?

?
?
ZZZ
?
?

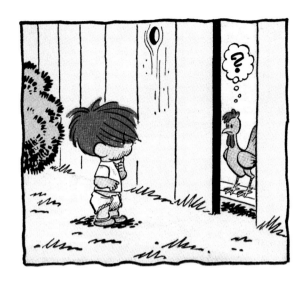

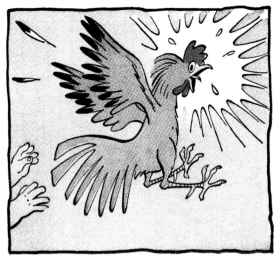

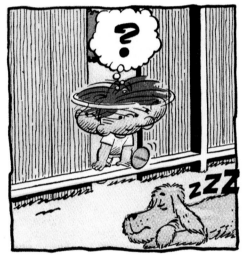

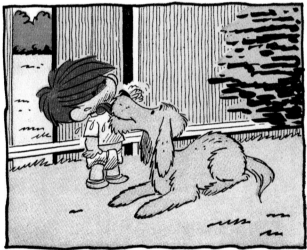

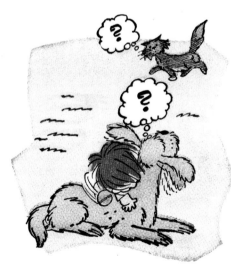

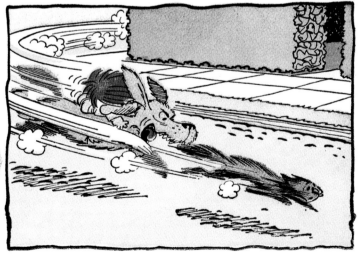

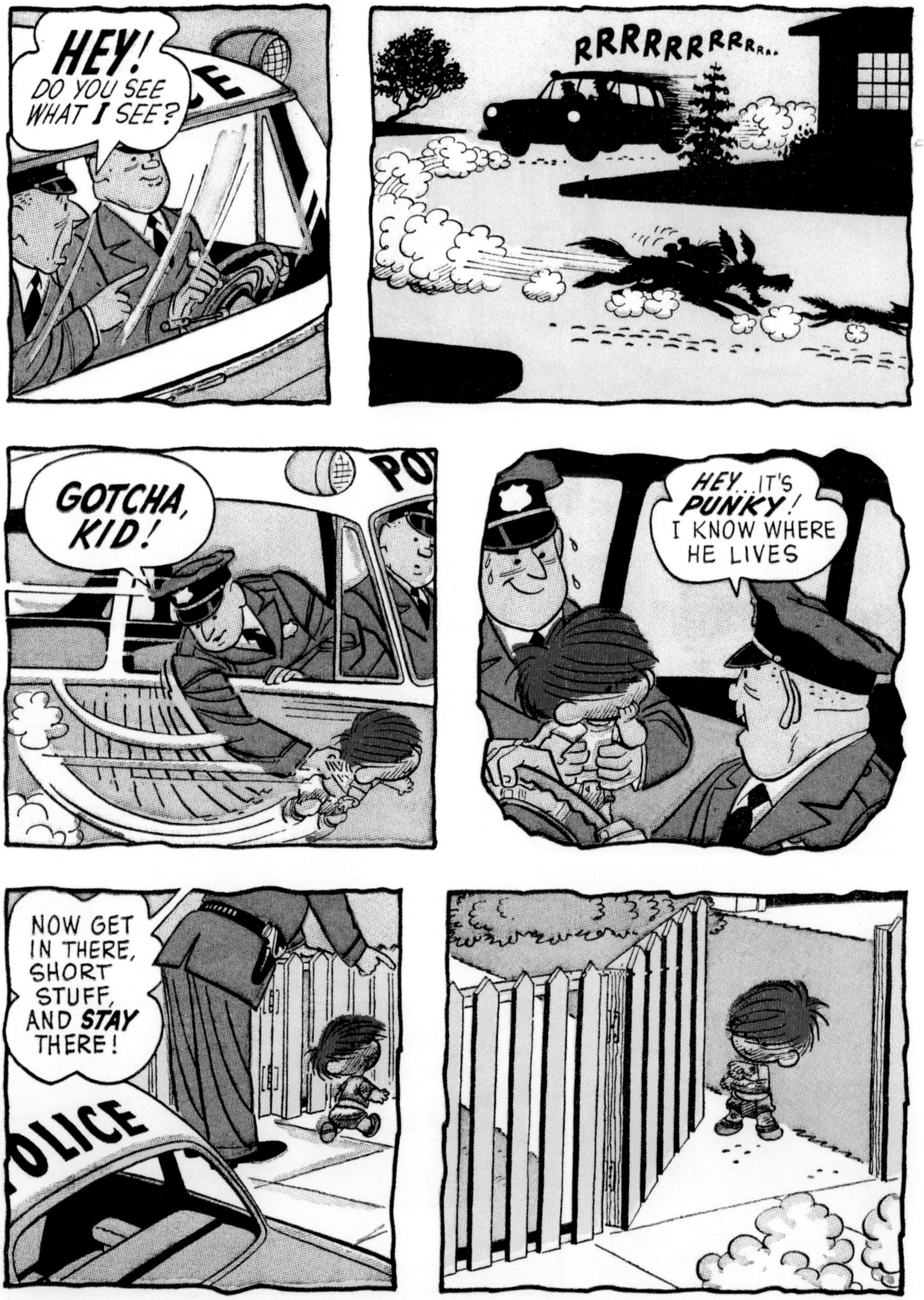
HEY!
DO YOU SEE WHAT I SEE?
RRRRRRRRRR...
GOTCHA, KID!
HEY... IT'S PUNKY! I KNOW WHERE HE LIVES
NOW GET IN THERE, SHORT STUFF, AND STAY THERE!
POLICE

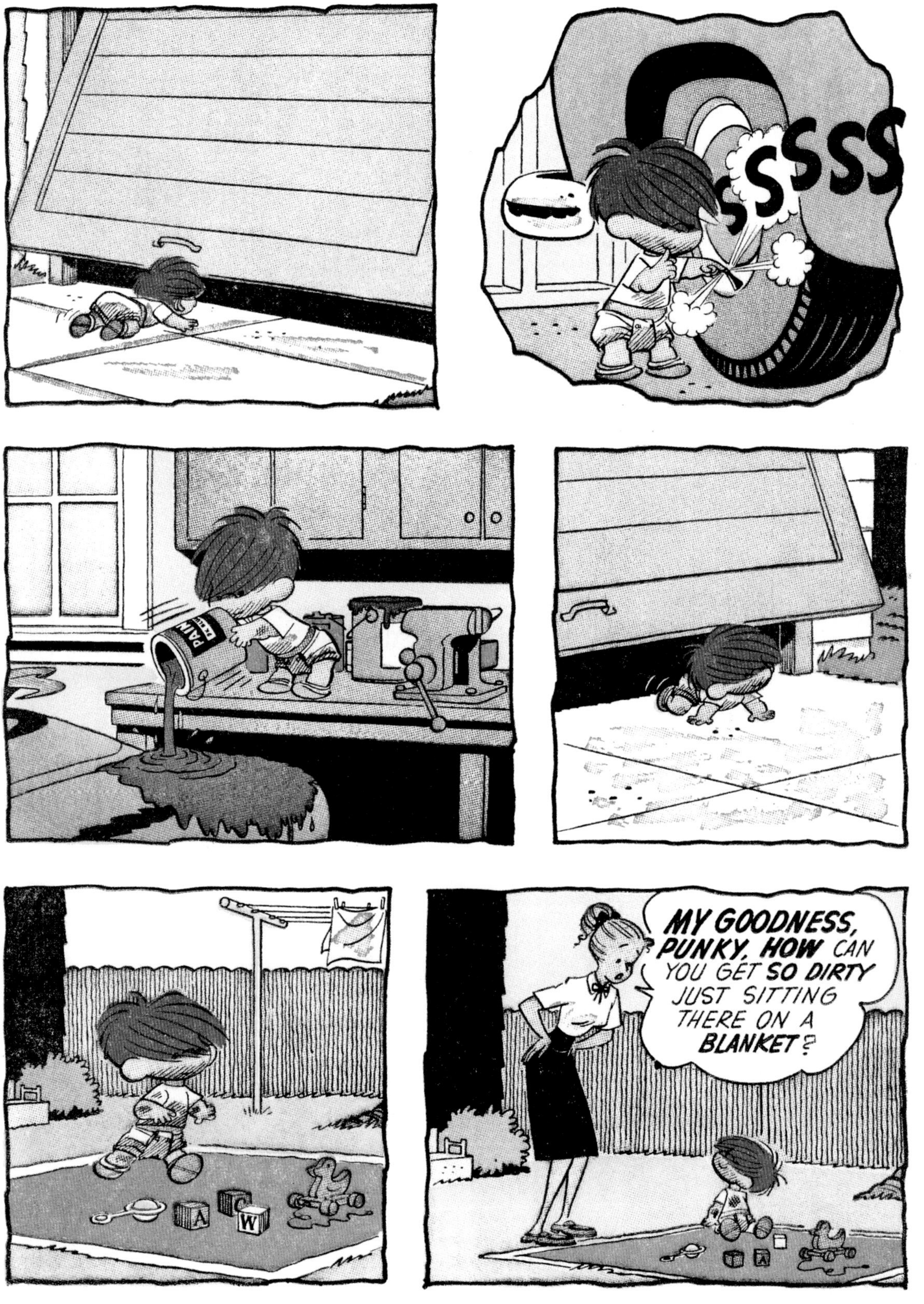
SSSSS
MY GOODNESS, PUNKY, HOW CAN YOU GET SO DIRTY JUST SITTING THERE ON A BLANKET?

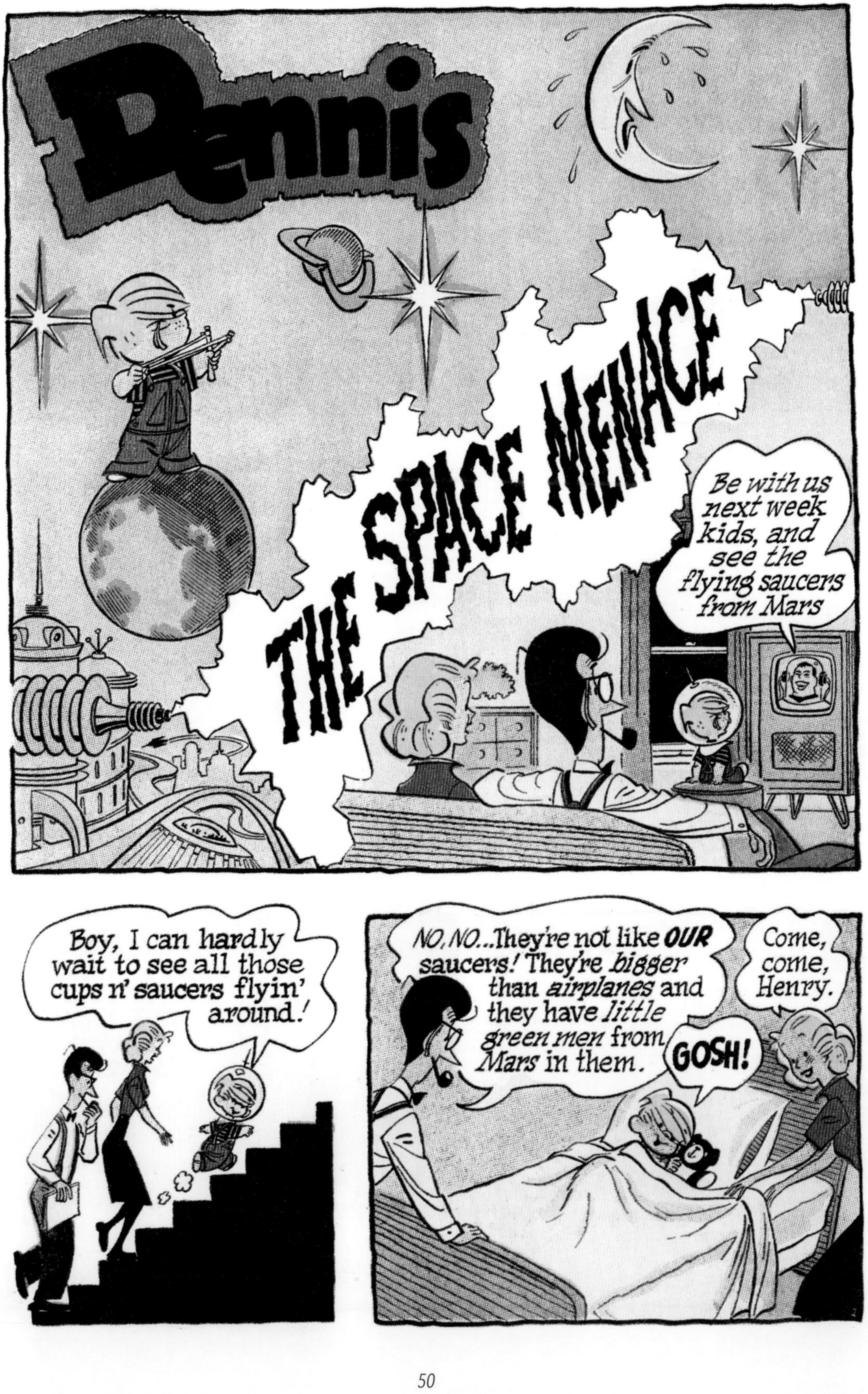
Dennis
THE SPACE MENACE
Be with us next week kids, and see the flying saucers from Mars
Boy, I can hardly wait to see all those cups n' saucers flyin' around.!
NO, NO...They're not like OUR saucers! They're bigger than airplanes and they have little green men from Mars in them.
Come, come, Henry.
GOSH!

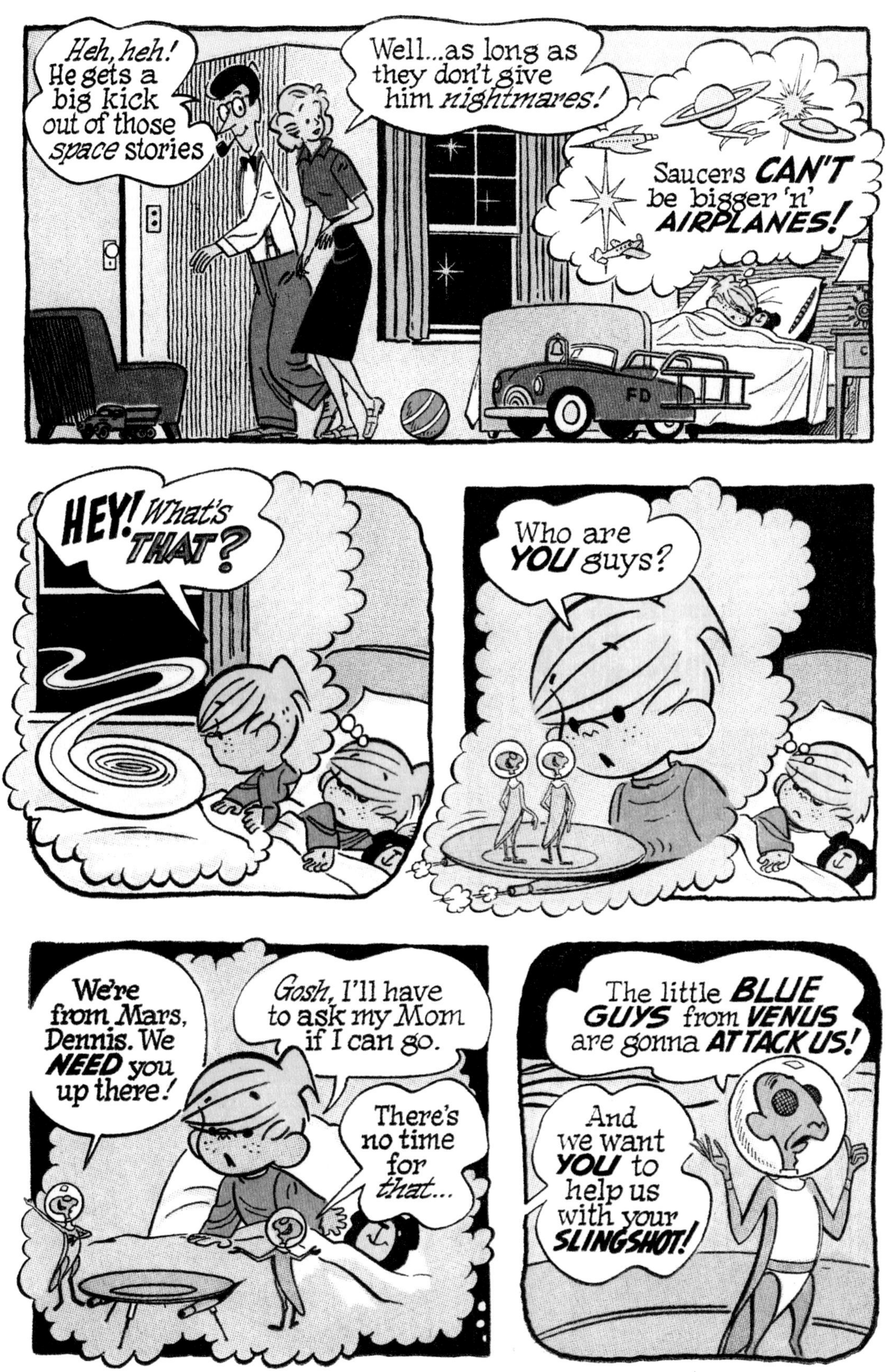

Heh, heh! He gets a big kick out of those *space* stories
Well...as long as they don't give him *nightmares!*
Saucers **CAN'T** be bigger 'n' **AIRPLANES!**
FD
HEY! What's **THAT?**
Who are **YOU** guys?
We're from Mars, Dennis. We **NEED** you up there!
Gosh, I'll have to ask my Mom if I can go.
There's no time for *that...*
The little **BLUE GUYS** from **VENUS** are gonna **ATTACK US!**
And we want **YOU** to help us with your **SLINGSHOT!**

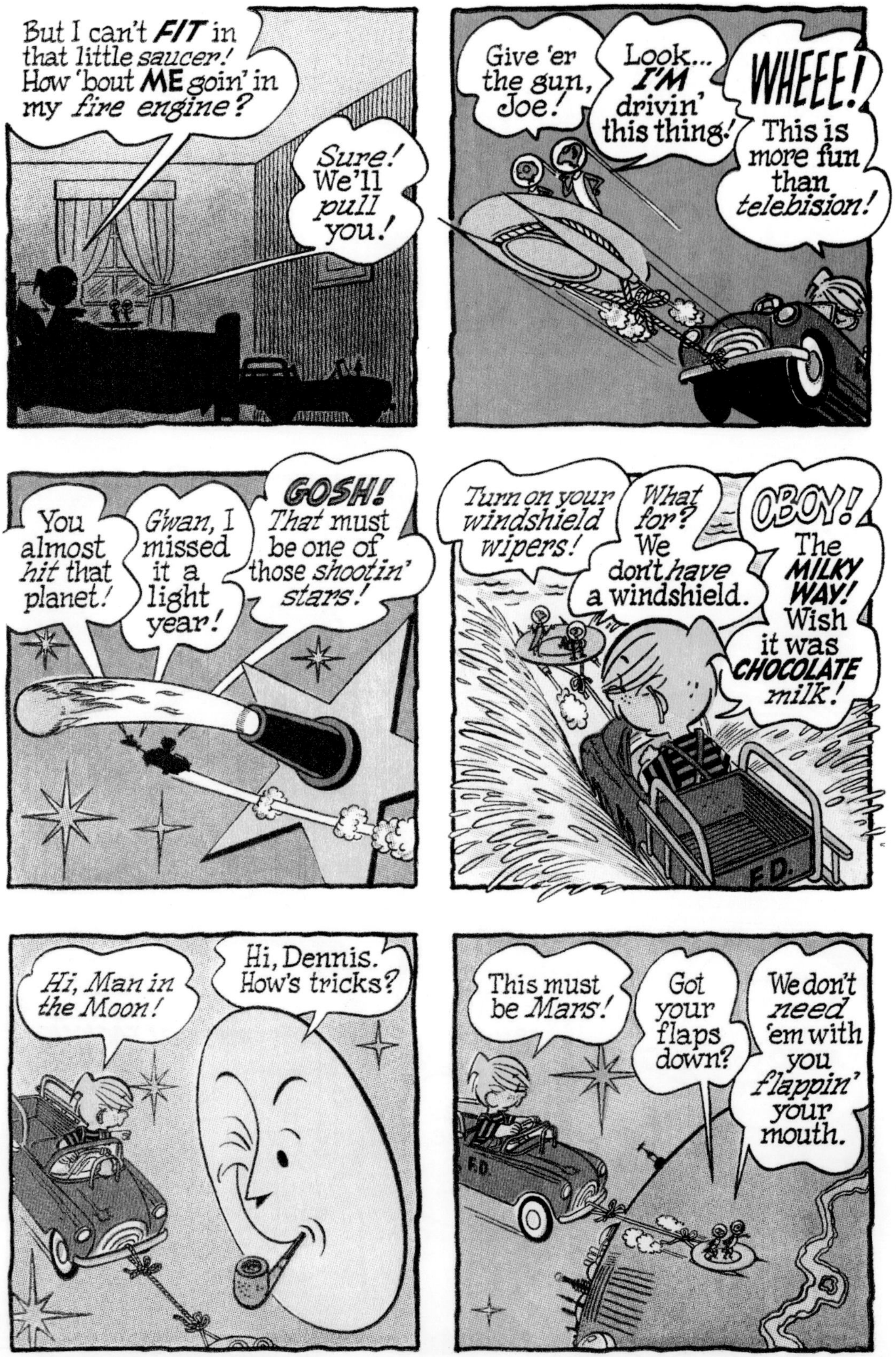
But I can't FIT in that little saucer! How 'bout ME goin' in my fire engine?
Sure! We'll pull you!
Give 'er the gun, Joe!
Look... I'M drivin' this thing!
WHEEE! This is more fun than telebision!
You almost hit that planet!
G'wan, I missed it a light year!
GOSH! That must be one of those shootin' stars!
Turn on your windshield wipers!
What for? We don't have a windshield.
OBOY! The MILKY WAY! Wish it was CHOCOLATE milk!
F.D.
Hi, Man in the Moon!
Hi, Dennis. How's tricks?
This must be Mars!
Got your flaps down?
We don't need 'em with you flappin' your mouth.
F.D.

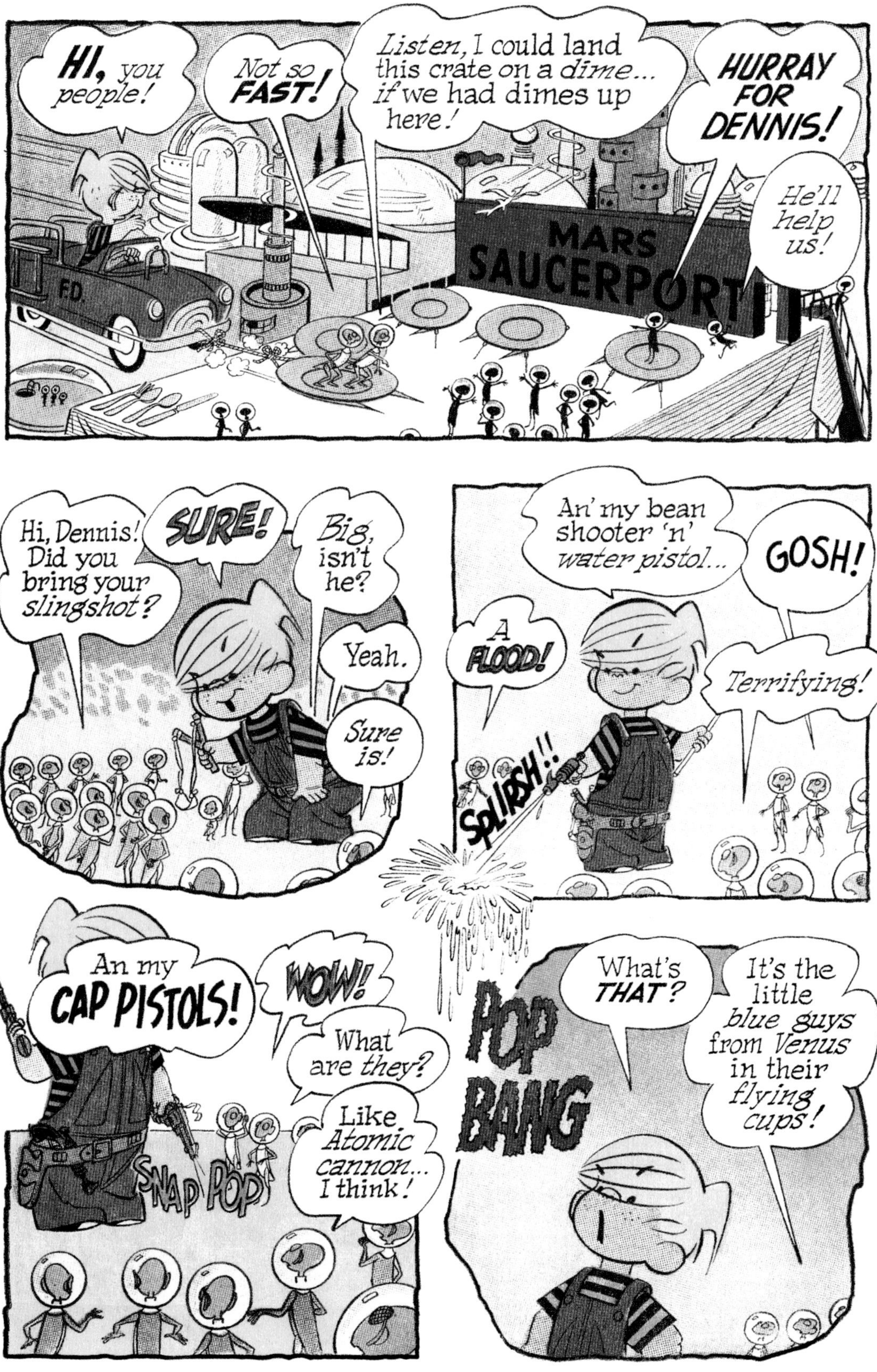
HI, you people!
Not so FAST!
Listen, I could land this crate on a dime... if we had dimes up here!
HURRAY FOR DENNIS!
He'll help us!
MARS SAUCERPORT
F.D.
Hi, Dennis! Did you bring your slingshot?
SURE!
Big, isn't he?
Yeah.
Sure is!
An' my bean shooter 'n' water pistol...
GOSH!
A FLOOD!
Terrifying!
SPLIRSH!!
An my CAP PISTOLS!
WOW!
What are they?
Like Atomic cannon... I think!
SNAP POP
POP BANG
What's THAT?
It's the little blue guys from Venus in their flying cups!

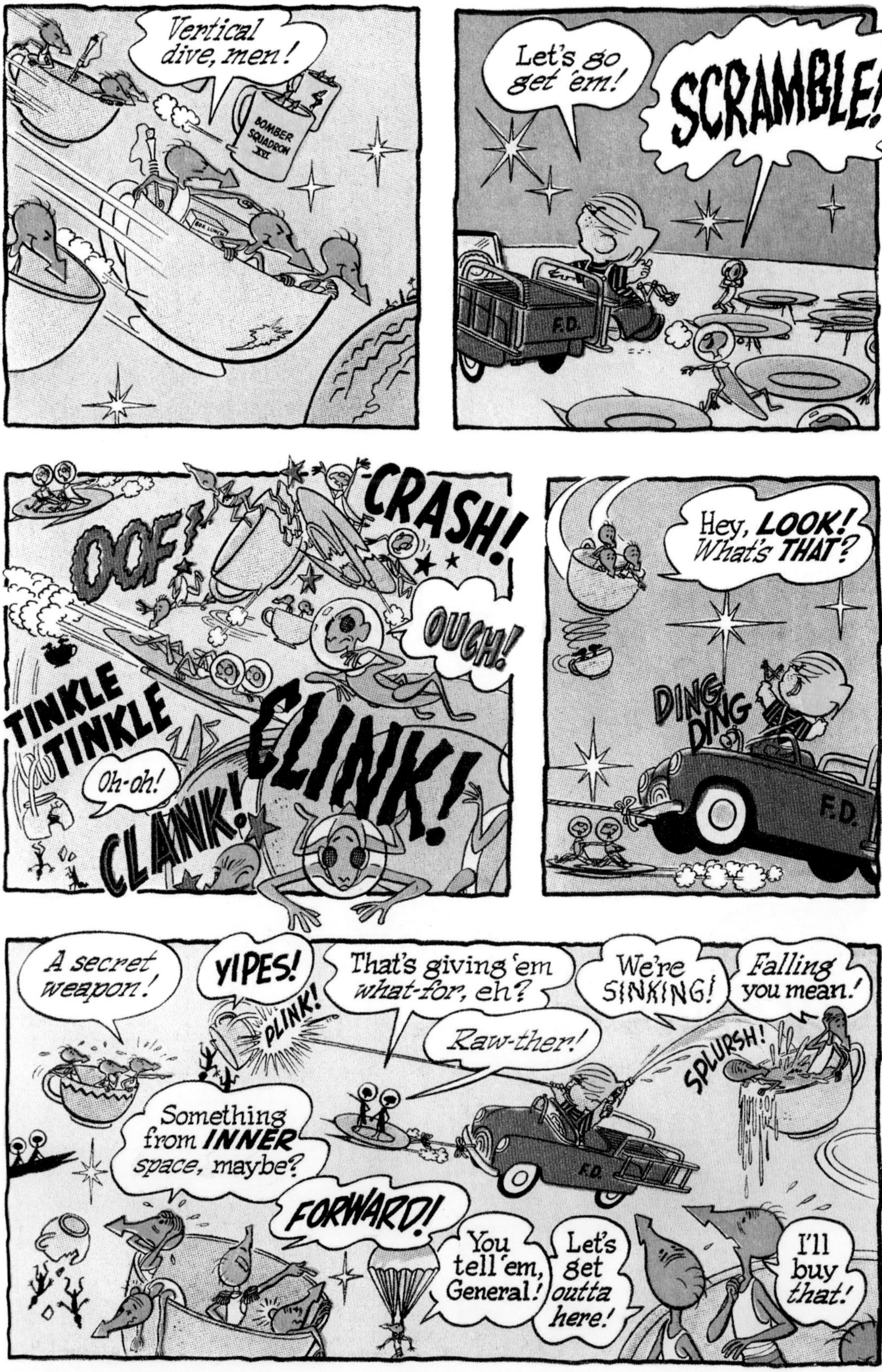
Vertical dive, men!
BOMBER SQUADRON XVI
Let's go get 'em!
SCRAMBLE!
F.D.
OOF!
CRASH!
OUGH!
TINKLE TINKLE
Oh-oh!
CLANK!
CLINK!
Hey, **LOOK!** *What's* **THAT?**
DING DING
F.D.
A secret weapon!
YIPES!
PLINK!
That's giving 'em *what-for*, eh?
Raw-ther!
We're SINKING!
Falling you mean!
SPLURSH!
Something from ***INNER*** *space*, maybe?
F.D.
FORWARD!
You tell 'em, General!
Let's get *outta here!*
I'll buy *that!*

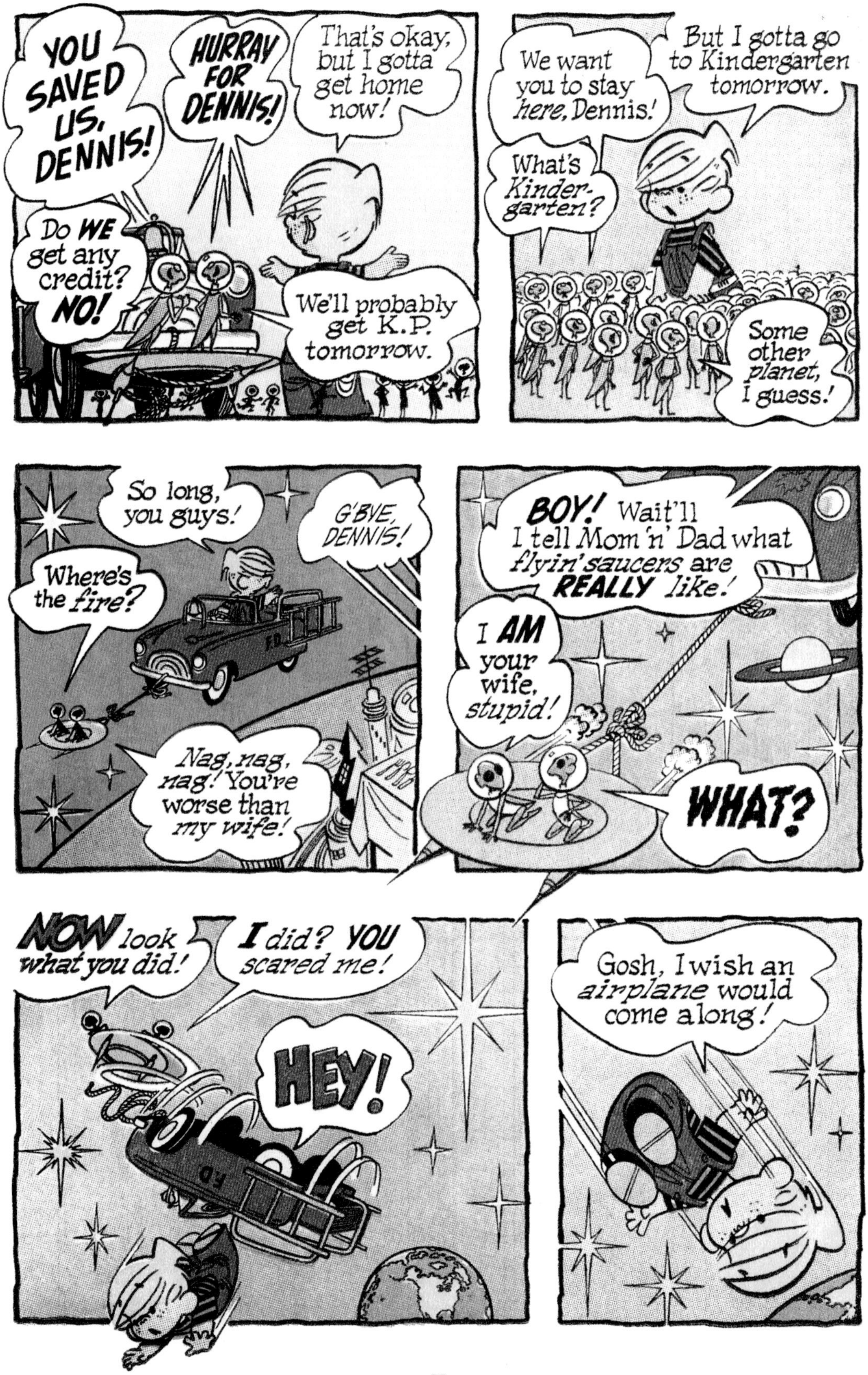
YOU SAVED US, DENNIS!
HURRAY FOR DENNIS!
That's okay, but I gotta get home now!
Do WE get any credit? NO!
We'll probably get K.P. tomorrow.
We want you to stay here, Dennis!
But I gotta go to Kindergarten tomorrow.
What's Kindergarten?
Some other planet, I guess!
So long, you guys!
G'BYE, DENNIS!
Where's the fire?
Nag, nag, nag! You're worse than my wife!
BOY! Wait'll I tell Mom 'n' Dad what flyin' saucers are REALLY like!
I AM your wife, stupid!
WHAT?
NOW look what you did!
I did? YOU scared me!
HEY!
Gosh, I wish an airplane would come along!

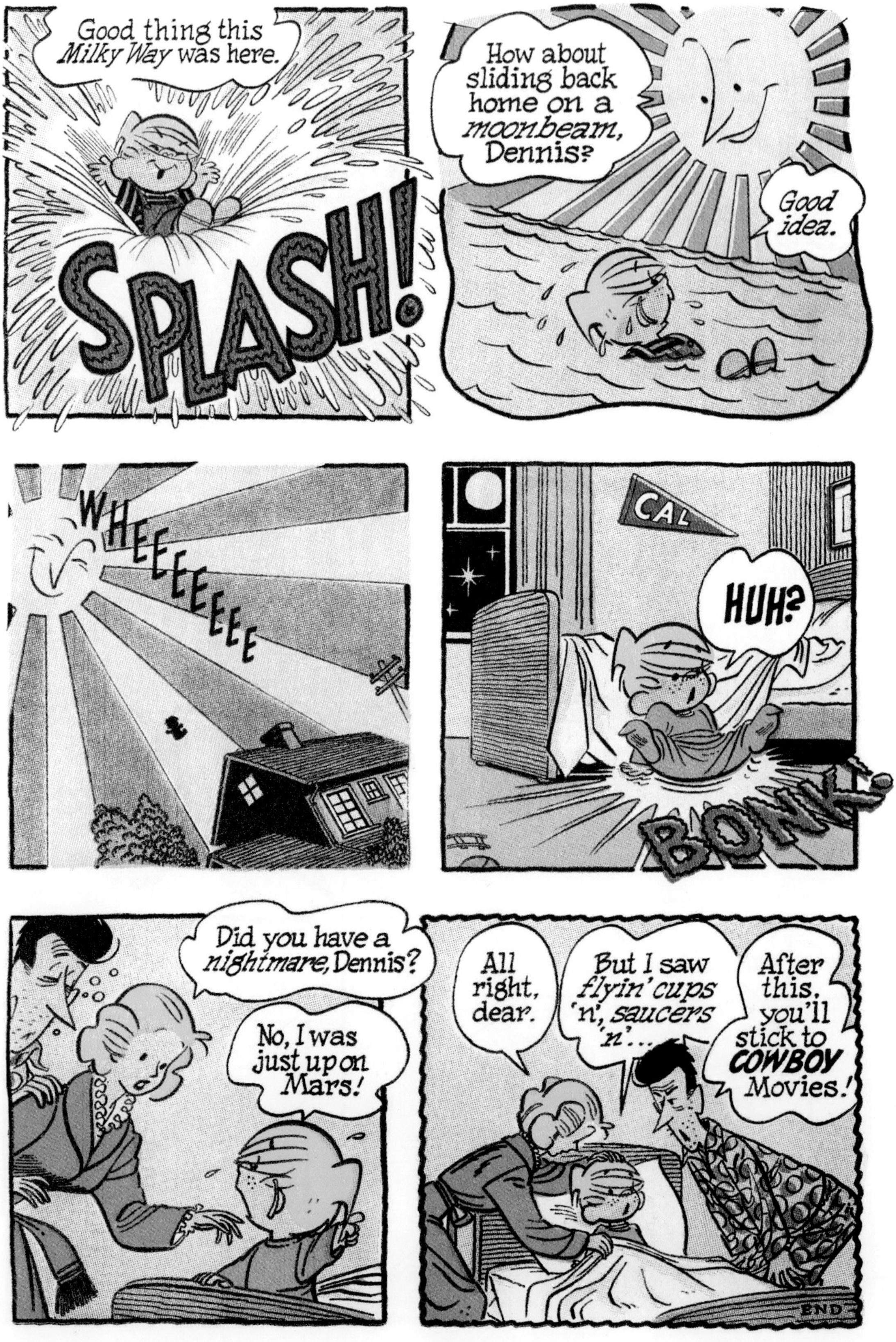

Good thing this Milky Way was here.
SPLASH!
How about sliding back home on a moonbeam, Dennis?
Good idea.
WHEEEEEEEE
CAL
HUH?
BONK!
Did you have a nightmare, Dennis?
No, I was just up on Mars!
All right, dear.
But I saw flyin' cups 'n' saucers 'n'...
After this, you'll stick to COWBOY Movies!

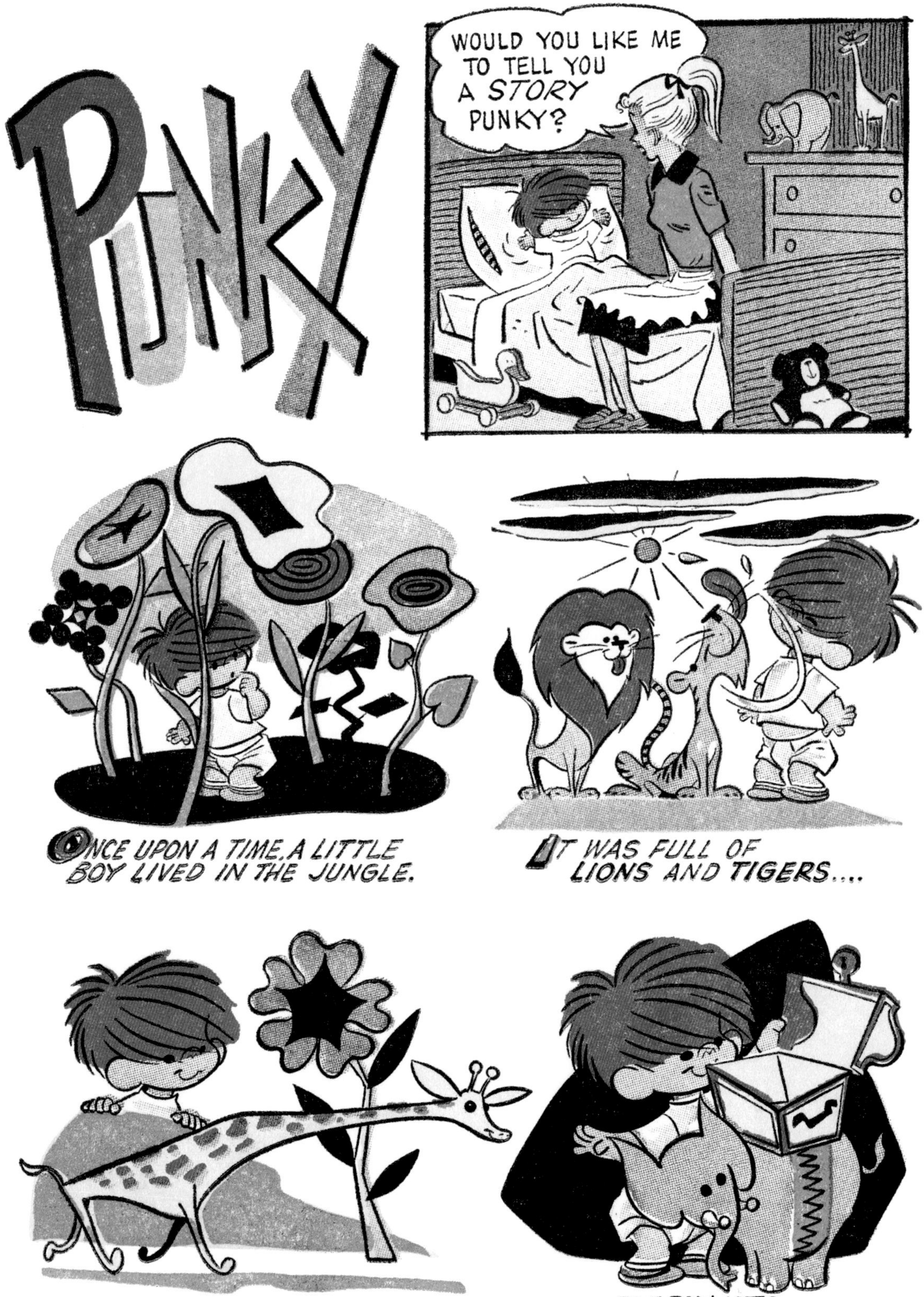
PUNKY
WOULD YOU LIKE ME TO TELL YOU A STORY PUNKY?
ONCE UPON A TIME, A LITTLE BOY LIVED IN THE JUNGLE.
IT WAS FULL OF LIONS AND TIGERS....
... AND GIRAFFES WITH LONG NECKS...
... AND ELEPHANTS WITH BIG TRUNKS

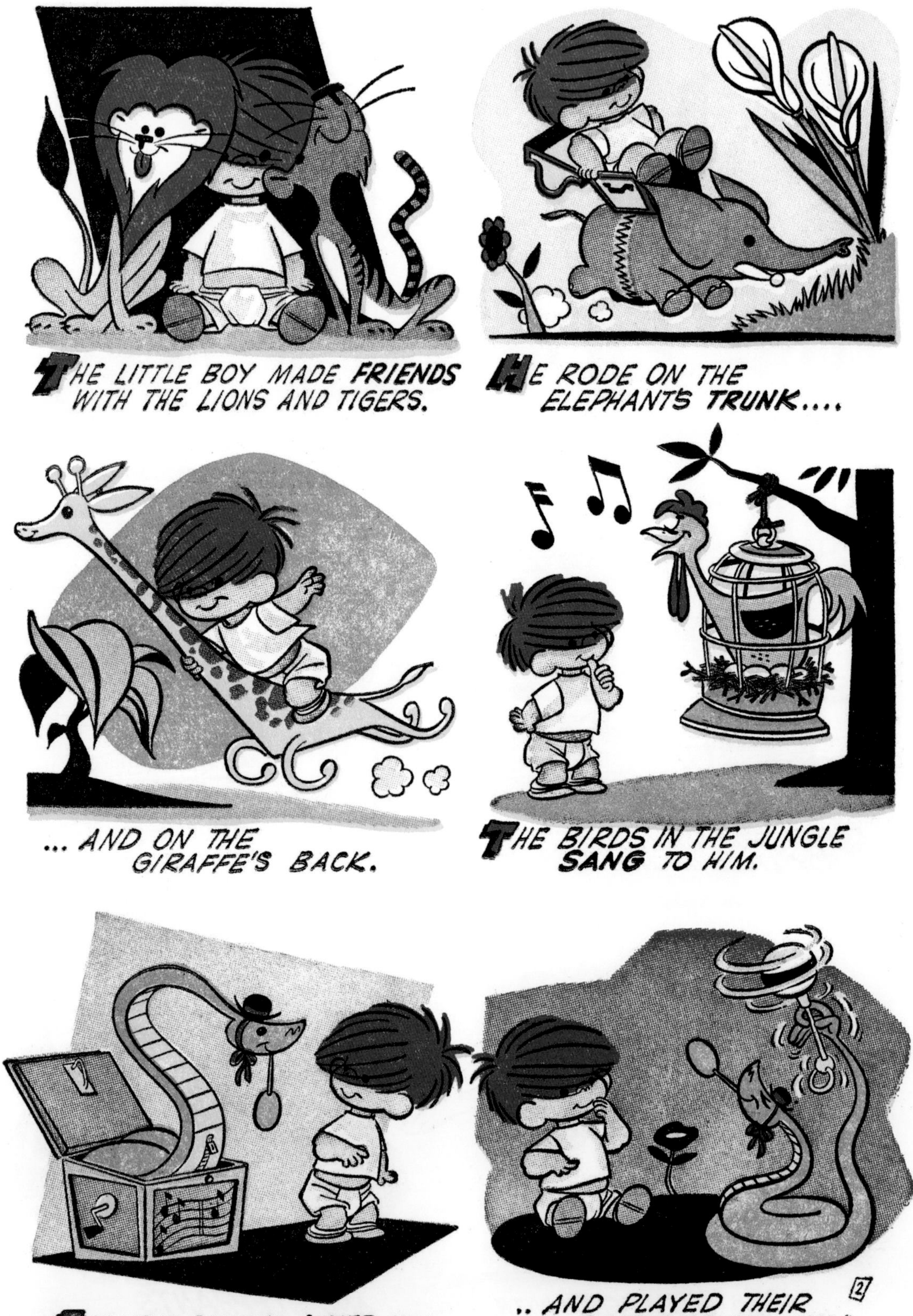
THE LITTLE BOY MADE FRIENDS WITH THE LIONS AND TIGERS.
HE RODE ON THE ELEPHANT'S TRUNK....
... AND ON THE GIRAFFE'S BACK.
THE BIRDS IN THE JUNGLE SANG TO HIM.
EVEN THE SNAKE'S LIKED HIM....
.. AND PLAYED THEIR RATTLES FOR HIM!
2

THEN ONE DAY ALL THE ANIMALS STARTED **RUNNING AWAY!**

THE LITTLE BOY ASKED WHAT WAS THE **MATTER**?

THEY SAID **THE JUNGLE'S ON FIRE!**

THE LITTLE BOY SAID **I'LL SAVE YOU!!!**

AND HE LED THEM **BACK** TO WHERE THE **FIRE** WAS.

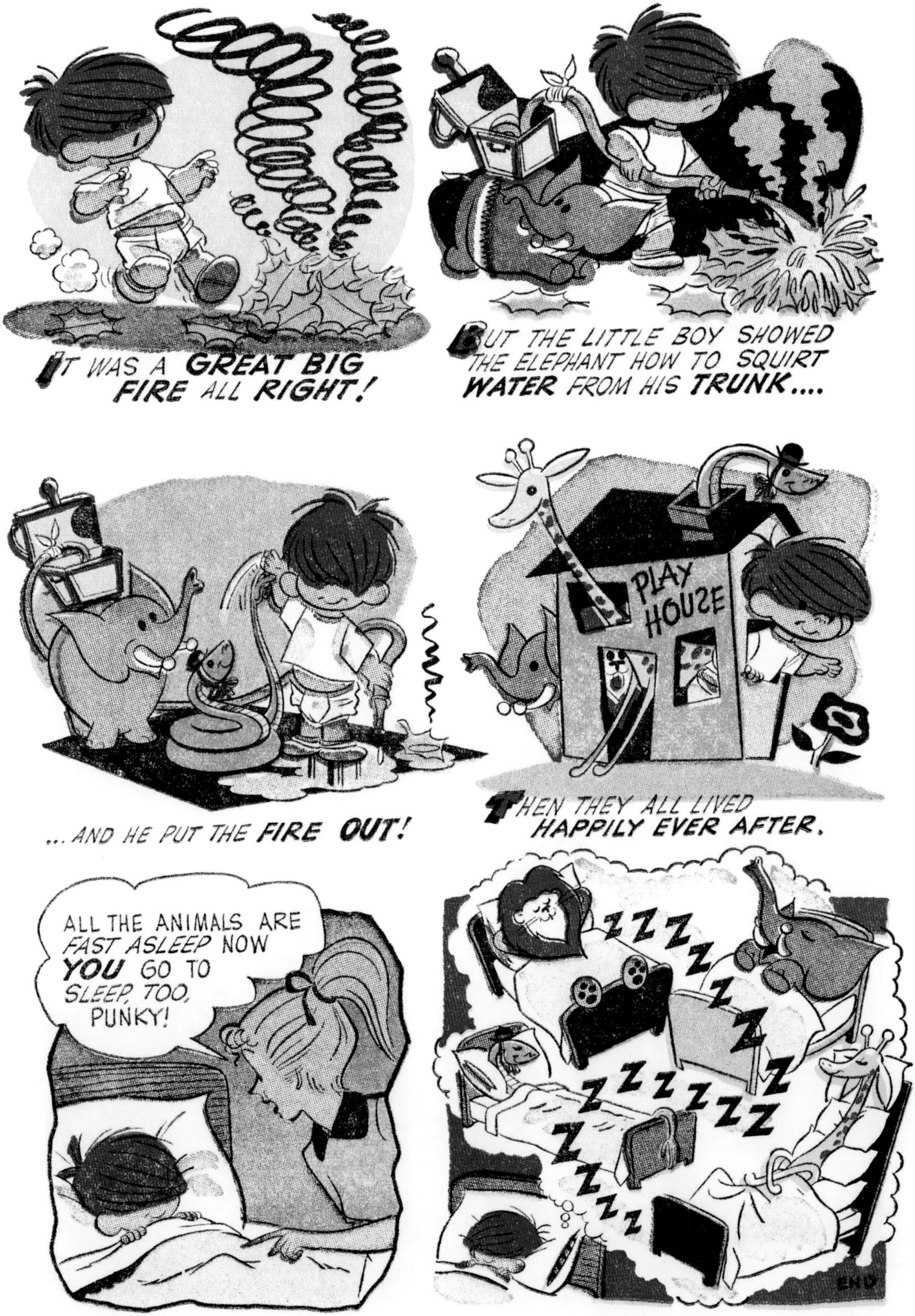
IT WAS A GREAT BIG FIRE ALL RIGHT!
BUT THE LITTLE BOY SHOWED THE ELEPHANT HOW TO SQUIRT WATER FROM HIS TRUNK....
...AND HE PUT THE FIRE OUT!
PLAY HOUSE
THEN THEY ALL LIVED HAPPILY EVER AFTER.
ALL THE ANIMALS ARE FAST ASLEEP NOW YOU GO TO SLEEP, TOO, PUNKY!
END

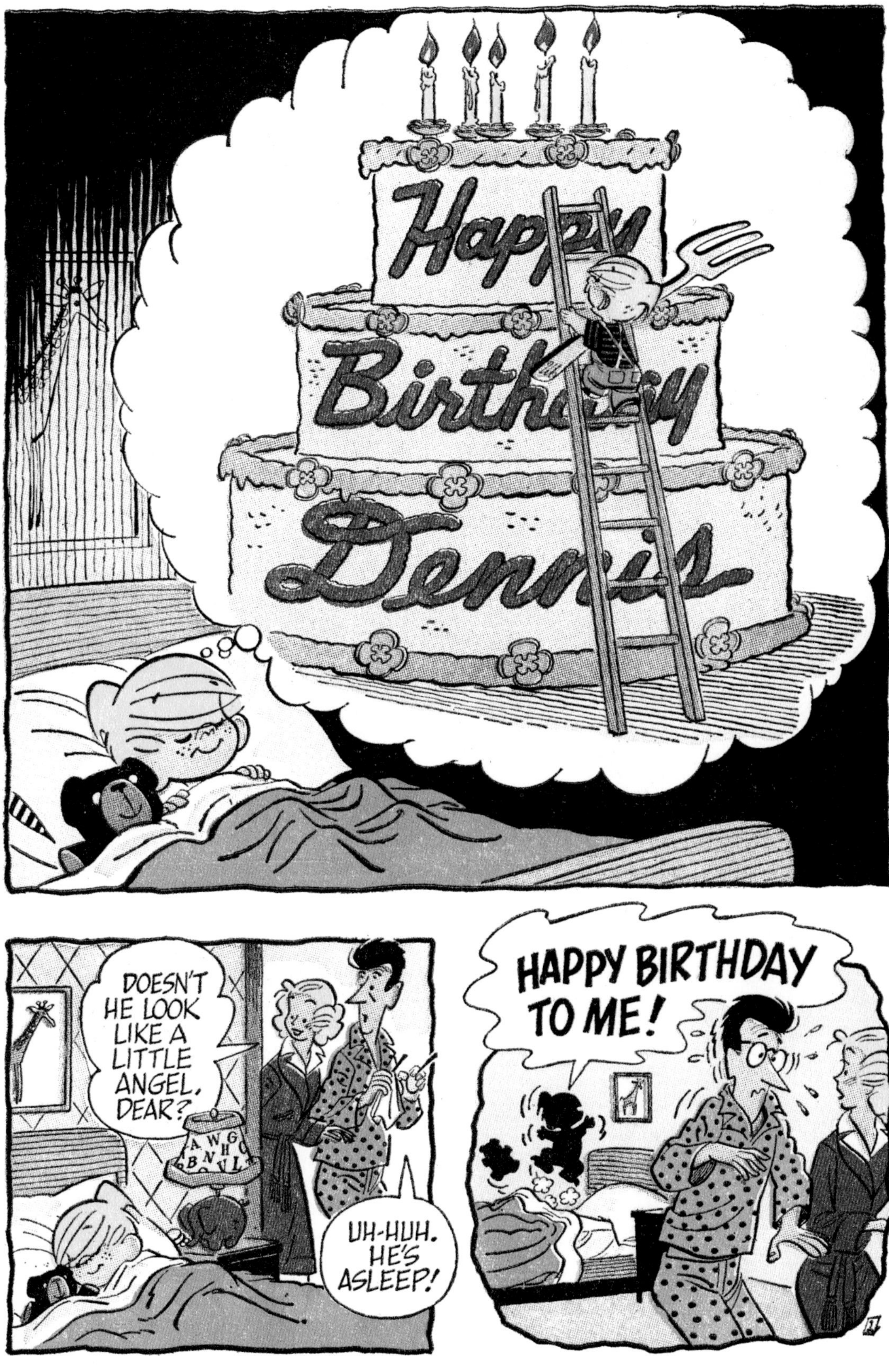
Happy Birthday Dennis
DOESN'T HE LOOK LIKE A LITTLE ANGEL, DEAR?
UH-HUH. HE'S ASLEEP!
HAPPY BIRTHDAY TO ME!

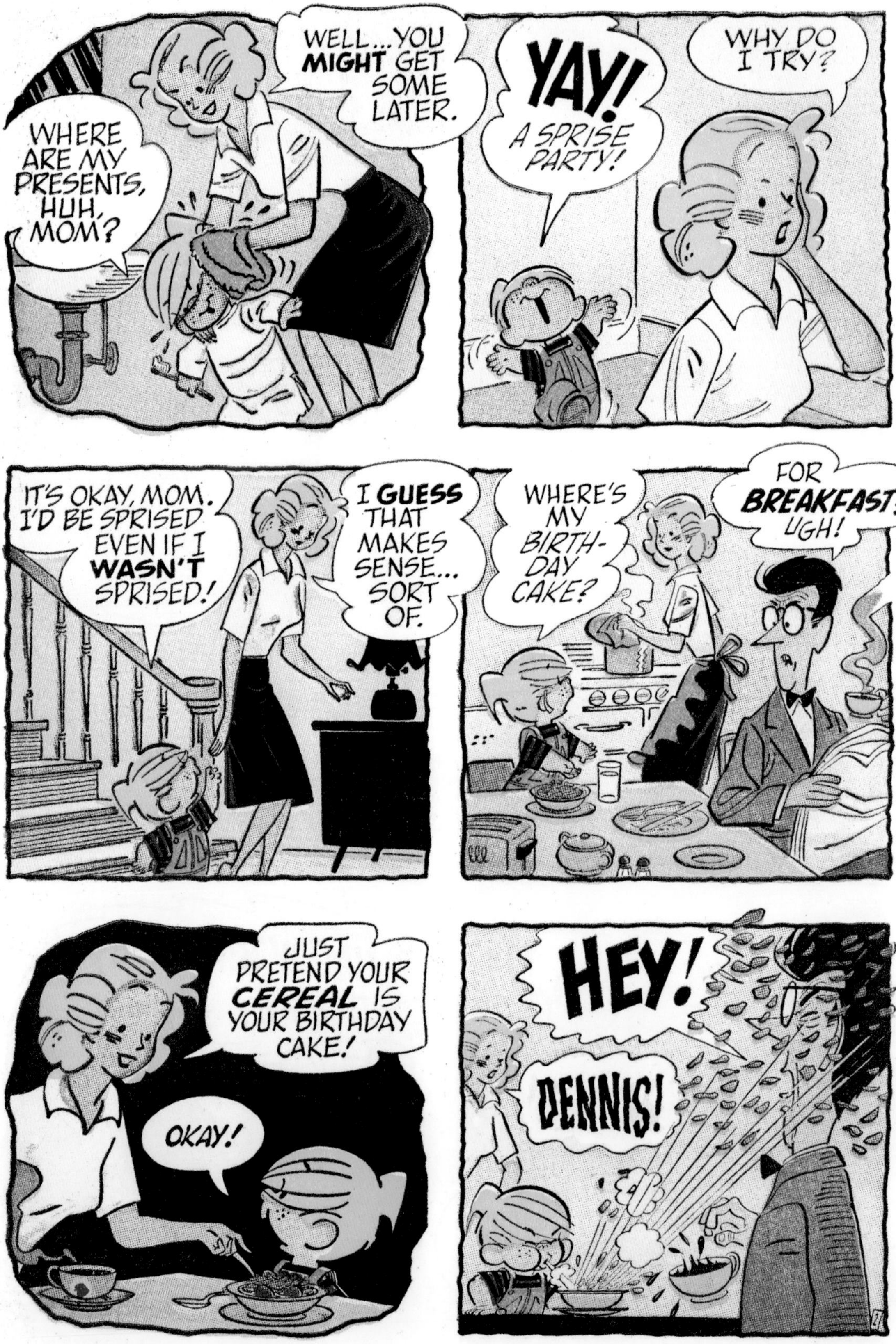
WHERE ARE MY PRESENTS, HUH, MOM?
WELL... YOU **MIGHT** GET SOME LATER.
YAY! A SPRISE PARTY!
WHY DO I TRY?
IT'S OKAY, MOM. I'D BE SPRISED EVEN IF I **WASN'T** SPRISED!
I **GUESS** THAT MAKES SENSE... SORT OF.
WHERE'S MY BIRTH-DAY CAKE?
FOR **BREAKFAST?** UGH!
JUST PRETEND YOUR **CEREAL** IS YOUR BIRTHDAY CAKE!
OKAY!
HEY!
DENNIS!

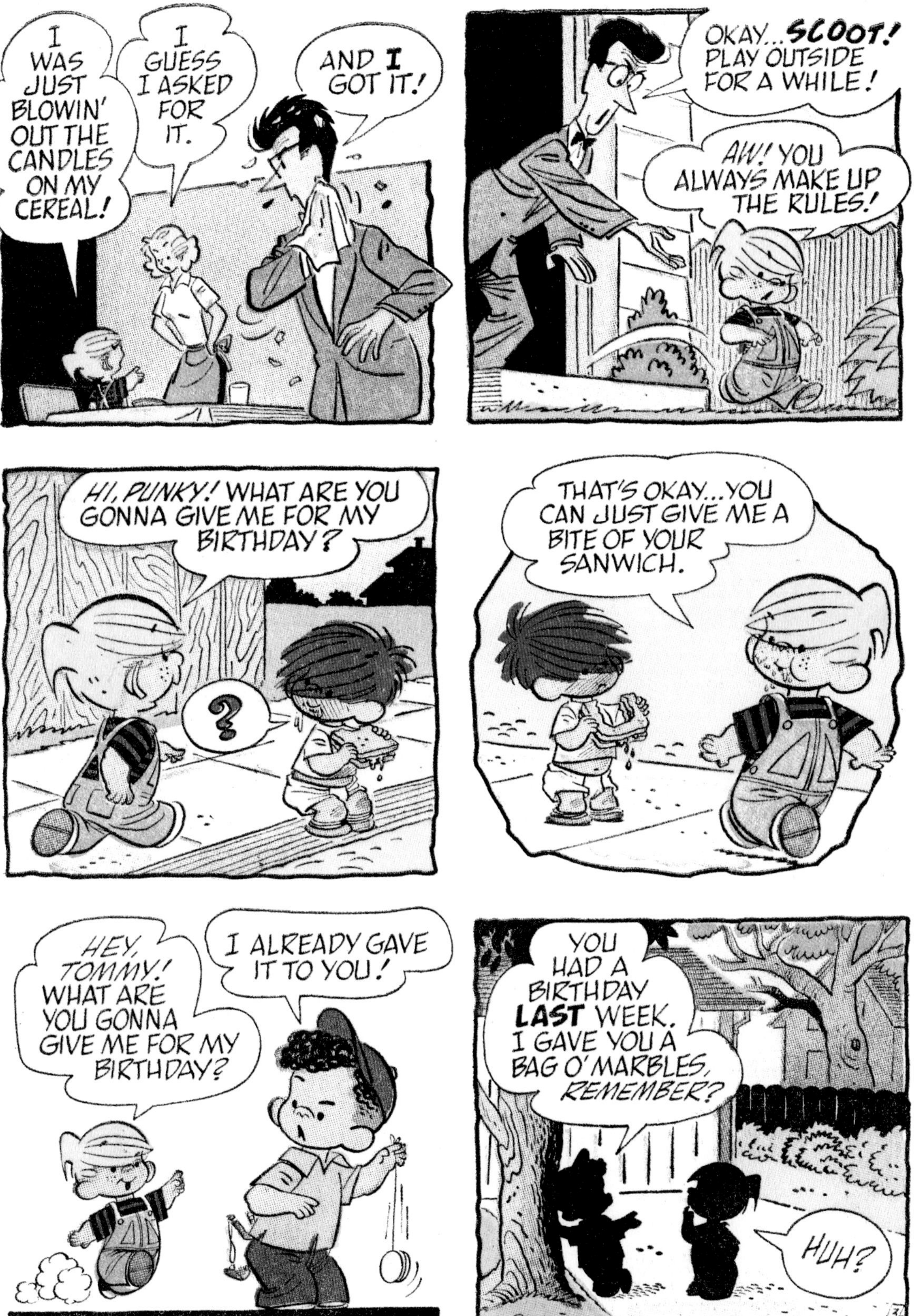
I WAS JUST BLOWIN' OUT THE CANDLES ON MY CEREAL!
I GUESS I ASKED FOR IT.
AND **I** GOT IT!
OKAY... **SCOOT!** PLAY OUTSIDE FOR A WHILE!
AW! YOU ALWAYS MAKE UP THE RULES!
HI, PUNKY! WHAT ARE YOU GONNA GIVE ME FOR MY BIRTHDAY?
?
THAT'S OKAY... YOU CAN JUST GIVE ME A BITE OF YOUR SANWICH.
HEY, TOMMY! WHAT ARE YOU GONNA GIVE ME FOR MY BIRTHDAY?
I ALREADY GAVE IT TO YOU!
YOU HAD A BIRTHDAY **LAST** WEEK. I GAVE YOU A BAG O' MARBLES, *REMEMBER?*
HUH?

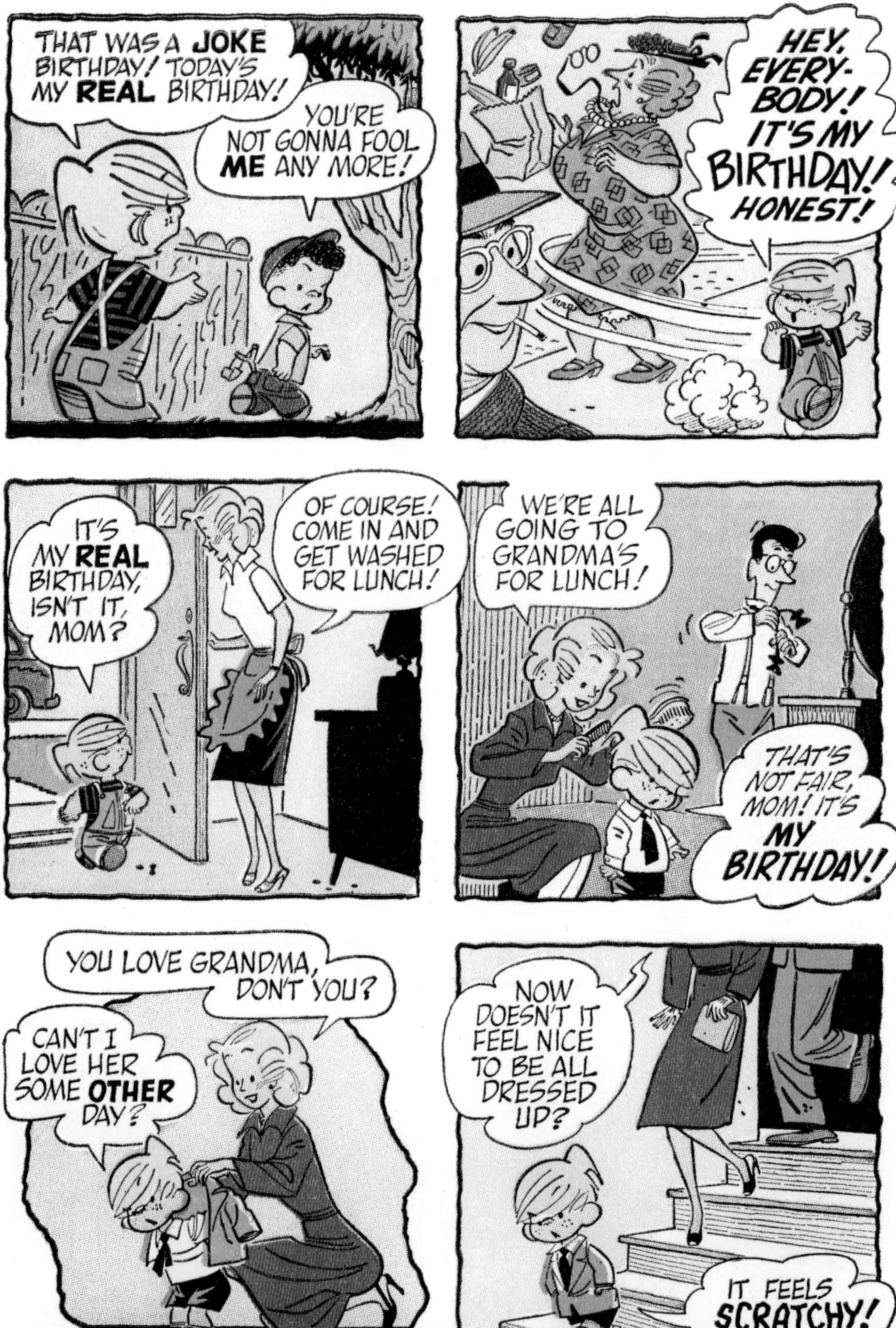
THAT WAS A JOKE BIRTHDAY! TODAY'S MY REAL BIRTHDAY!
YOU'RE NOT GONNA FOOL ME ANY MORE!
HEY, EVERY-BODY! IT'S MY BIRTHDAY! HONEST!
IT'S MY REAL BIRTHDAY, ISN'T IT, MOM?
OF COURSE! COME IN AND GET WASHED FOR LUNCH!
WE'RE ALL GOING TO GRANDMA'S FOR LUNCH!
THAT'S NOT FAIR, MOM! IT'S MY BIRTHDAY!
YOU LOVE GRANDMA, DON'T YOU?
CAN'T I LOVE HER SOME OTHER DAY?
NOW DOESN'T IT FEEL NICE TO BE ALL DRESSED UP?
IT FEELS SCRATCHY!

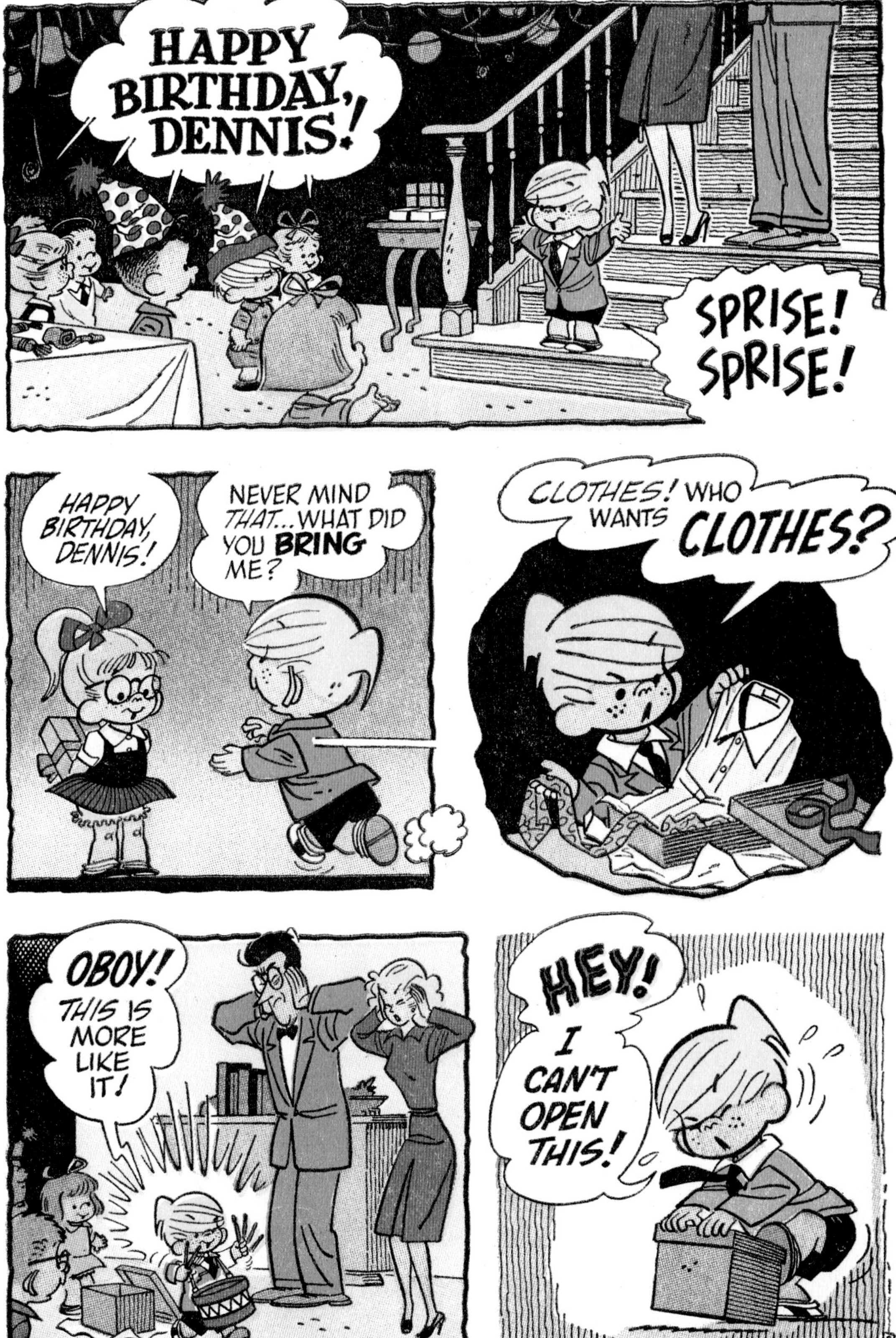
HAPPY BIRTHDAY, DENNIS!
SPRISE! SPRISE!
HAPPY BIRTHDAY, DENNIS!
NEVER MIND THAT...WHAT DID YOU BRING ME?
CLOTHES! WHO WANTS CLOTHES?
OBOY! THIS IS MORE LIKE IT!
HEY! I CAN'T OPEN THIS!
5

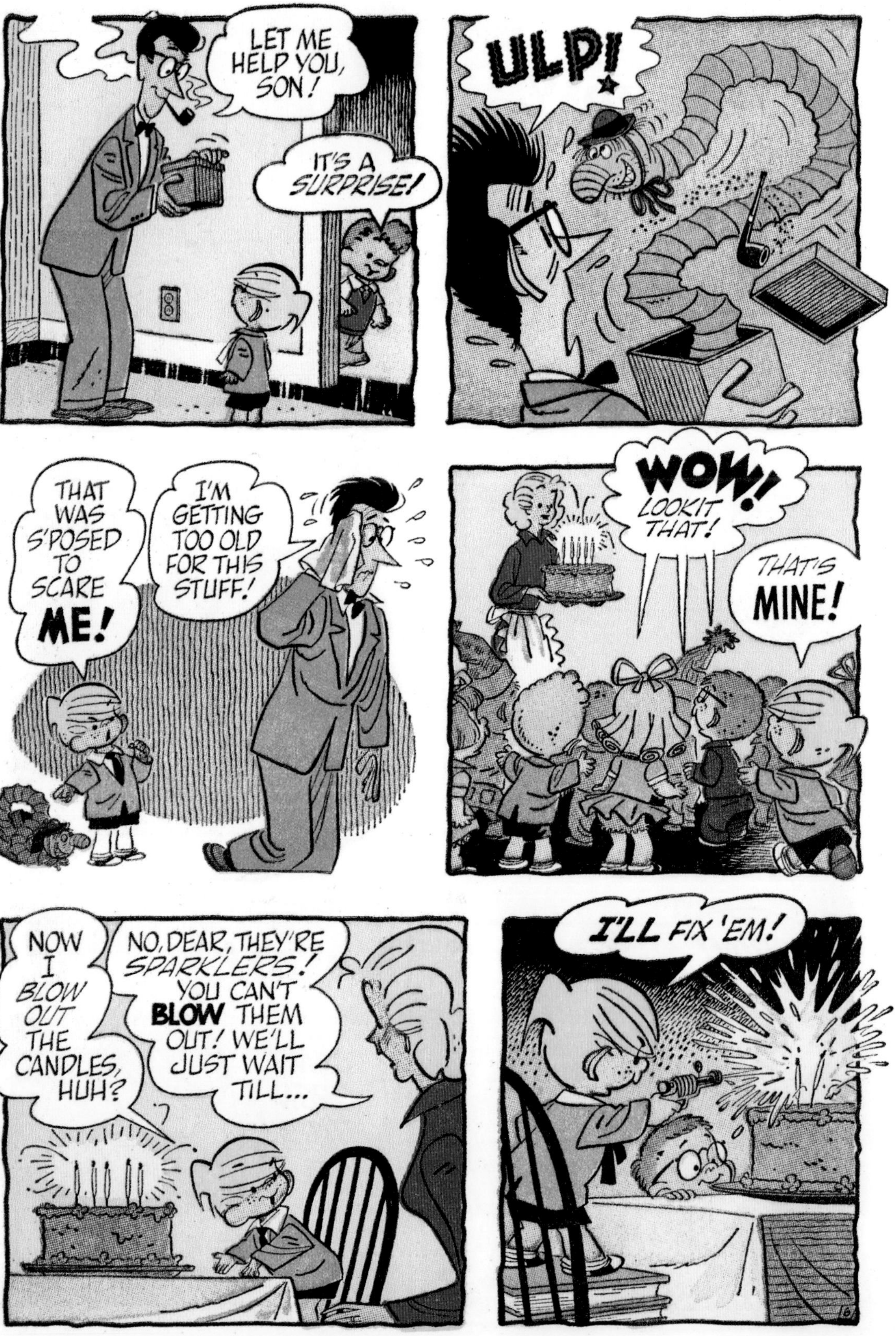
LET ME HELP YOU, SON!
IT'S A SURPRISE!
ULP!
THAT WAS S'POSED TO SCARE ME!
I'M GETTING TOO OLD FOR THIS STUFF!
WOW! LOOKIT THAT!
THAT'S MINE!
NOW I BLOW OUT THE CANDLES, HUH?
NO, DEAR, THEY'RE SPARKLERS! YOU CAN'T BLOW THEM OUT! WE'LL JUST WAIT TILL...
I'LL FIX 'EM!

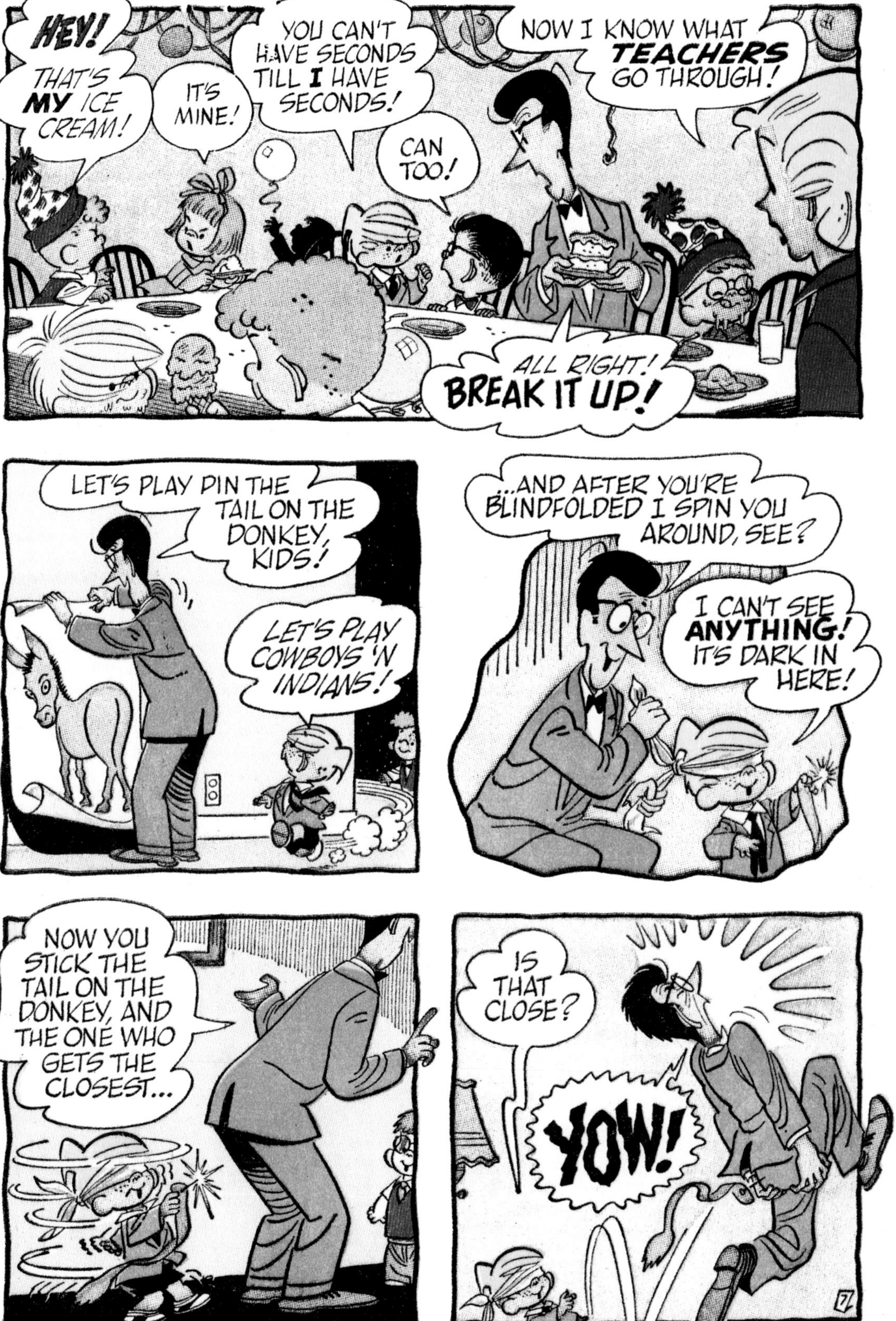
HEY! THAT'S MY ICE CREAM!
IT'S MINE!
YOU CAN'T HAVE SECONDS TILL I HAVE SECONDS!
CAN TOO!
NOW I KNOW WHAT TEACHERS GO THROUGH!
ALL RIGHT! BREAK IT UP!
LET'S PLAY PIN THE TAIL ON THE DONKEY, KIDS!
LET'S PLAY COWBOYS 'N INDIANS!
...AND AFTER YOU'RE BLINDFOLDED I SPIN YOU AROUND, SEE?
I CAN'T SEE ANYTHING! IT'S DARK IN HERE!
NOW YOU STICK THE TAIL ON THE DONKEY, AND THE ONE WHO GETS THE CLOSEST...
IS THAT CLOSE?
YOW!
7

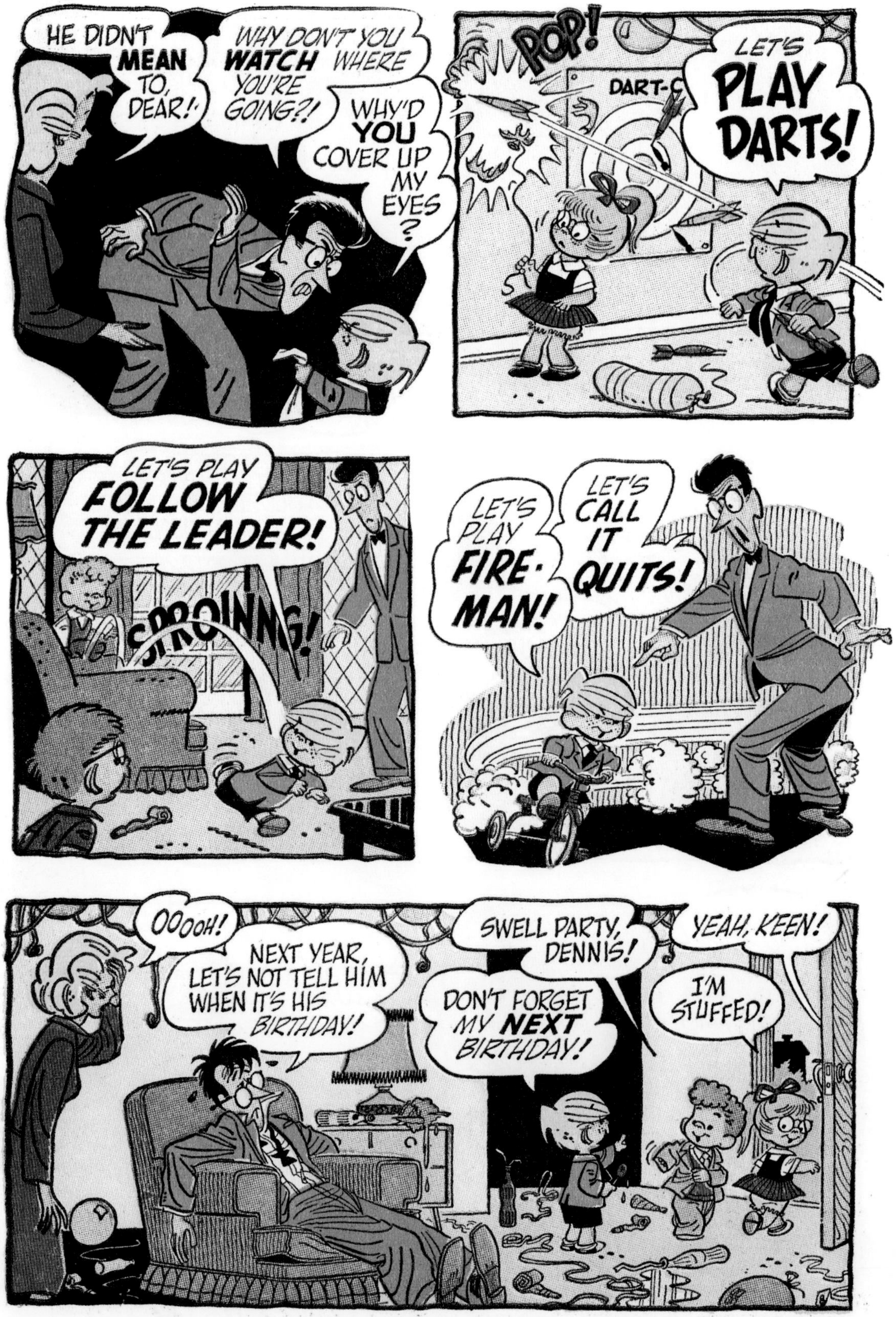
HE DIDN'T MEAN TO, DEAR!
WHY DON'T YOU WATCH WHERE YOU'RE GOING?!
WHY'D YOU COVER UP MY EYES?
POP!
DART-C
LET'S PLAY DARTS!
LET'S PLAY FOLLOW THE LEADER!
SPROINNG!
LET'S PLAY FIRE-MAN!
LET'S CALL IT QUITS!
OOOOH!
NEXT YEAR, LET'S NOT TELL HIM WHEN IT'S HIS BIRTHDAY!
SWELL PARTY, DENNIS!
DON'T FORGET MY NEXT BIRTHDAY!
YEAH, KEEN!
I'M STUFFED!

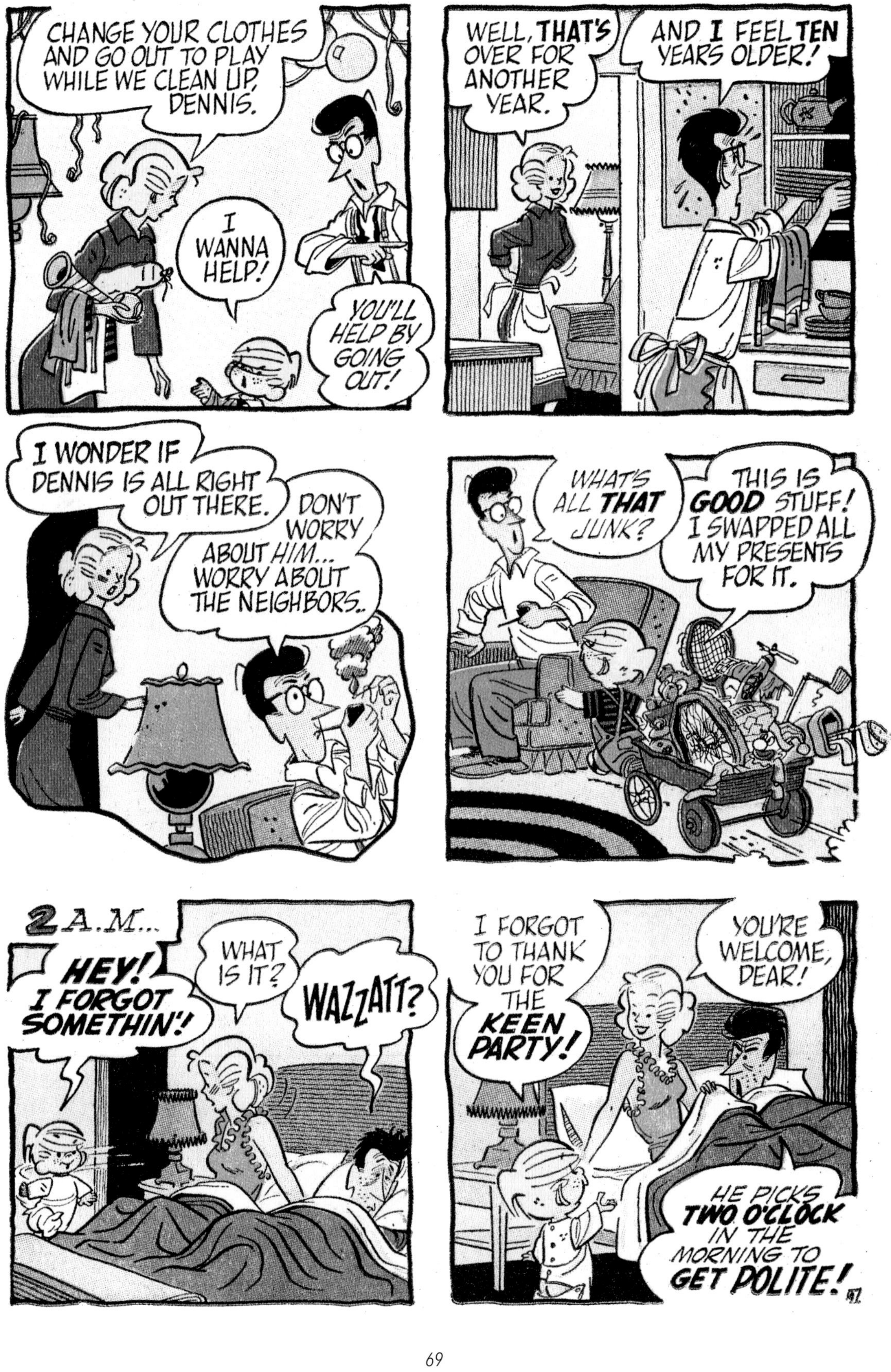
CHANGE YOUR CLOTHES AND GO OUT TO PLAY WHILE WE CLEAN UP, DENNIS.
I WANNA HELP!
YOU'LL HELP BY GOING OUT!
WELL, THAT'S OVER FOR ANOTHER YEAR.
AND I FEEL TEN YEARS OLDER!
I WONDER IF DENNIS IS ALL RIGHT OUT THERE.
DON'T WORRY ABOUT HIM... WORRY ABOUT THE NEIGHBORS..
WHAT'S ALL THAT JUNK?
THIS IS GOOD STUFF! I SWAPPED ALL MY PRESENTS FOR IT.
2 A.M...
HEY! I FORGOT SOMETHIN'!
WHAT IS IT?
WAZZATT?
I FORGOT TO THANK YOU FOR THE KEEN PARTY!
YOU'RE WELCOME, DEAR!
HE PICKS TWO O'CLOCK IN THE MORNING TO GET POLITE!

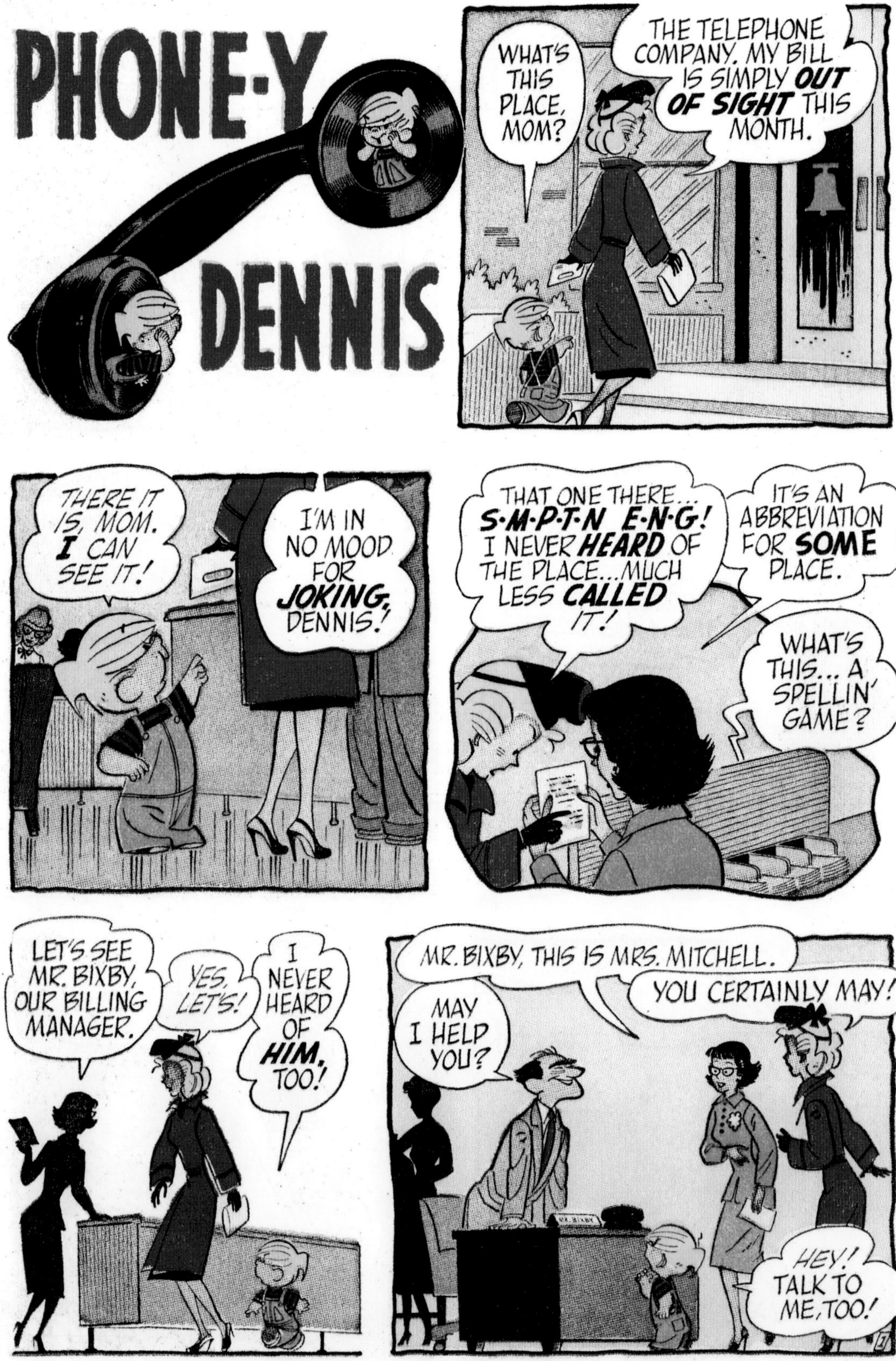
PHONE-Y DENNIS
WHAT'S THIS PLACE, MOM?
THE TELEPHONE COMPANY. MY BILL IS SIMPLY OUT OF SIGHT THIS MONTH.
THERE IT IS, MOM. I CAN SEE IT!
I'M IN NO MOOD FOR JOKING, DENNIS!
THAT ONE THERE... S·M·P·T·N E·N·G! I NEVER HEARD OF THE PLACE...MUCH LESS CALLED IT!
IT'S AN ABBREVIATION FOR SOME PLACE.
WHAT'S THIS... A SPELLIN' GAME?
LET'S SEE MR. BIXBY, OUR BILLING MANAGER.
YES, LET'S!
I NEVER HEARD OF HIM, TOO!
MR. BIXBY, THIS IS MRS. MITCHELL.
MAY I HELP YOU?
YOU CERTAINLY MAY!
HEY! TALK TO ME, TOO!

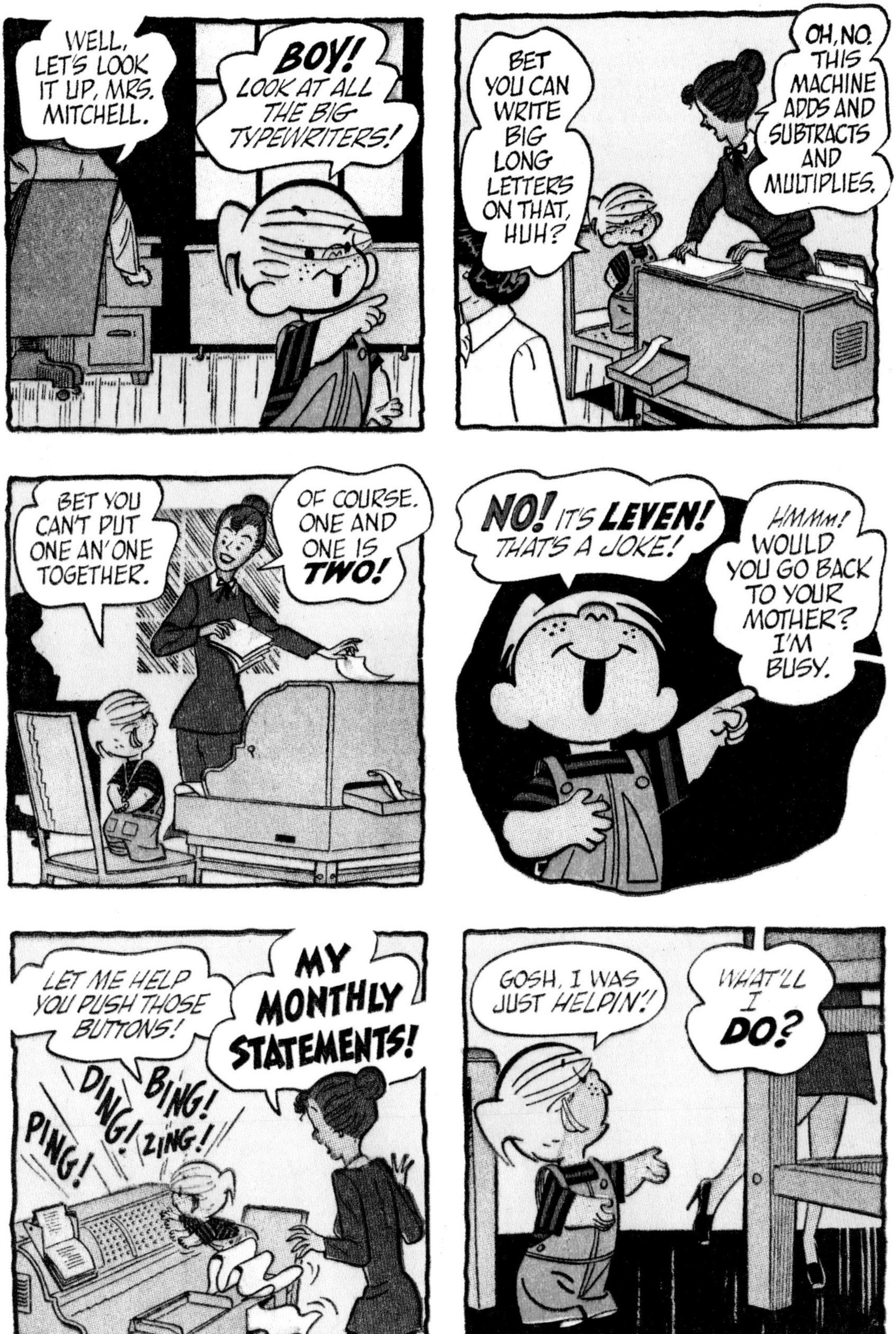
WELL, LET'S LOOK IT UP, MRS. MITCHELL.
BOY! LOOK AT ALL THE BIG TYPEWRITERS!
BET YOU CAN WRITE BIG LONG LETTERS ON THAT, HUH?
OH, NO. THIS MACHINE ADDS AND SUBTRACTS AND MULTIPLIES.
BET YOU CAN'T PUT ONE AN' ONE TOGETHER.
OF COURSE. ONE AND ONE IS TWO!
NO! IT'S LEVEN! THAT'S A JOKE!
HMMM! WOULD YOU GO BACK TO YOUR MOTHER? I'M BUSY.
LET ME HELP YOU PUSH THOSE BUTTONS!
MY MONTHLY STATEMENTS!
DING!
BING!
ZING!
PING!
GOSH, I WAS JUST HELPIN'!
WHAT'LL I DO?

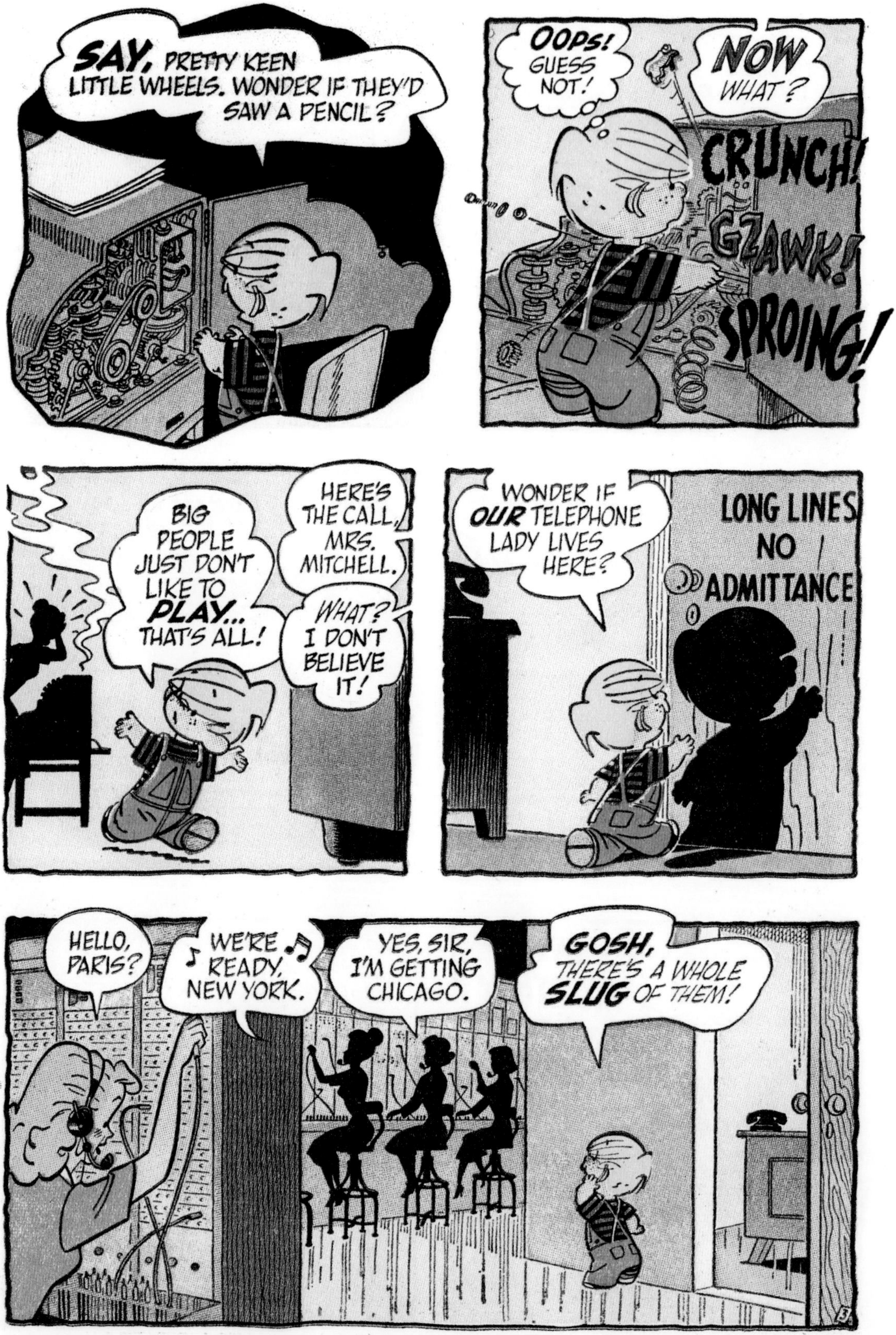
SAY, PRETTY KEEN LITTLE WHEELS. WONDER IF THEY'D SAW A PENCIL?
OOPS! GUESS NOT!
NOW WHAT?
CRUNCH!
GZAWK!
SPROING!
BIG PEOPLE JUST DON'T LIKE TO PLAY... THAT'S ALL!
HERE'S THE CALL, MRS. MITCHELL.
WHAT? I DON'T BELIEVE IT!
WONDER IF OUR TELEPHONE LADY LIVES HERE?
LONG LINES NO ADMITTANCE
HELLO, PARIS?
WE'RE READY, NEW YORK.
YES, SIR, I'M GETTING CHICAGO.
GOSH, THERE'S A WHOLE SLUG OF THEM!
3

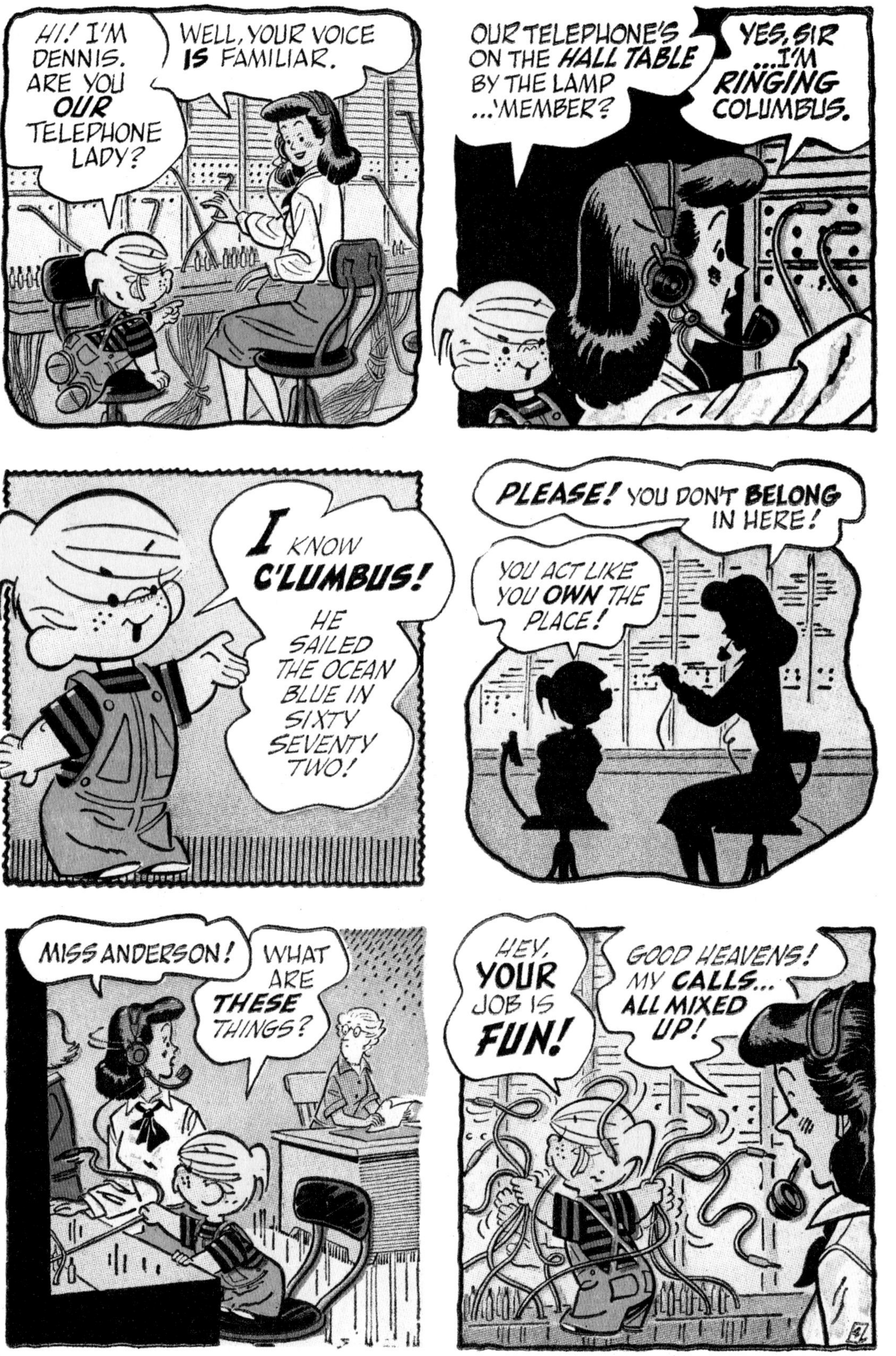
HI! I'M DENNIS. ARE YOU OUR TELEPHONE LADY?
WELL, YOUR VOICE IS FAMILIAR.
OUR TELEPHONE'S ON THE HALL TABLE BY THE LAMP ...'MEMBER?
YES, SIR ...I'M RINGING COLUMBUS.
I KNOW C'LUMBUS!
HE SAILED THE OCEAN BLUE IN SIXTY SEVENTY TWO!
PLEASE! YOU DON'T BELONG IN HERE!
YOU ACT LIKE YOU OWN THE PLACE!
MISS ANDERSON!
WHAT ARE THESE THINGS?
HEY, YOUR JOB IS FUN!
GOOD HEAVENS! MY CALLS... ALL MIXED UP!

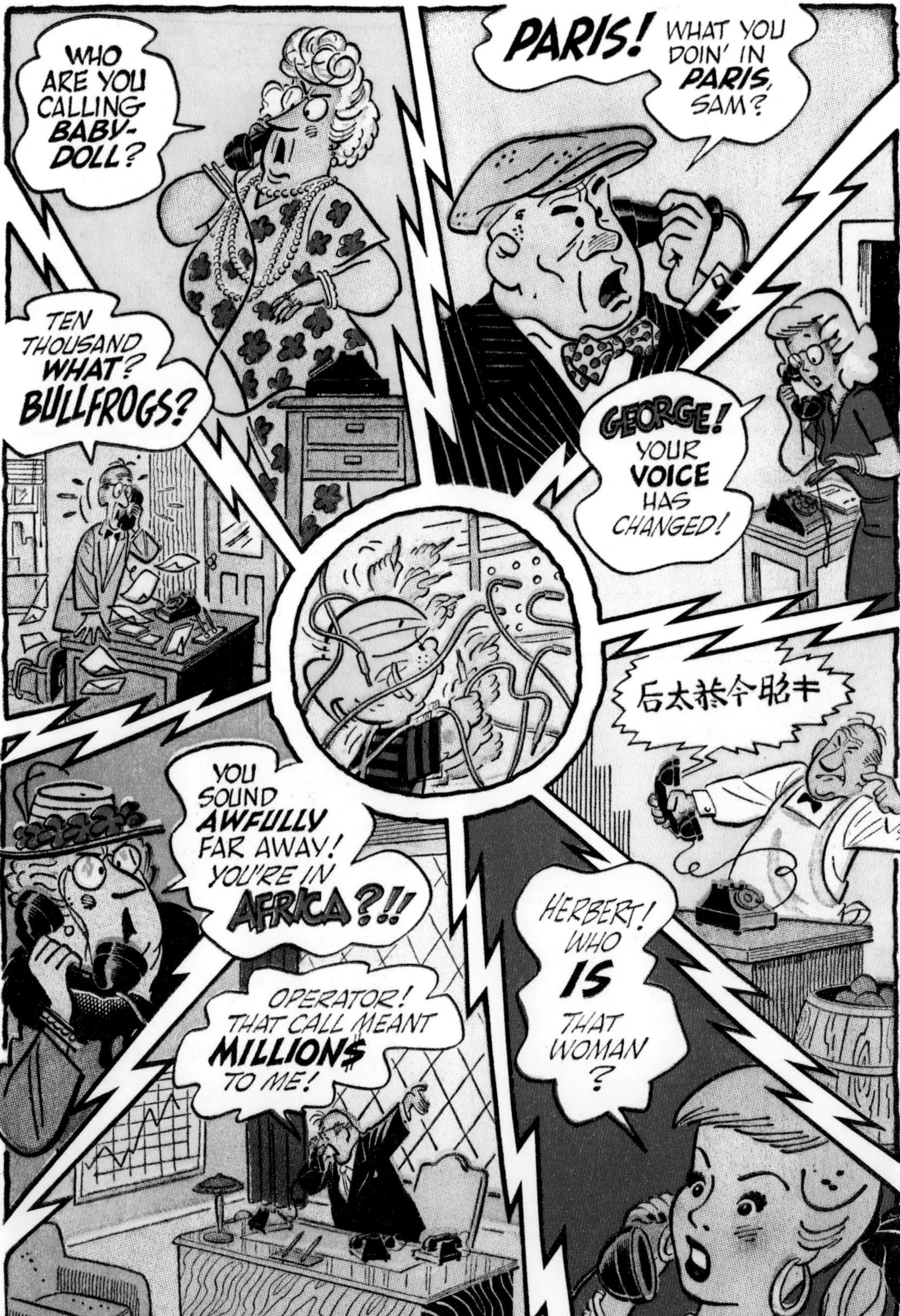

WHO ARE YOU CALLING BABY-DOLL?
PARIS! WHAT YOU DOIN' IN PARIS, SAM?
TEN THOUSAND WHAT? BULLFROGS?
GEORGE! YOUR VOICE HAS CHANGED!
YOU SOUND AWFULLY FAR AWAY! YOU'RE IN AFRICA?!!
OPERATOR! THAT CALL MEANT MILLION$ TO ME!
HERBERT! WHO IS THAT WOMAN?

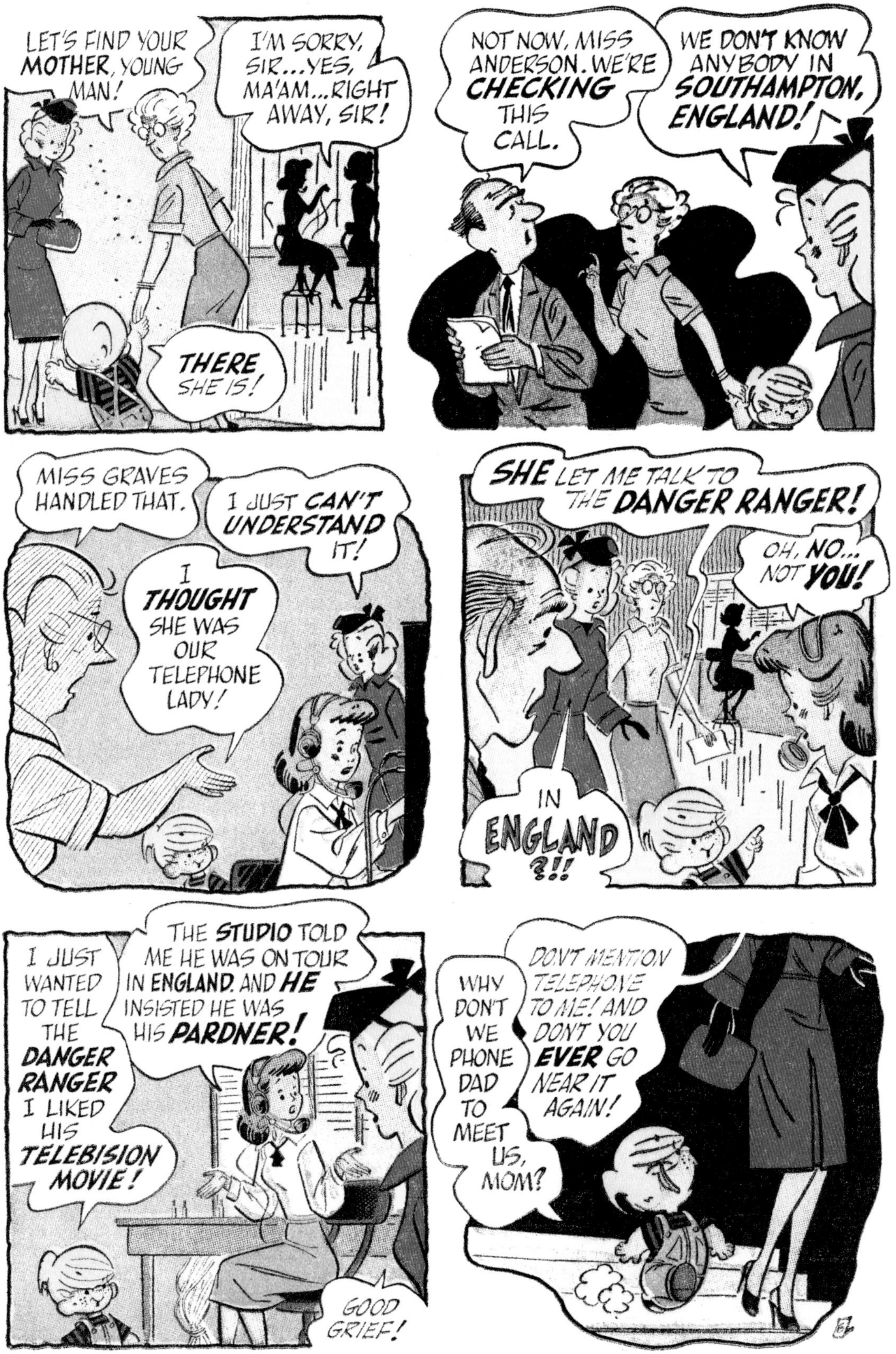
LET'S FIND YOUR MOTHER, YOUNG MAN!
I'M SORRY, SIR... YES, MA'AM... RIGHT AWAY, SIR!
THERE SHE IS!
NOT NOW, MISS ANDERSON. WE'RE CHECKING THIS CALL.
WE DON'T KNOW ANYBODY IN SOUTHAMPTON, ENGLAND!
MISS GRAVES HANDLED THAT.
I JUST CAN'T UNDERSTAND IT!
I THOUGHT SHE WAS OUR TELEPHONE LADY!
SHE LET ME TALK TO THE DANGER RANGER!
OH, NO... NOT YOU!
IN ENGLAND ?!!
I JUST WANTED TO TELL THE DANGER RANGER I LIKED HIS TELEBISION MOVIE!
THE STUDIO TOLD ME HE WAS ON TOUR IN ENGLAND. AND HE INSISTED HE WAS HIS PARDNER!
GOOD GRIEF!
WHY DON'T WE PHONE DAD TO MEET US, MOM?
DON'T MENTION TELEPHONE TO ME! AND DON'T YOU EVER GO NEAR IT AGAIN!

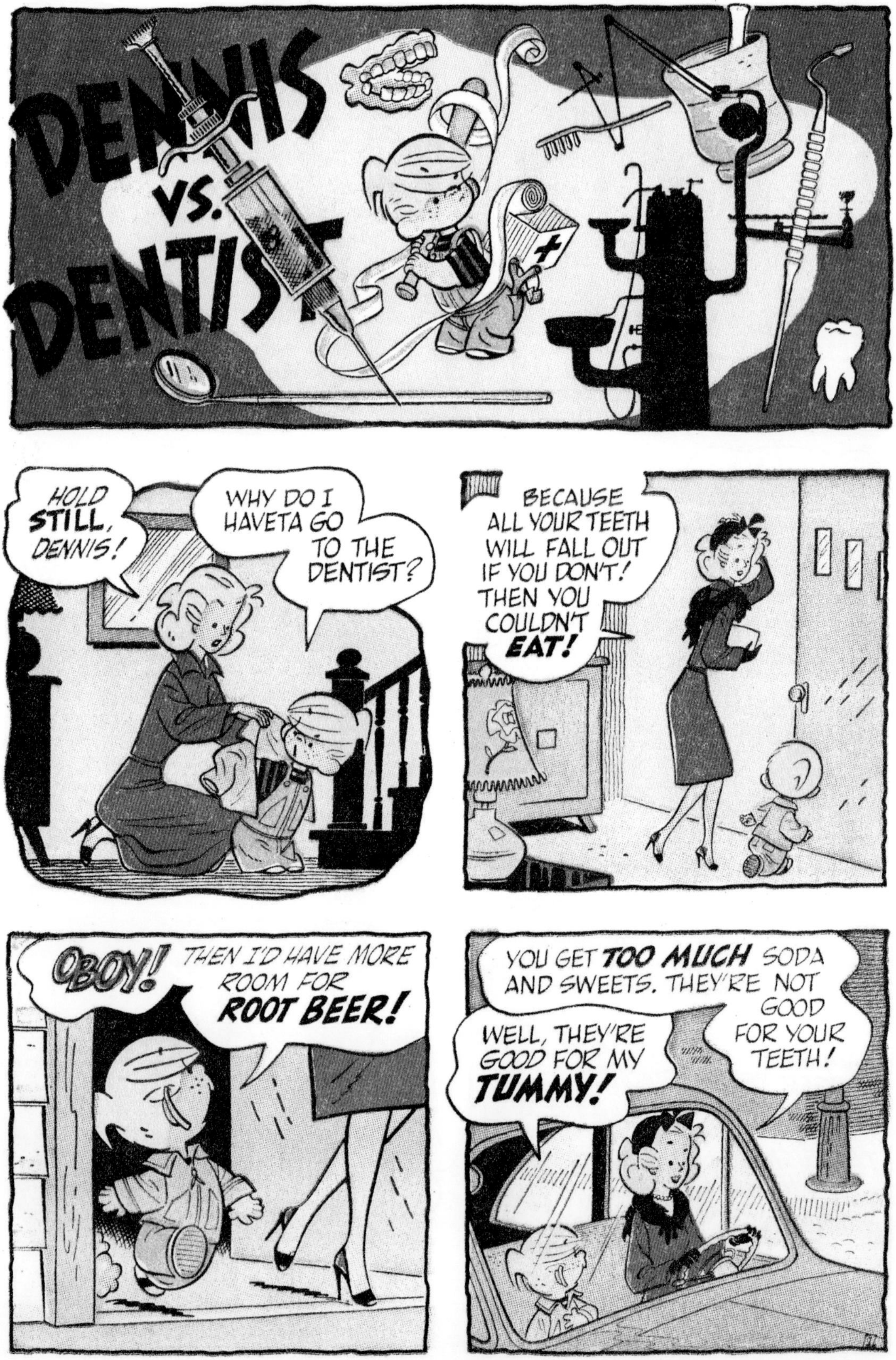
DENNIS vs. DENTIST
HOLD STILL, DENNIS!
WHY DO I HAVETA GO TO THE DENTIST?
BECAUSE ALL YOUR TEETH WILL FALL OUT IF YOU DON'T! THEN YOU COULDN'T EAT!
OBOY!
THEN I'D HAVE MORE ROOM FOR ROOT BEER!
YOU GET TOO MUCH SODA AND SWEETS. THEY'RE NOT GOOD FOR YOUR TEETH!
WELL, THEY'RE GOOD FOR MY TUMMY!

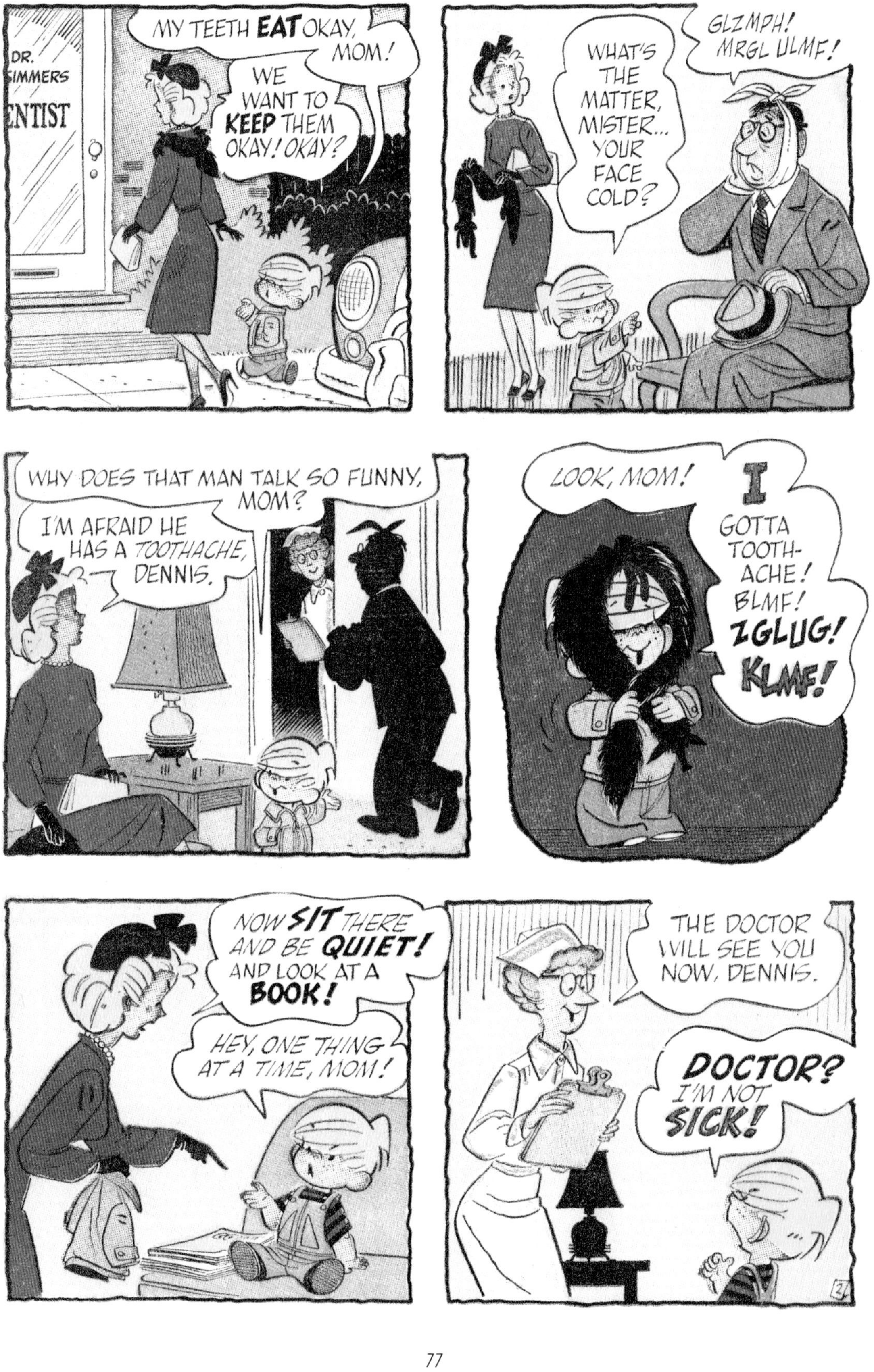
DR.
SIMMERS
ENTIST
MY TEETH EAT OKAY, MOM!
WE WANT TO KEEP THEM OKAY! OKAY?
GLZMPH! MRGL ULMF!
WHAT'S THE MATTER, MISTER... YOUR FACE COLD?
WHY DOES THAT MAN TALK SO FUNNY, MOM?
I'M AFRAID HE HAS A TOOTHACHE, DENNIS.
LOOK, MOM!
I GOTTA TOOTH-ACHE! BLMF! ZGLUG! KLMF!
NOW SIT THERE AND BE QUIET! AND LOOK AT A BOOK!
HEY, ONE THING AT A TIME, MOM!
THE DOCTOR WILL SEE YOU NOW, DENNIS.
DOCTOR? I'M NOT SICK!

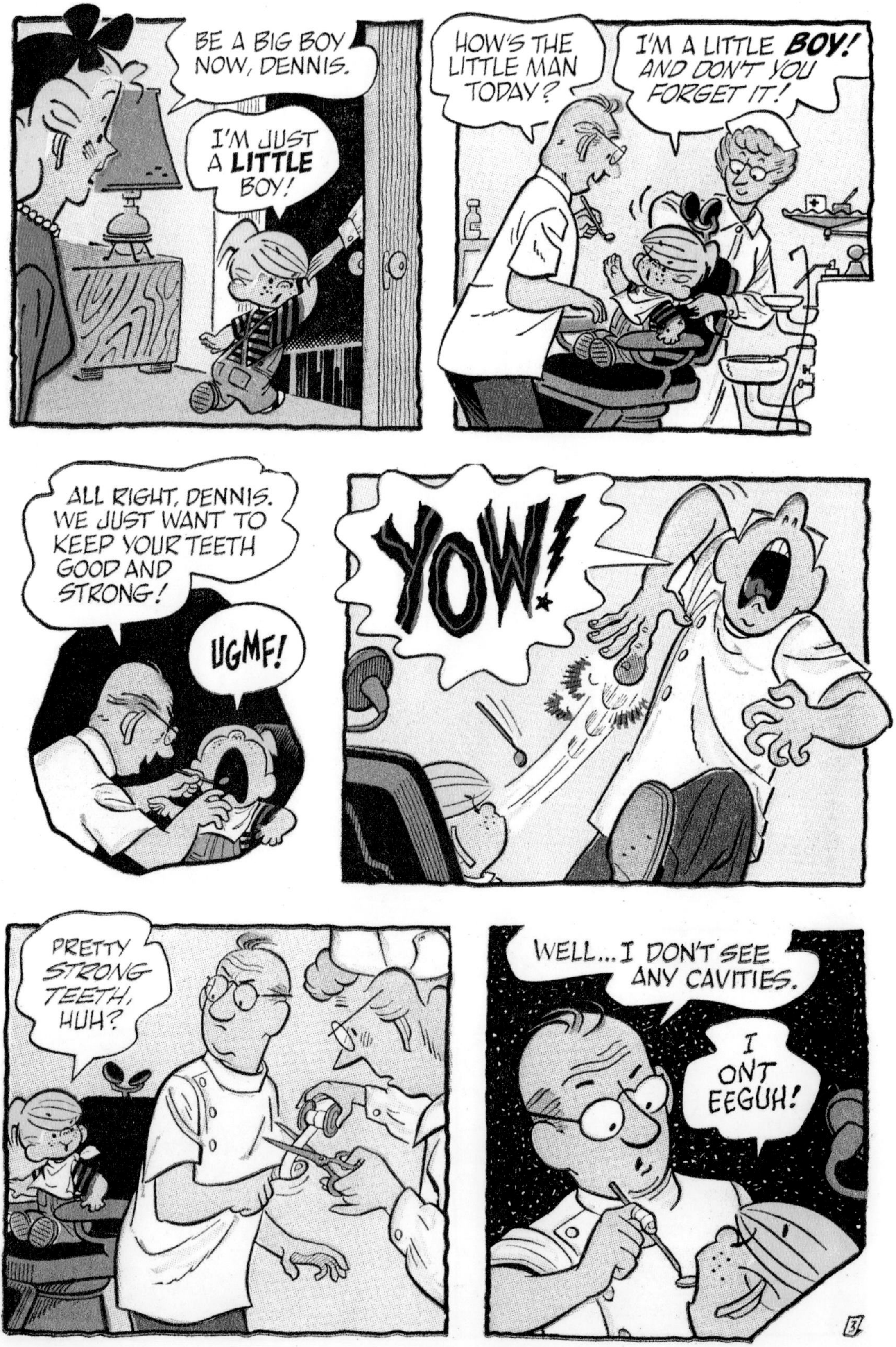
BE A BIG BOY NOW, DENNIS.
I'M JUST A LITTLE BOY!
HOW'S THE LITTLE MAN TODAY?
I'M A LITTLE BOY! AND DON'T YOU FORGET IT!
ALL RIGHT, DENNIS. WE JUST WANT TO KEEP YOUR TEETH GOOD AND STRONG!
UGMF!
YOW!
PRETTY STRONG TEETH, HUH?
WELL... I DON'T SEE ANY CAVITIES.
I ONT EEGUH!
3

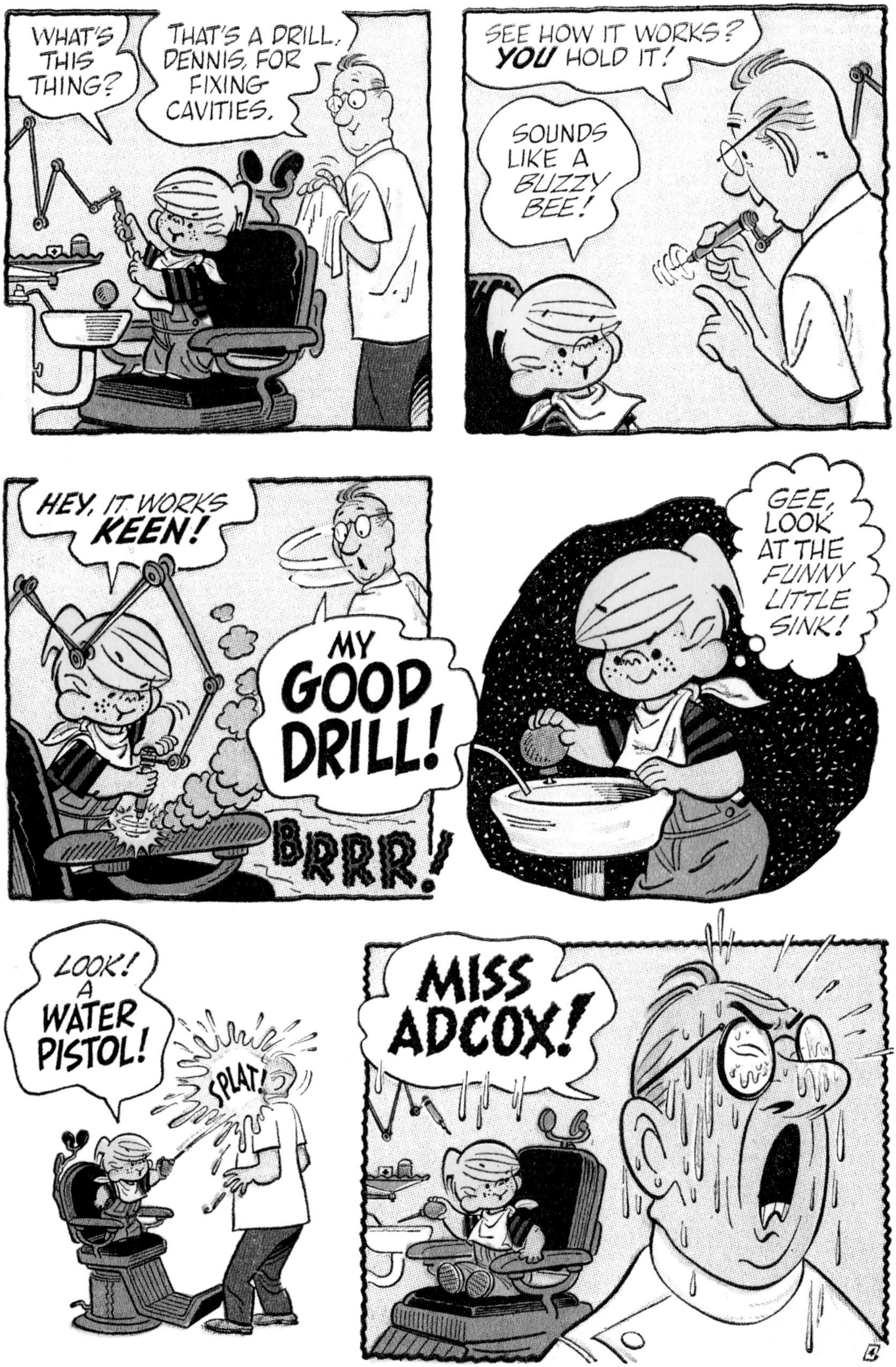
WHAT'S THIS THING?
THAT'S A DRILL, DENNIS, FOR FIXING CAVITIES.
SEE HOW IT WORKS? YOU HOLD IT!
SOUNDS LIKE A BUZZY BEE!
HEY, IT WORKS KEEN!
MY GOOD DRILL!
BRRRR!
GEE, LOOK AT THE FUNNY LITTLE SINK!
LOOK! A WATER PISTOL!
SPLAT!
MISS ADCOX!

WHAT'S **THAT** FUNNY PICTURE?
FIRST PERMANENT MOLAR
ENAMEL
DENTIN
PULP
PULP CANAL
THAT'S A **TOOTH,** DENNIS.
WOW! MUST BE A *ELEPHANT'S!*
IT'S JUST A BIG DRAWING OF ONE OF **OUR** TEETH.
HERE'S THE PULP, SEE... AND THIS IS THE ENAMEL... AND THIS...
IRST
RMANENT
OLAR
ENAMEL
DENTIN
PULP
PULP CANAL
UH-HUH.
MY DENTURES!
BOY, THE GOOD FAIRY MUST GIVE YOU ***LOTSA*** *QUARTERS!*
THESE ARE **FALSE** TEETH FOR PEOPLE WHO LOSE ALL THEIR OWN TEETH.
MY GRAN'PA HAS SOME... BUT THEY'RE ALWAYS ***THIRSTY!***
WHAT? ***THIRSTY?***
YEAH! HE HAS TO KEEP 'EM IN A *GLASS OF WATER!*
5

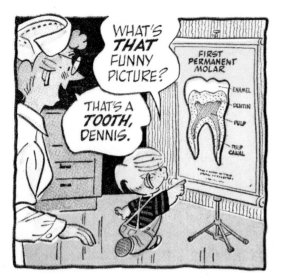

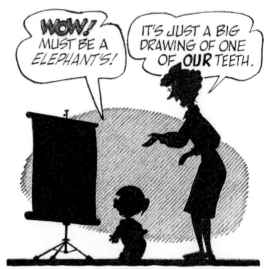

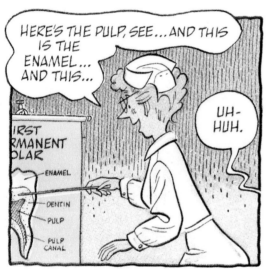

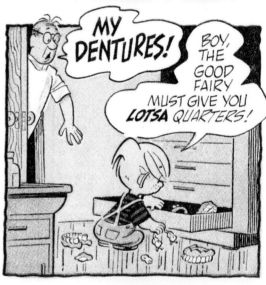

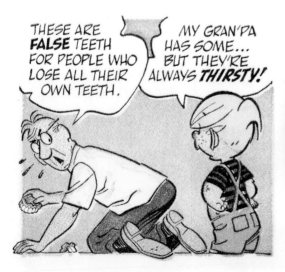

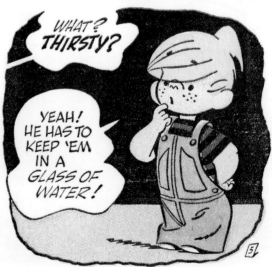

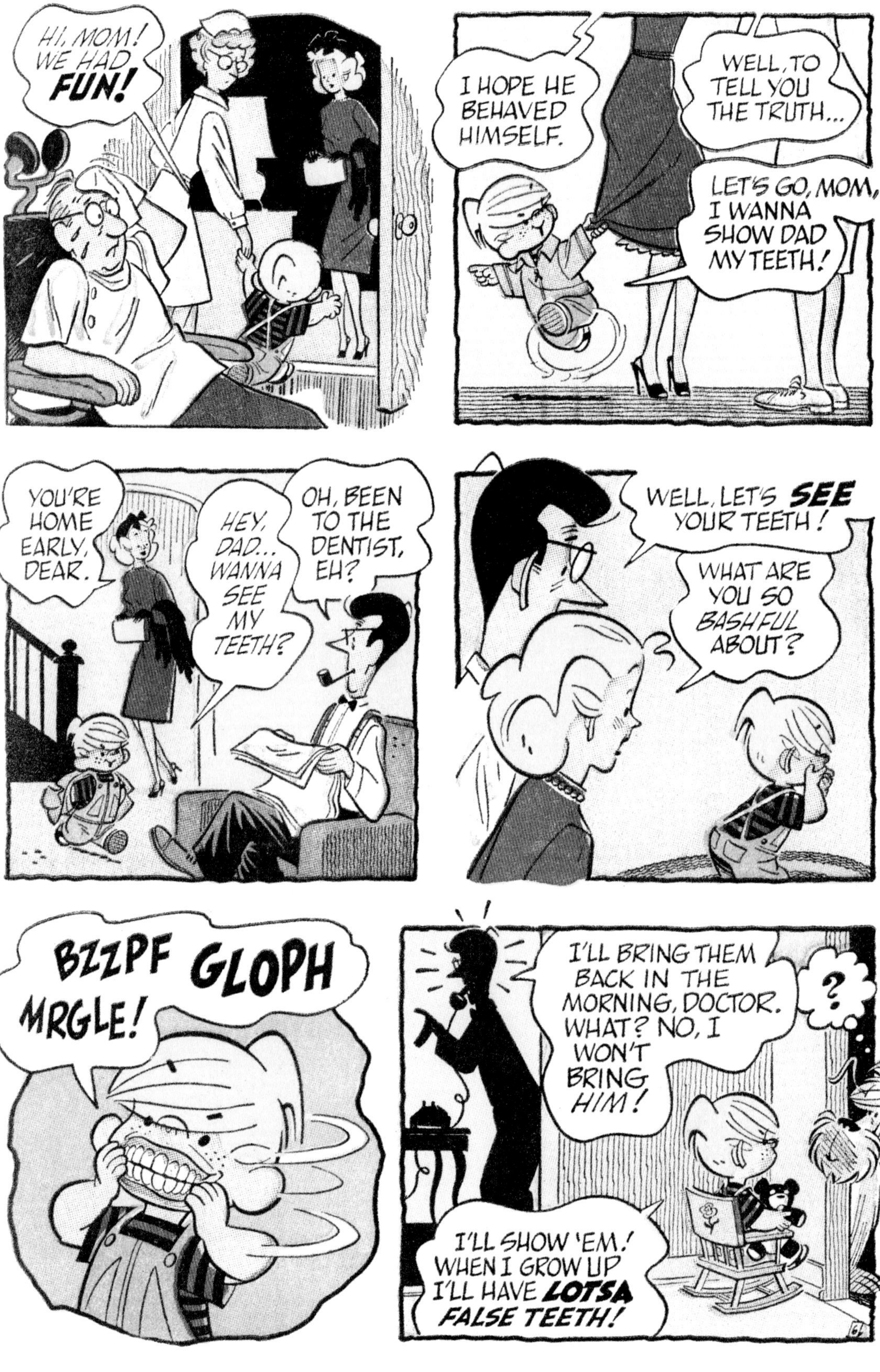
HI, MOM! WE HAD FUN!
I HOPE HE BEHAVED HIMSELF.
WELL, TO TELL YOU THE TRUTH...
LET'S GO, MOM, I WANNA SHOW DAD MY TEETH!
YOU'RE HOME EARLY, DEAR.
HEY, DAD... WANNA SEE MY TEETH?
OH, BEEN TO THE DENTIST, EH?
WELL, LET'S SEE YOUR TEETH!
WHAT ARE YOU SO BASHFUL ABOUT?
BZZPF GLOPH MRGLE!
I'LL BRING THEM BACK IN THE MORNING, DOCTOR. WHAT? NO, I WON'T BRING HIM!
?
I'LL SHOW 'EM! WHEN I GROW UP I'LL HAVE LOTSA FALSE TEETH!

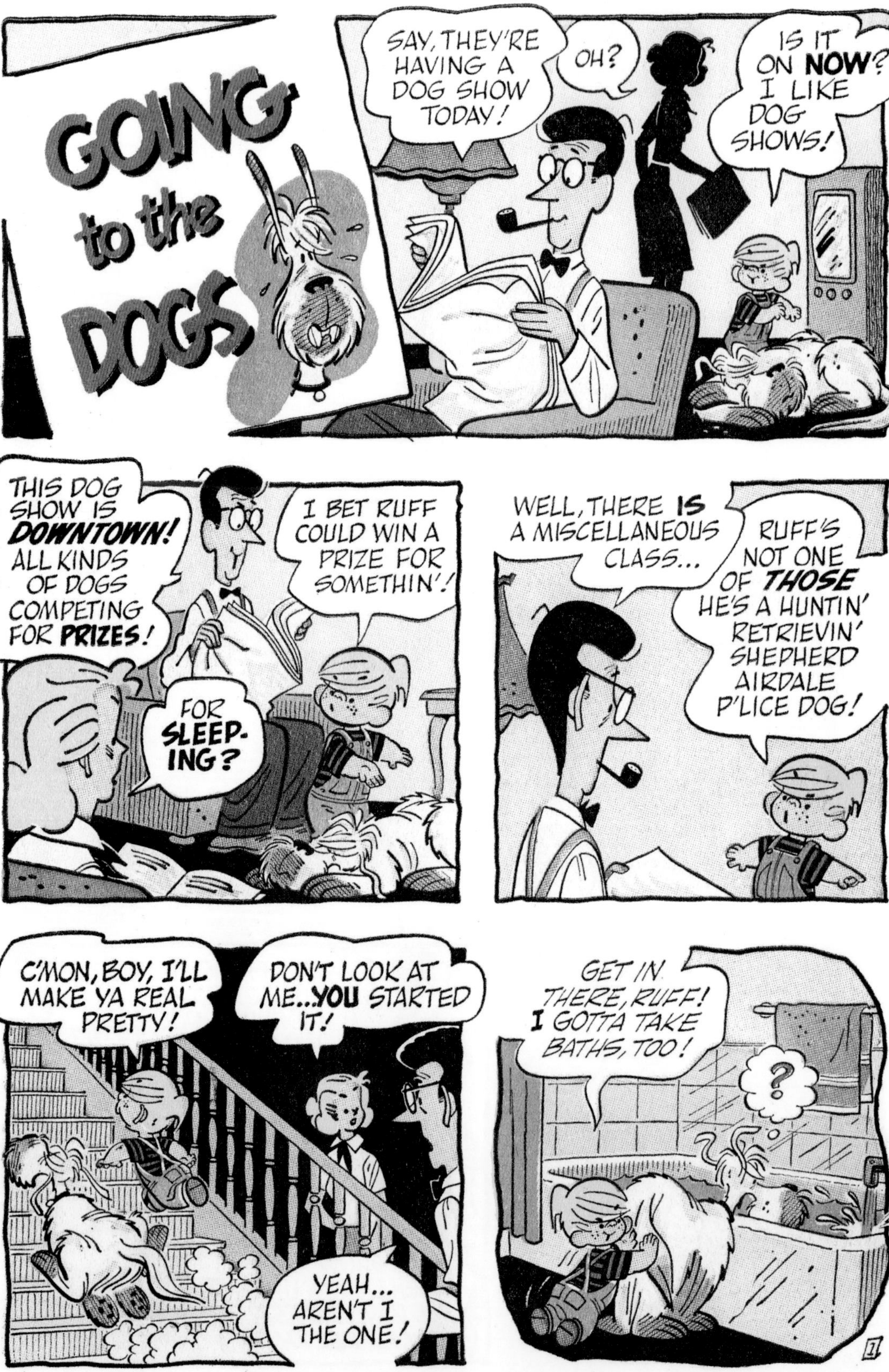
GOING to the DOGS
SAY, THEY'RE HAVING A DOG SHOW TODAY!
OH?
IS IT ON NOW? I LIKE DOG SHOWS!
THIS DOG SHOW IS DOWNTOWN! ALL KINDS OF DOGS COMPETING FOR PRIZES!
I BET RUFF COULD WIN A PRIZE FOR SOMETHIN'!
FOR SLEEPING?
WELL, THERE IS A MISCELLANEOUS CLASS...
RUFF'S NOT ONE OF THOSE HE'S A HUNTIN' RETRIEVIN' SHEPHERD AIRDALE P'LICE DOG!
C'MON, BOY, I'LL MAKE YA REAL PRETTY!
DON'T LOOK AT ME...YOU STARTED IT!
YEAH... AREN'T I THE ONE!
GET IN THERE, RUFF! I GOTTA TAKE BATHS, TOO!
?
1

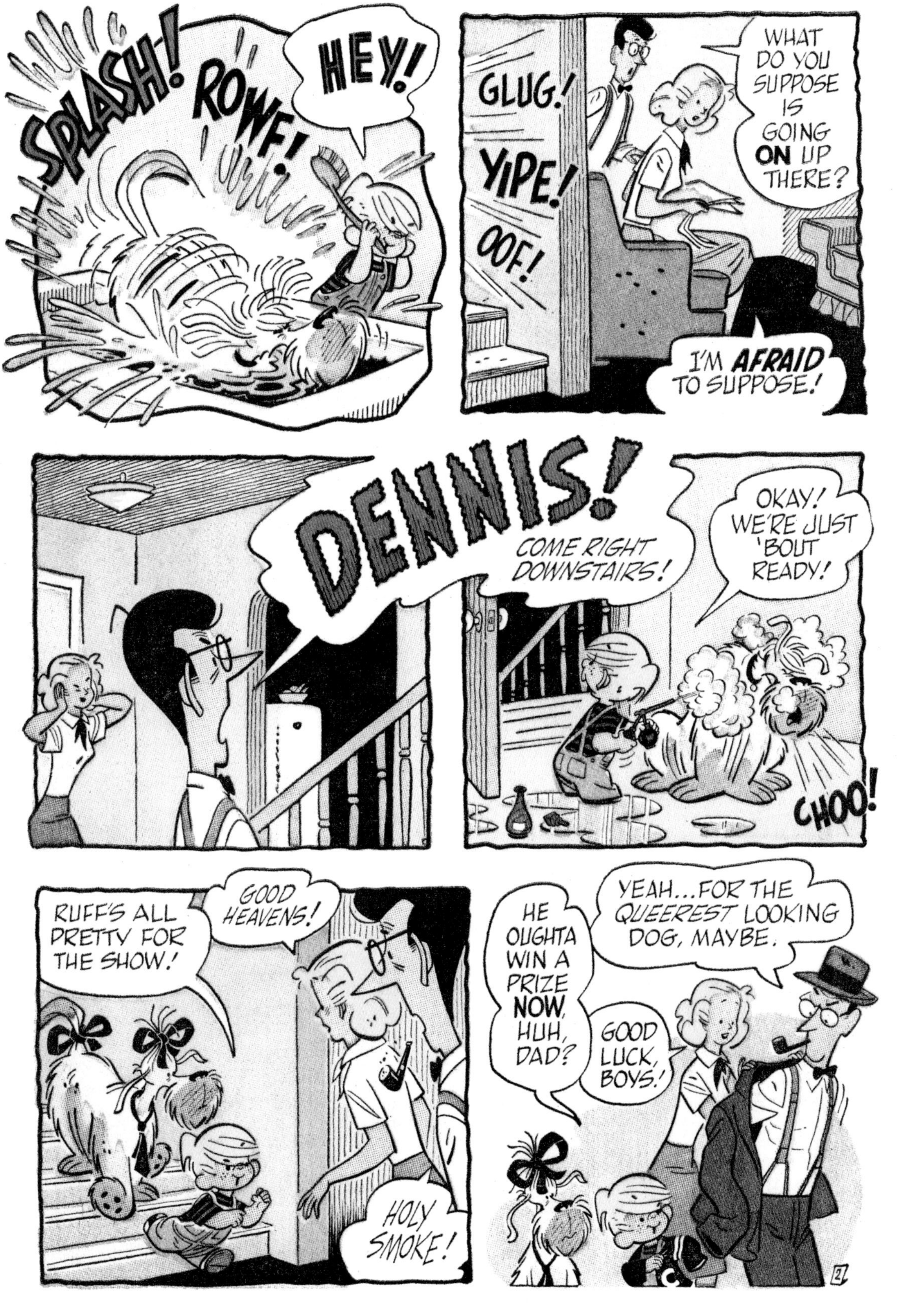
SPLASH!
ROWF!
HEY!
GLUG!
YIPE!
OOF!
WHAT DO YOU SUPPOSE IS GOING **ON** UP THERE?
I'M **AFRAID** TO SUPPOSE!
DENNIS!
COME RIGHT DOWNSTAIRS!
OKAY! WE'RE JUST 'BOUT READY!
CHOO!
RUFF'S ALL PRETTY FOR THE SHOW!
GOOD HEAVENS!
HOLY SMOKE!
HE OUGHTA WIN A PRIZE **NOW**, HUH, DAD?
YEAH...FOR THE *QUEEREST* LOOKING DOG, MAYBE.
GOOD LUCK, BOYS!
2

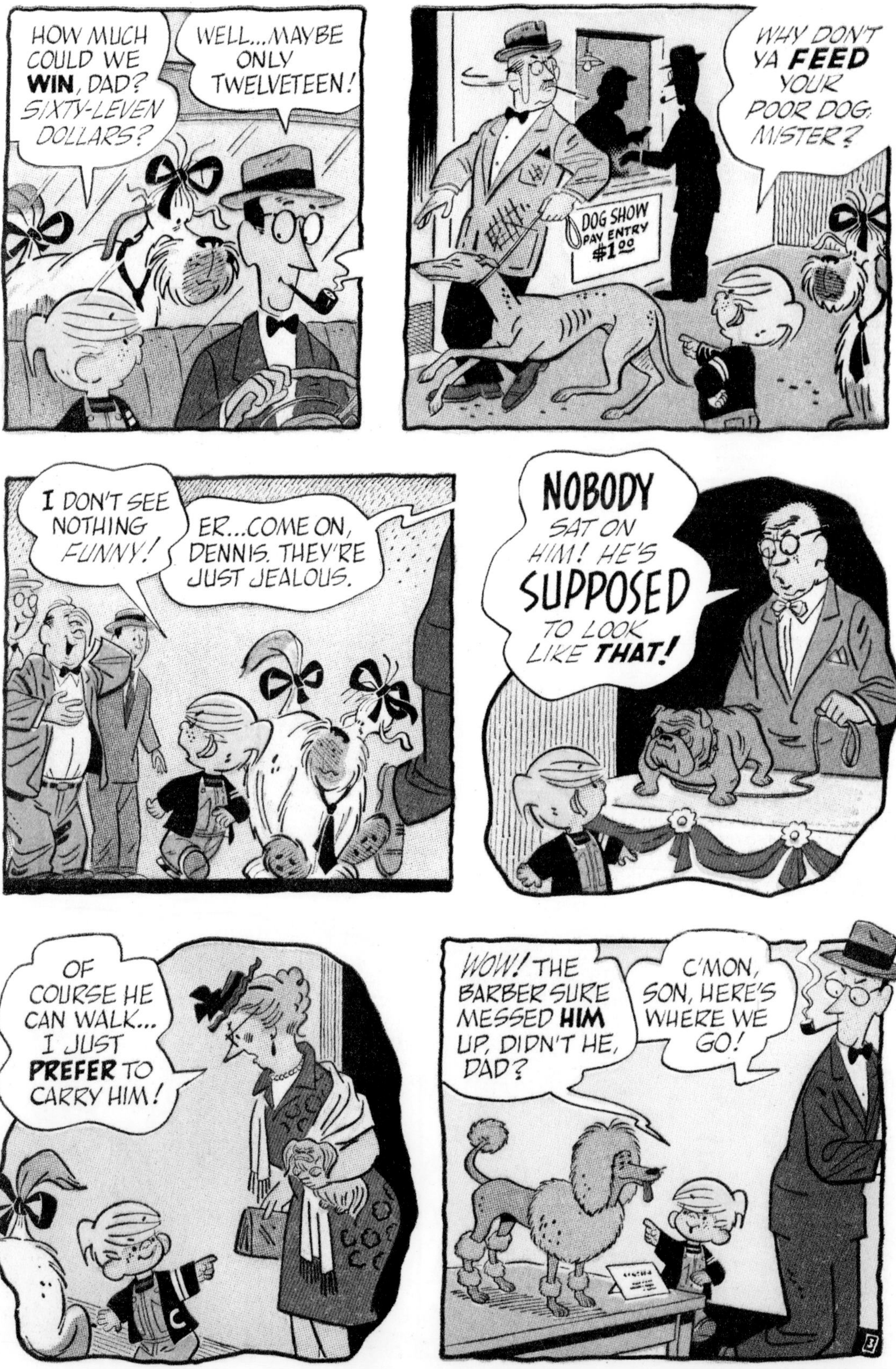
HOW MUCH COULD WE WIN, DAD? SIXTY-LEVEN DOLLARS?
WELL... MAYBE ONLY TWELVETEEN!
DOG SHOW PAY ENTRY $1.00
WHY DON'T YA FEED YOUR POOR DOG, MISTER?
I DON'T SEE NOTHING FUNNY!
ER... COME ON, DENNIS. THEY'RE JUST JEALOUS.
NOBODY SAT ON HIM! HE'S SUPPOSED TO LOOK LIKE THAT!
OF COURSE HE CAN WALK... I JUST PREFER TO CARRY HIM!
WOW! THE BARBER SURE MESSED HIM UP, DIDN'T HE, DAD?
C'MON, SON, HERE'S WHERE WE GO!

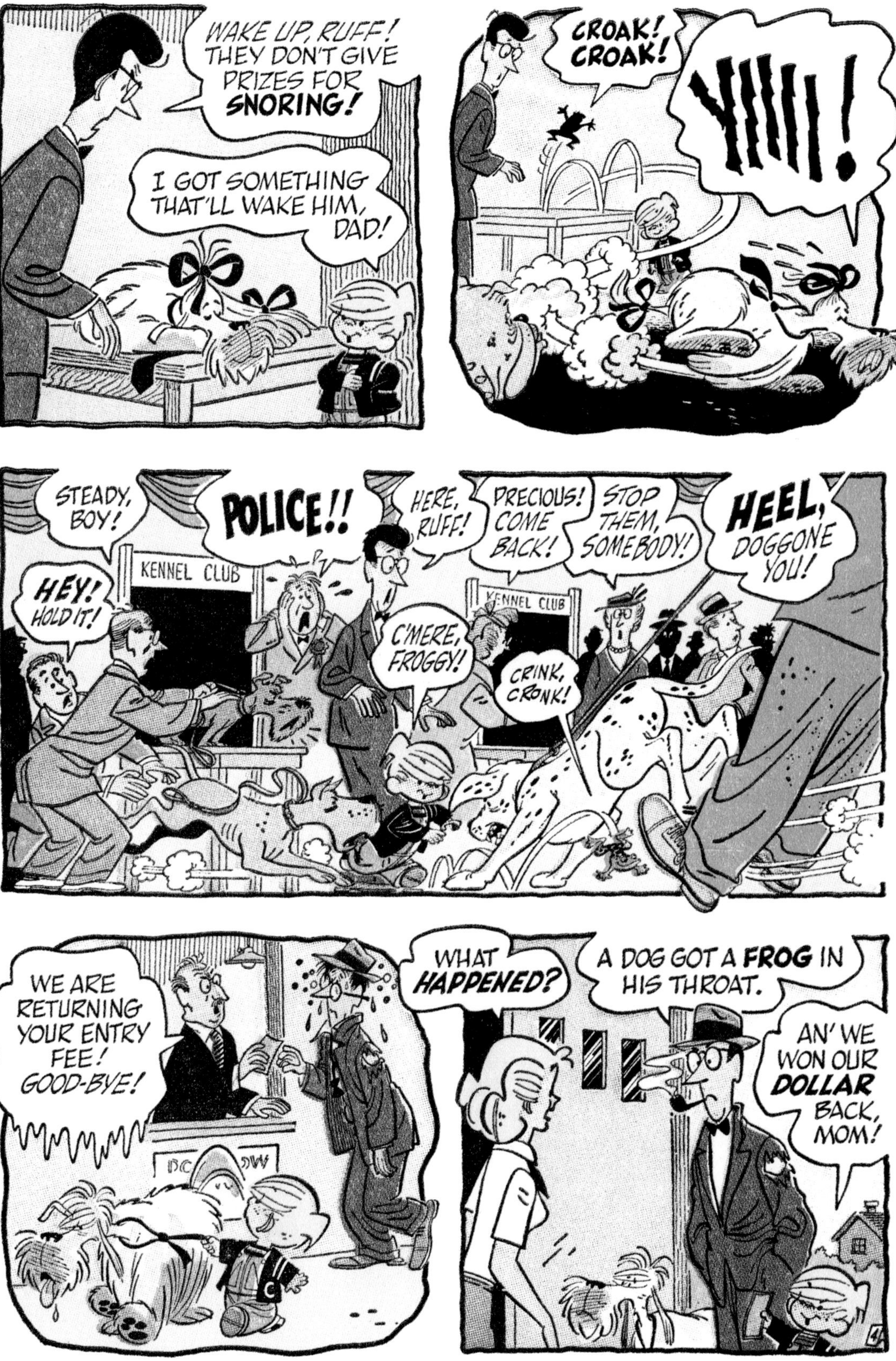
WAKE UP, RUFF! THEY DON'T GIVE PRIZES FOR SNORING!
I GOT SOMETHING THAT'LL WAKE HIM, DAD!
CROAK! CROAK!
YIIII!
STEADY, BOY!
POLICE!!
HERE, RUFF!
PRECIOUS! COME BACK!
STOP THEM, SOMEBODY!
HEEL, DOGGONE YOU!
HEY! HOLD IT!
KENNEL CLUB
KENNEL CLUB
C'MERE, FROGGY!
CRINK, CRONK!
WE ARE RETURNING YOUR ENTRY FEE! GOOD-BYE!
WHAT HAPPENED?
A DOG GOT A FROG IN HIS THROAT.
AN' WE WON OUR DOLLAR BACK, MOM!

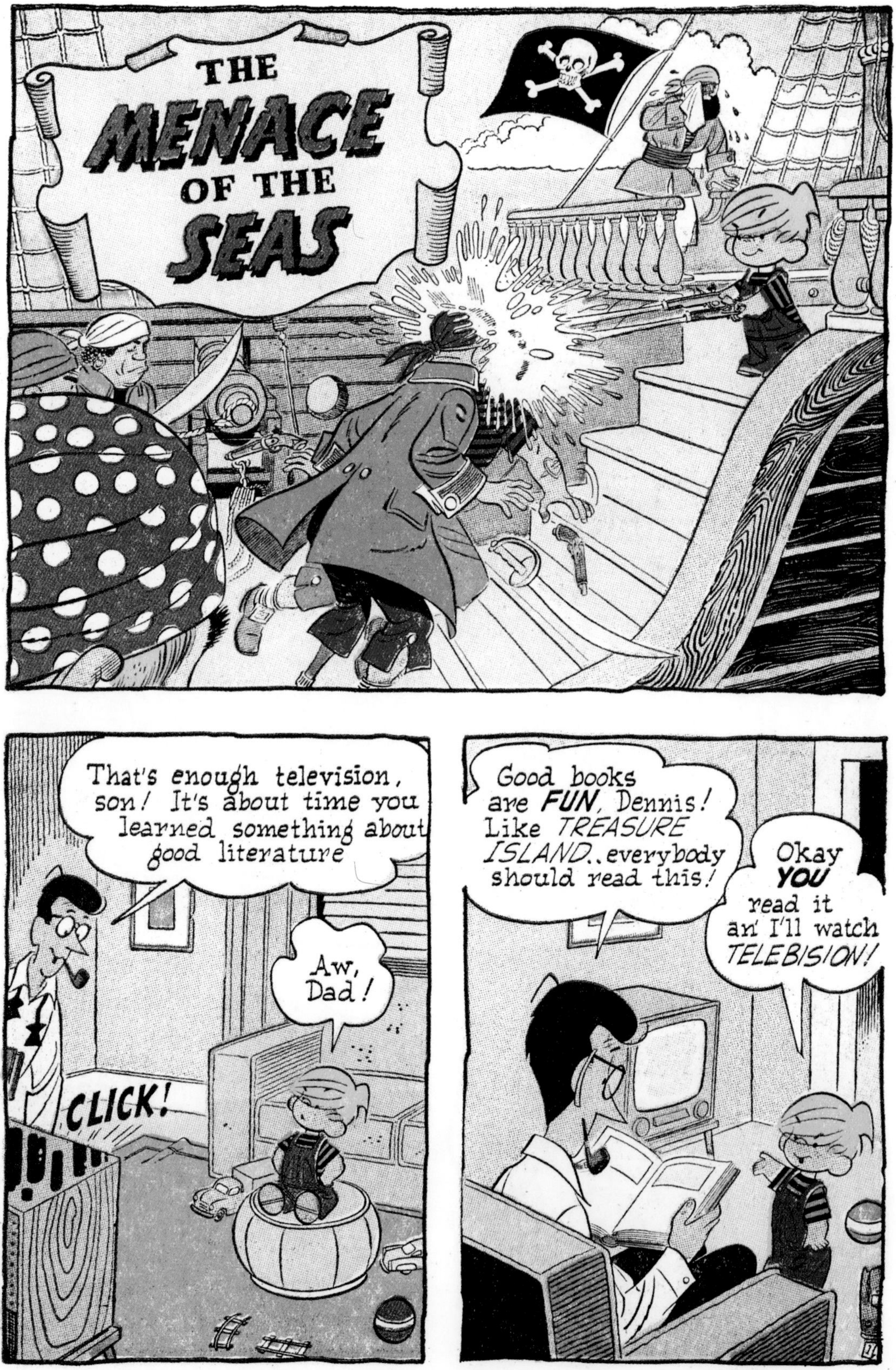
THE MENACE OF THE SEAS
That's enough television, son! It's about time you learned something about good literature
Aw, Dad!
CLICK!
Good books are FUN, Dennis! Like TREASURE ISLAND.. everybody should read this!
Okay YOU read it an' I'll watch TELEBISION!

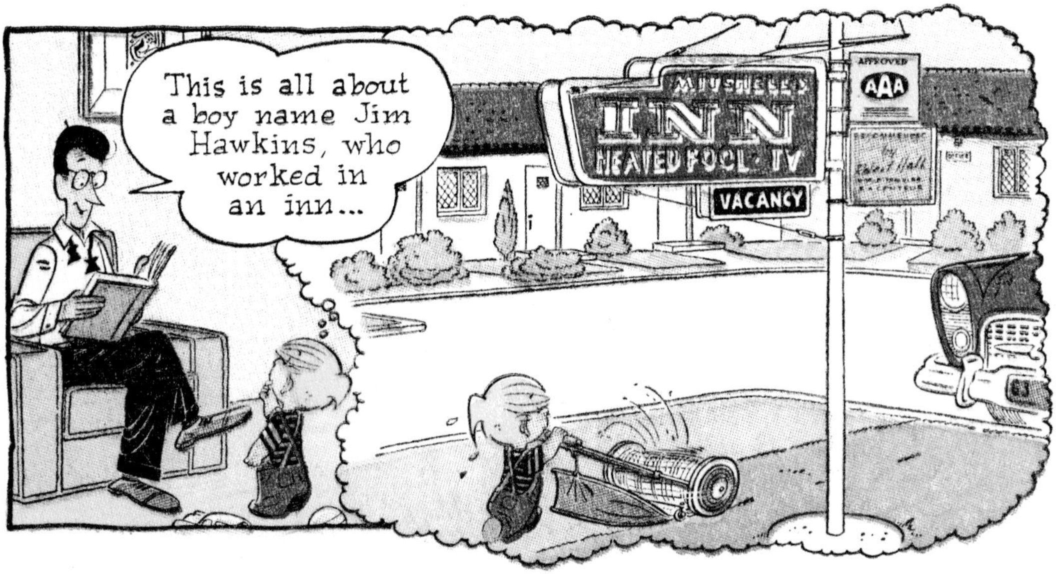

This is all about a boy name Jim Hawkins, who worked in an inn...
APPROVED
AAA
INN
VACANCY

ONE DAY A MAN WHO HAD BEEN A PIRATE CAME TO STAY AT THE INN...

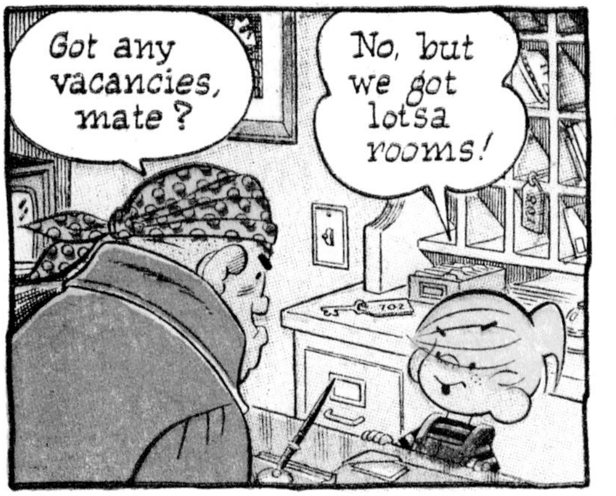

Got any vacancies, mate?
No, but we got lotsa rooms!

... AND JIM FOUND OUT THAT HE HAD A TREASURE MAP!

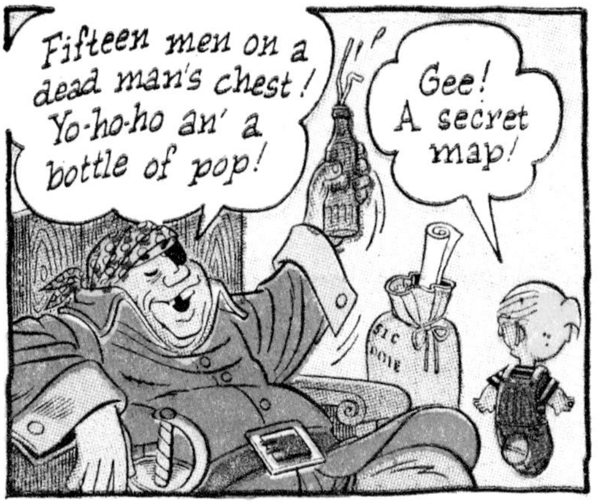

Fifteen men on a dead man's chest! Yo-ho-ho an' a bottle of pop!
Gee! A secret map!

THEN SOME OTHER MEN CAME TO STEAL THE MAP...

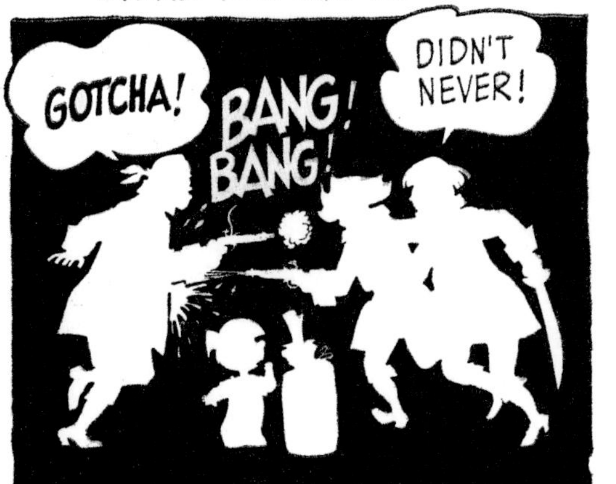

GOTCHA!
BANG! BANG!
DIDN'T NEVER!

... BUT JIM RAN AWAY WITH IT TO HIS FRIEND SQUIRE TRELAWNEY.

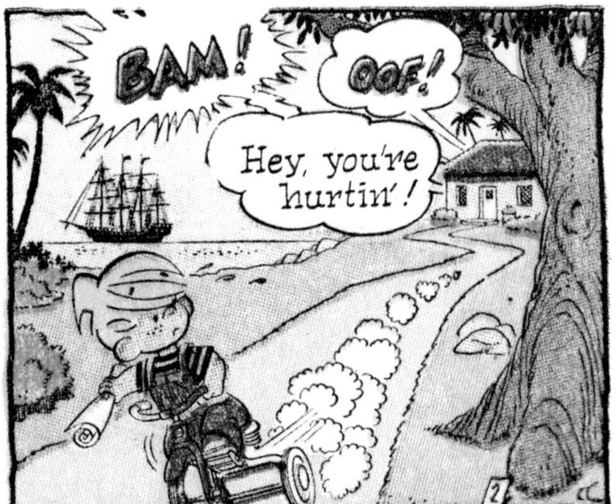

BAM!
OOF!
Hey, you're hurtin'!

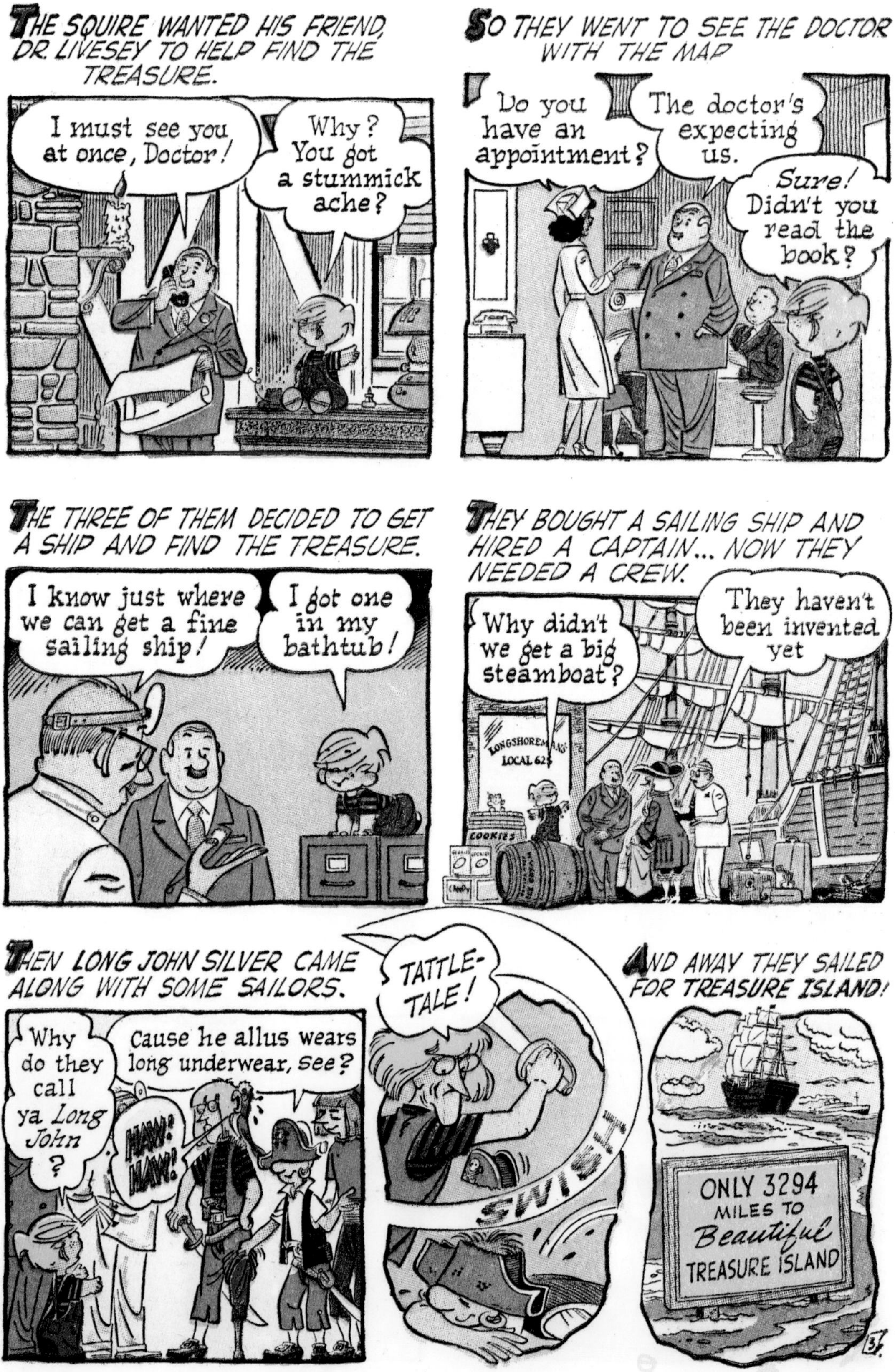
THE SQUIRE WANTED HIS FRIEND, DR. LIVESEY TO HELP FIND THE TREASURE.
I must see you at once, Doctor!
Why? You got a stummick ache?
SO THEY WENT TO SEE THE DOCTOR WITH THE MAP
Do you have an appointment?
The doctor's expecting us.
Sure! Didn't you read the book?
THE THREE OF THEM DECIDED TO GET A SHIP AND FIND THE TREASURE.
I know just where we can get a fine sailing ship!
I got one in my bathtub!
THEY BOUGHT A SAILING SHIP AND HIRED A CAPTAIN... NOW THEY NEEDED A CREW.
Why didn't we get a big steamboat?
They haven't been invented yet
LONGSHOREMAN'S LOCAL 625
COOKIES
THEN LONG JOHN SILVER CAME ALONG WITH SOME SAILORS.
Why do they call ya Long John?
Cause he allus wears long underwear, see?
HAW! HAW!
TATTLE-TALE!
SWISH
AND AWAY THEY SAILED FOR TREASURE ISLAND!
ONLY 3294 MILES TO Beautiful TREASURE ISLAND
3

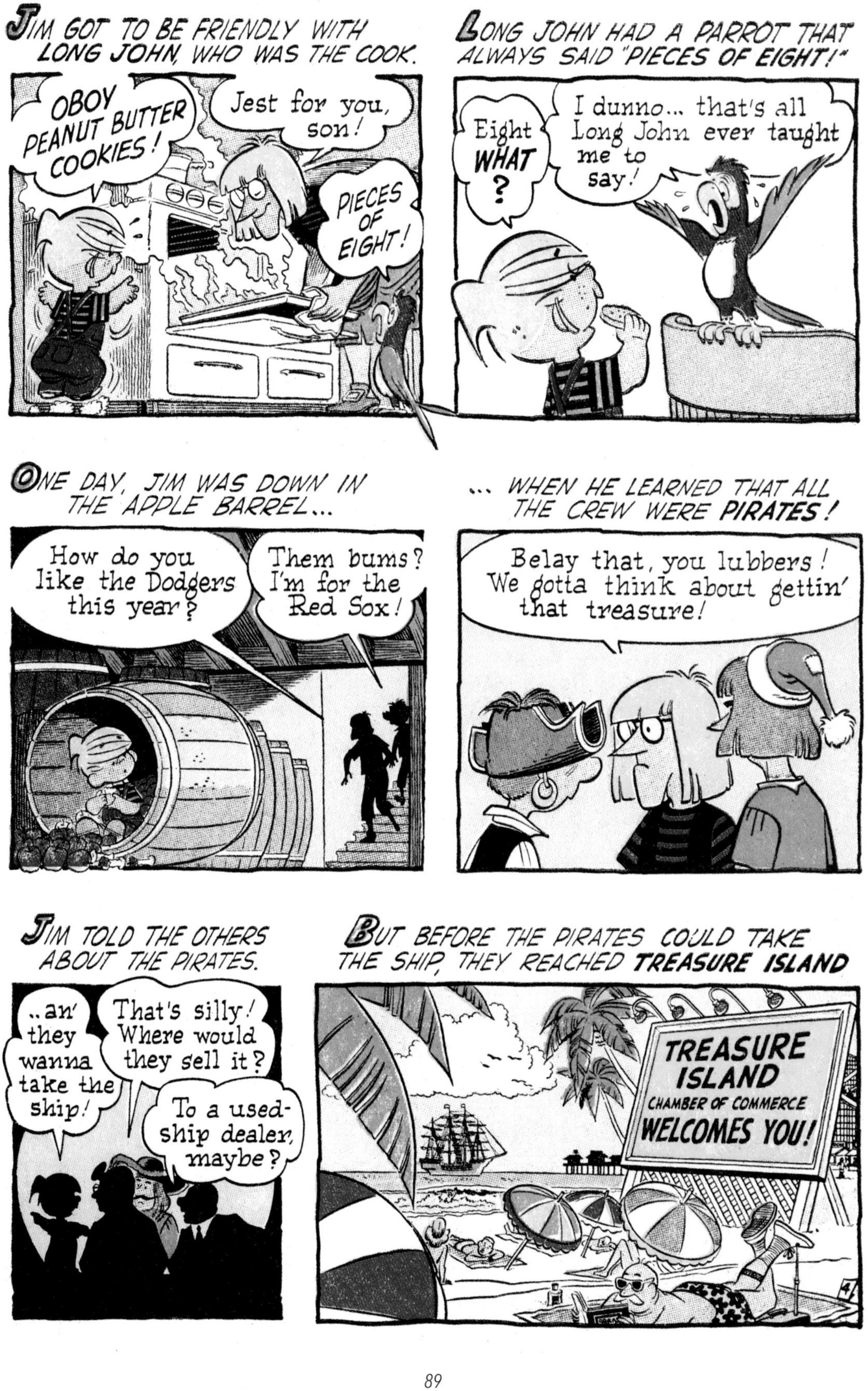
JIM GOT TO BE FRIENDLY WITH LONG JOHN, WHO WAS THE COOK.
OBOY PEANUT BUTTER COOKIES!
Jest for you, son!
PIECES OF EIGHT!
LONG JOHN HAD A PARROT THAT ALWAYS SAID "PIECES OF EIGHT!"
Eight WHAT ?
I dunno... that's all Long John ever taught me to say!
ONE DAY, JIM WAS DOWN IN THE APPLE BARREL...
How do you like the Dodgers this year?
Them bums? I'm for the Red Sox!
... WHEN HE LEARNED THAT ALL THE CREW WERE PIRATES!
Belay that, you lubbers! We gotta think about gettin' that treasure!
JIM TOLD THE OTHERS ABOUT THE PIRATES.
..an' they wanna take the ship!
That's silly! Where would they sell it?
To a used-ship dealer, maybe?
BUT BEFORE THE PIRATES COULD TAKE THE SHIP, THEY REACHED TREASURE ISLAND
TREASURE ISLAND
CHAMBER OF COMMERCE
WELCOMES YOU!
4

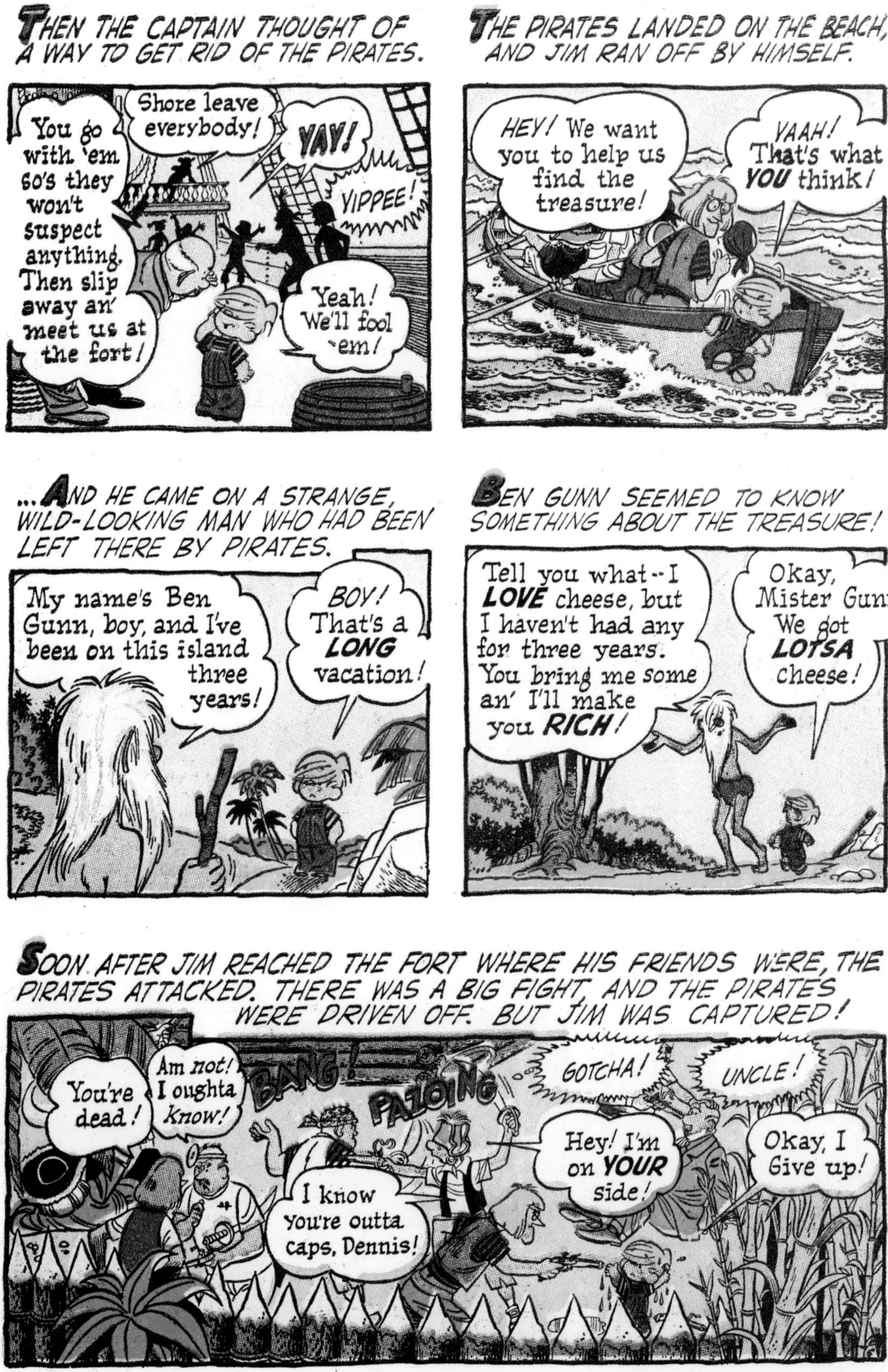
THEN THE CAPTAIN THOUGHT OF A WAY TO GET RID OF THE PIRATES.
You go with 'em so's they won't suspect anything. Then slip away an' meet us at the fort!
Shore leave everybody!
YAY!
YIPPEE!
Yeah! We'll fool 'em!
THE PIRATES LANDED ON THE BEACH, AND JIM RAN OFF BY HIMSELF.
HEY! We want you to help us find the treasure!
YAAH! That's what YOU think!
...AND HE CAME ON A STRANGE, WILD-LOOKING MAN WHO HAD BEEN LEFT THERE BY PIRATES.
My name's Ben Gunn, boy, and I've been on this island three years!
BOY! That's a LONG vacation!
BEN GUNN SEEMED TO KNOW SOMETHING ABOUT THE TREASURE!
Tell you what--I LOVE cheese, but I haven't had any for three years. You bring me some an' I'll make you RICH!
Okay, Mister Gunn! We got LOTSA cheese!
SOON AFTER JIM REACHED THE FORT WHERE HIS FRIENDS WERE, THE PIRATES ATTACKED. THERE WAS A BIG FIGHT, AND THE PIRATES WERE DRIVEN OFF. BUT JIM WAS CAPTURED!
You're dead!
Am not! I oughta know!
BANG!
PAZOING
GOTCHA!
UNCLE!
I know you're outta caps, Dennis!
Hey! I'm on YOUR side!
Okay, I give up!

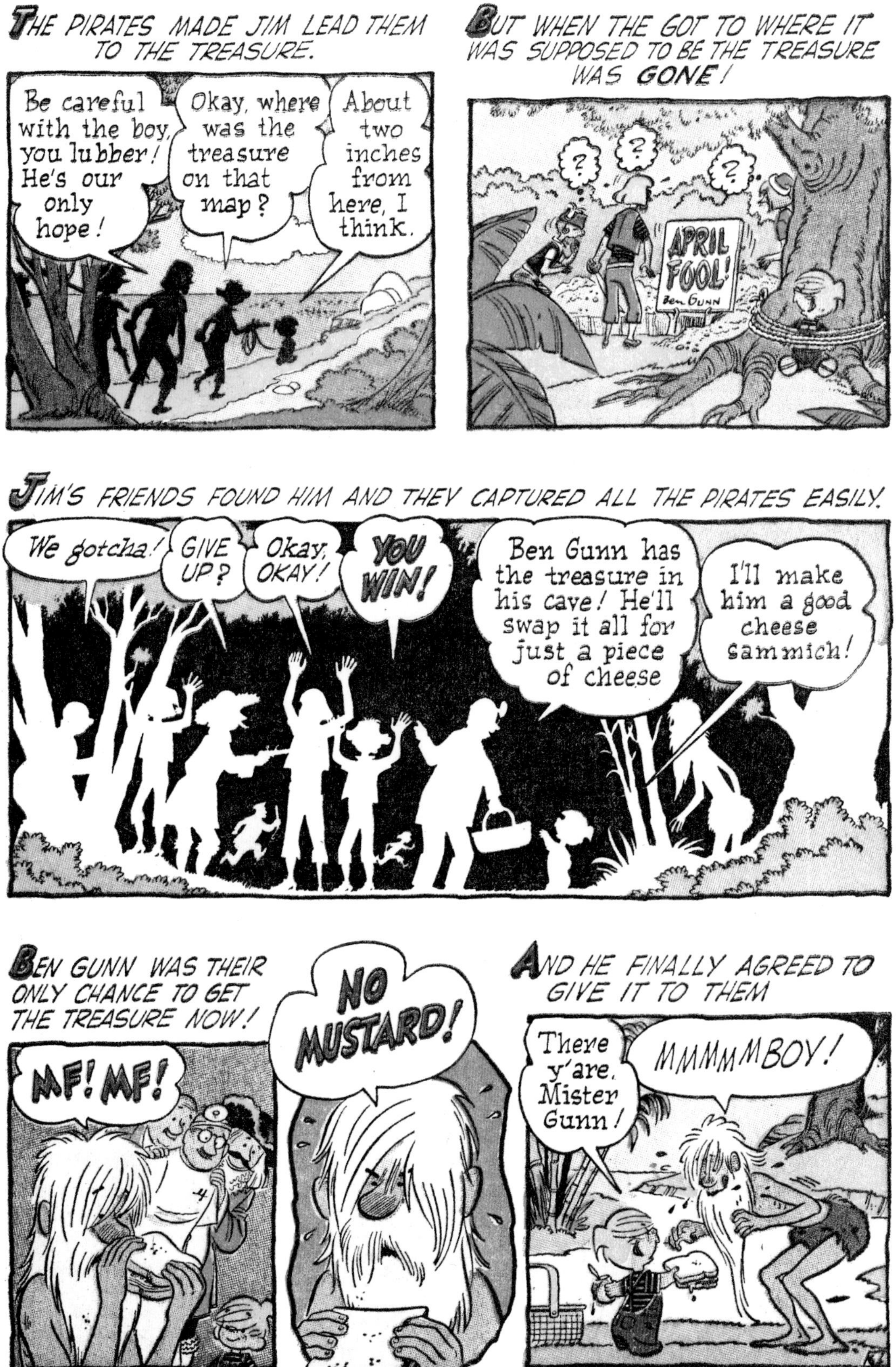
THE PIRATES MADE JIM LEAD THEM TO THE TREASURE.
Be careful with the boy, you lubber! He's our only hope!
Okay, where was the treasure on that map?
About two inches from here, I think.
BUT WHEN THE GOT TO WHERE IT WAS SUPPOSED TO BE THE TREASURE WAS GONE!
?
?
?
APRIL FOOL! Ben Gunn
JIM'S FRIENDS FOUND HIM AND THEY CAPTURED ALL THE PIRATES EASILY.
We gotcha!
GIVE UP?
Okay, OKAY!
YOU WIN!
Ben Gunn has the treasure in his cave! He'll swap it all for just a piece of cheese
I'll make him a good cheese sammich!
BEN GUNN WAS THEIR ONLY CHANCE TO GET THE TREASURE NOW!
MF! MF!
NO MUSTARD!
AND HE FINALLY AGREED TO GIVE IT TO THEM
There y'are, Mister Gunn!
MMMMMBOY!

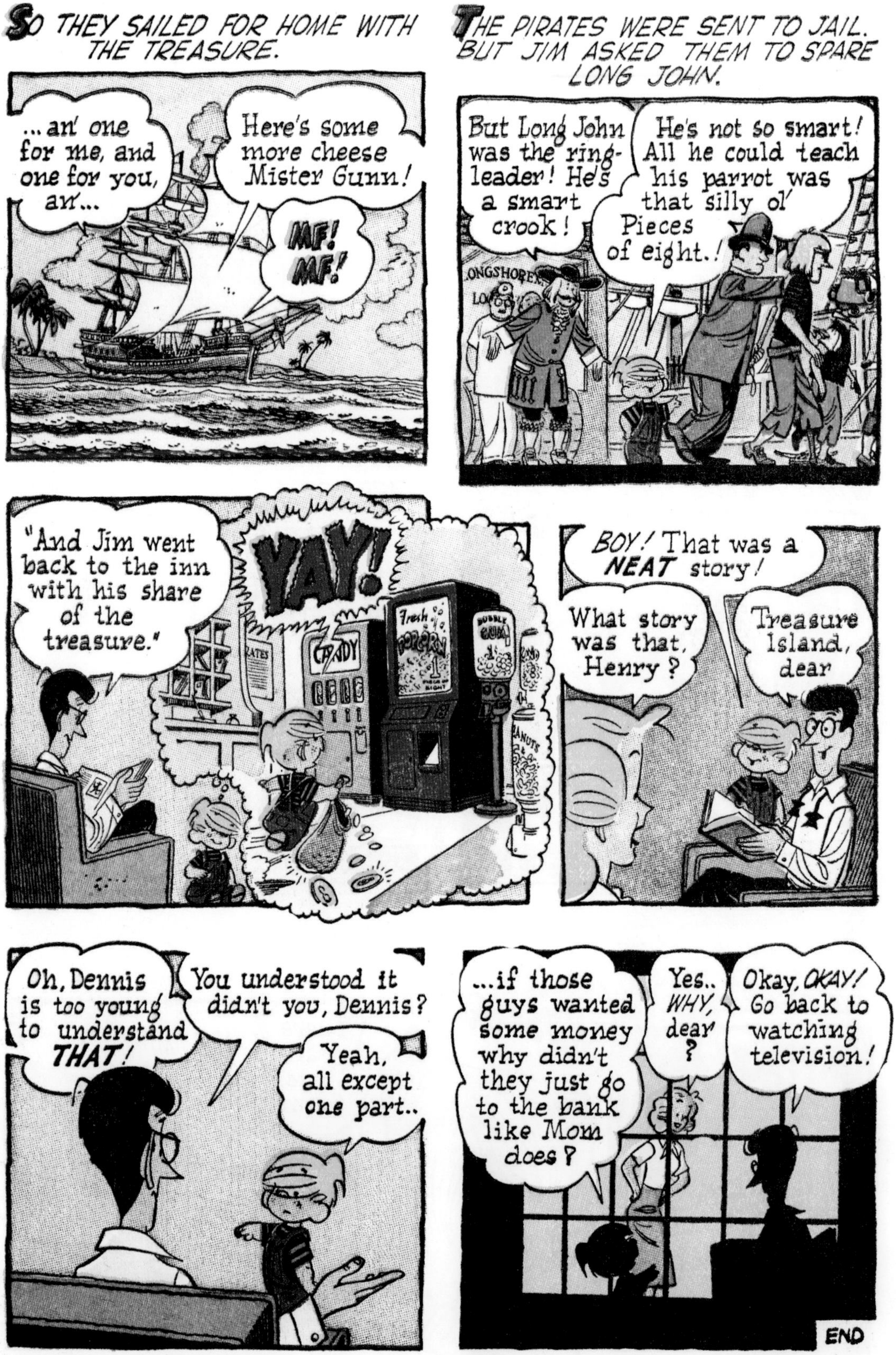
SO THEY SAILED FOR HOME WITH THE TREASURE.
...an' one for me, and one for you, an'...
Here's some more cheese Mister Gunn!
MF! MF!
THE PIRATES WERE SENT TO JAIL. BUT JIM ASKED THEM TO SPARE LONG JOHN.
But Long John was the ring-leader! He's a smart crook!
He's not so smart! All he could teach his parrot was that silly ol' Pieces of eight.!
LONGSHOREM
"And Jim went back to the inn with his share of the treasure."
YAY!
CANDY
Fresh POPCORN
BUBBLE GUM
PEANUTS
BOY! That was a NEAT story!
What story was that, Henry?
Treasure Island, dear
Oh, Dennis is too young to understand THAT!
You understood it didn't you, Dennis?
Yeah, all except one part..
...if those guys wanted some money why didn't they just go to the bank like Mom does?
Yes.. WHY, dear?
Okay, OKAY! Go back to watching television!
END

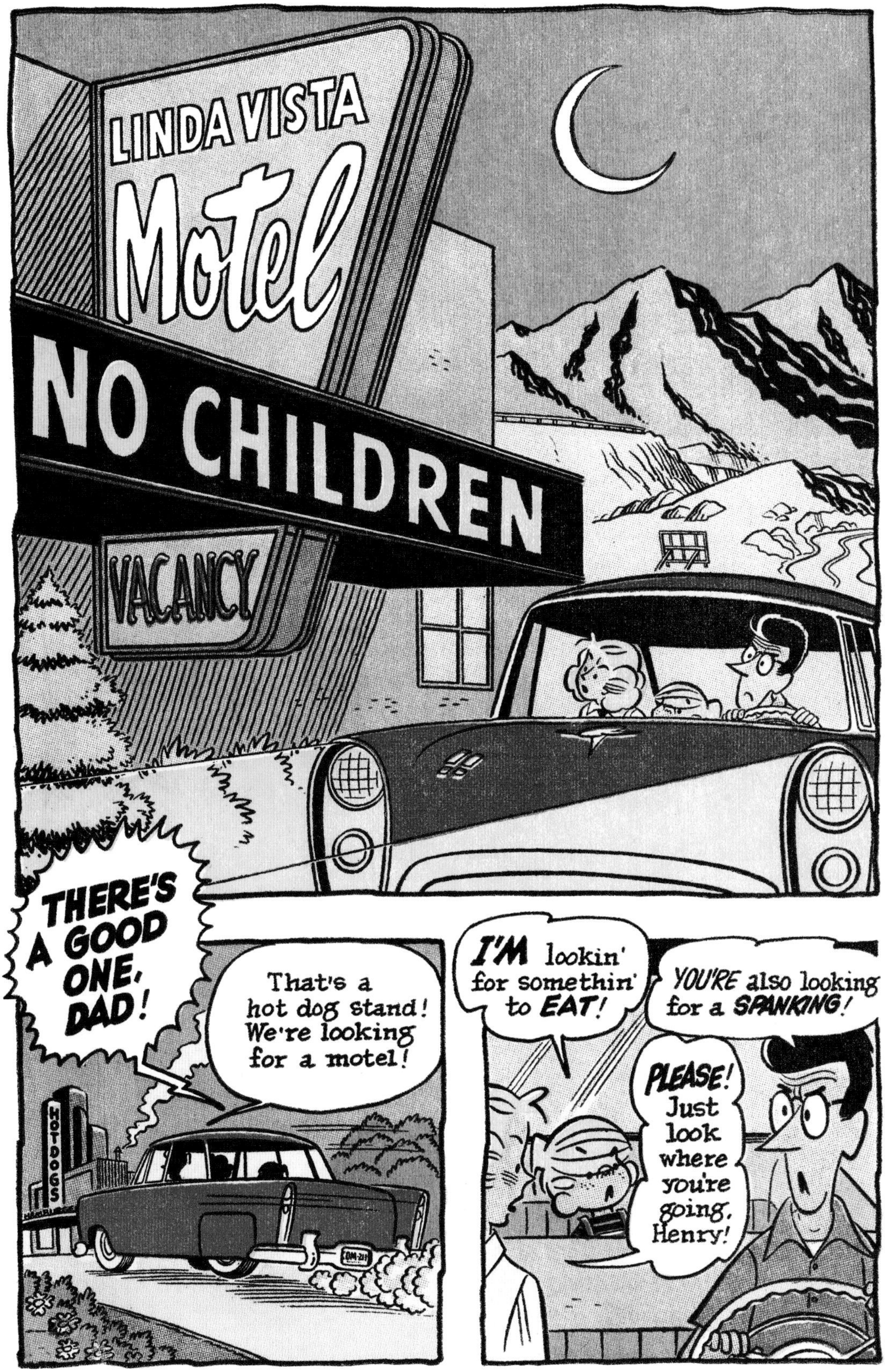
LINDA VISTA
Motel
NO CHILDREN
VACANCY
THERE'S A GOOD ONE, DAD!
HOT DOGS
That's a hot dog stand! We're looking for a motel!
I'M lookin' for somethin' to EAT!
YOU'RE also looking for a SPANKING!
PLEASE! Just look where you're going, Henry!

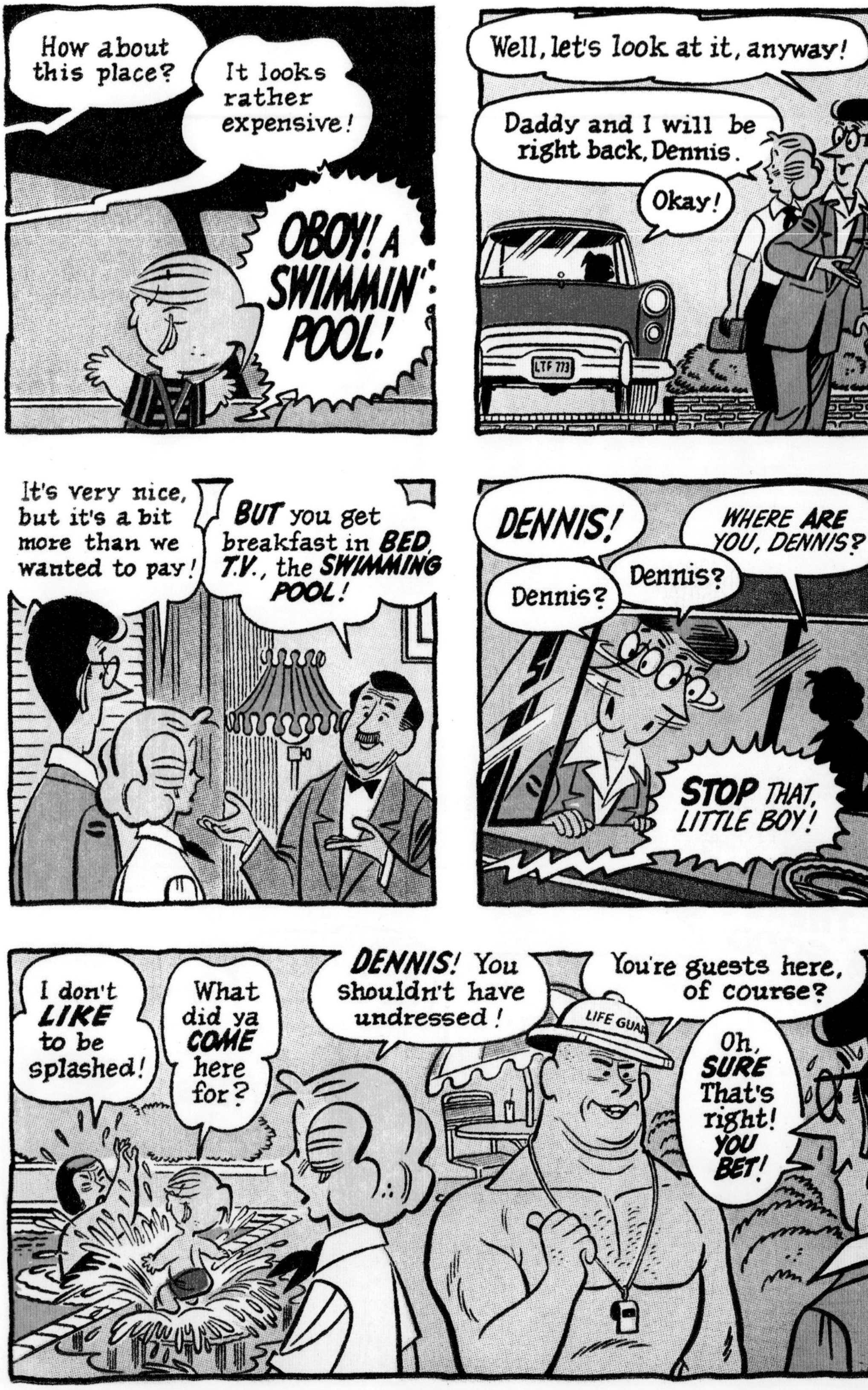
How about this place?
It looks rather expensive!
OBOY! A SWIMMIN' POOL!
Well, let's look at it, anyway!
Daddy and I will be right back, Dennis.
Okay!
LTF 773
It's very nice, but it's a bit more than we wanted to pay!
BUT you get breakfast in BED, T.V., the SWIMMING POOL!
DENNIS!
WHERE ARE YOU, DENNIS?
Dennis?
Dennis?
STOP THAT, LITTLE BOY!
I don't LIKE to be splashed!
What did ya COME here for?
DENNIS! You shouldn't have undressed!
You're guests here, of course?
Oh, SURE That's right! YOU BET!

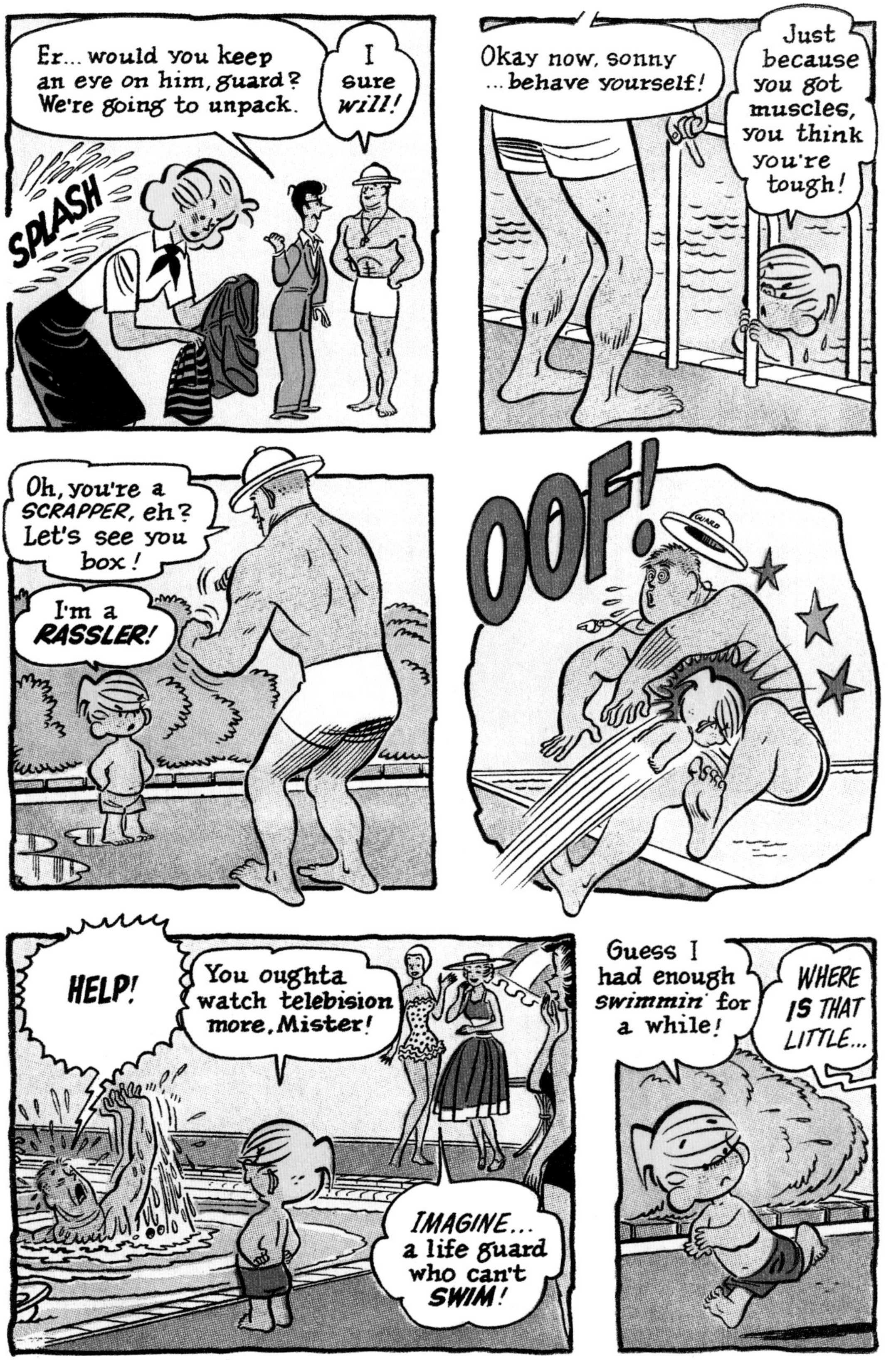
Er... would you keep an eye on him, guard? We're going to unpack.
I sure will!
SPLASH
Okay now, sonny ...behave yourself!
Just because you got muscles, you think you're tough!
Oh, you're a SCRAPPER, eh? Let's see you box!
I'm a RASSLER!
OOF!
GUARD
HELP!
You oughta watch telebision more, Mister!
IMAGINE... a life guard who can't SWIM!
Guess I had enough swimmin' for a while!
WHERE IS THAT LITTLE...

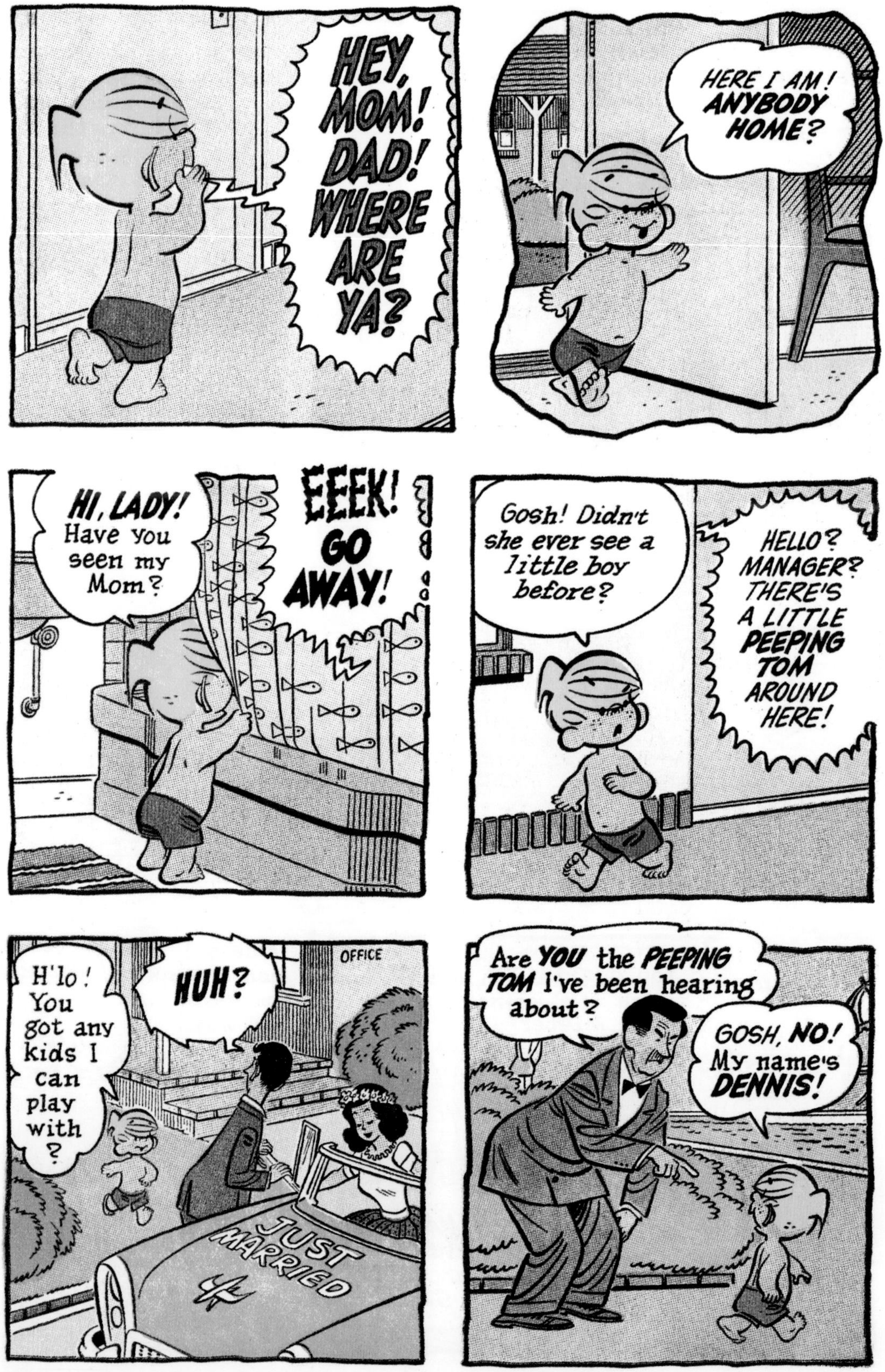
HEY, MOM! DAD! WHERE ARE YA?
HERE I AM! ANYBODY HOME?
HI, LADY! Have you seen my Mom?
EEEK! GO AWAY!
Gosh! Didn't she ever see a little boy before?
HELLO? MANAGER? THERE'S A LITTLE PEEPING TOM AROUND HERE!
OFFICE
H'lo! You got any kids I can play with?
HUH?
JUST MARRIED
Are YOU the PEEPING TOM I've been hearing about?
GOSH, NO! My name's DENNIS!

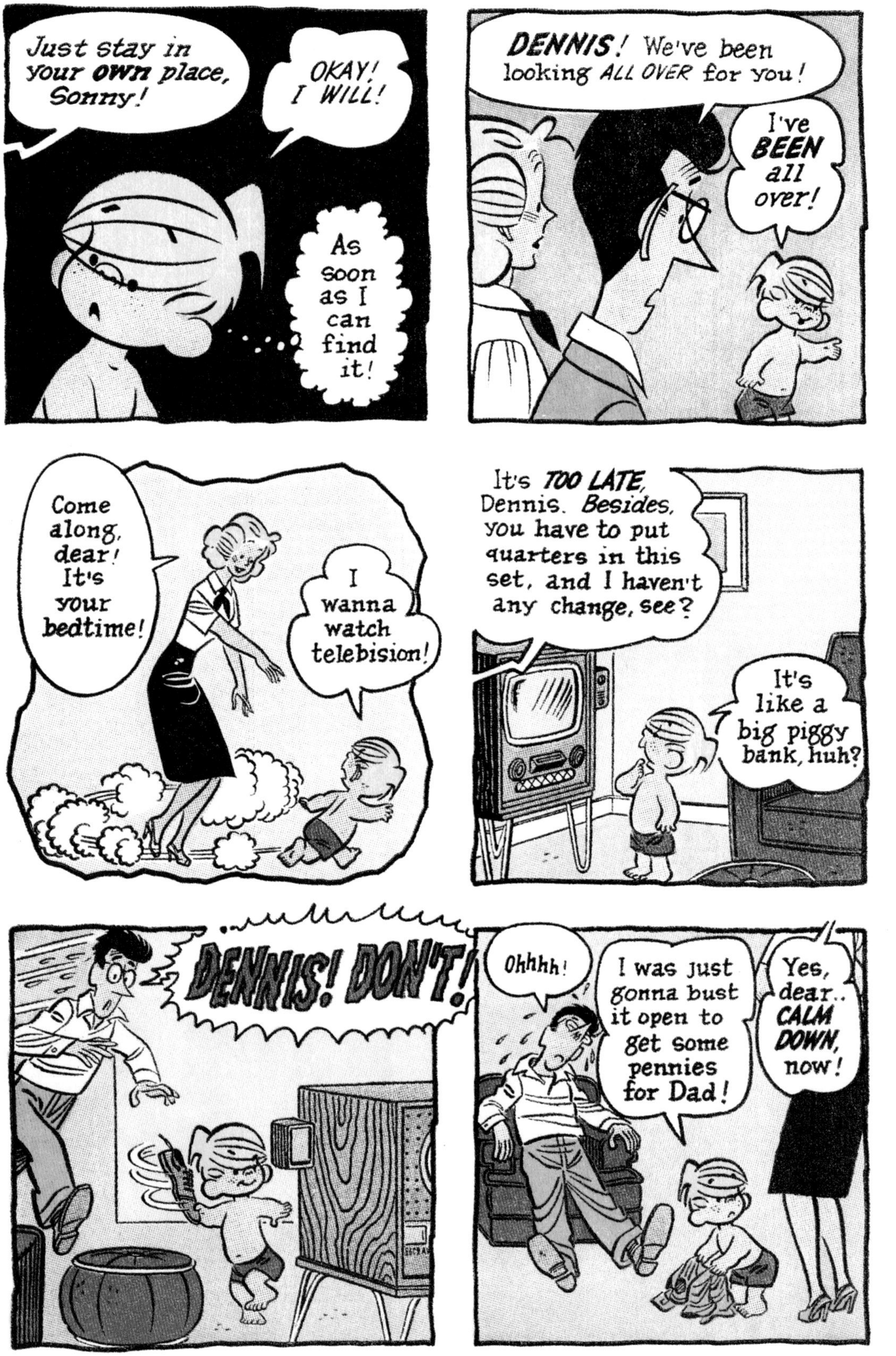

Just stay in your OWN place, Sonny!
OKAY! I WILL!
As soon as I can find it!
DENNIS! We've been looking ALL OVER for you!
I've BEEN all over!
Come along, dear! It's your bedtime!
I wanna watch telebision!
It's TOO LATE, Dennis. Besides, you have to put quarters in this set, and I haven't any change, see?
It's like a big piggy bank, huh?
DENNIS! DON'T!
Ohhhh!
I was just gonna bust it open to get some pennies for Dad!
Yes, dear.. CALM DOWN, now!

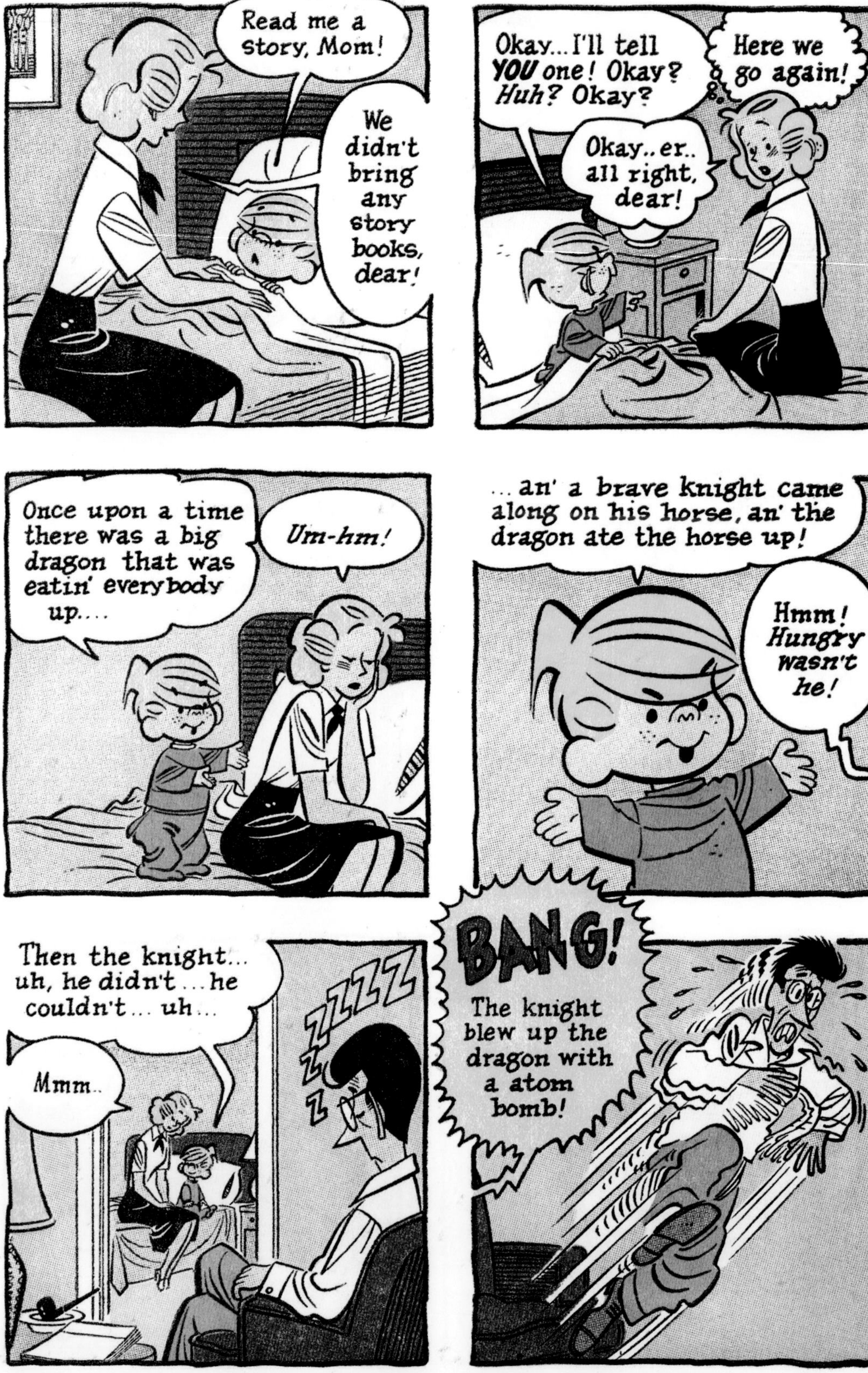
Read me a story, Mom!
We didn't bring any story books, dear!
Okay... I'll tell YOU one! Okay? Huh? Okay?
Here we go again!
Okay.. er.. all right, dear!
Once upon a time there was a big dragon that was eatin' everybody up....
Um-hm!
... an' a brave knight came along on his horse, an' the dragon ate the horse up!
Hmm! Hungry wasn't he!
Then the knight... uh, he didn't ... he couldn't ... uh ...
Mmm..
ZZZZZZZ
BANG!
The knight blew up the dragon with a atom bomb!

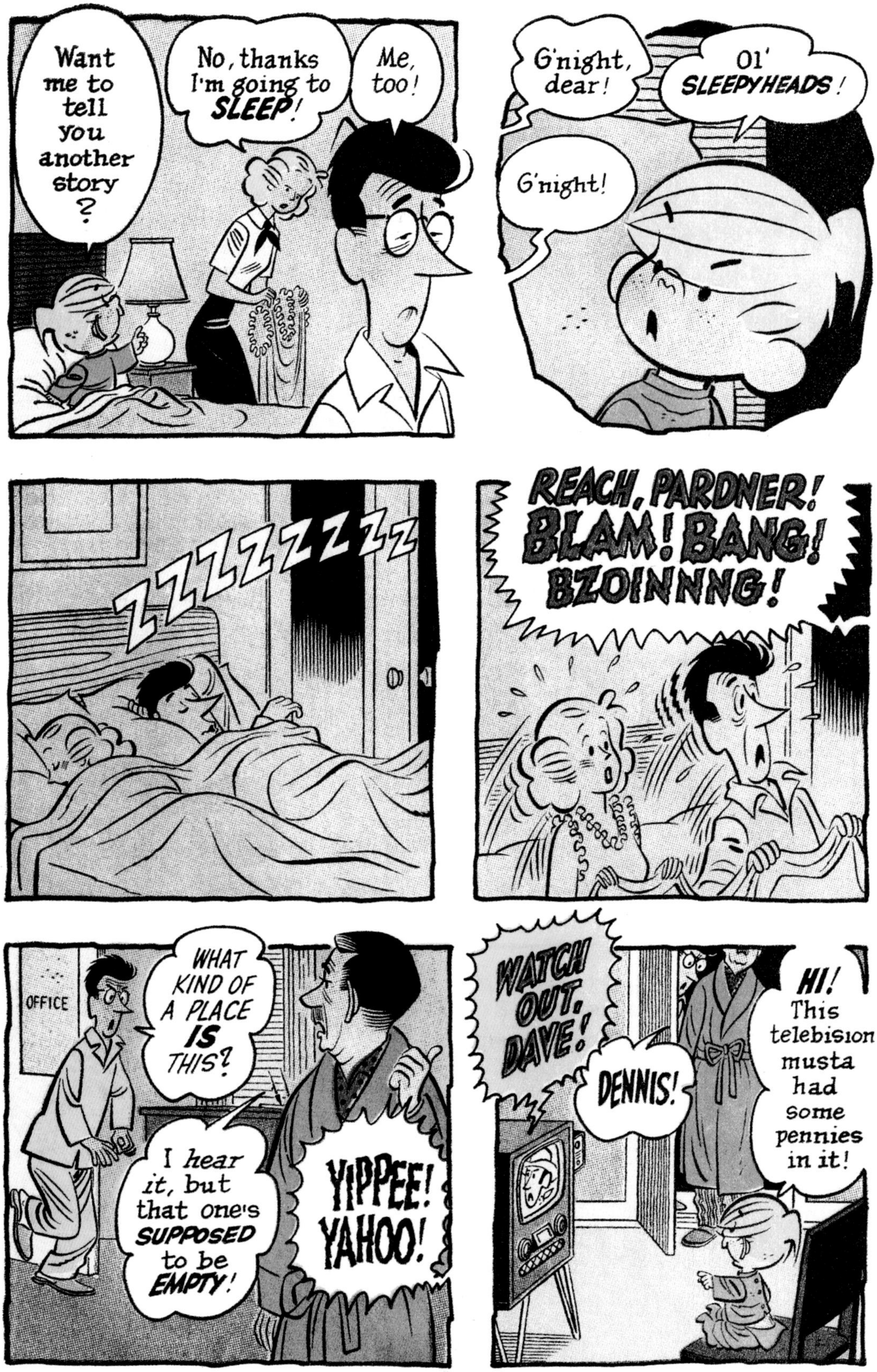
Want me to tell you another story?
No, thanks I'm going to SLEEP!
Me, too!
G'night, dear!
G'night!
Ol' SLEEPYHEADS!
ZZZZZZZZZ
REACH, PARDNER! BLAM! BANG! BZOINNNG!
OFFICE
WHAT KIND OF A PLACE IS THIS?
I hear it, but that one's SUPPOSED to be EMPTY!
YIPPEE! YAHOO!
WATCH OUT, DAVE!
DENNIS!
HI! This telebision musta had some pennies in it!

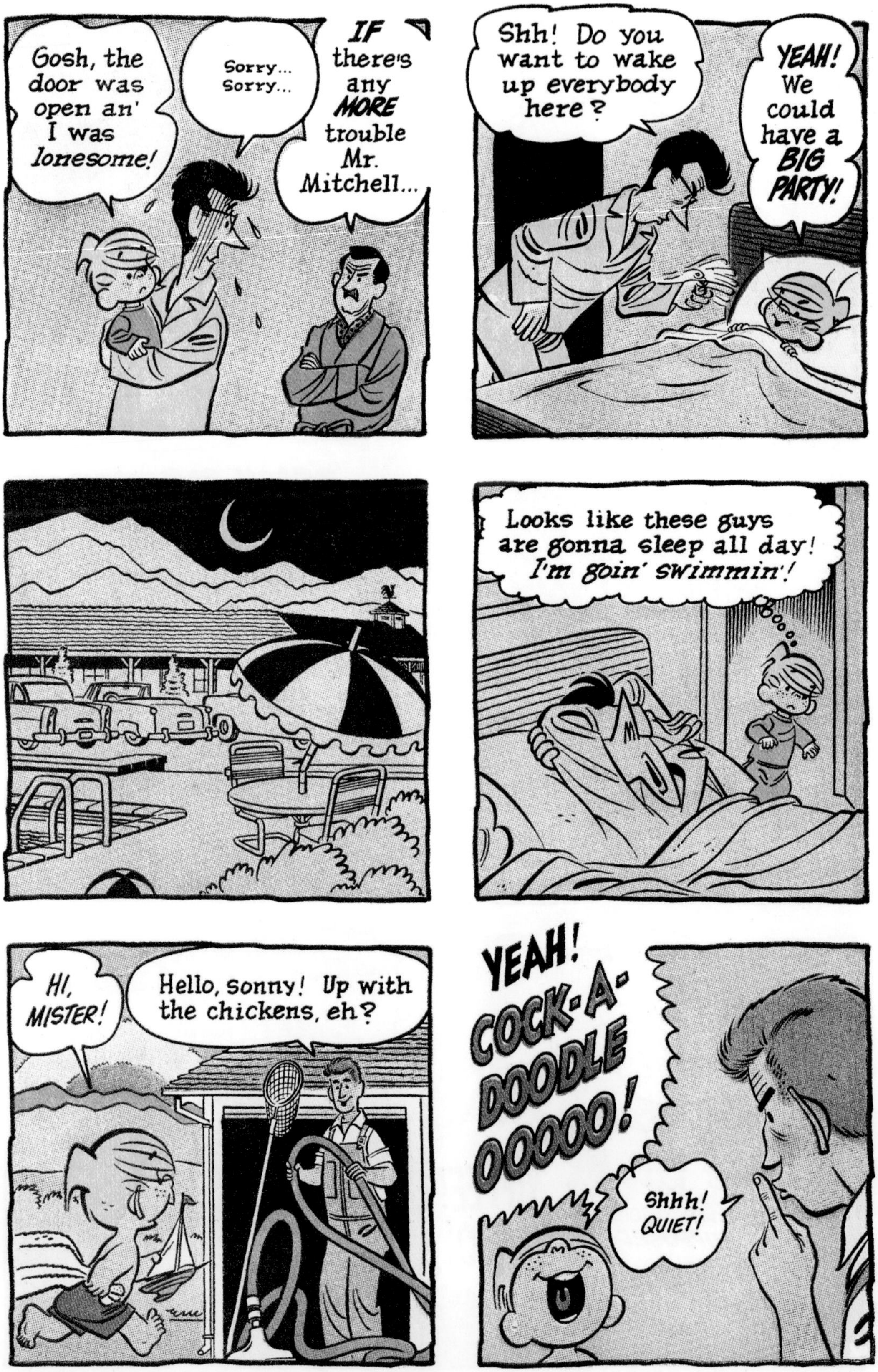
Gosh, the door was open an' I was *lonesome!*
Sorry... Sorry...
IF there's any *MORE* trouble Mr. Mitchell...
Shh! Do you want to wake up everybody here?
YEAH! We could have a *BIG PARTY!*
Looks like these guys are gonna sleep all day! *I'm goin' swimmin'!*
HI, MISTER!
Hello, sonny! Up with the chickens, eh?
YEAH! COCK-A-DOODLE OOOOO!
Shhh! QUIET!

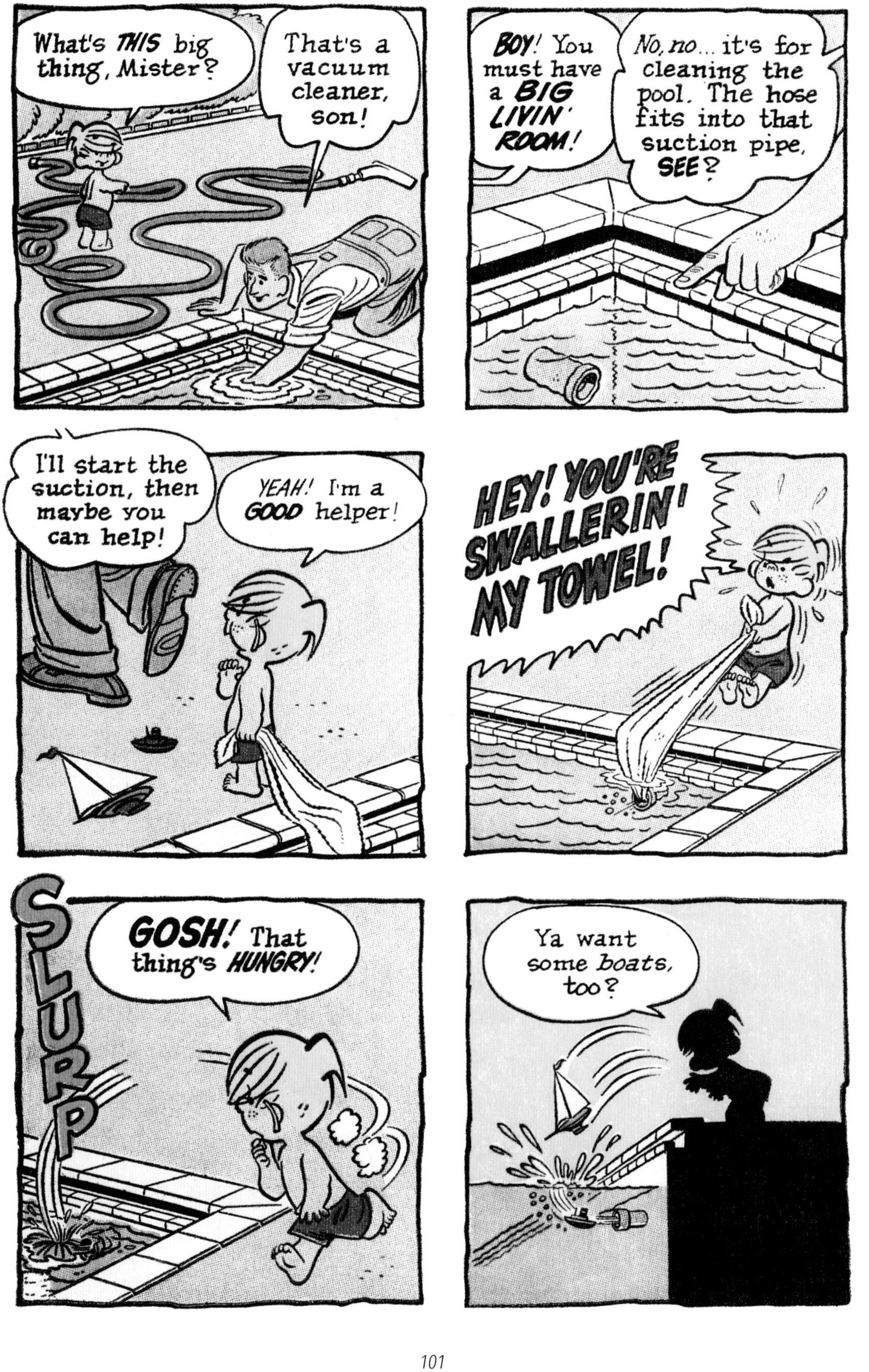
What's THIS big thing, Mister?
That's a vacuum cleaner, son!
BOY! You must have a BIG LIVIN' ROOM!
No, no... it's for cleaning the pool. The hose fits into that suction pipe, SEE?
I'll start the suction, then maybe you can help!
YEAH! I'm a GOOD helper!
HEY! YOU'RE SWALLERIN' MY TOWEL!
SLURP
GOSH! That thing's HUNGRY!
Ya want some boats, too?

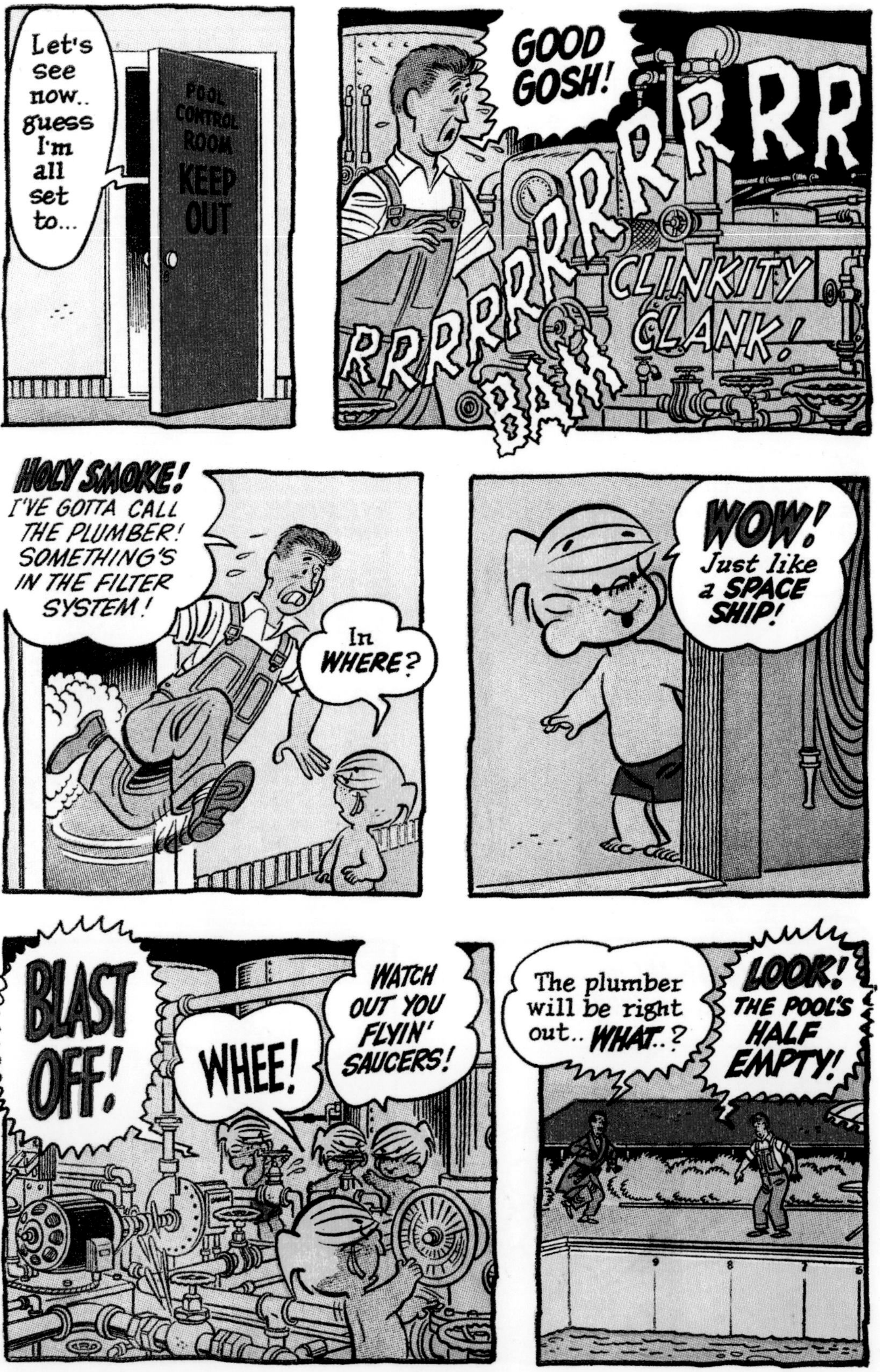
Let's see now.. guess I'm all set to...
POOL CONTROL ROOM KEEP OUT
GOOD GOSH!
RRRRRRRRRRRRRR
CLINKITY CLANK!
BAM
HOLY SMOKE! I'VE GOTTA CALL THE PLUMBER! SOMETHING'S IN THE FILTER SYSTEM!
In WHERE?
WOW! Just like a SPACE SHIP!
BLAST OFF!
WHEE!
WATCH OUT YOU FLYIN' SAUCERS!
The plumber will be right out.. WHAT..?
LOOK! THE POOL'S HALF EMPTY!

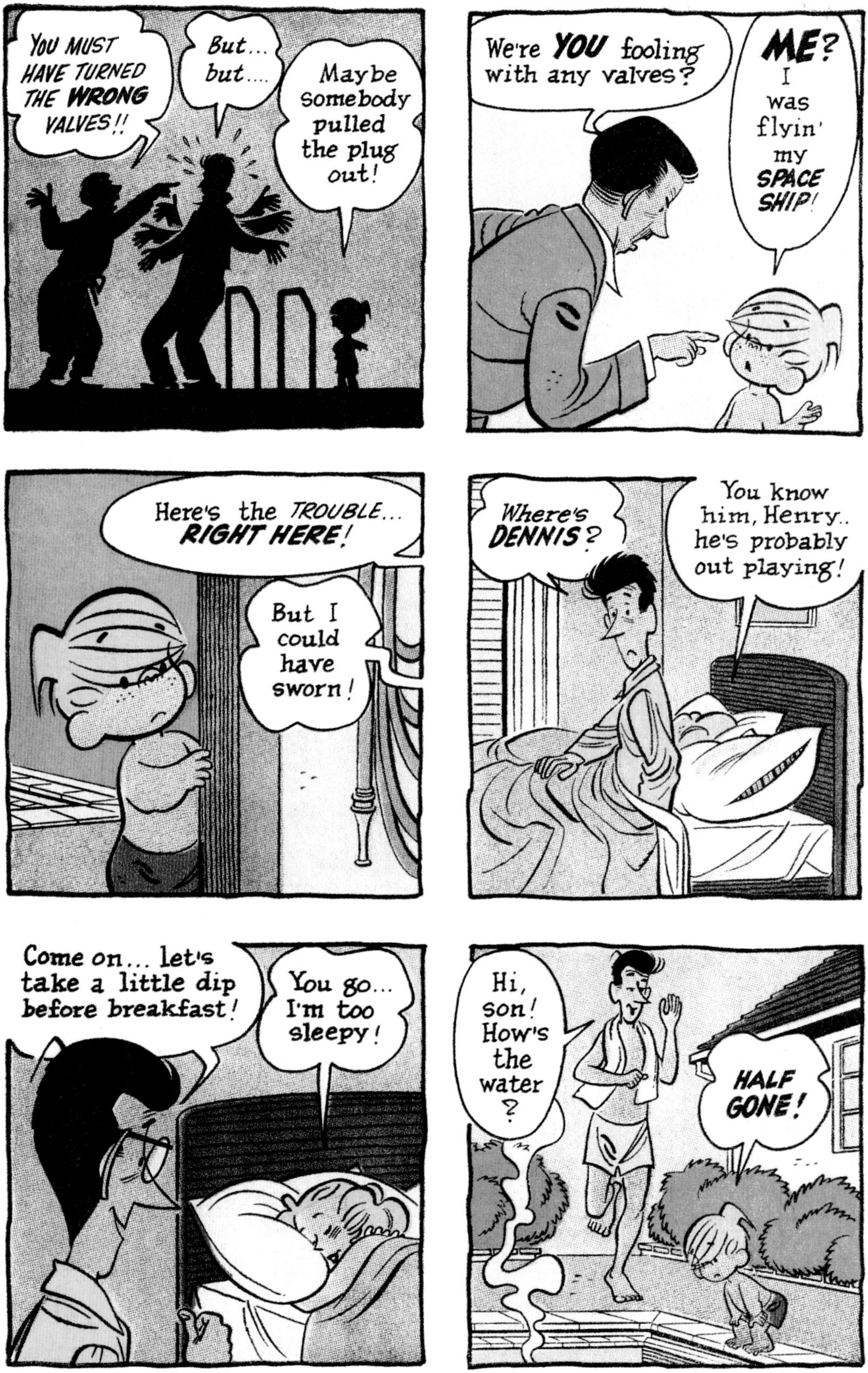

YOU MUST HAVE TURNED THE WRONG VALVES!!
But... but....
Maybe somebody pulled the plug out!
We're YOU fooling with any valves?
ME? I was flyin' my SPACE SHIP!
Here's the TROUBLE... RIGHT HERE!
But I could have sworn!
Where's DENNIS?
You know him, Henry.. he's probably out playing!
Come on... let's take a little dip before breakfast!
You go... I'm too sleepy!
Hi, son! How's the water?
HALF GONE!

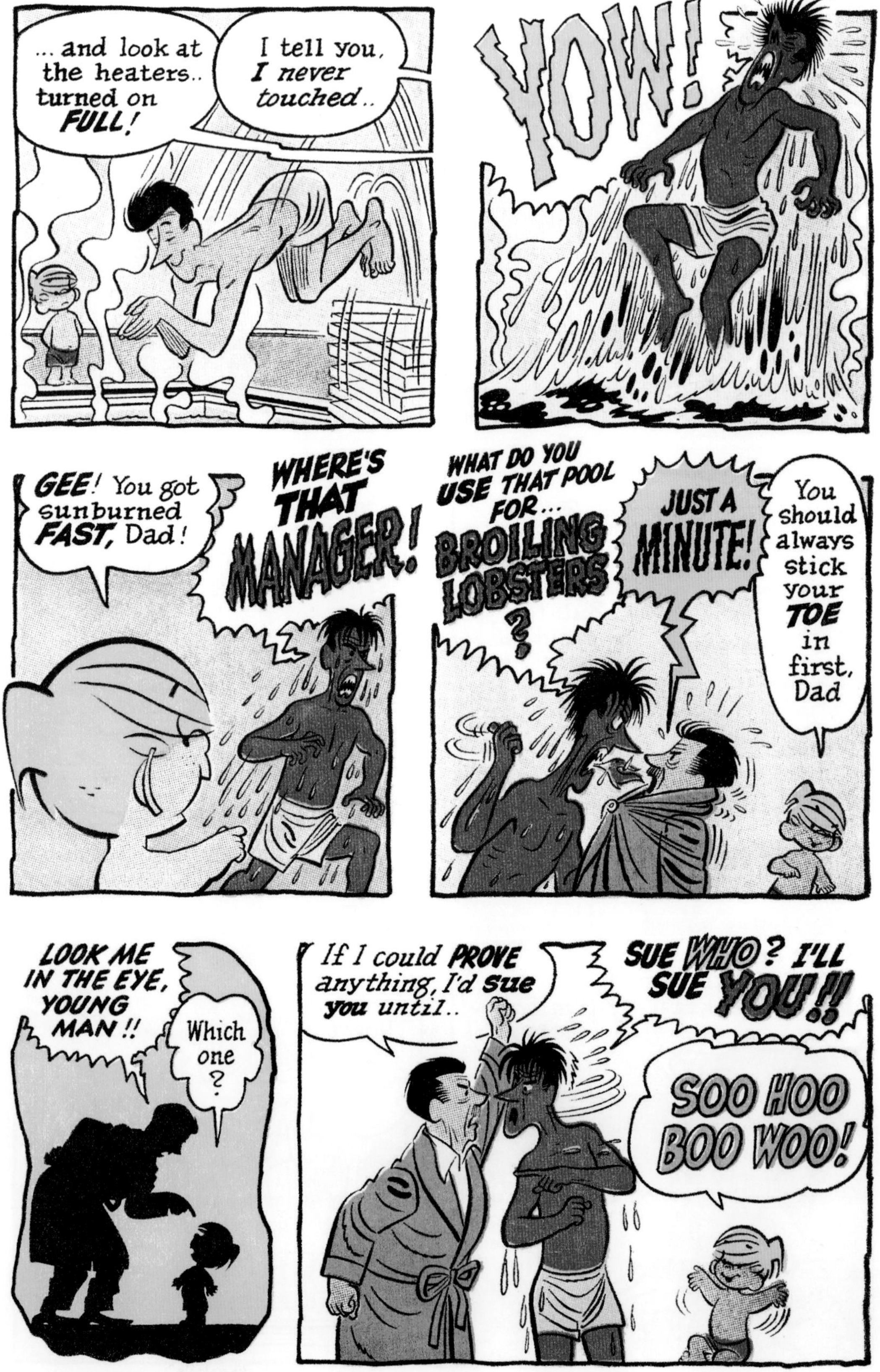
... and look at the heaters.. turned on FULL!
I tell you, I never touched..
YOW!
GEE! You got sunburned FAST, Dad!
WHERE'S THAT MANAGER!
WHAT DO YOU USE THAT POOL FOR... BROILING LOBSTERS?
JUST A MINUTE!
You should always stick your TOE in first, Dad
LOOK ME IN THE EYE, YOUNG MAN!!
Which one?
If I could PROVE anything, I'd sue you until..
SUE WHO? I'LL SUE YOU!!
SOO HOO BOO WOO!

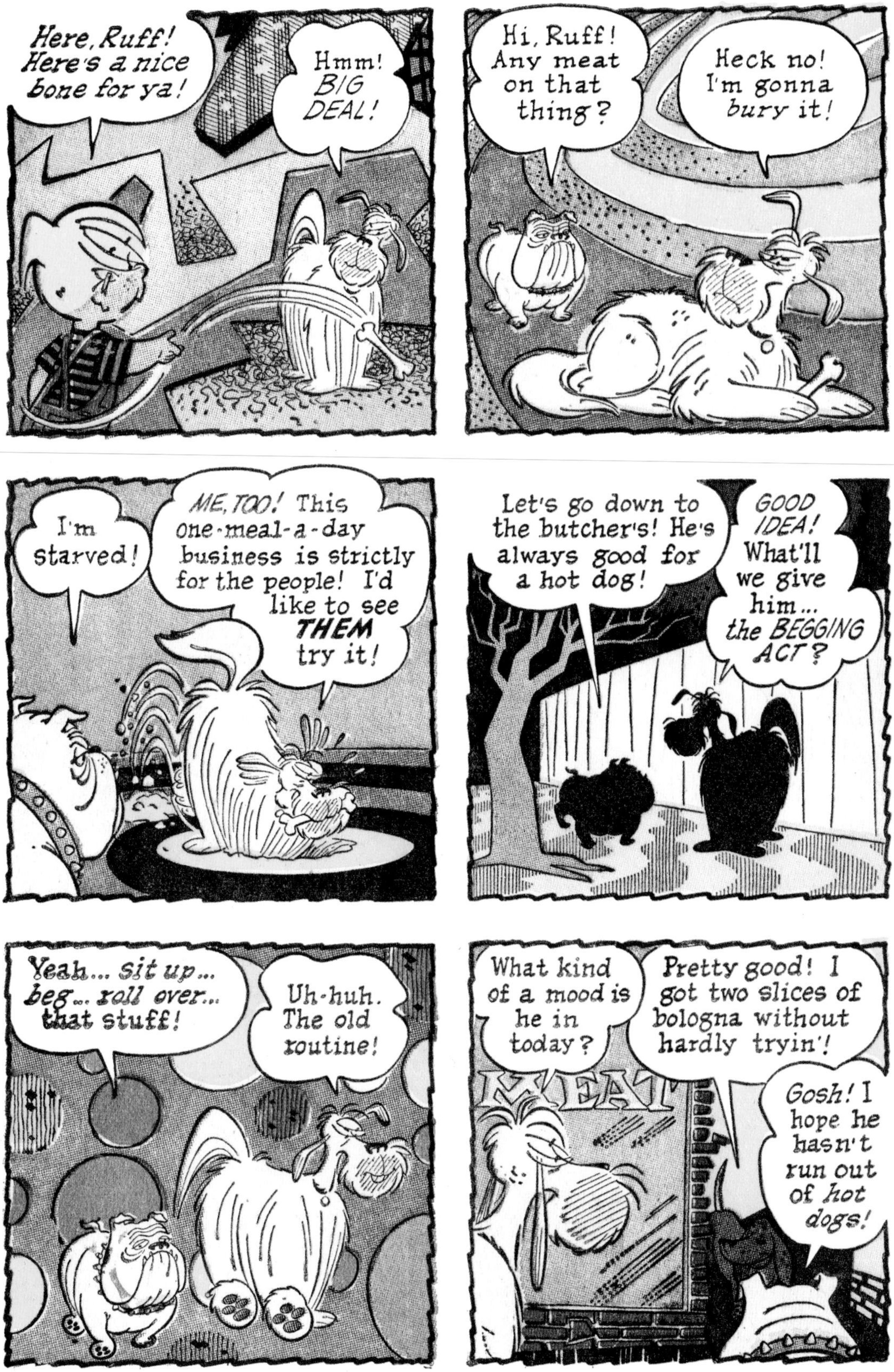
Here, Ruff! Here's a nice bone for ya!
Hmm! BIG DEAL!
Hi, Ruff! Any meat on that thing?
Heck no! I'm gonna bury it!
I'm starved!
ME, TOO! This one-meal-a-day business is strictly for the people! I'd like to see THEM try it!
Let's go down to the butcher's! He's always good for a hot dog!
GOOD IDEA! What'll we give him... the BEGGING ACT?
Yeah... sit up... beg... roll over... that stuff!
Uh-huh. The old routine!
What kind of a mood is he in today?
Pretty good! I got two slices of bologna without hardly tryin'!
Gosh! I hope he hasn't run out of hot dogs!

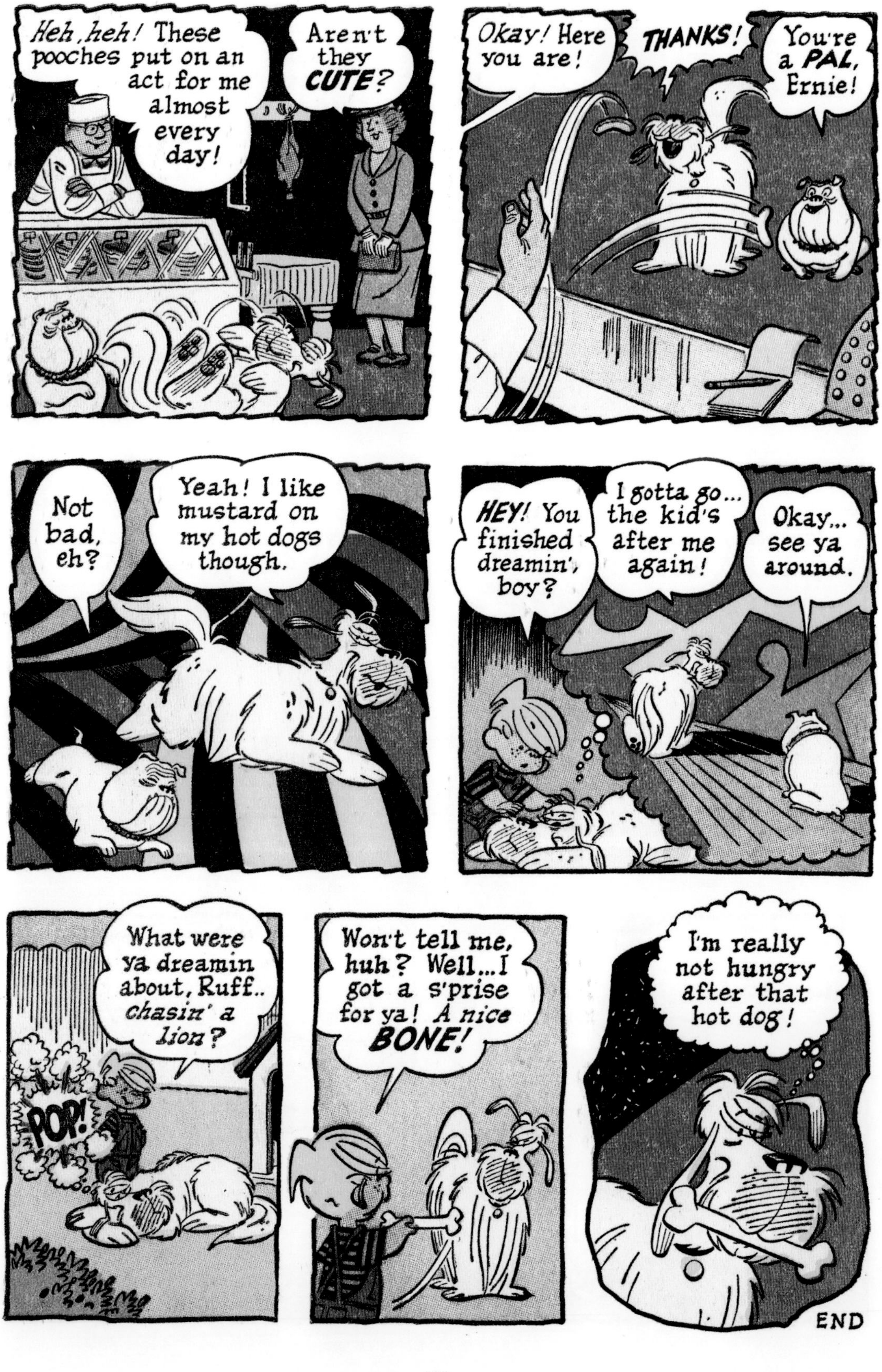
Heh, heh! These pooches put on an act for me almost every day!
Aren't they CUTE?
Okay! Here you are!
THANKS!
You're a PAL, Ernie!
Not bad, eh?
Yeah! I like mustard on my hot dogs though.
HEY! You finished dreamin', boy?
I gotta go... the kid's after me again!
Okay... see ya around.
What were ya dreamin about, Ruff.. chasin' a lion?
POP!
Won't tell me, huh? Well...I got a s'prise for ya! A nice BONE!
I'm really not hungry after that hot dog!
END

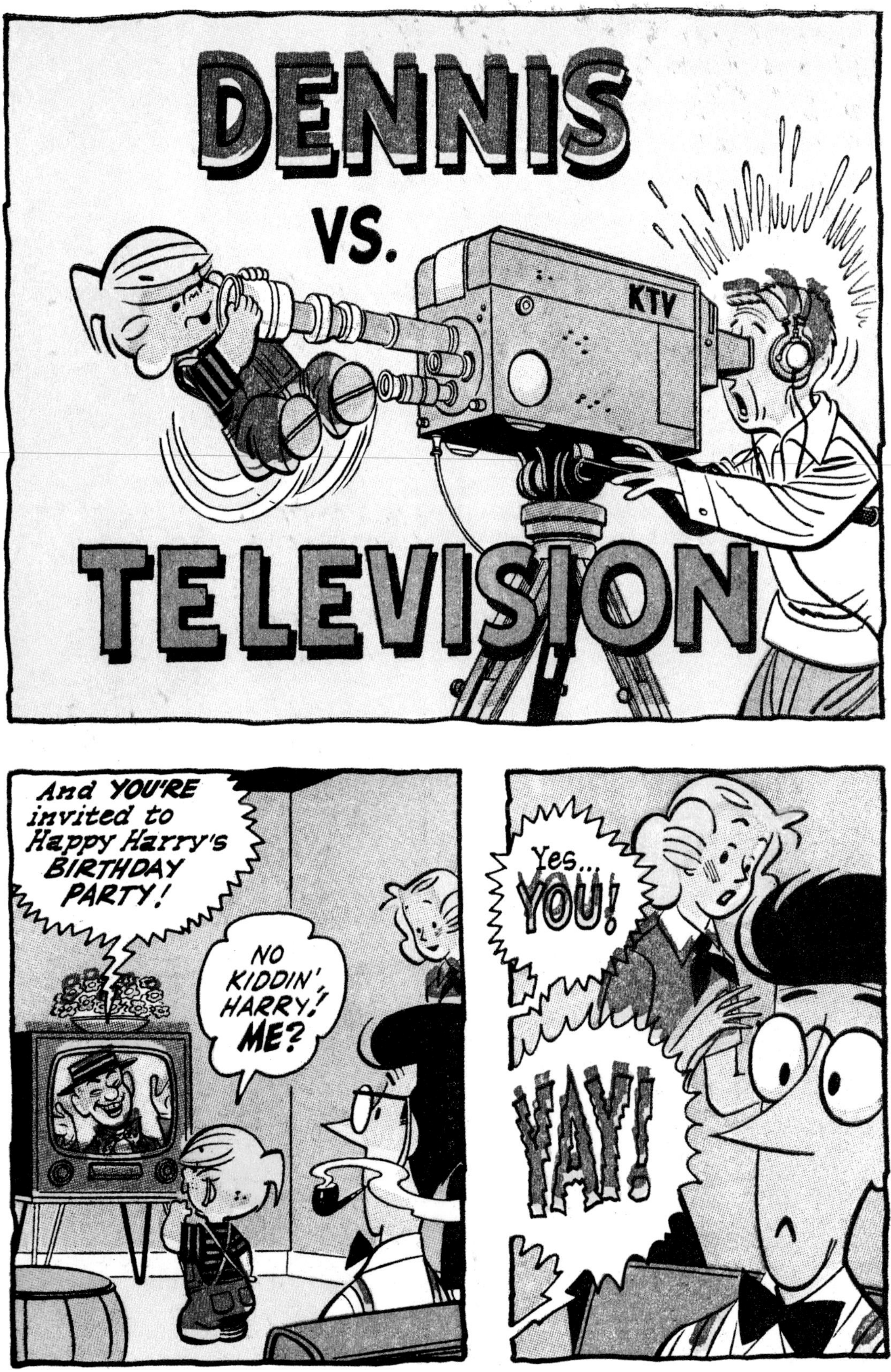
DENNIS VS. TELEVISION
KTV
And YOU'RE invited to Happy Harry's BIRTHDAY PARTY!
NO KIDDIN', HARRY! ME?
Yes... YOU!
YAY!

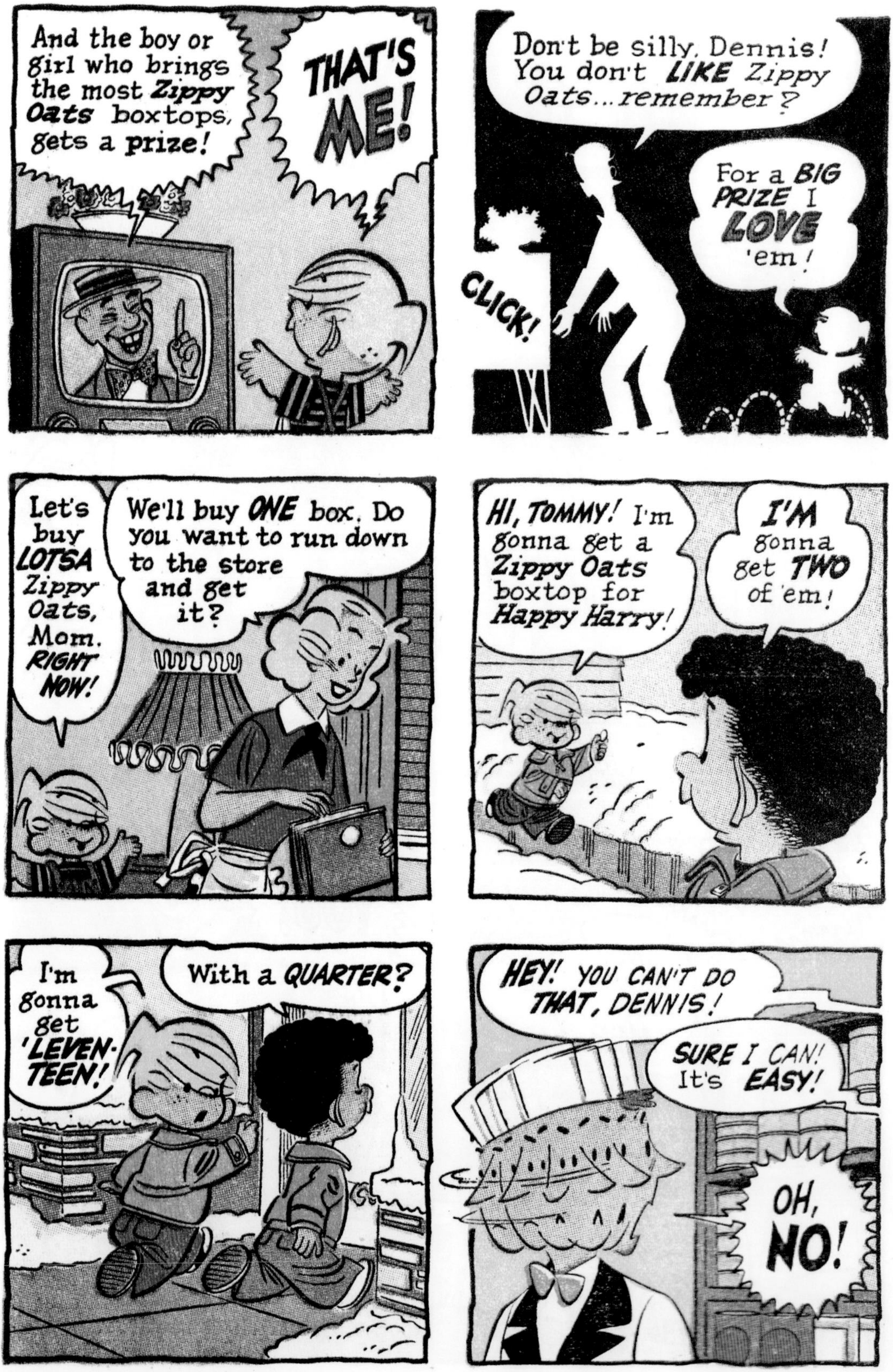
And the boy or girl who brings the most Zippy Oats boxtops, gets a prize!
THAT'S ME!
Don't be silly, Dennis! You don't LIKE Zippy Oats...remember?
For a BIG PRIZE I LOVE 'em!
CLICK!
Let's buy LOTSA Zippy Oats, Mom. RIGHT NOW!
We'll buy ONE box. Do you want to run down to the store and get it?
HI, TOMMY! I'm gonna get a Zippy Oats boxtop for Happy Harry!
I'M gonna get TWO of 'em!
I'm gonna get 'LEVEN-TEEN!
With a QUARTER?
HEY! YOU CAN'T DO THAT, DENNIS!
SURE I CAN! It's EASY!
OH, NO!

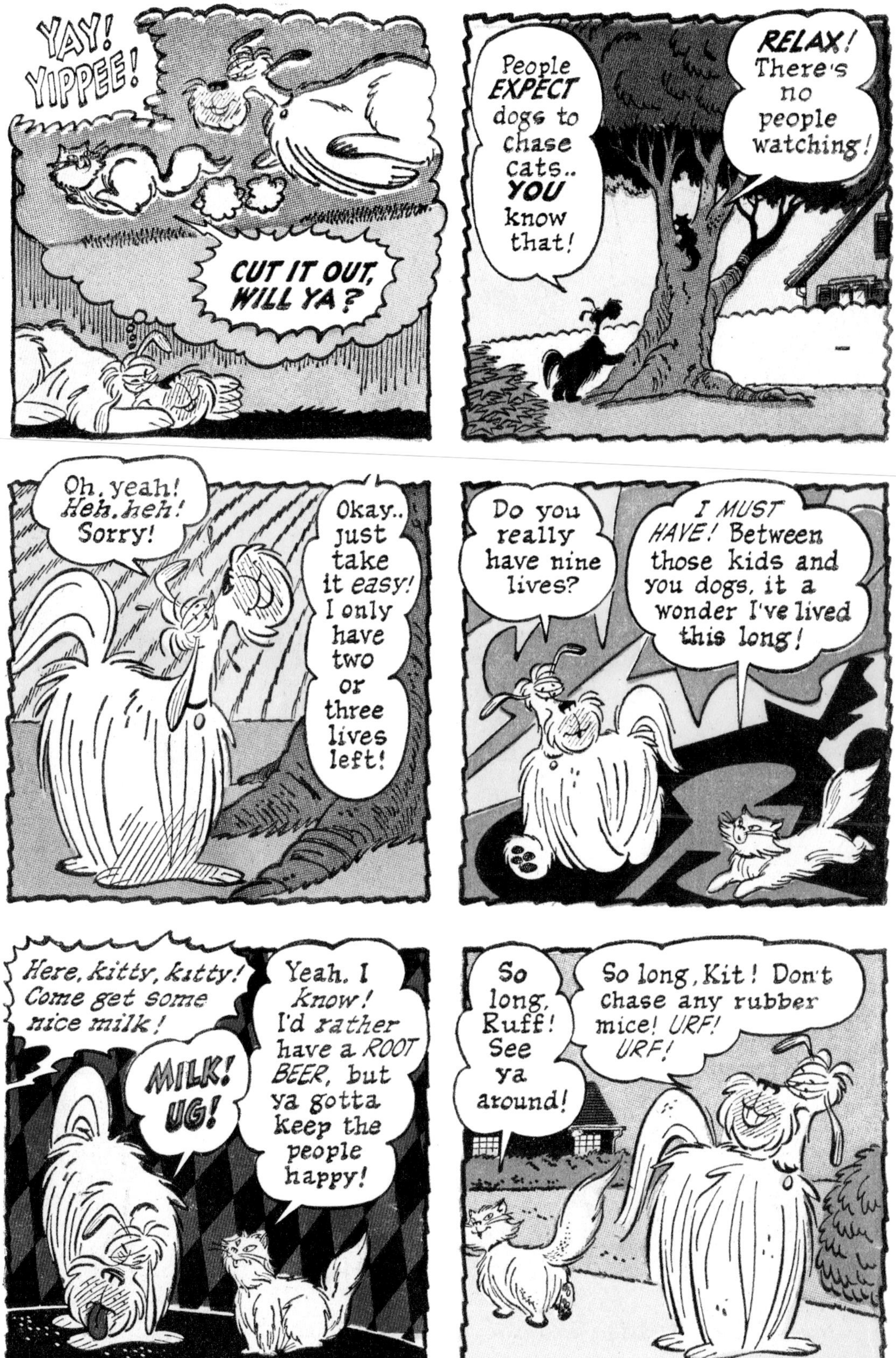
YAY! YIPPEE!
CUT IT OUT, WILL YA?
People EXPECT dogs to chase cats.. YOU know that!
RELAX! There's no people watching!
Oh, yeah! Heh, heh! Sorry!
Okay.. just take it easy! I only have two or three lives left!
Do you really have nine lives?
I MUST HAVE! Between those kids and you dogs, it a wonder I've lived this long!
Here, kitty, kitty! Come get some nice milk!
MILK! UG!
Yeah. I know! I'd rather have a ROOT BEER, but ya gotta keep the people happy!
So long, Ruff! See ya around!
So long, Kit! Don't chase any rubber mice! URF! URF!

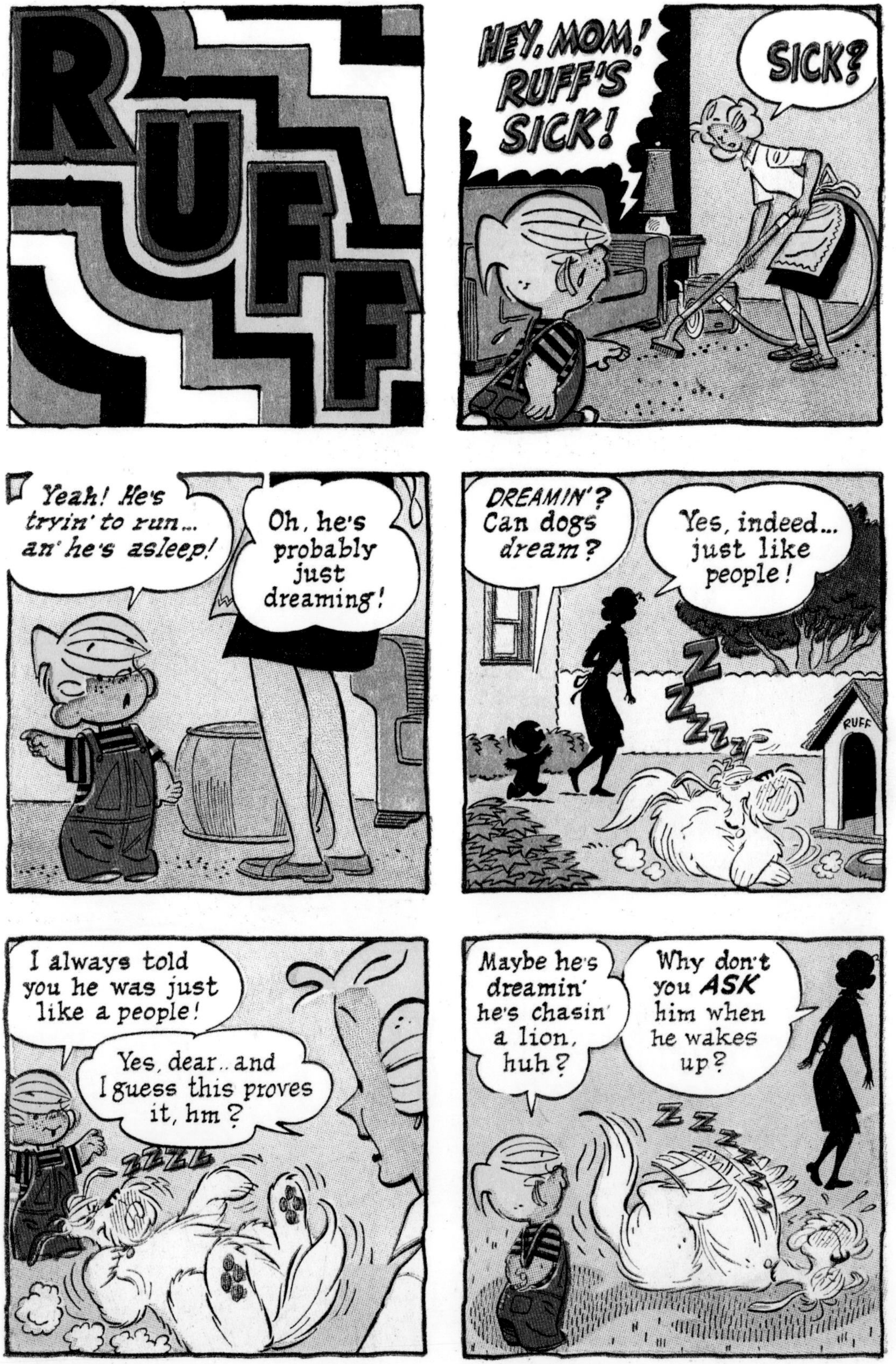
RUFF
HEY, MOM! RUFF'S SICK!
SICK?
Yeah! He's tryin' to run... an' he's asleep!
Oh, he's probably just dreaming!
DREAMIN'? Can dogs dream?
Yes, indeed... just like people!
RUFF
I always told you he was just like a people!
Yes, dear.. and I guess this proves it, hm?
Maybe he's dreamin' he's chasin' a lion, huh?
Why don't you ASK him when he wakes up?

I don't think the grocery man liked what you did, Dennis!
Well, gosh! I gotta keep *Happy Harry* happy, don't I?
Hi! Here's a note from the grocery man!
A note?
It's a **BILL!**
FOR 42 BOXES OF ZIPPY OATS!
What does this mean, Dennis?
You **CAN'T** have **42** boxes of cereal in that little box!
Who wants the boxes? I got the **TOPS!**
Up to bed with you! And no dinner for you tonight!
Not even some *Zippy Oats!*

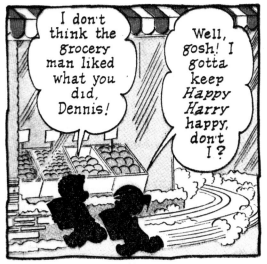

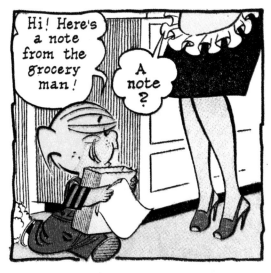

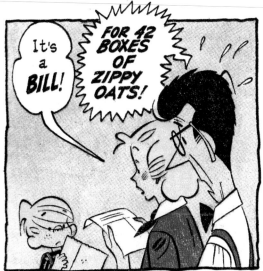

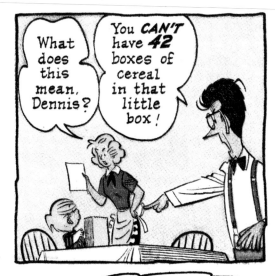

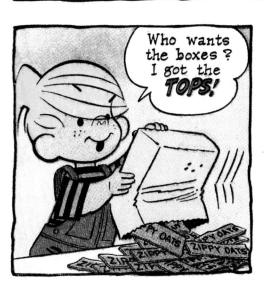

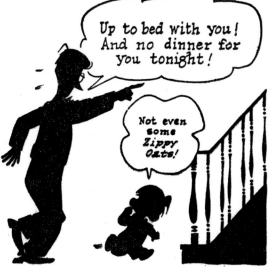

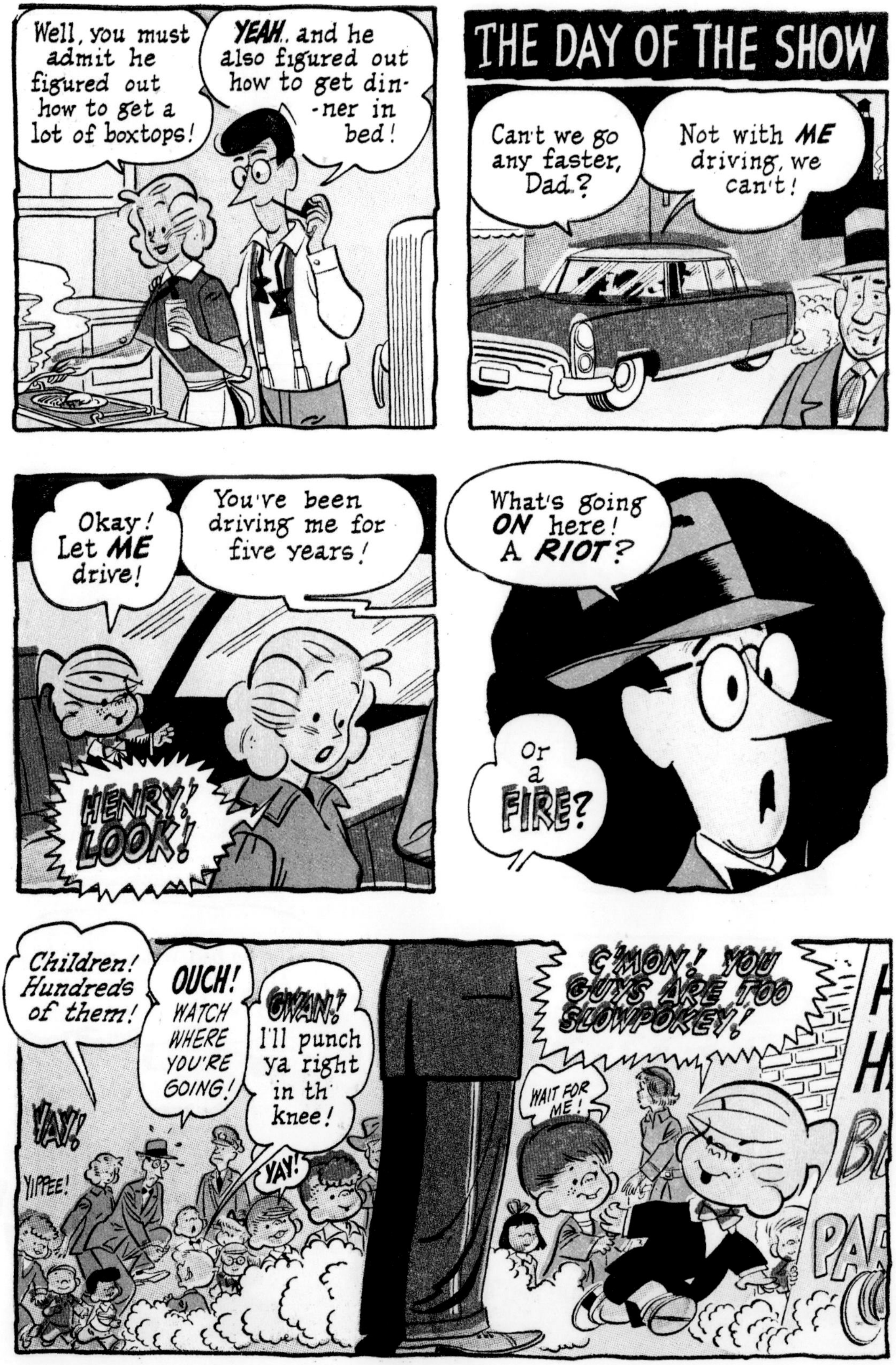
Well, you must admit he figured out how to get a lot of boxtops!
YEAH.. and he also figured out how to get din--ner in bed!
THE DAY OF THE SHOW
Can't we go any faster, Dad?
Not with ME driving, we can't!
Okay! Let ME drive!
You've been driving me for five years!
HENRY! LOOK!
What's going ON here! A RIOT?
Or a FIRE?
Children! Hundreds of them!
OUCH! WATCH WHERE YOU'RE GOING!
G'WAN! I'll punch ya right in th' knee!
YAY!
YIPPEE!
YAY!
C'MON! YOU GUYS ARE TOO SLOWPOKEY!
WAIT FOR ME!

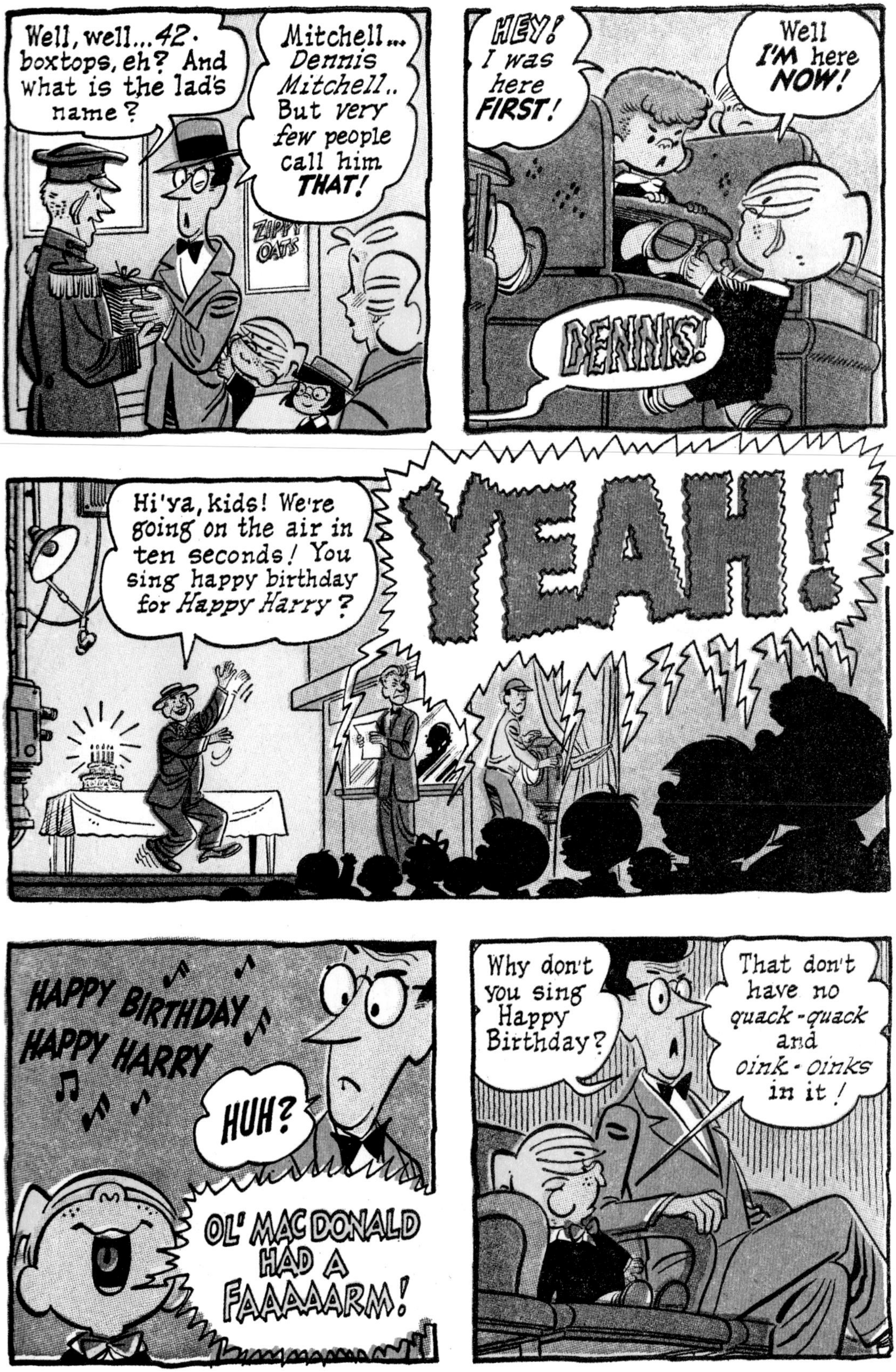

Well, well...42. boxtops, eh? And what is the lad's name?
Mitchell... Dennis Mitchell.. But very few people call him THAT!
ZIPPY OATS
HEY! I was here FIRST!
Well I'M here NOW!
DENNIS!
Hi'ya, kids! We're going on the air in ten seconds! You sing happy birthday for Happy Harry?
YEAH!
HAPPY BIRTHDAY HAPPY HARRY
HUH?
OL' MAC DONALD HAD A FAAAAARM!
Why don't you sing Happy Birthday?
That don't have no quack-quack and oink-oinks in it!

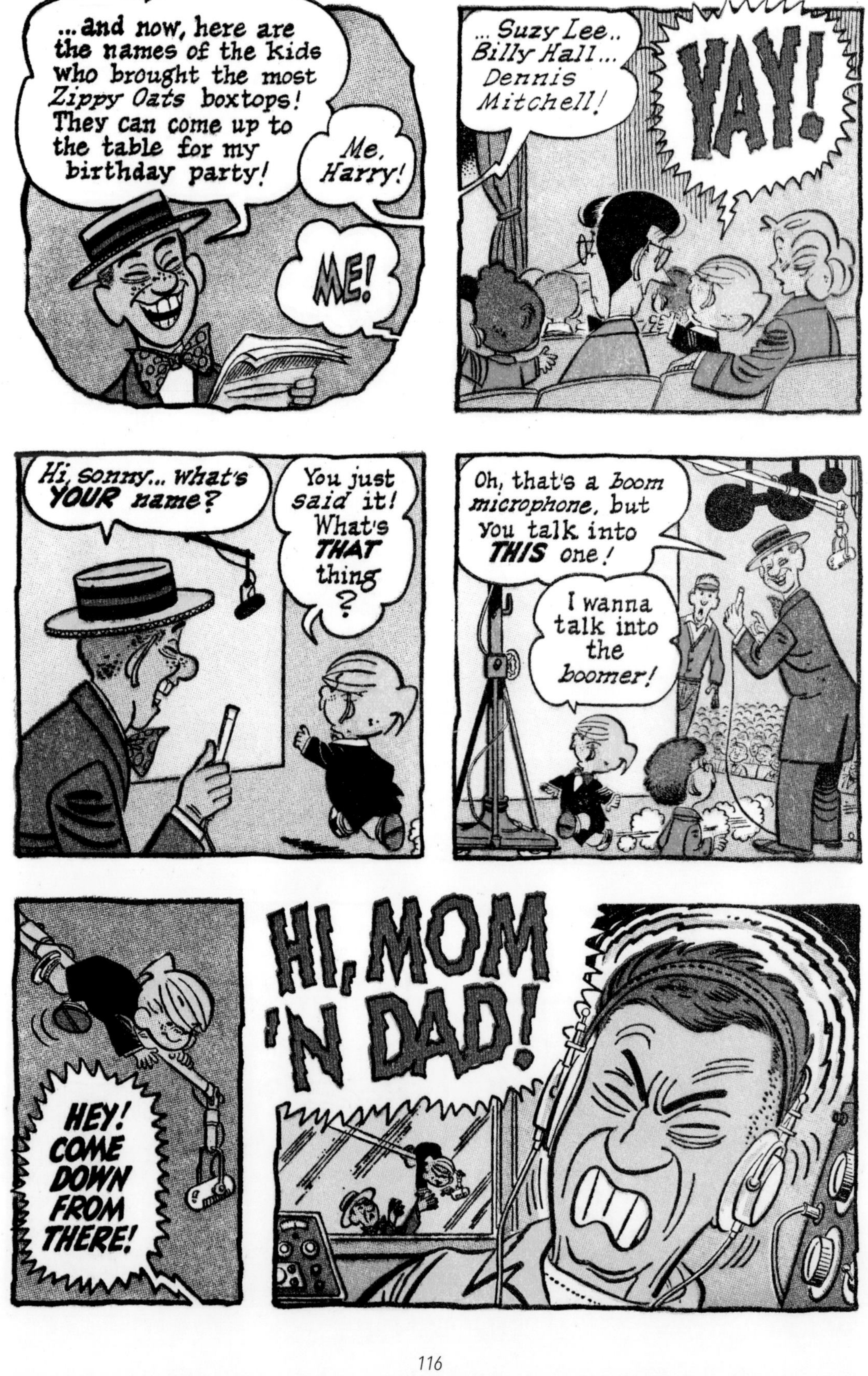
...and now, here are the names of the kids who brought the most Zippy Oats boxtops! They can come up to the table for my birthday party!
Me, Harry!
ME!
...Suzy Lee.. Billy Hall... Dennis Mitchell!
YAY!
Hi, sonny... what's YOUR name?
You just said it! What's THAT thing?
Oh, that's a boom microphone, but you talk into THIS one!
I wanna talk into the boomer!
HEY! COME DOWN FROM THERE!
HI, MOM 'N DAD!

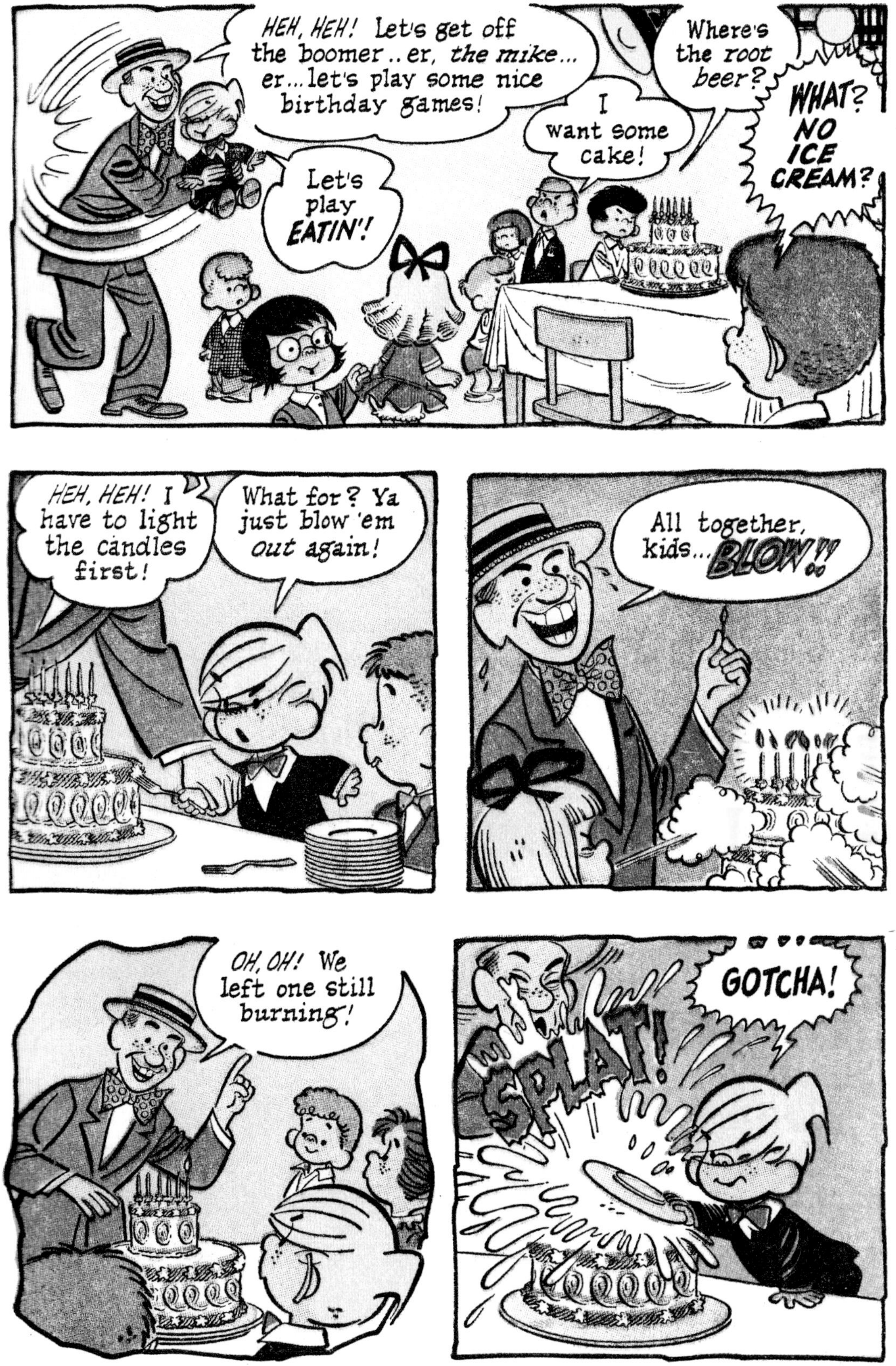
HEH, HEH! Let's get off the boomer.. er, the mike... er...let's play some nice birthday games!
Let's play EATIN'!
I want some cake!
Where's the root beer?
WHAT? NO ICE CREAM?
HEH, HEH! I have to light the candles first!
What for? Ya just blow 'em out again!
All together, kids... BLOW!!
OH, OH! We left one still burning!
GOTCHA!
SPLAT!

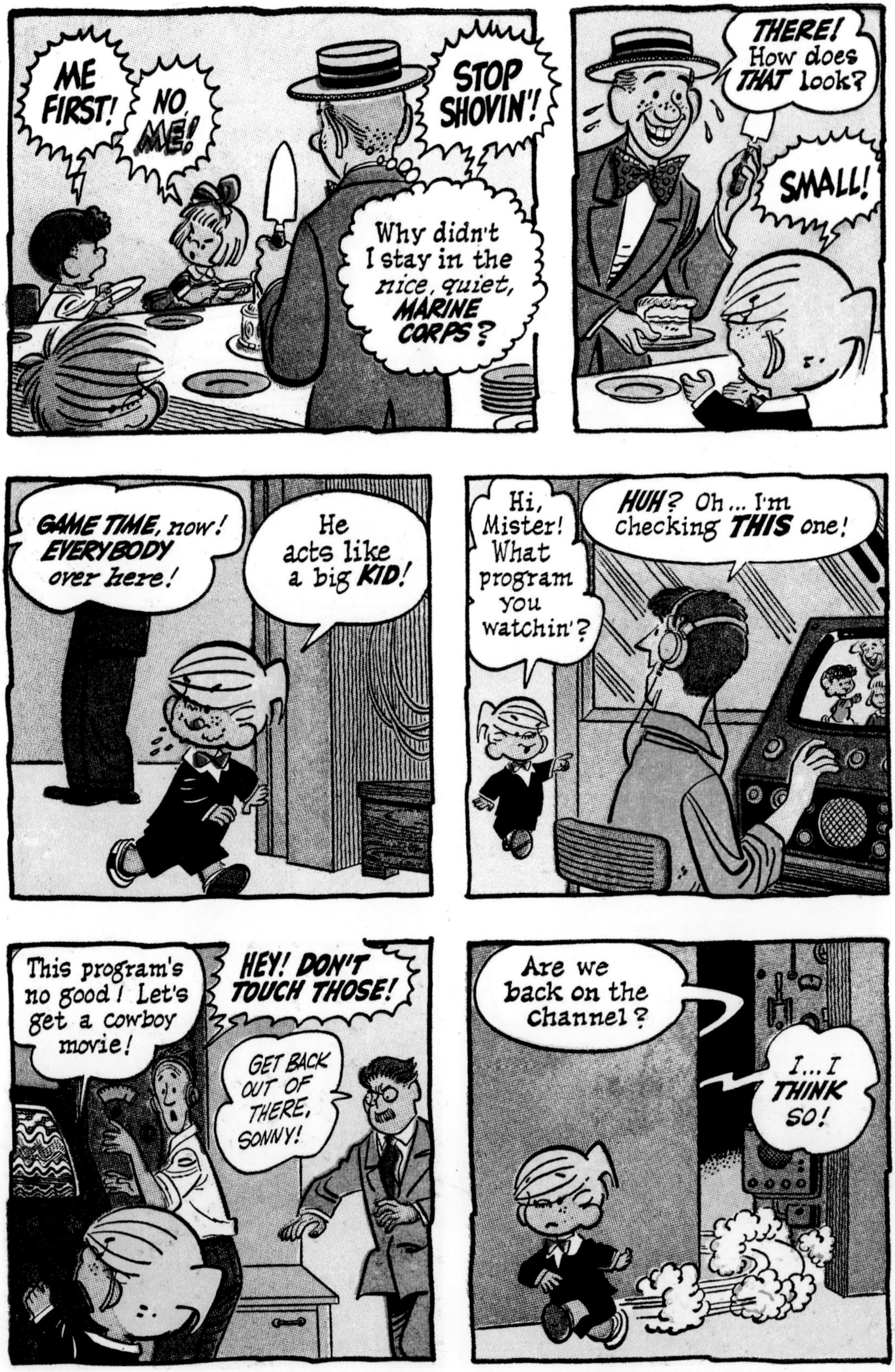
ME FIRST!
NO, ME!
STOP SHOVIN'!
Why didn't I stay in the nice, quiet, MARINE CORPS?
THERE! How does THAT look?
SMALL!
GAME TIME, now! EVERYBODY over here!
He acts like a big KID!
Hi, Mister! What program you watchin'?
HUH? Oh... I'm checking THIS one!
This program's no good! Let's get a cowboy movie!
HEY! DON'T TOUCH THOSE!
GET BACK OUT OF THERE, SONNY!
Are we back on the channel?
I... I THINK SO!

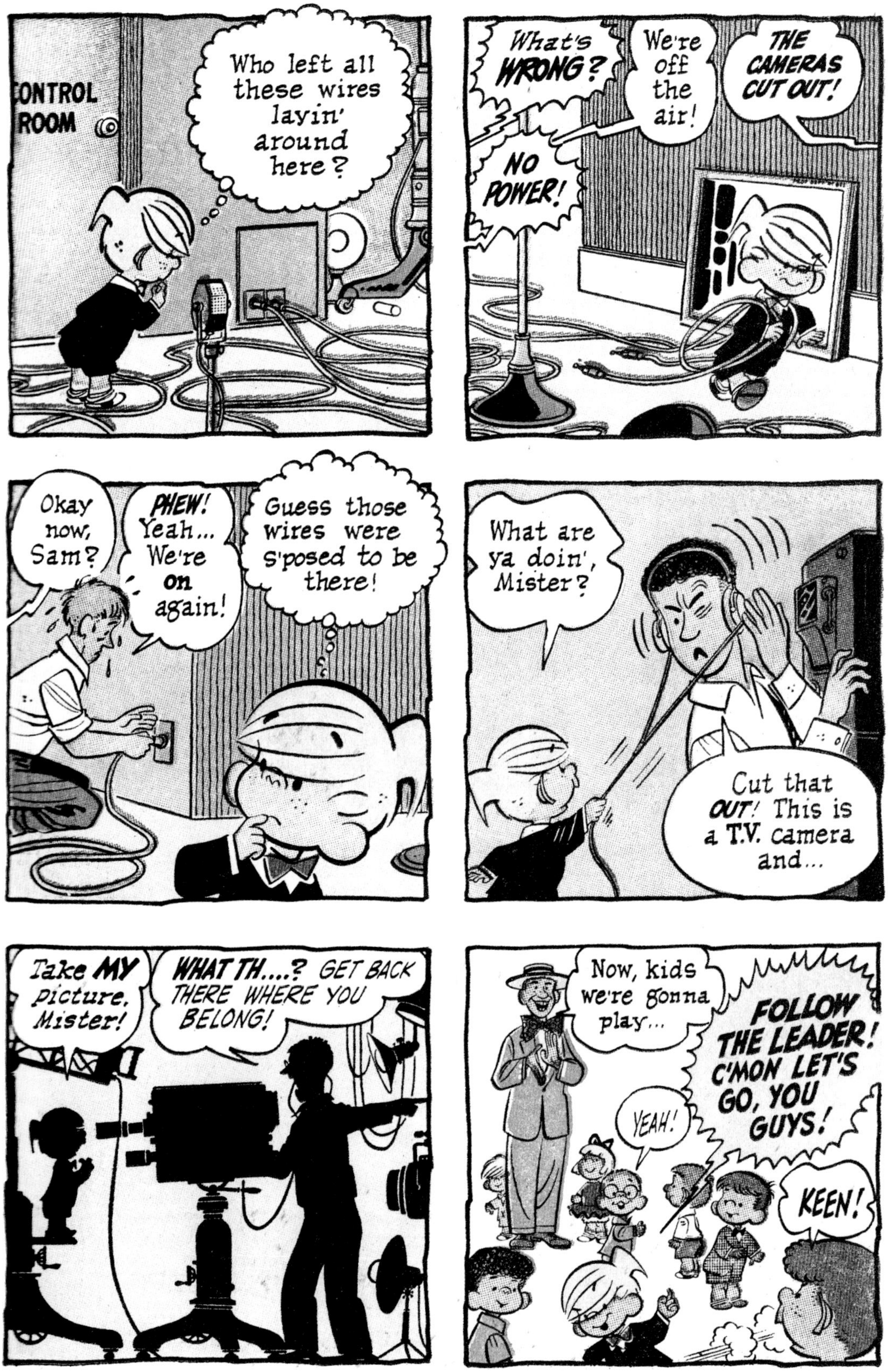
CONTROL ROOM
Who left all these wires layin' around here?
What's WRONG?
We're off the air!
THE CAMERAS CUT OUT!
NO POWER!
Okay now, Sam?
PHEW! Yeah... We're on again!
Guess those wires were s'posed to be there!
What are ya doin', Mister?
Cut that OUT! This is a T.V. camera and...
Take MY picture, Mister!
WHAT TH....? GET BACK THERE WHERE YOU BELONG!
Now, kids we're gonna play...
FOLLOW THE LEADER! C'MON LET'S GO, YOU GUYS!
YEAH!
KEEN!

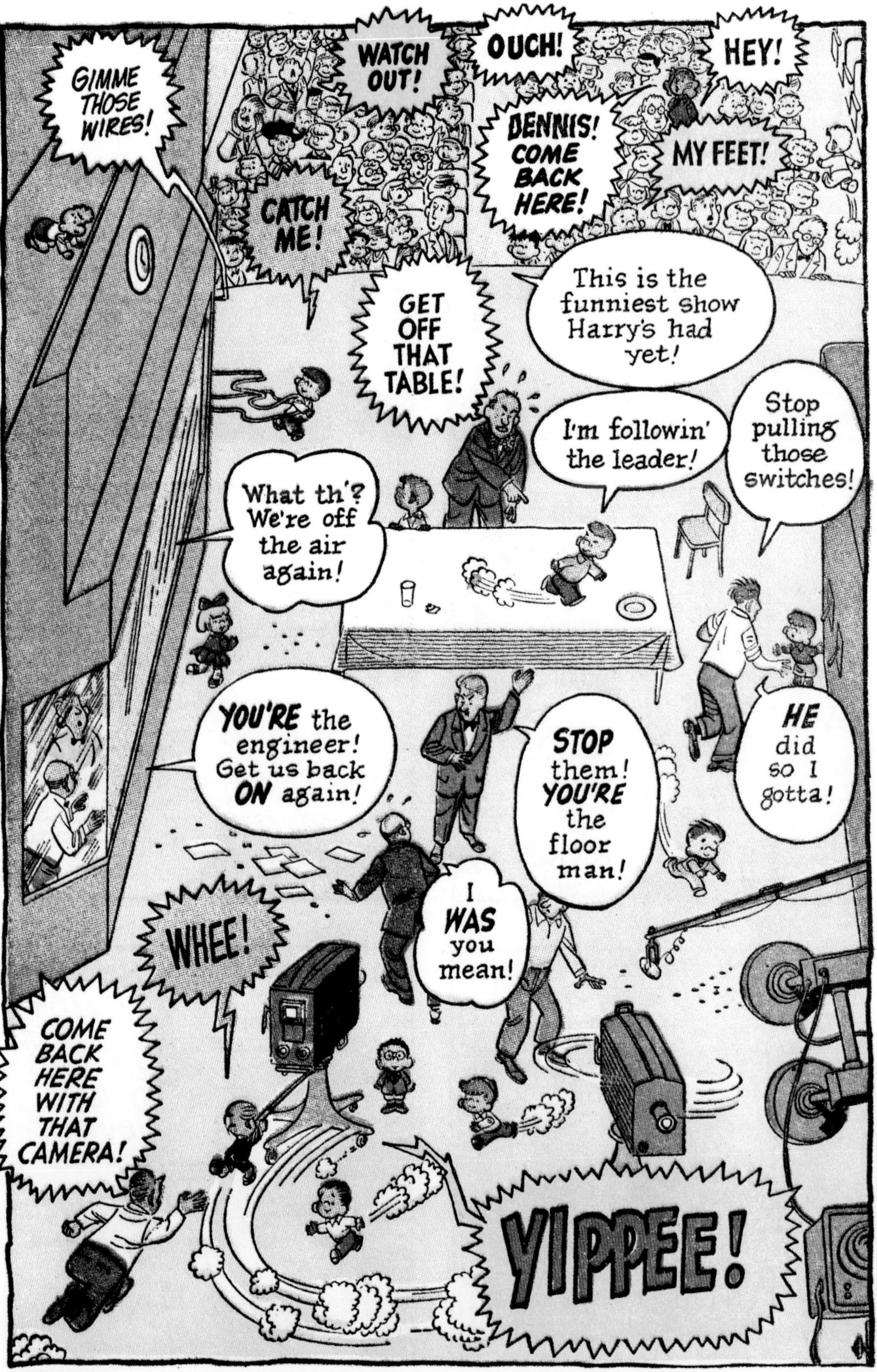
GIMME THOSE WIRES!
WATCH OUT!
OUCH!
HEY!
DENNIS! COME BACK HERE!
MY FEET!
CATCH ME!
GET OFF THAT TABLE!
This is the funniest show Harry's had yet!
I'm followin' the leader!
Stop pulling those switches!
What th'? We're off the air again!
YOU'RE the engineer! Get us back ON again!
STOP them! YOU'RE the floor man!
HE did so I gotta!
I WAS you mean!
WHEE!
COME BACK HERE WITH THAT CAMERA!
YIPPEE!

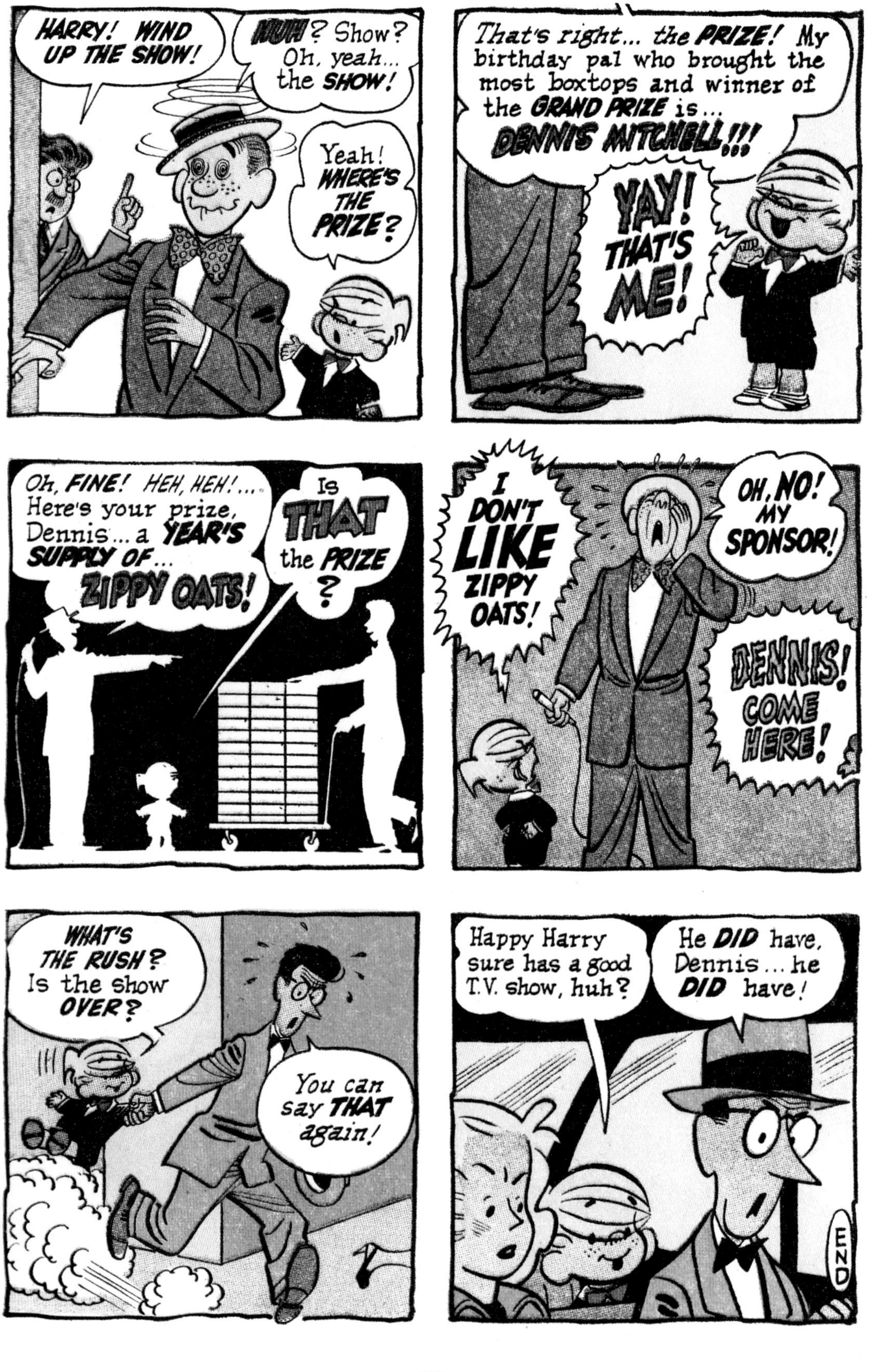

HARRY! WIND UP THE SHOW!
HUH? Show? Oh, yeah... the SHOW!
Yeah! WHERE'S THE PRIZE?
That's right... the PRIZE! My birthday pal who brought the most boxtops and winner of the GRAND PRIZE is... DENNIS MITCHELL!!!
YAY! THAT'S ME!
Oh, FINE! HEH, HEH!... Here's your prize, Dennis... a YEAR'S SUPPLY OF... ZIPPY OATS!
Is THAT the PRIZE?
I DON'T LIKE ZIPPY OATS!
OH, NO! MY SPONSOR!
DENNIS! COME HERE!
WHAT'S THE RUSH? Is the show OVER?
You can say THAT again!
Happy Harry sure has a good T.V. show, huh?
He DID have, Dennis... he DID have!
END

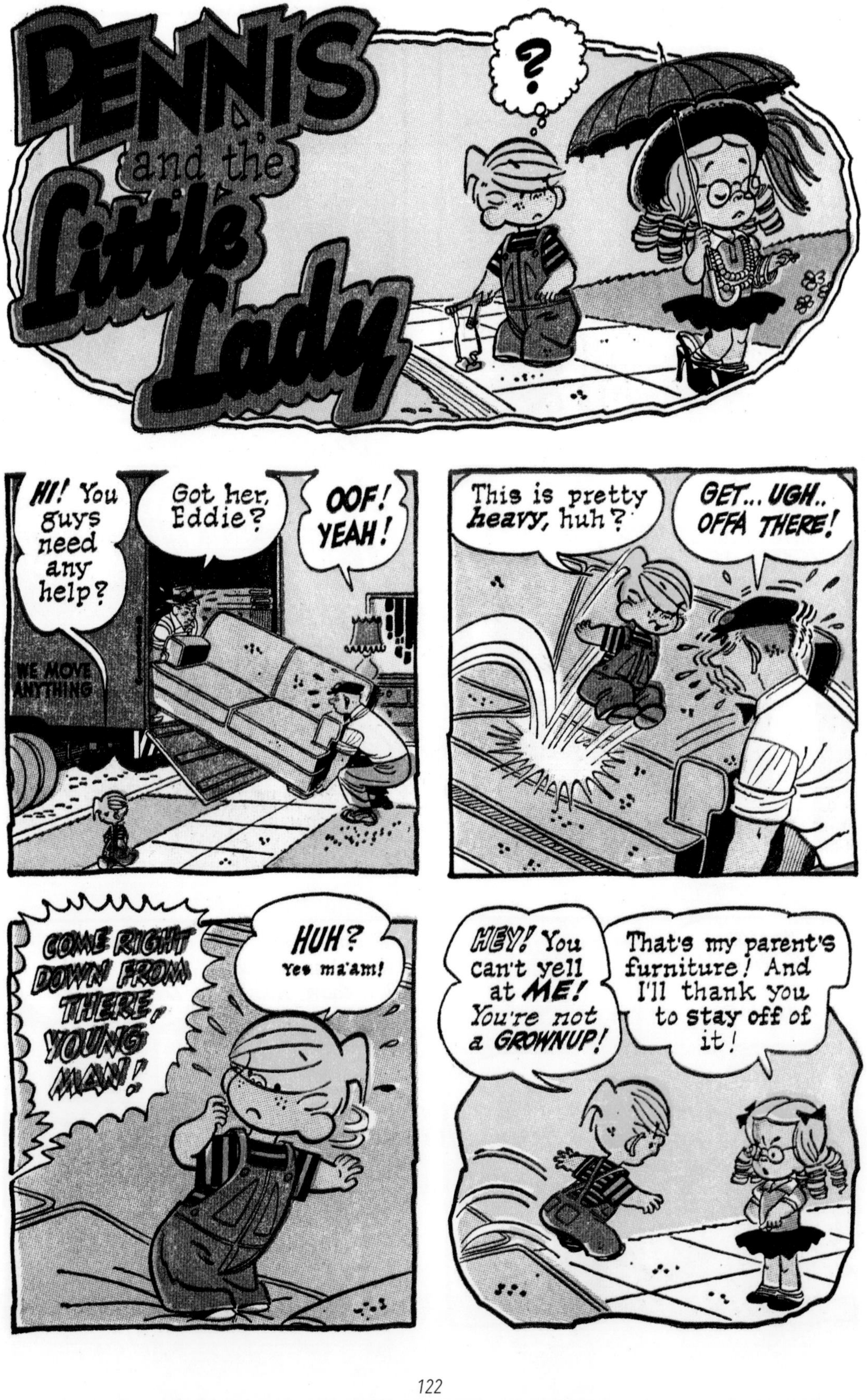
DENNIS
and the
Little Lady
?
HI! You guys need any help?
Got her, Eddie?
OOF! YEAH!
WE MOVE ANYTHING
This is pretty heavy, huh?
GET... UGH.. OFFA THERE!
COME RIGHT DOWN FROM THERE, YOUNG MAN!
HUH? Yes ma'am!
HEY! You can't yell at ME! You're not a GROWNUP!
That's my parent's furniture! And I'll thank you to stay off of it!

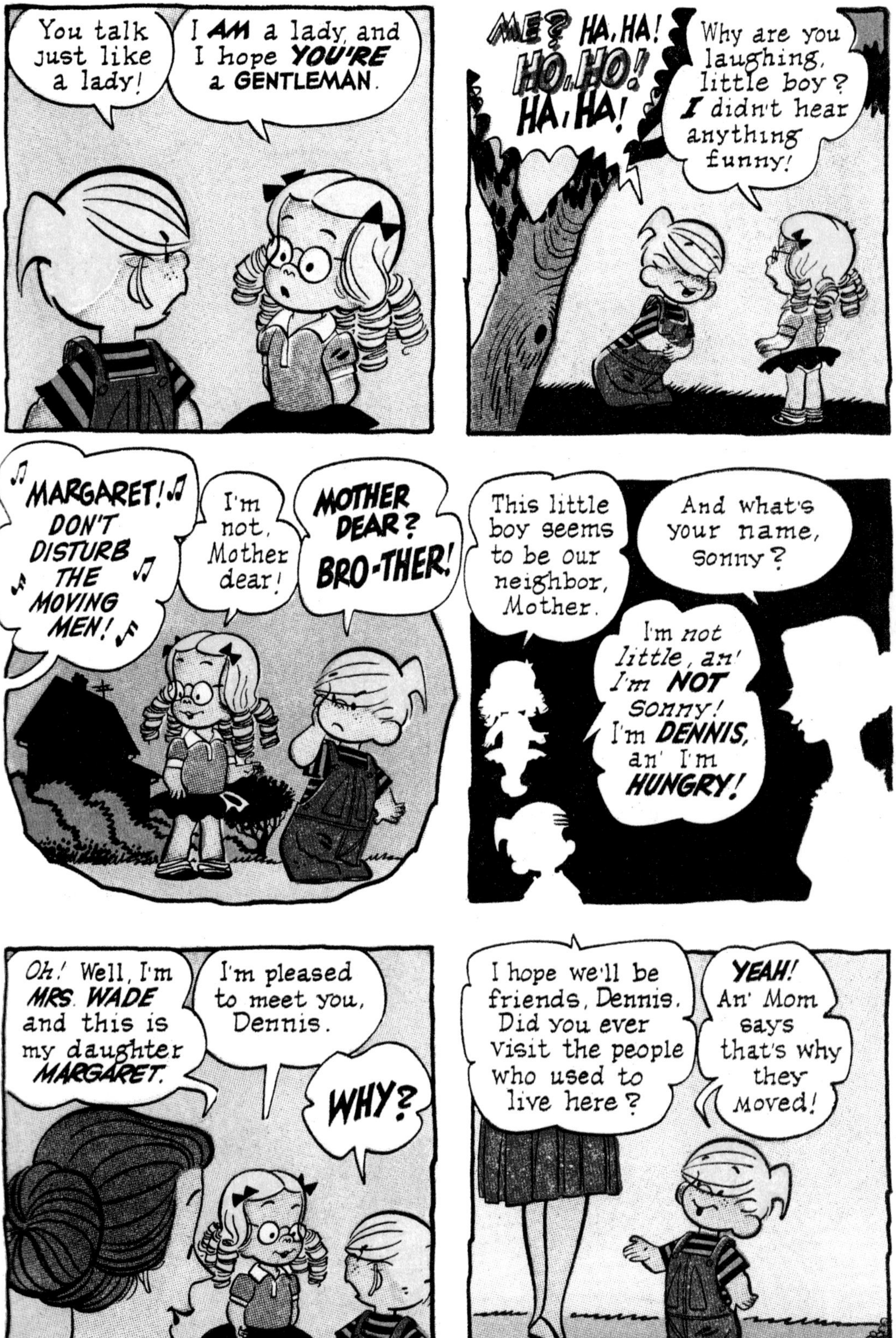

You talk just like a lady!
I AM a lady, and I hope YOU'RE a GENTLEMAN.
ME? HA, HA! HO, HO! HA, HA!
Why are you laughing, little boy? I didn't hear anything funny!
MARGARET! DON'T DISTURB THE MOVING MEN!
I'm not, Mother dear!
MOTHER DEAR? BRO-THER!
This little boy seems to be our neighbor, Mother.
And what's your name, sonny?
I'm not little, an' I'm NOT sonny! I'm DENNIS, an' I'm HUNGRY!
Oh! Well, I'm MRS. WADE and this is my daughter MARGARET.
I'm pleased to meet you, Dennis.
WHY?
I hope we'll be friends, Dennis. Did you ever visit the people who used to live here?
YEAH! An' Mom says that's why they moved!

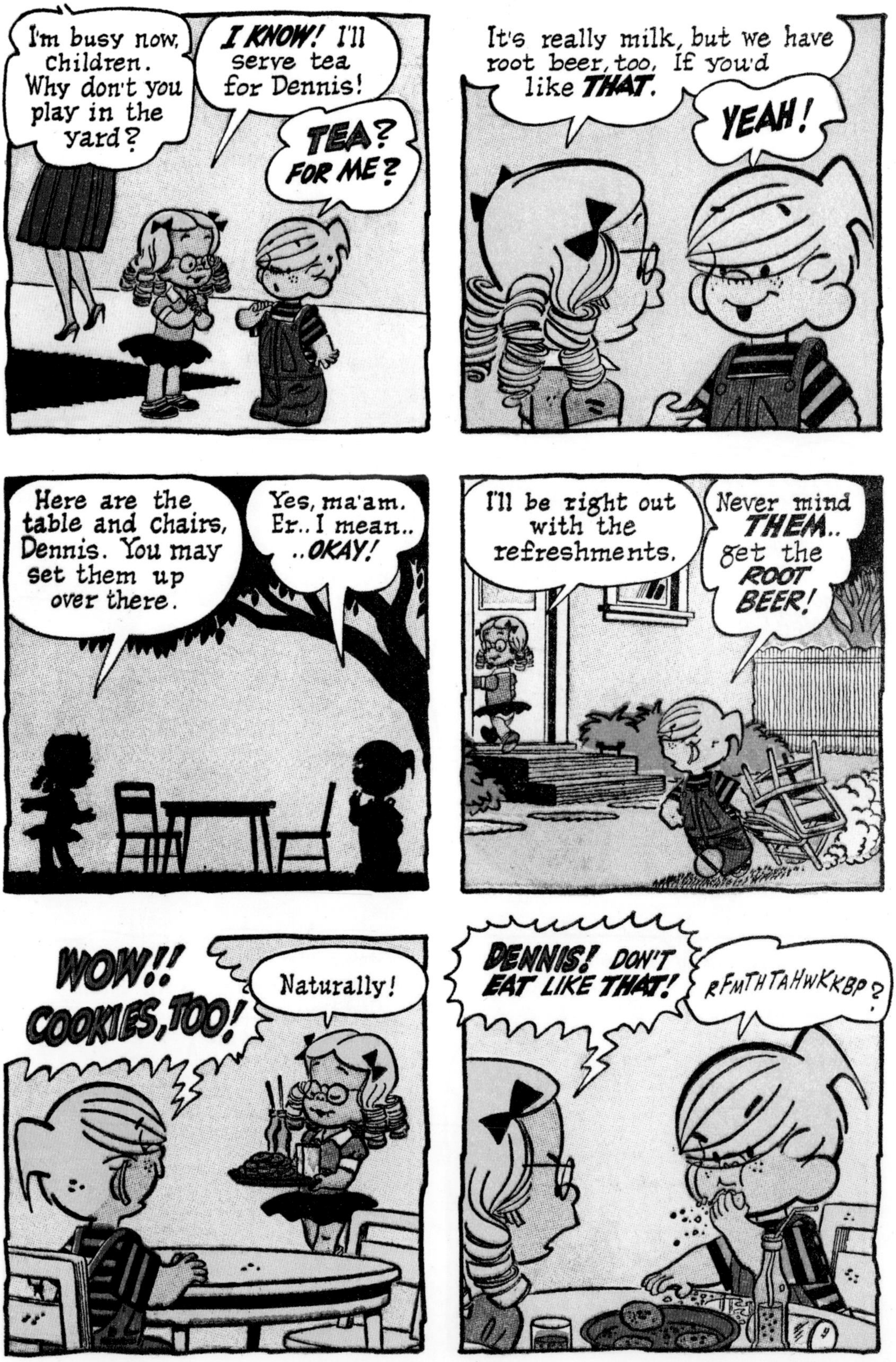
I'm busy now, children. Why don't you play in the yard?
I KNOW! I'll serve tea for Dennis!
TEA? FOR ME?
It's really milk, but we have root beer, too, If you'd like THAT.
YEAH!
Here are the table and chairs, Dennis. You may set them up over there.
Yes, ma'am. Er.. I mean.. ..OKAY!
I'll be right out with the refreshments.
Never mind THEM.. get the ROOT BEER!
WOW!! COOKIES, TOO!
Naturally!
DENNIS! DON'T EAT LIKE THAT!
RFMTHTAHWKKBP?

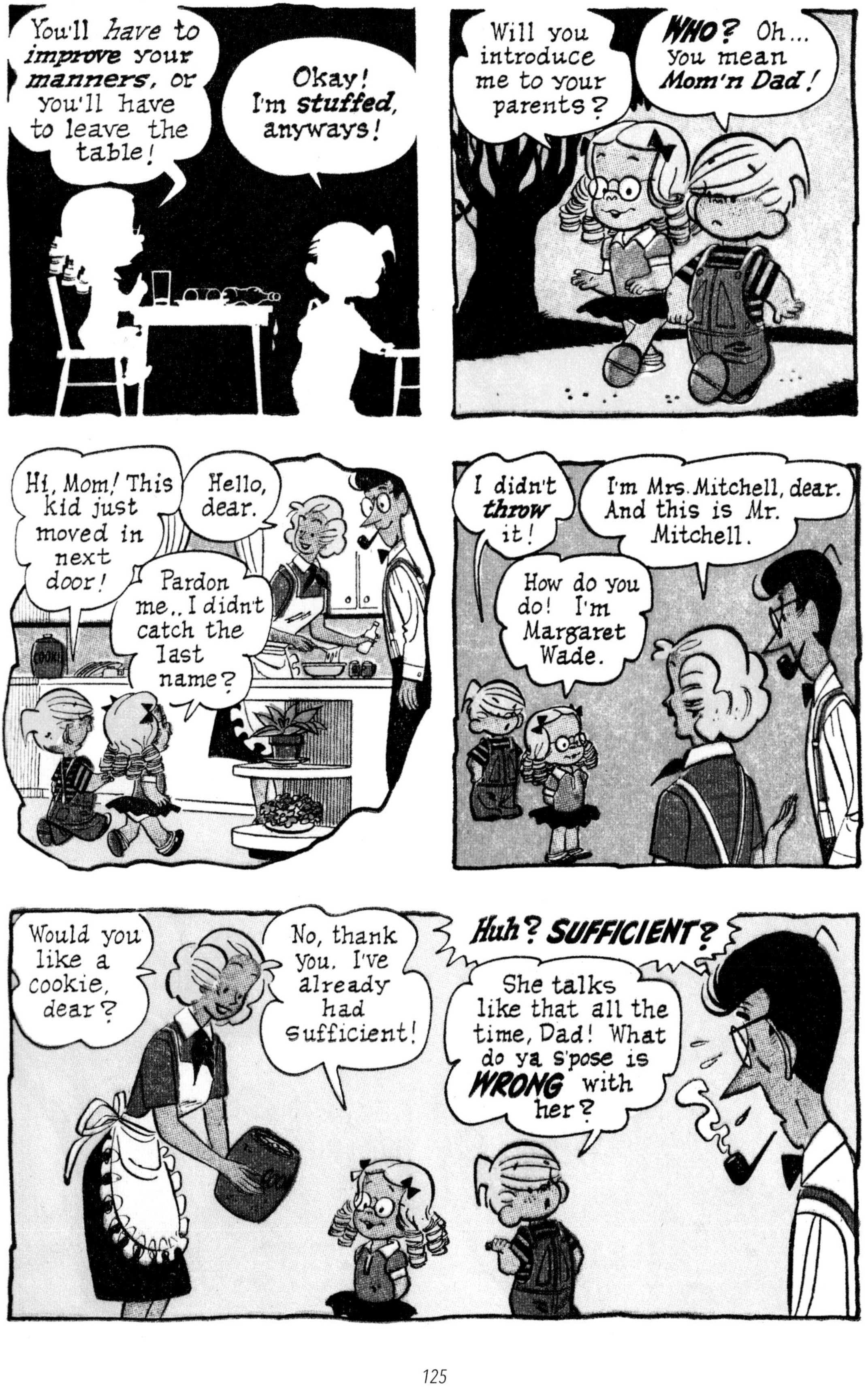

You'll *have* to **improve** your **manners**, or you'll have to leave the table!
Okay! I'm **stuffed**, anyways!
Will you introduce me to your parents?
WHO? Oh... You mean **Mom'n Dad!**
Hi, Mom! This kid just moved in next door!
Hello, dear.
Pardon me.. I didn't catch the last name?
I didn't **throw** it!
I'm Mrs. Mitchell, dear. And this is Mr. Mitchell.
How do you do! I'm Margaret Wade.
Would you like a cookie, dear?
No, thank you. I've already had sufficient!
Huh? SUFFICIENT?
She talks like that all the time, Dad! What do ya s'pose is **WRONG** with her?

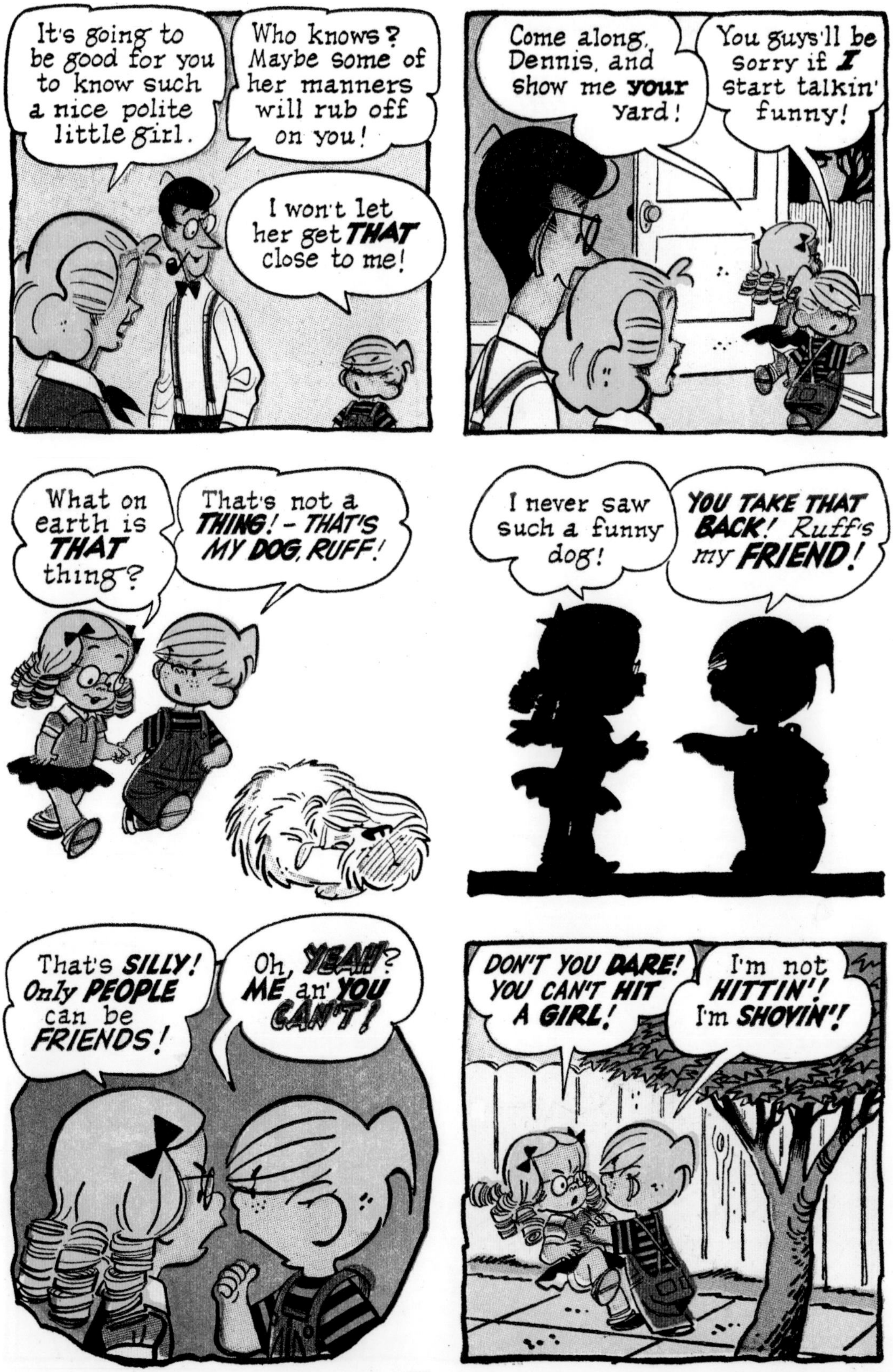
It's going to be good for you to know such a nice polite little girl.
Who knows? Maybe some of her manners will rub off on you!
I won't let her get THAT close to me!
Come along, Dennis, and show me your yard!
You guys'll be sorry if I start talkin' funny!
What on earth is THAT thing?
That's not a THING! - THAT'S MY DOG, RUFF!
I never saw such a funny dog!
YOU TAKE THAT BACK! Ruff's my FRIEND!
That's SILLY! Only PEOPLE can be FRIENDS!
Oh, YEAH? ME an' YOU CAN'T!
DON'T YOU DARE! YOU CAN'T HIT A GIRL!
I'm not HITTIN'! I'm SHOVIN'!

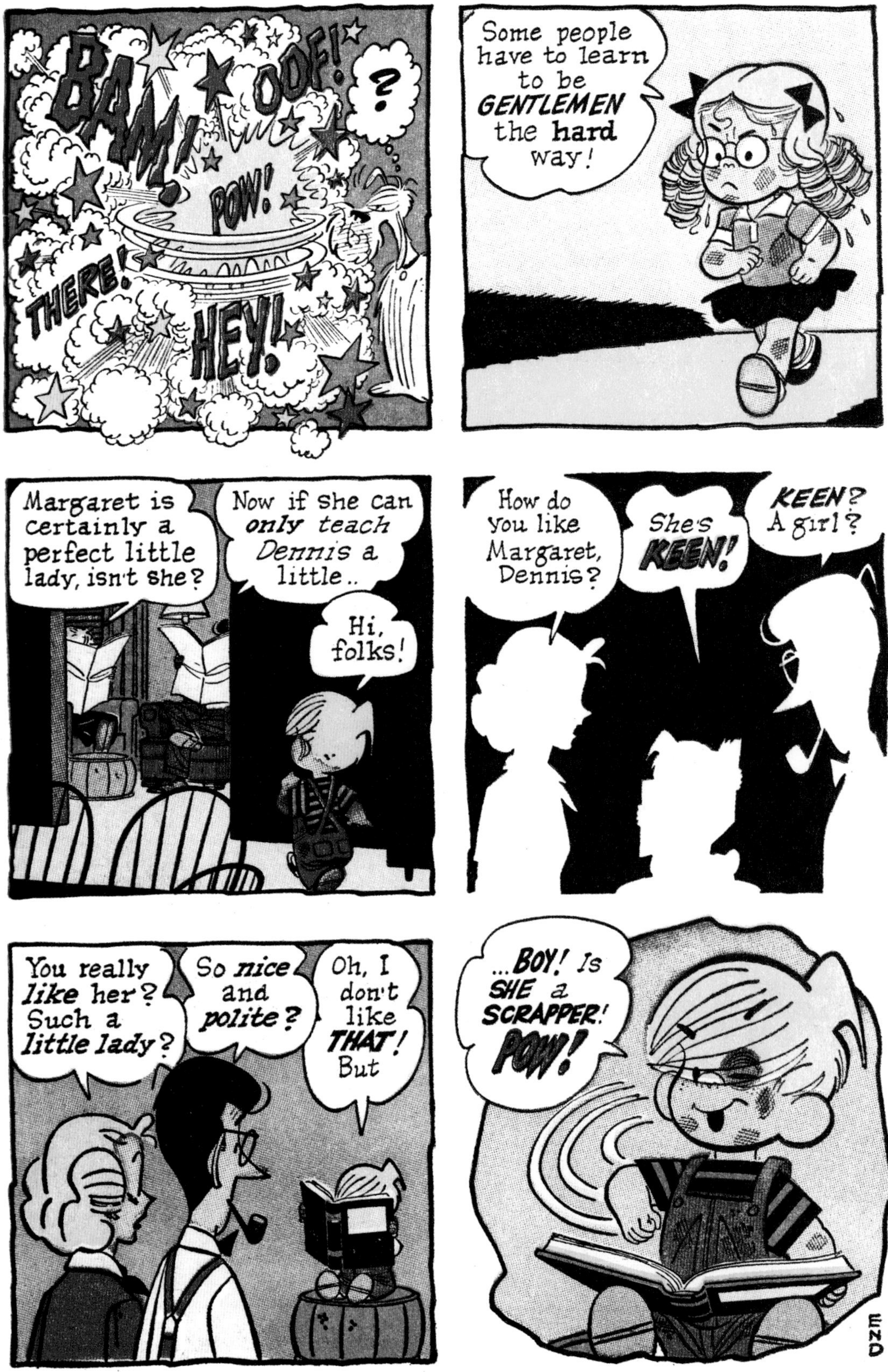
BAM!
OOF!
?
POW!
THERE!
HEY!
Some people have to learn to be GENTLEMEN the hard way!
Margaret is certainly a perfect little lady, isn't she?
Now if she can only teach Dennis a little..
Hi, folks!
How do you like Margaret, Dennis?
She's KEEN!
KEEN? A girl?
You really like her? Such a little lady?
So nice and polite?
Oh, I don't like THAT! But
...BOY! Is SHE a SCRAPPER! POW!
END

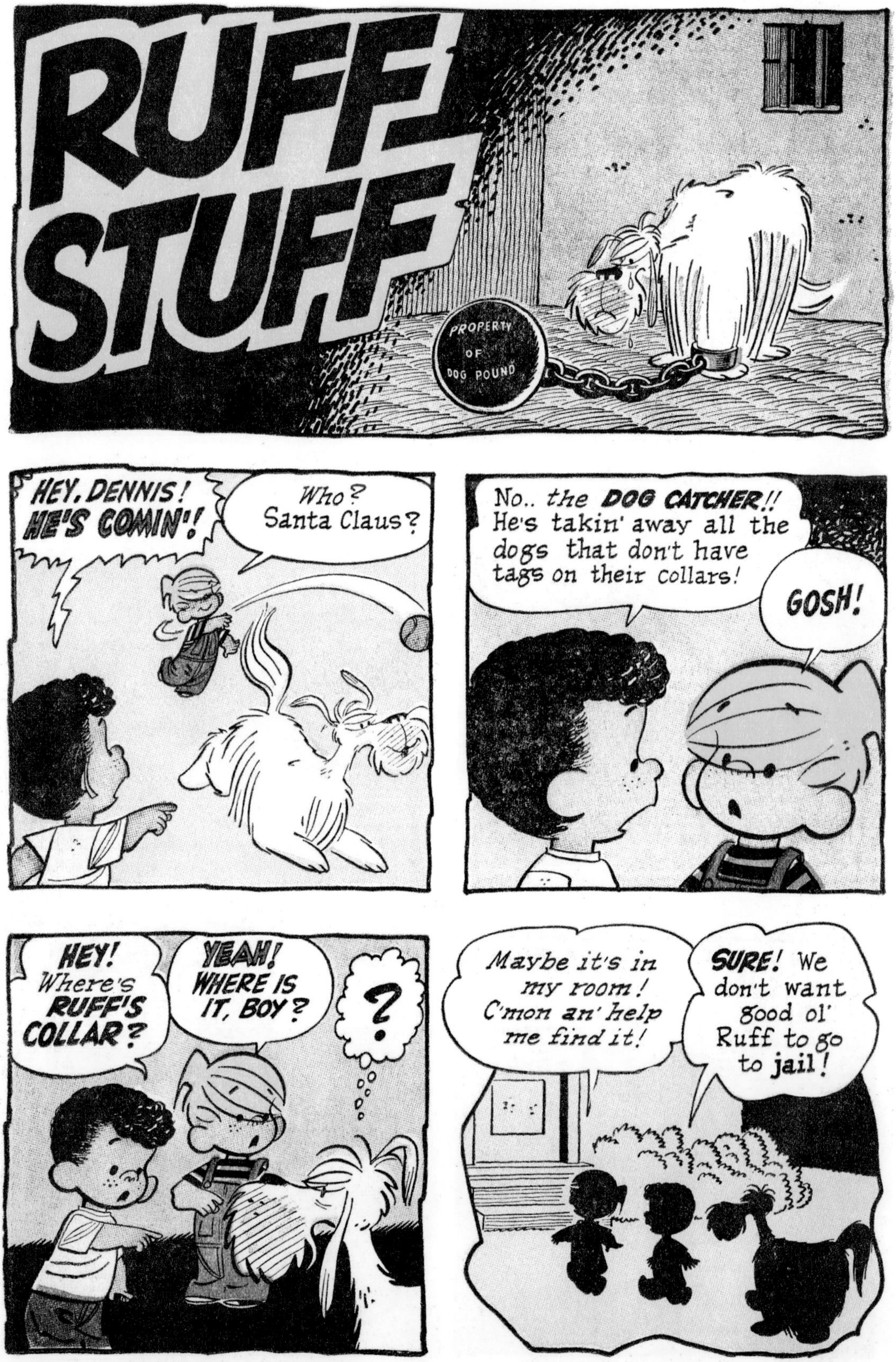
RUFF STUFF
PROPERTY OF DOG POUND
HEY, DENNIS! HE'S COMIN'!
Who? Santa Claus?
No.. the DOG CATCHER!! He's takin' away all the dogs that don't have tags on their collars!
GOSH!
HEY! Where's RUFF'S COLLAR?
YEAH! WHERE IS IT, BOY?
?
Maybe it's in my room! C'mon an' help me find it!
SURE! We don't want good ol' Ruff to go to jail!

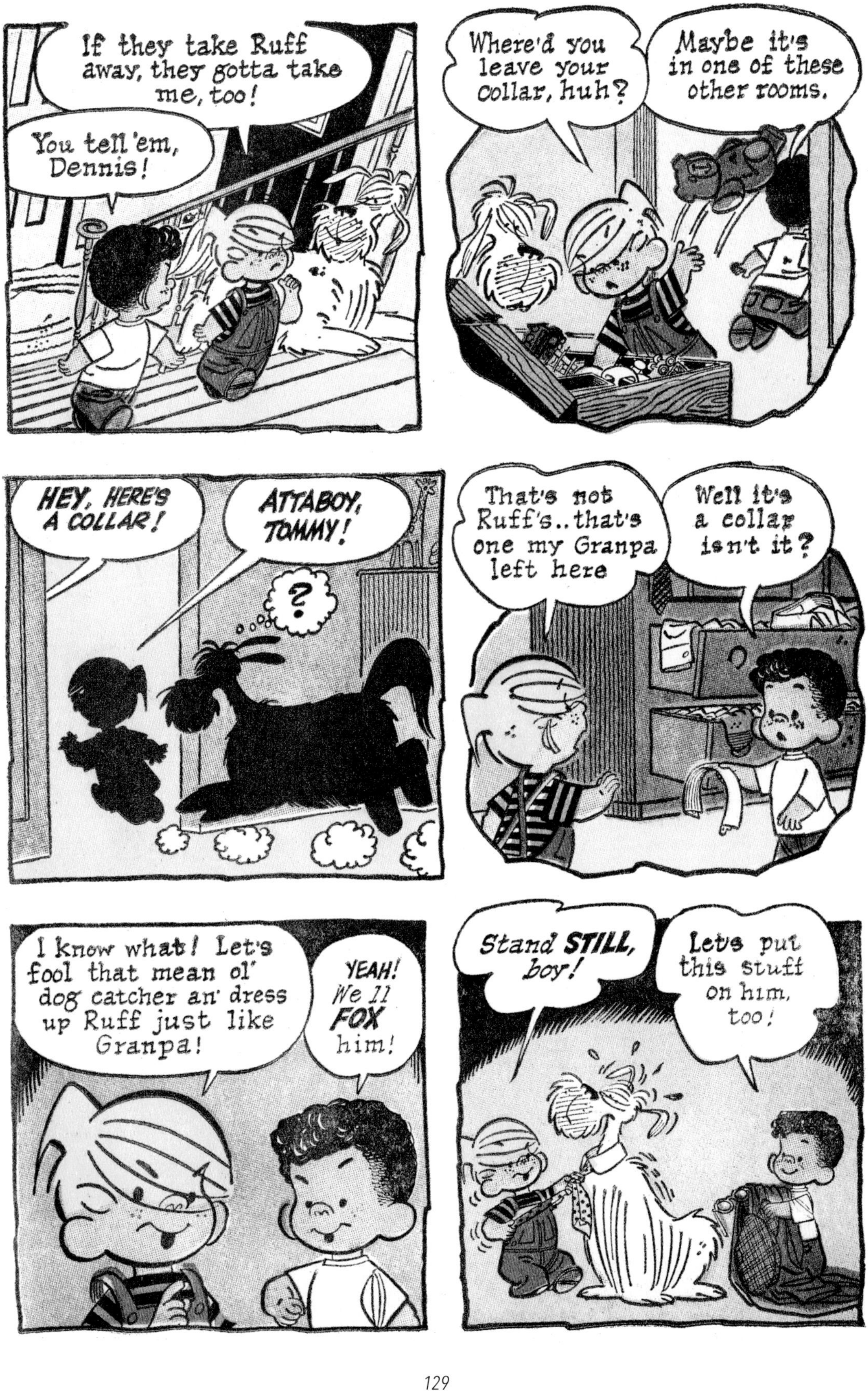
If they take Ruff away, they gotta take me, too!
You tell 'em, Dennis!
Where'd you leave your collar, huh?
Maybe it's in one of these other rooms.
HEY, HERE'S A COLLAR!
ATTABOY, TOMMY!
?
That's not Ruff's..that's one my Granpa left here
Well it's a collar isn't it?
I know what! Let's fool that mean ol' dog catcher an' dress up Ruff just like Granpa!
YEAH! We'll FOX him!
Stand STILL, boy!
Let's put this stuff on him, too!

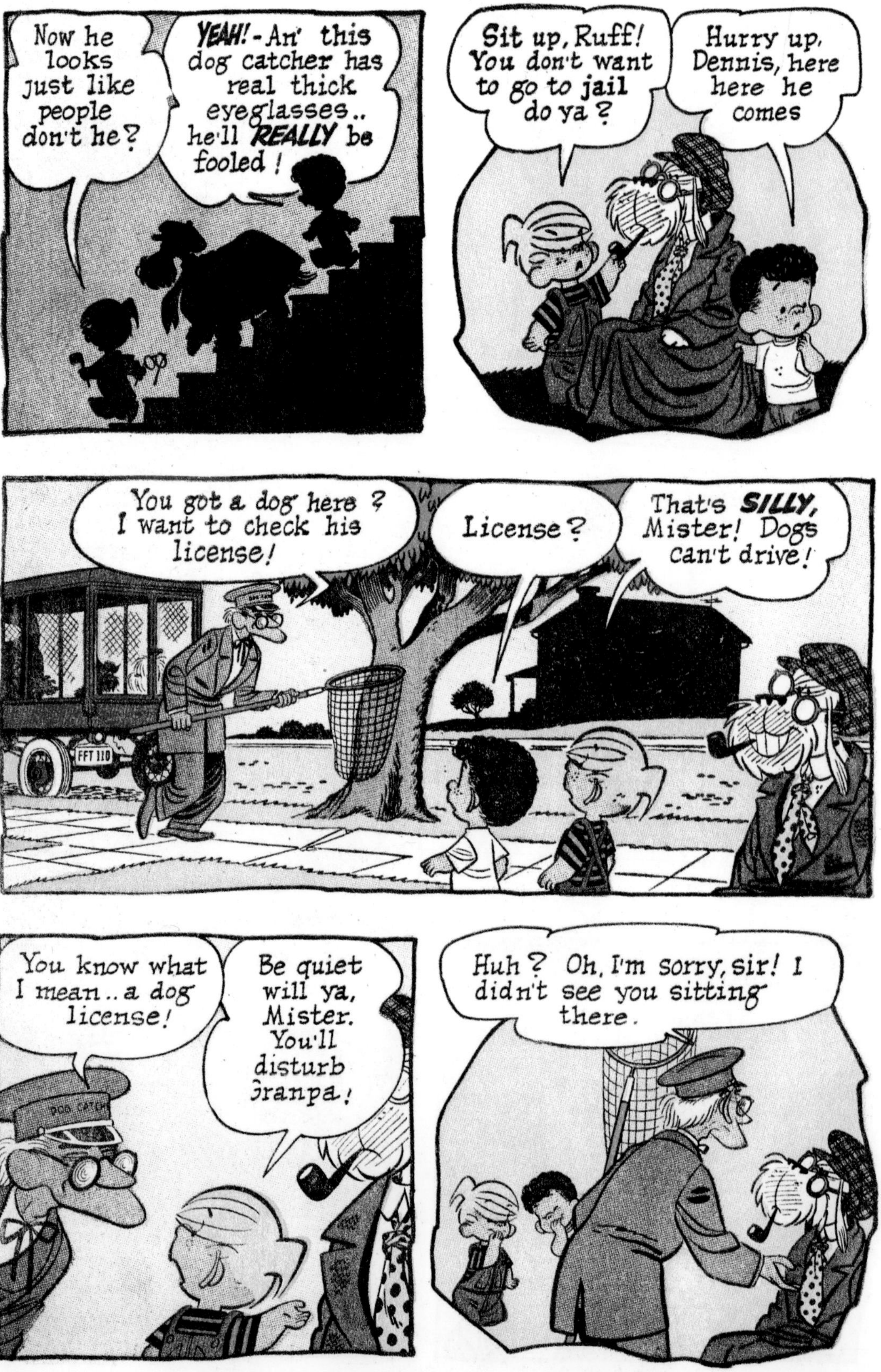
Now he looks just like people don't he?
YEAH! - An' this dog catcher has real thick eyeglasses.. he'll REALLY be fooled!
Sit up, Ruff! You don't want to go to jail do ya?
Hurry up, Dennis, here here he comes
You got a dog here? I want to check his license!
License?
That's SILLY, Mister! Dogs can't drive!
FFT 110
You know what I mean.. a dog license!
Be quiet will ya, Mister. You'll disturb Granpa!
Huh? Oh, I'm sorry, sir! I didn't see you sitting there.

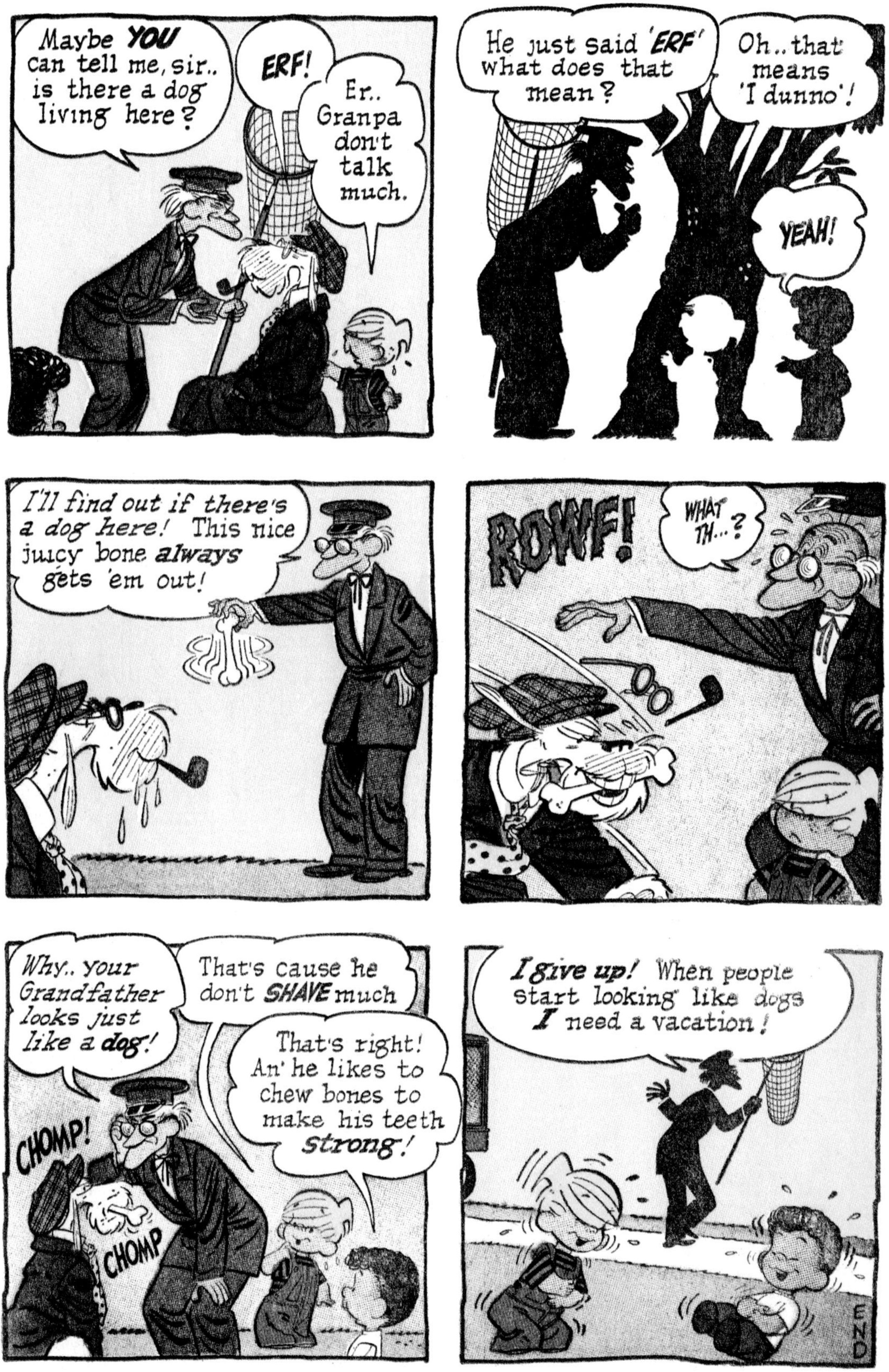
Maybe YOU can tell me, sir.. is there a dog living here?
ERF!
Er.. Granpa don't talk much.
He just said 'ERF' what does that mean?
Oh.. that means 'I dunno'!
YEAH!
I'll find out if there's a dog here! This nice juicy bone always gets 'em out!
ROWF!
WHAT TH...?
Why.. your Grandfather looks just like a dog!
That's cause he don't SHAVE much
That's right! An' he likes to chew bones to make his teeth strong!
CHOMP!
CHOMP
I give up! When people start looking like dogs I need a vacation!
END

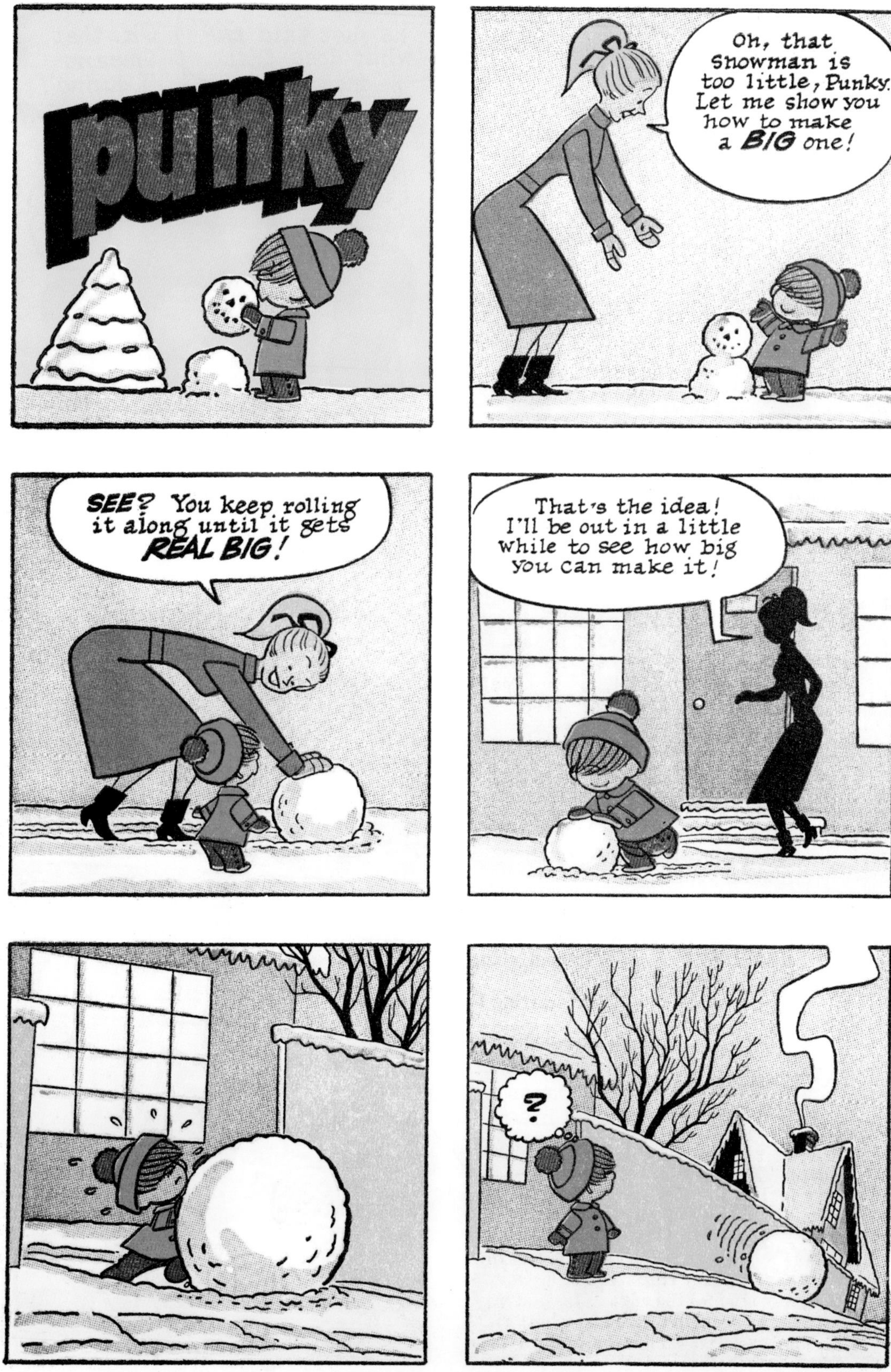
punky
Oh, that Snowman is too little, Punky. Let me show you how to make a BIG one!
SEE? You keep rolling it along until it gets REAL BIG!
That's the idea! I'll be out in a little while to see how big you can make it!
?

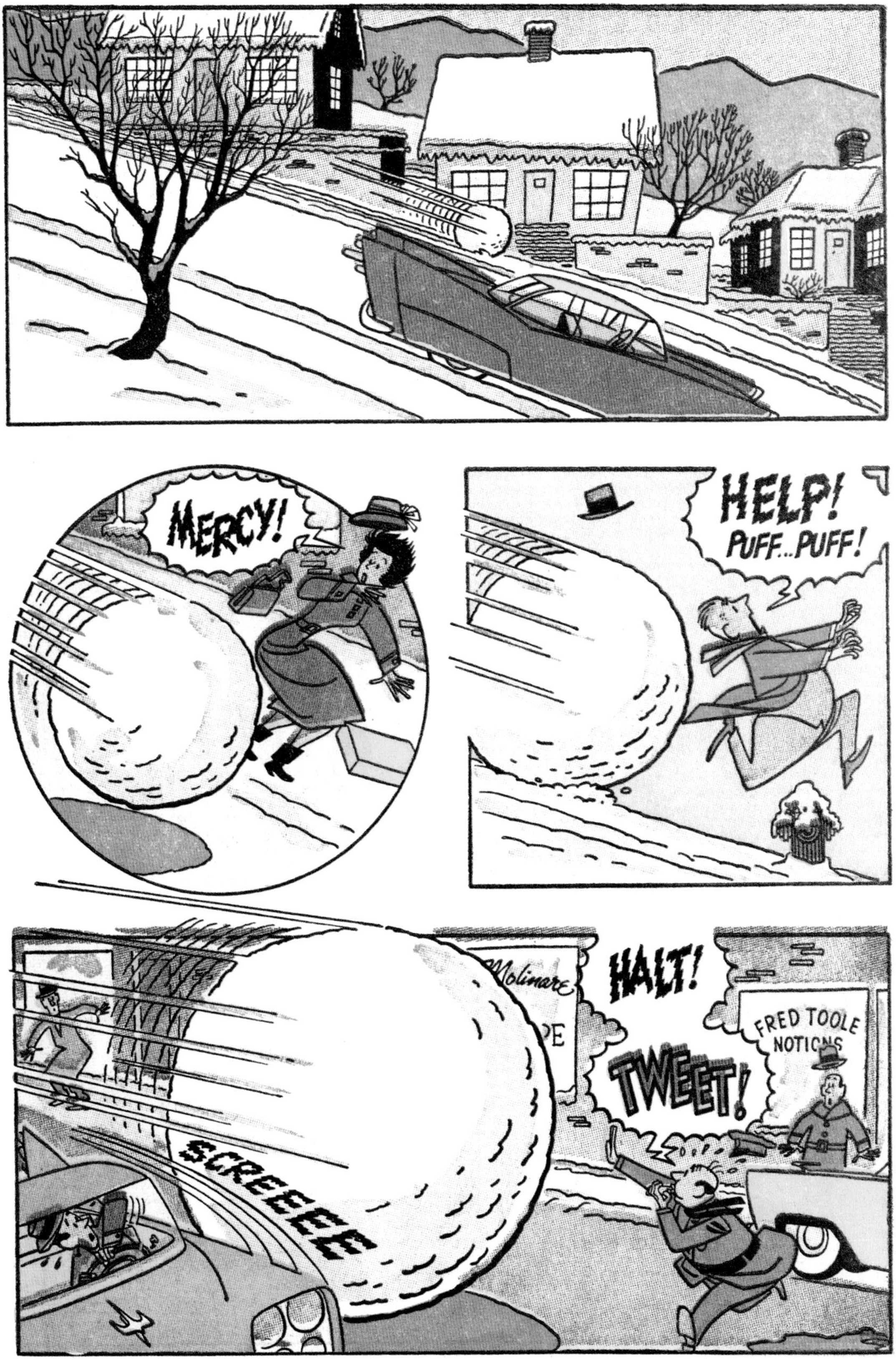
MERCY!
HELP!
PUFF...PUFF!
Molinare
HALT!
FRED TOOLE NOTIONS
TWEET!
SCREEEEE

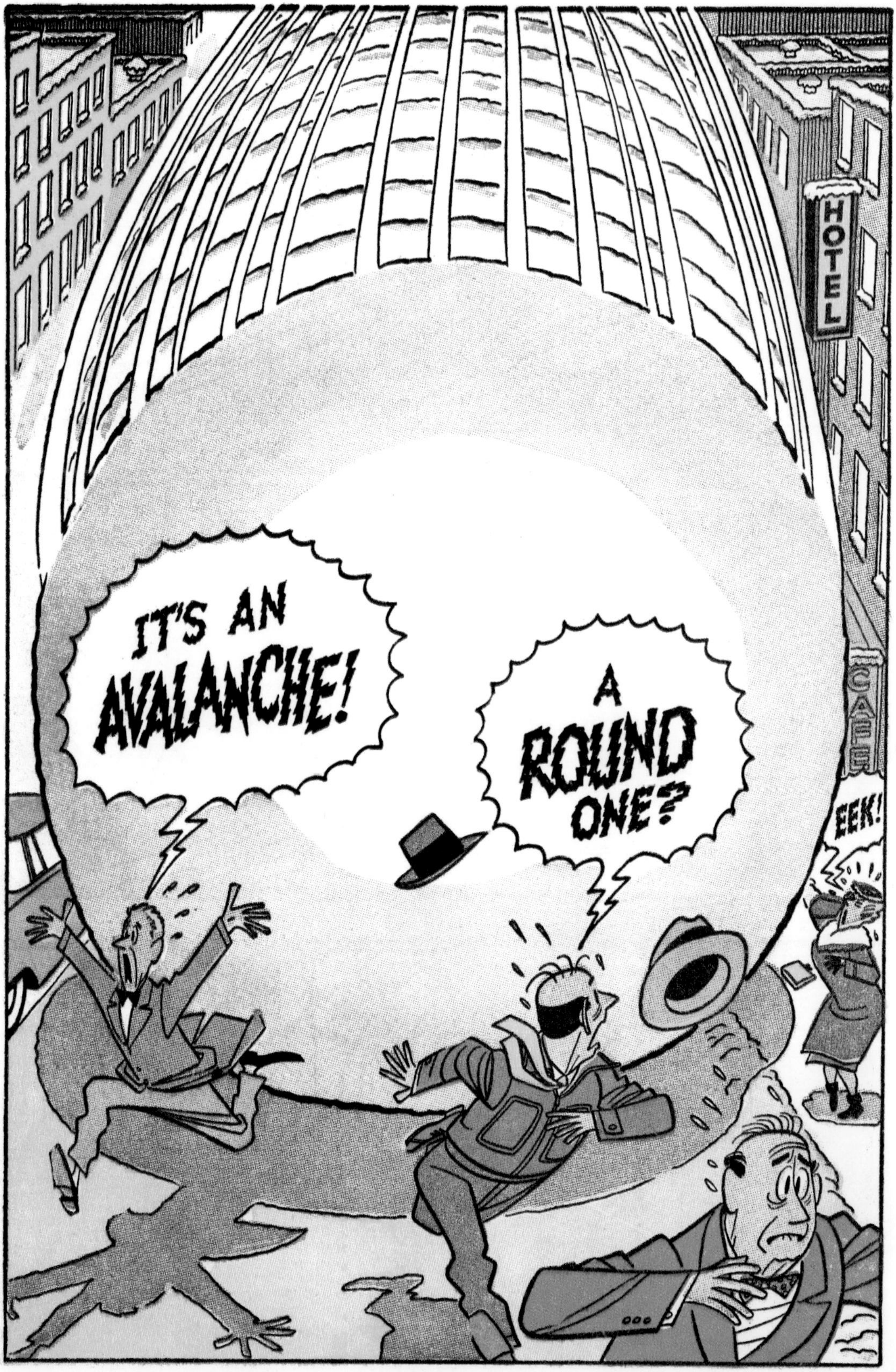
HOTEL
CAFE
IT'S AN AVALANCHE!
A ROUND ONE?
EEK!

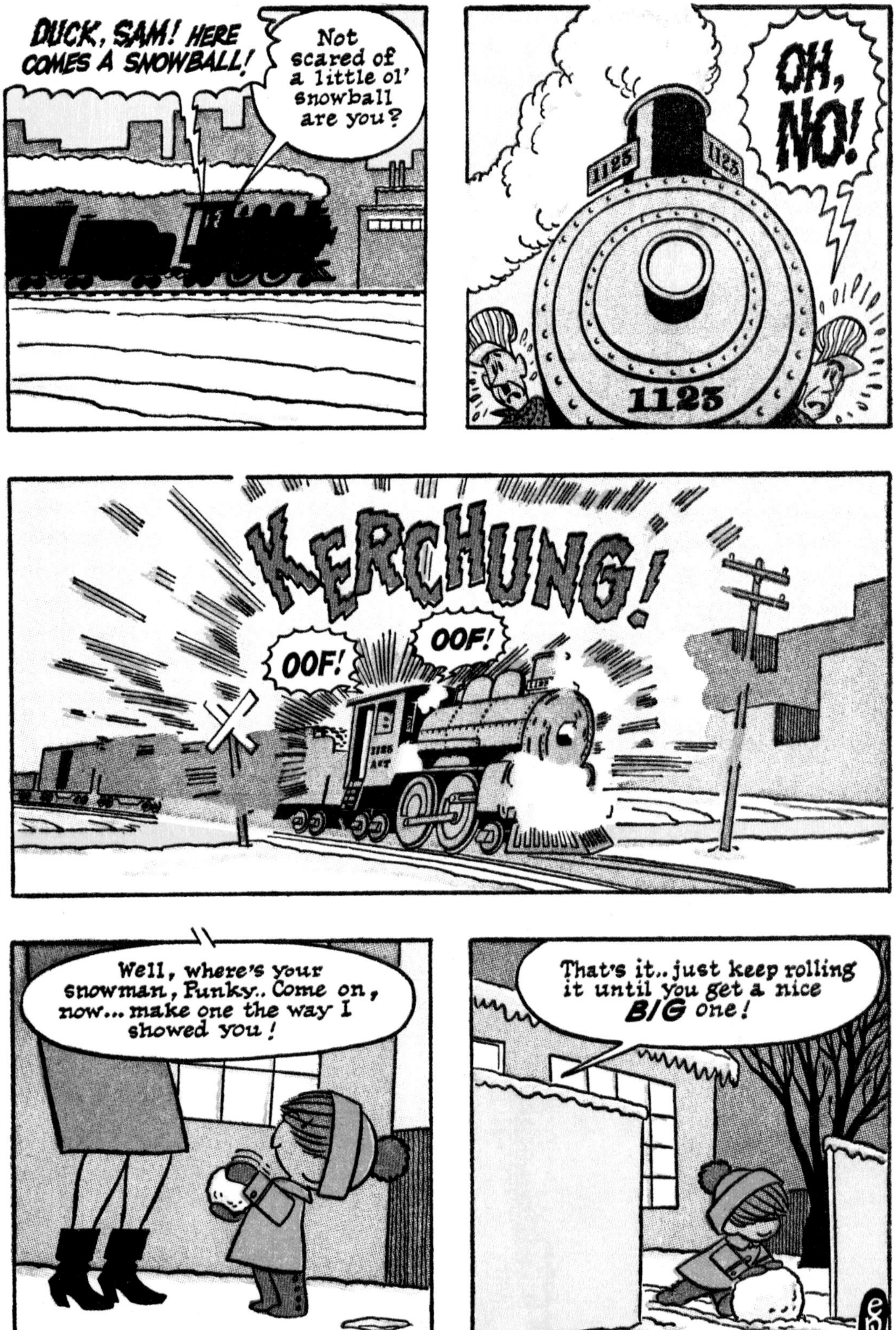
DUCK, SAM! HERE COMES A SNOWBALL!
Not scared of a little ol' snowball are you?
OH, NO!
1125
1123
1123
KERCHUNG!
OOF!
OOF!
Well, where's your snowman, Punky.. Come on, now... make one the way I showed you!
That's it.. just keep rolling it until you get a nice BIG one!
end

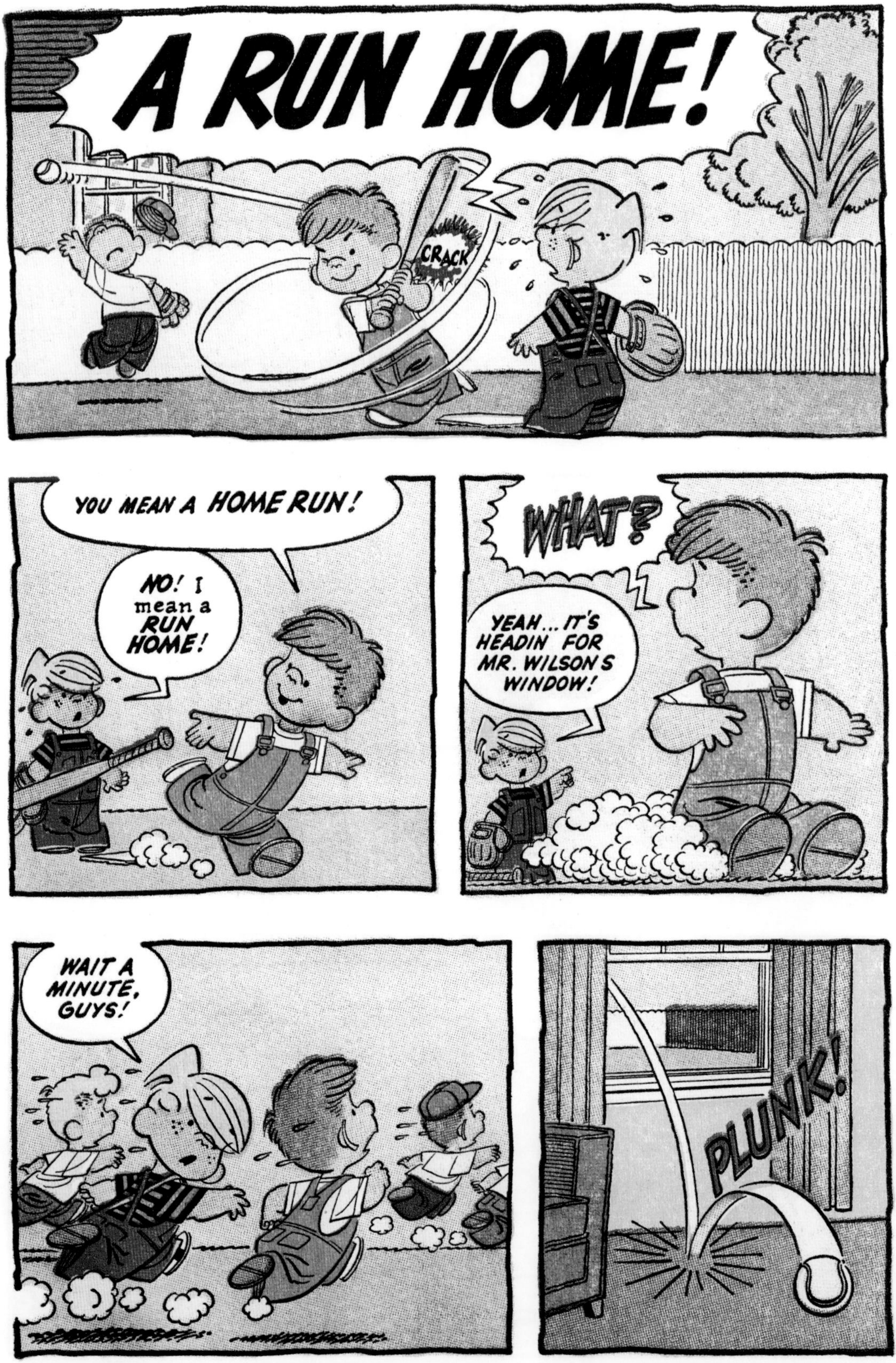
A RUN HOME!
CRACK
YOU MEAN A HOME RUN!
NO! I mean a RUN HOME!
WHAT?
YEAH... IT'S HEADIN' FOR MR. WILSON'S WINDOW!
WAIT A MINUTE, GUYS!
PLUNK!

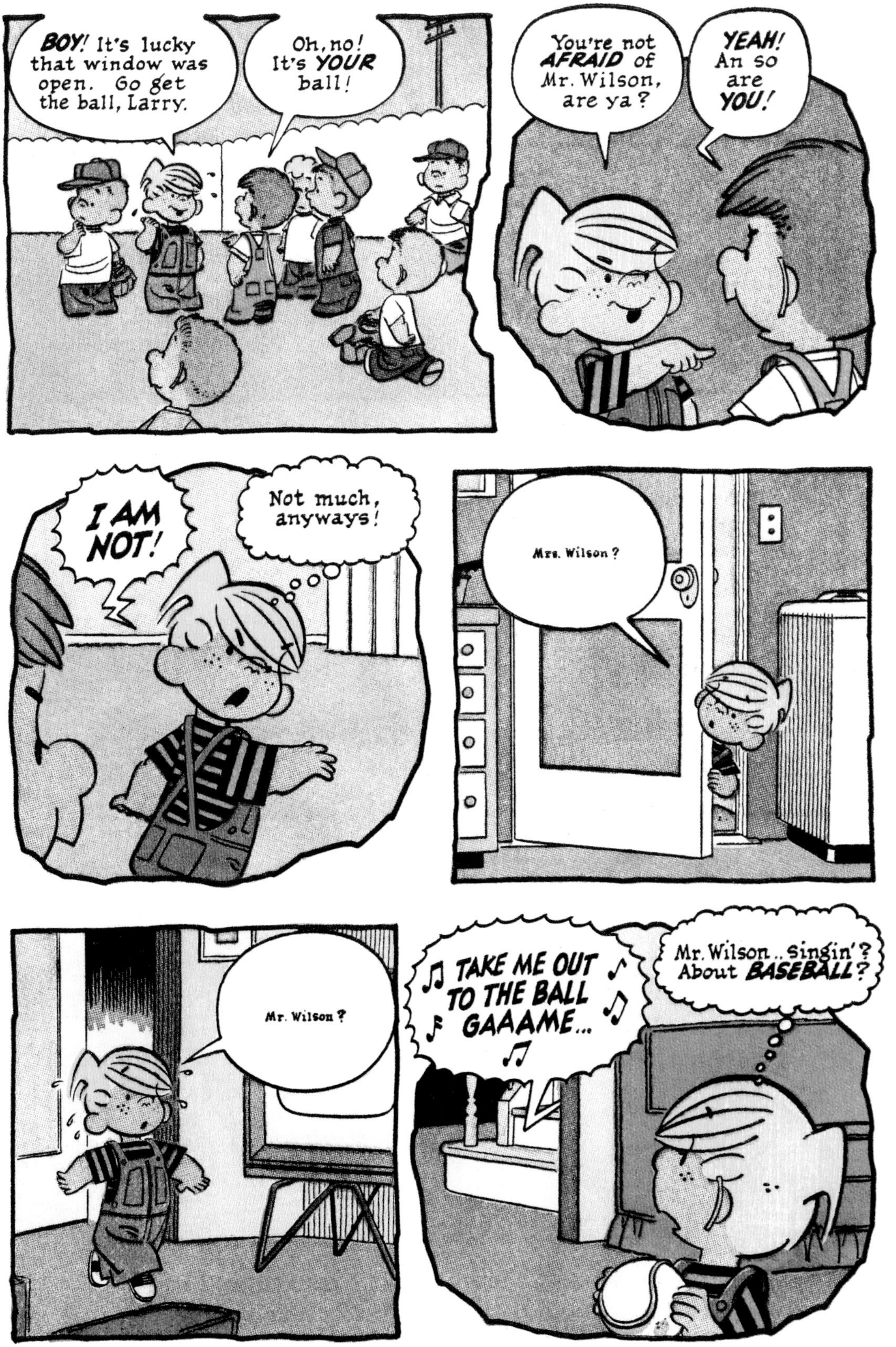
BOY! It's lucky that window was open. Go get the ball, Larry.
Oh, no! It's YOUR ball!
You're not AFRAID of Mr. Wilson, are ya?
YEAH! An so are YOU!
I AM NOT!
Not much, anyways!
Mrs. Wilson?
Mr. Wilson?
TAKE ME OUT TO THE BALL GAAAME...
Mr. Wilson.. Singin'? About BASEBALL?

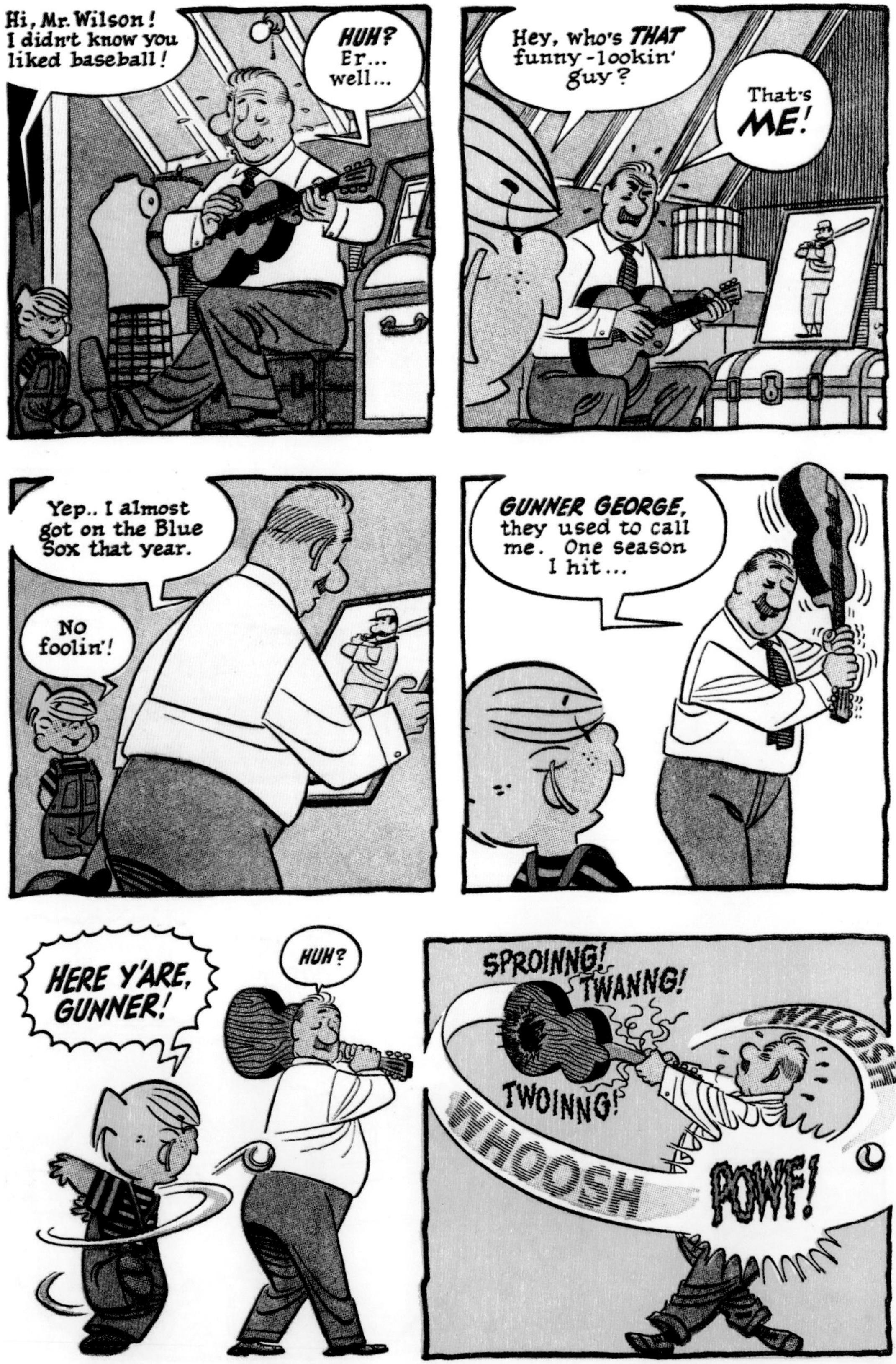
Hi, Mr. Wilson! I didn't know you liked baseball!
HUH? Er... well...
Hey, who's THAT funny-lookin' guy?
That's ME!
Yep.. I almost got on the Blue Sox that year.
No foolin'!
GUNNER GEORGE, they used to call me. One season I hit...
HERE Y'ARE, GUNNER!
HUH?
SPROINNG!
TWANNG!
TWOINNG!
WHOOSH
WHOOSH
POWF!

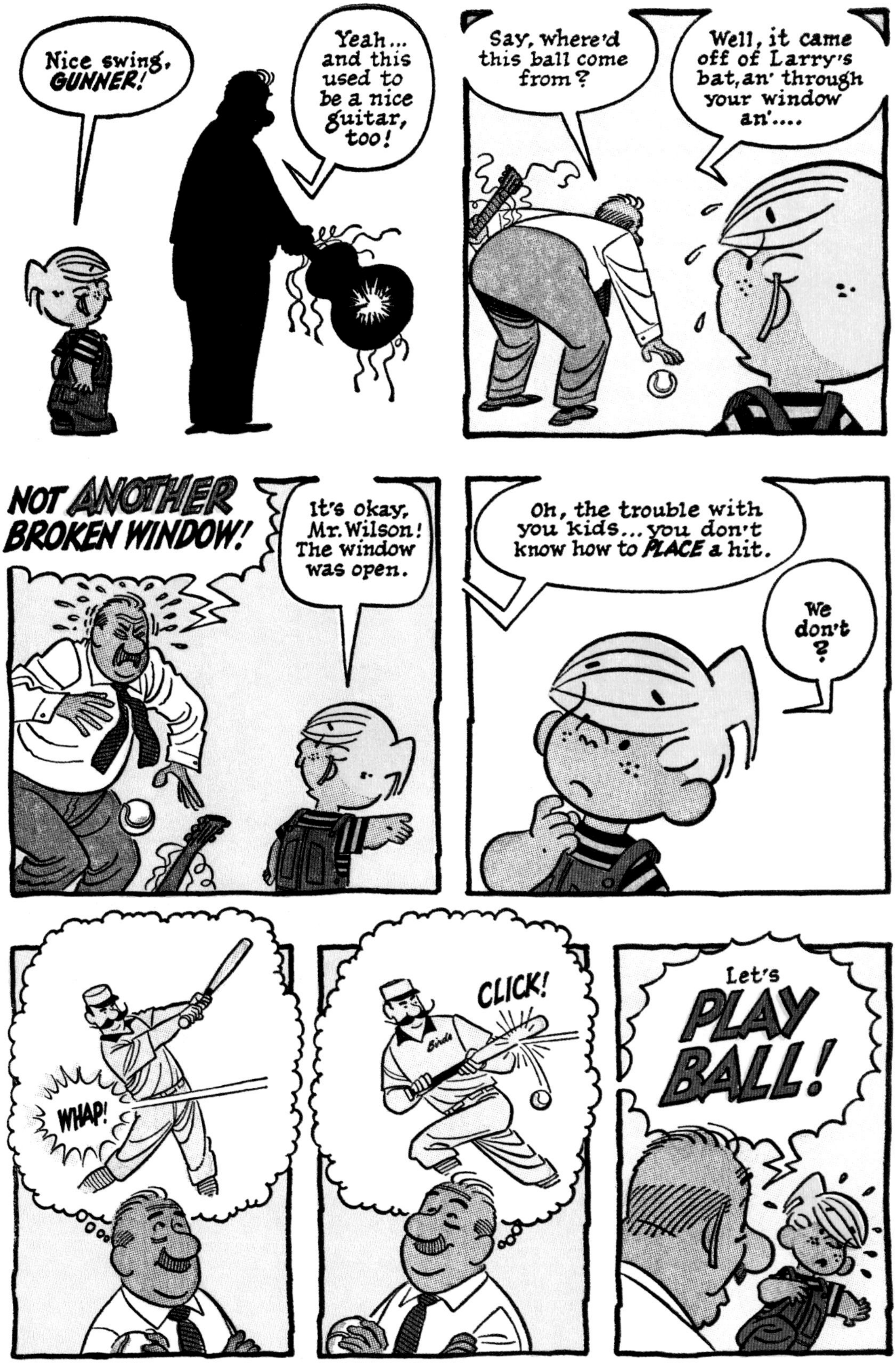
Nice swing, GUNNER!
Yeah... and this used to be a nice guitar, too!
Say, where'd this ball come from?
Well, it came off of Larry's bat, an' through your window an'....
NOT ANOTHER BROKEN WINDOW!
It's okay, Mr. Wilson! The window was open.
Oh, the trouble with you kids... you don't know how to PLACE a hit.
We don't?
WHAP!
CLICK!
Let's PLAY BALL!

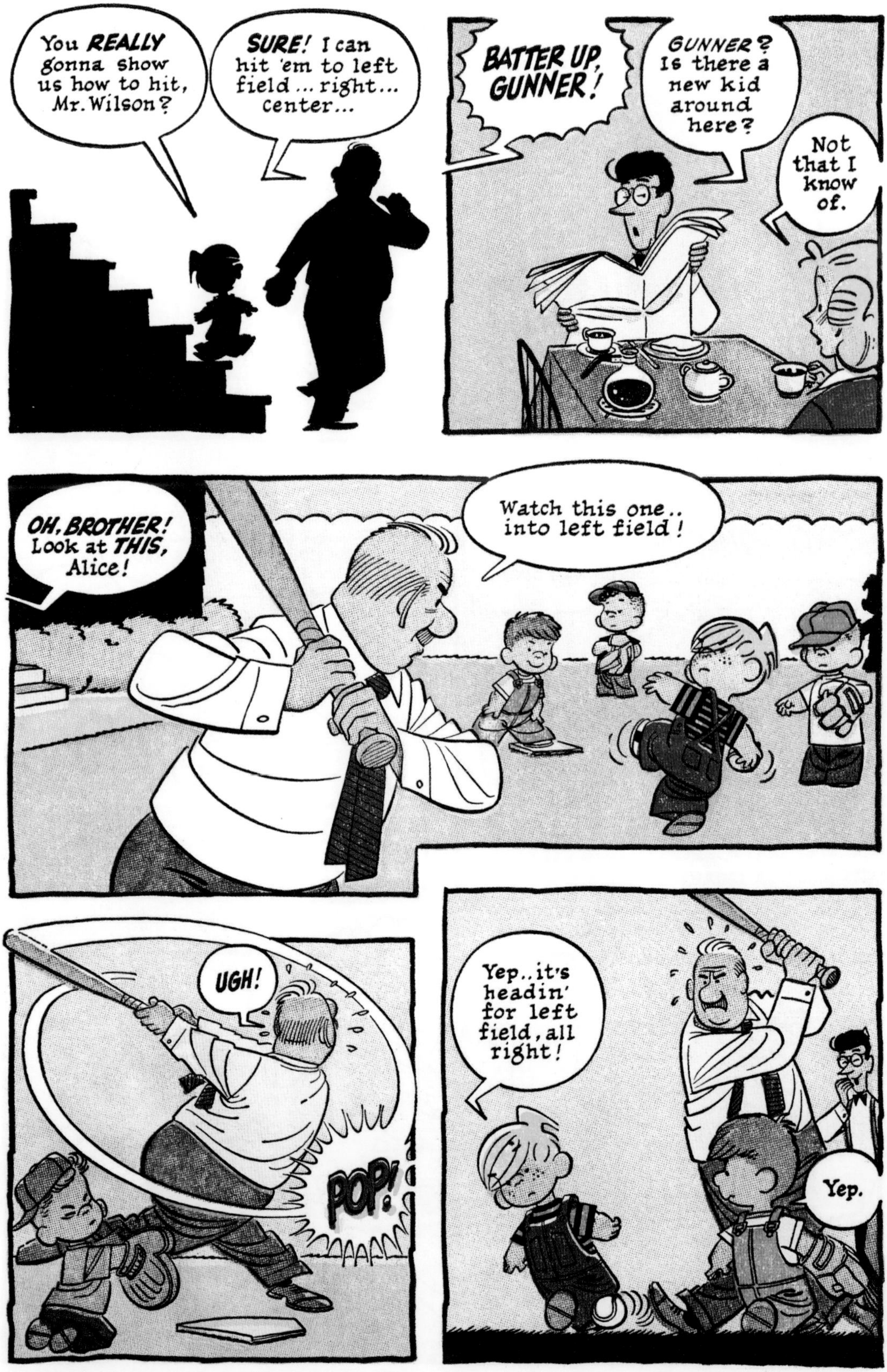
You REALLY gonna show us how to hit, Mr. Wilson?
SURE! I can hit 'em to left field ... right ... center ...
BATTER UP, GUNNER!
GUNNER? Is there a new kid around here?
Not that I know of.
OH, BROTHER! Look at THIS, Alice!
Watch this one .. into left field!
UGH!
POP!
Yep .. it's headin' for left field, all right!
Yep.

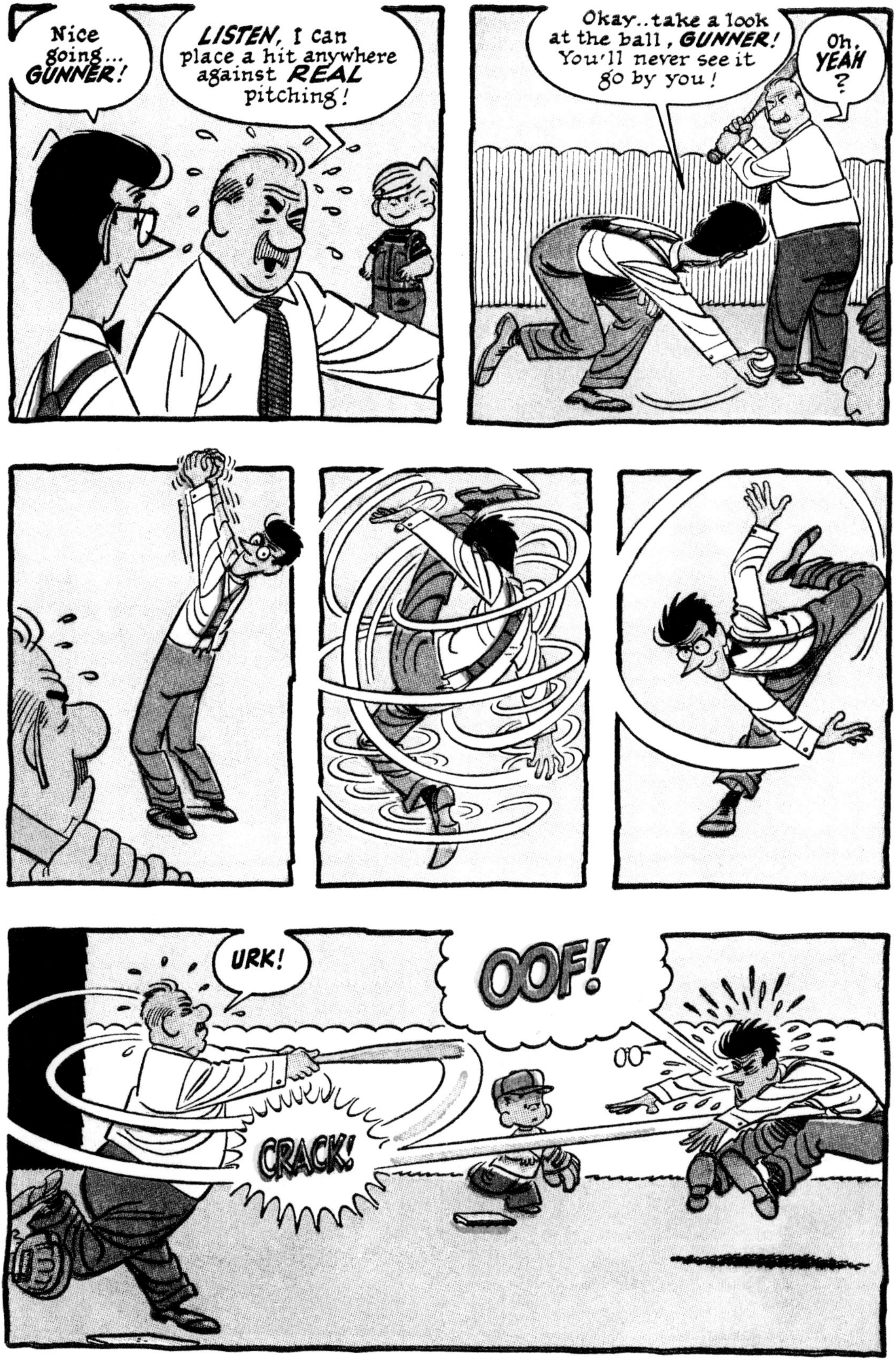
Nice going... GUNNER!
LISTEN, I can place a hit anywhere against REAL pitching!
Okay..take a look at the ball, GUNNER! You'll never see it go by you!
Oh, YEAH?
URK!
OOF!
CRACK!

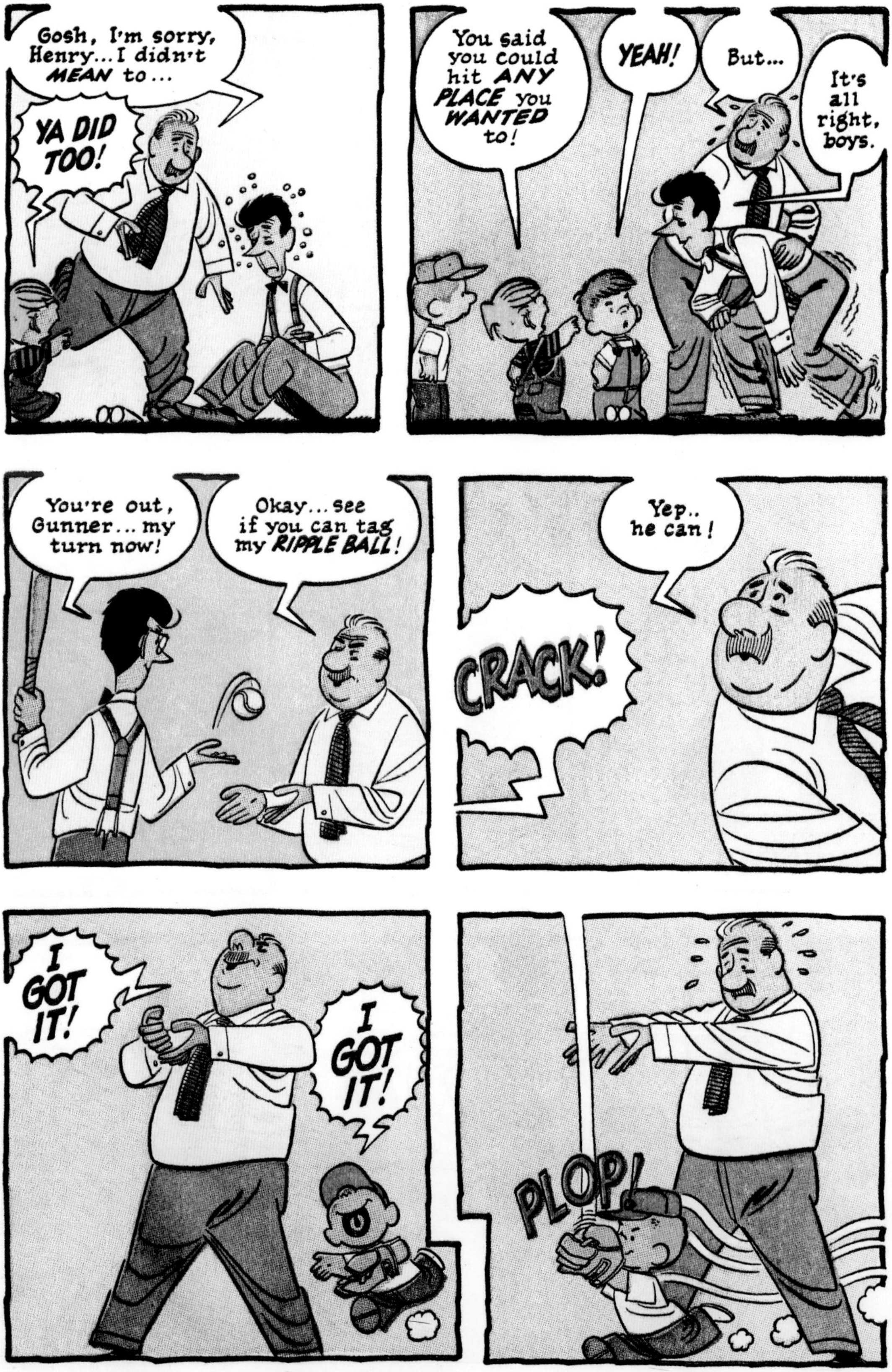
Gosh, I'm sorry, Henry...I didn't MEAN to...
YA DID TOO!
You said you could hit ANY PLACE you WANTED to!
YEAH!
But...
It's all right, boys.
You're out, Gunner... my turn now!
Okay... see if you can tag my RIPPLE BALL!
Yep.. he can!
CRACK!
I GOT IT!
I GOT IT!
PLOP!

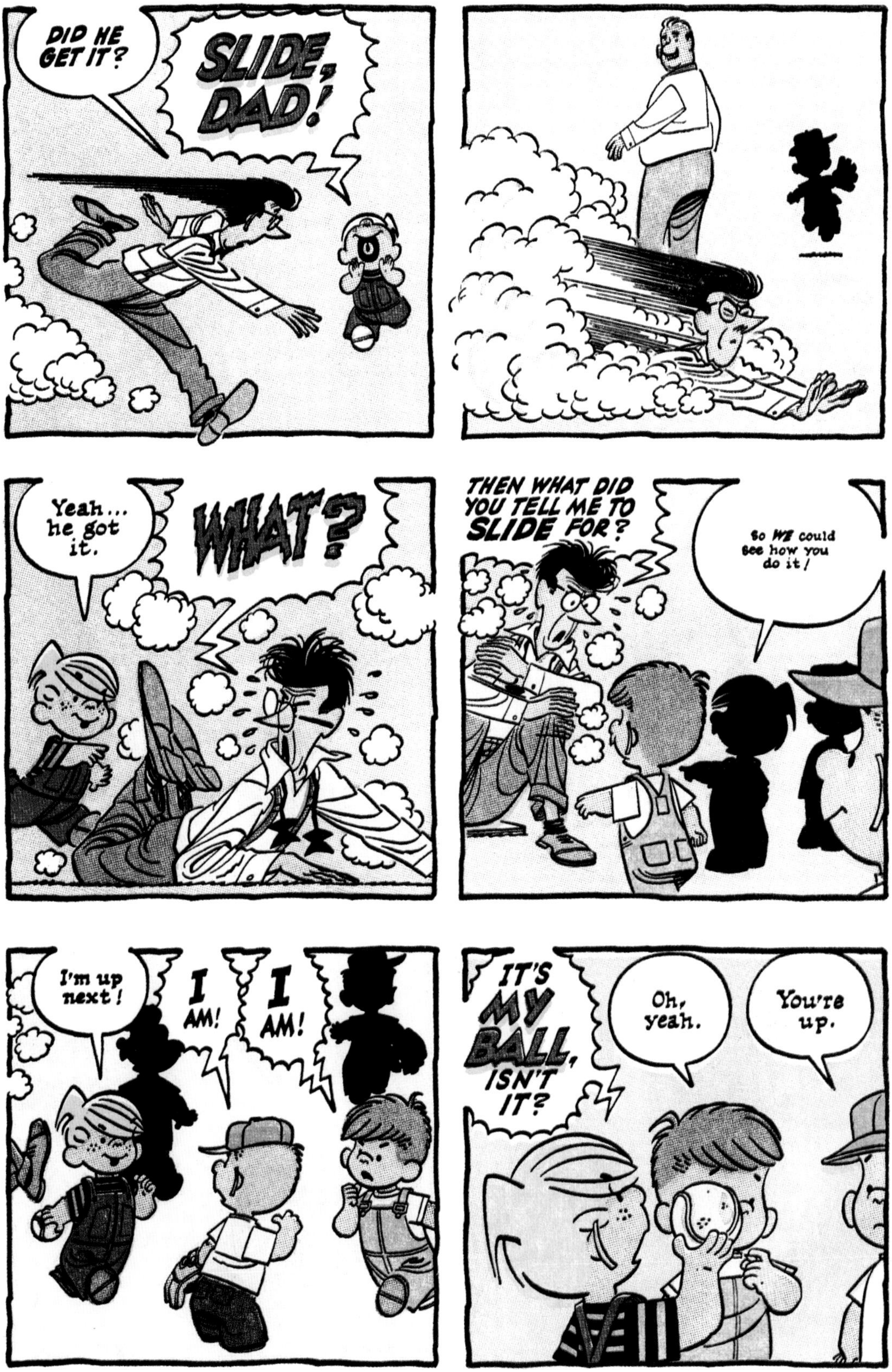
DID HE GET IT?
SLIDE, DAD!
Yeah... he got it.
WHAT?
THEN WHAT DID YOU TELL ME TO SLIDE FOR?
So WE could see how you do it!
I'm up next!
I AM!
I AM!
IT'S MY BALL, ISN'T IT?
Oh, yeah.
You're up.

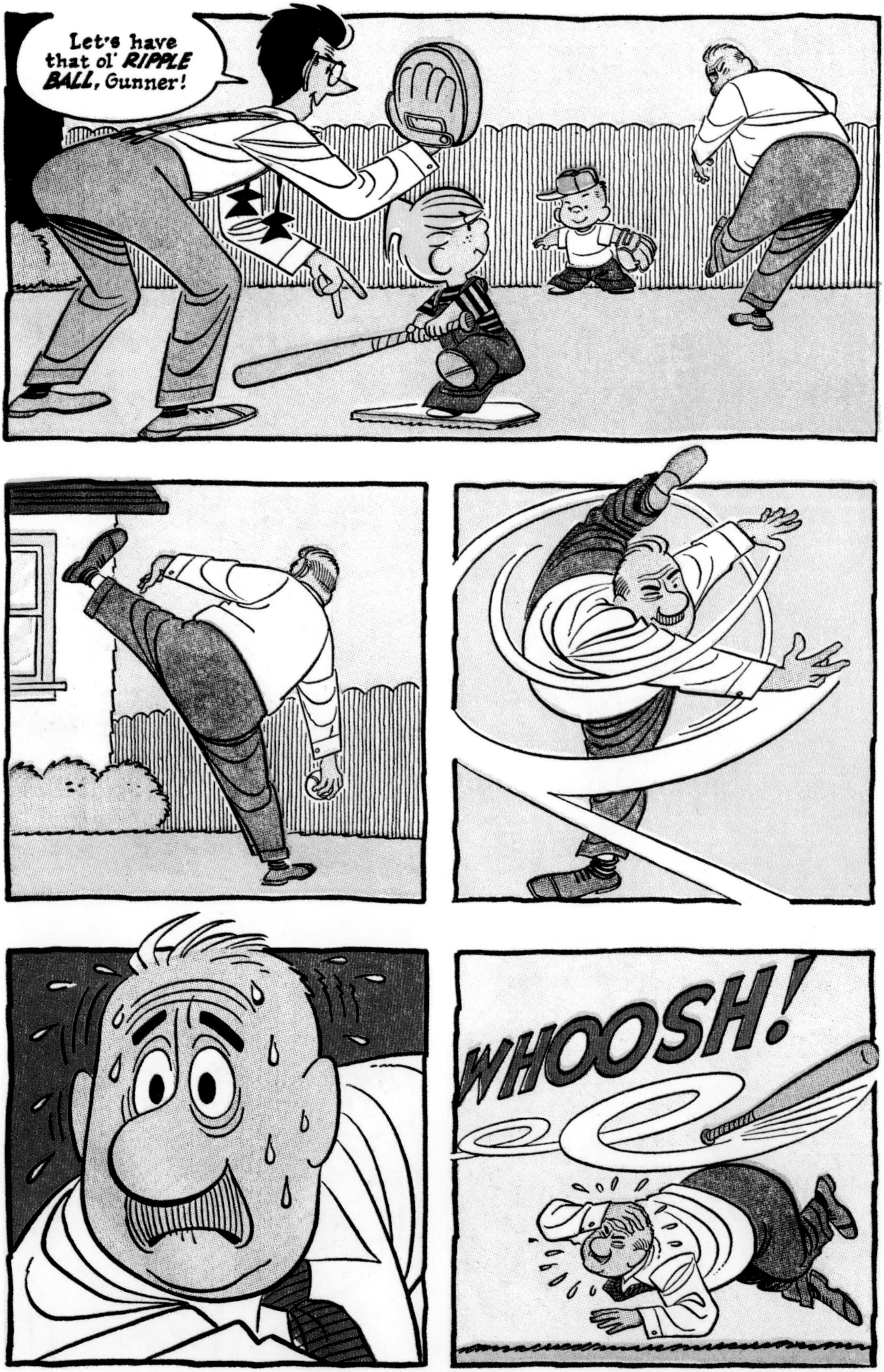
Let's have that ol' RIPPLE BALL, Gunner!
WHOOSH!

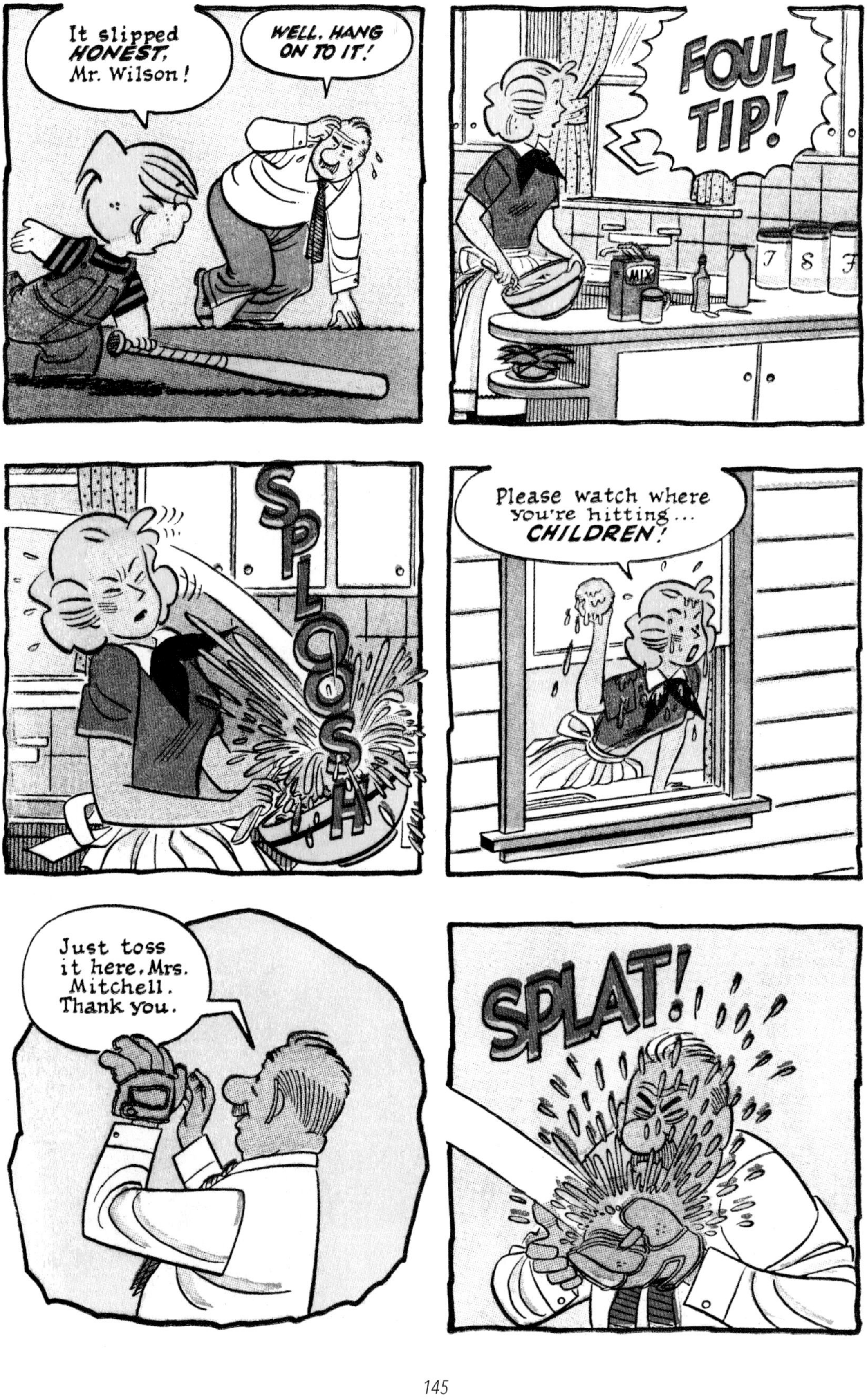

It slipped HONEST, Mr. Wilson!
WELL, HANG ON TO IT!
FOUL TIP!
MIX
SPLOOSH
Please watch where you're hitting... CHILDREN!
Just toss it here, Mrs. Mitchell. Thank you.
SPLAT!

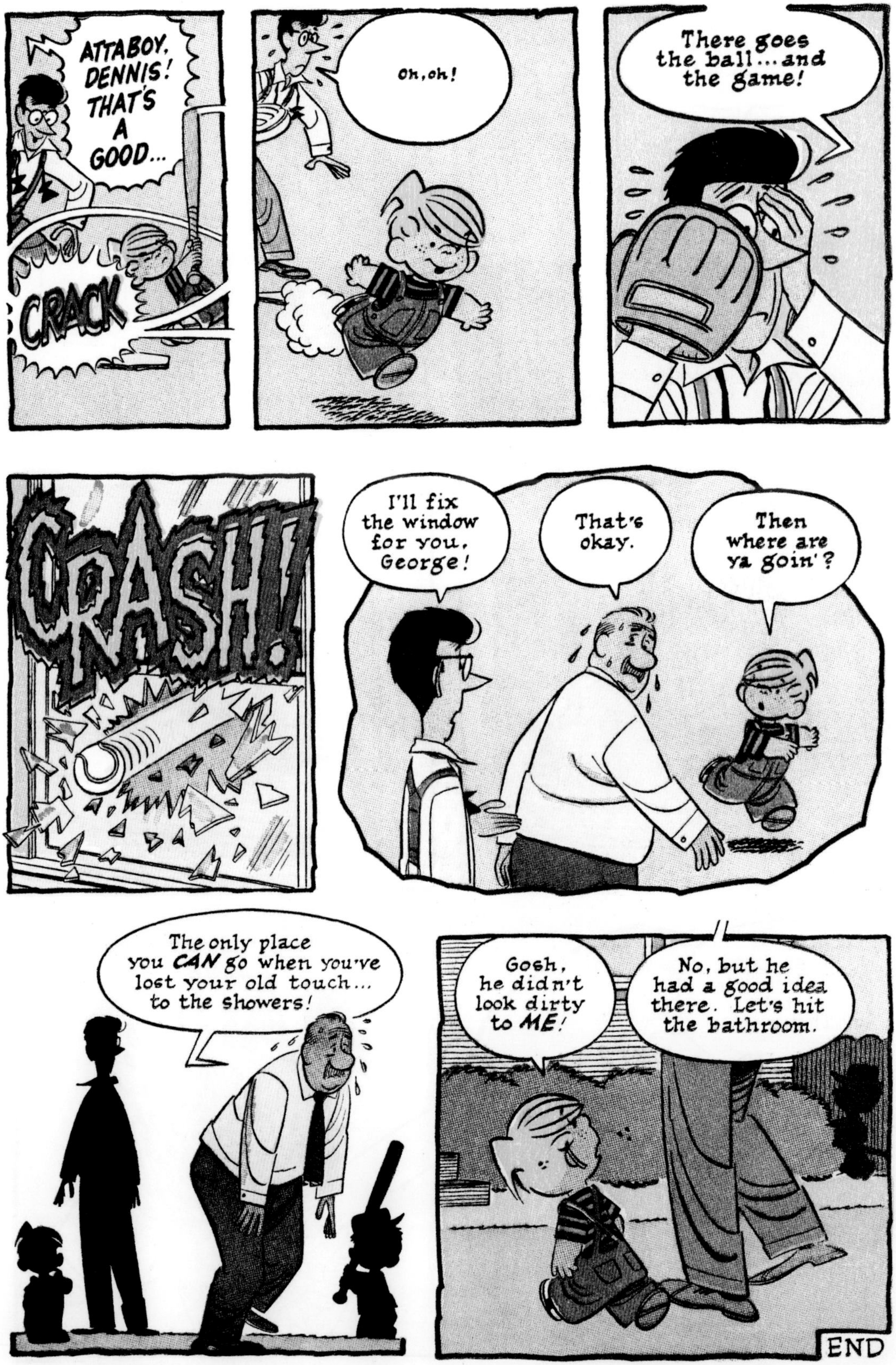
ATTABOY, DENNIS! THAT'S A GOOD...
CRACK
Oh, oh!
There goes the ball...and the game!
CRASH!
I'll fix the window for you, George!
That's okay.
Then where are ya goin'?
The only place you CAN go when you've lost your old touch... to the showers!
Gosh, he didn't look dirty to ME!
No, but he had a good idea there. Let's hit the bathroom.
END

RUNNING WILD!

Hey, Dad! Let's play somethin'!
HUH? WHAZZAT?
PLAY? At FIVE o'clock in the morning?
No... NOW!
Why don't you play jumping in bed?
OKAY!
OOF!!

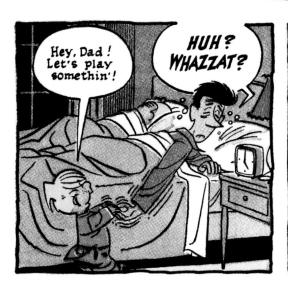

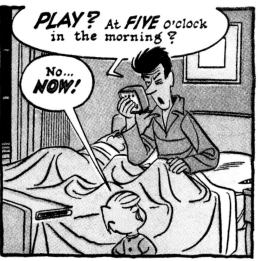

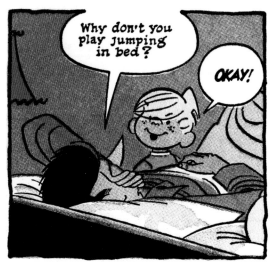

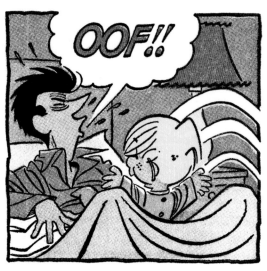

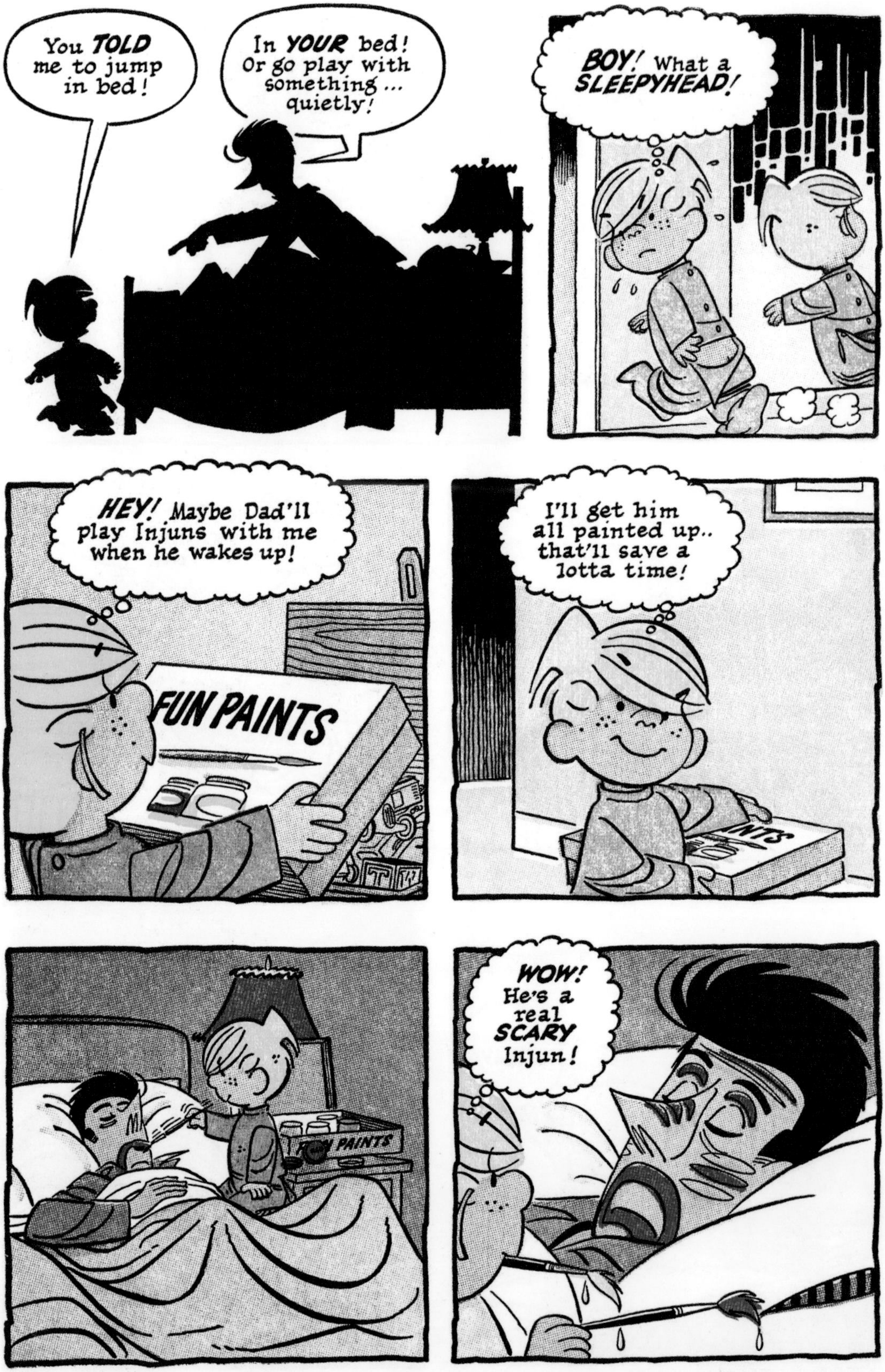
You TOLD me to jump in bed!
In YOUR bed! Or go play with something ... quietly!
BOY! What a SLEEPYHEAD!
HEY! Maybe Dad'll play Injuns with me when he wakes up!
FUN PAINTS
I'll get him all painted up.. that'll save a lotta time!
FUN PAINTS
WOW! He's a real SCARY Injun!

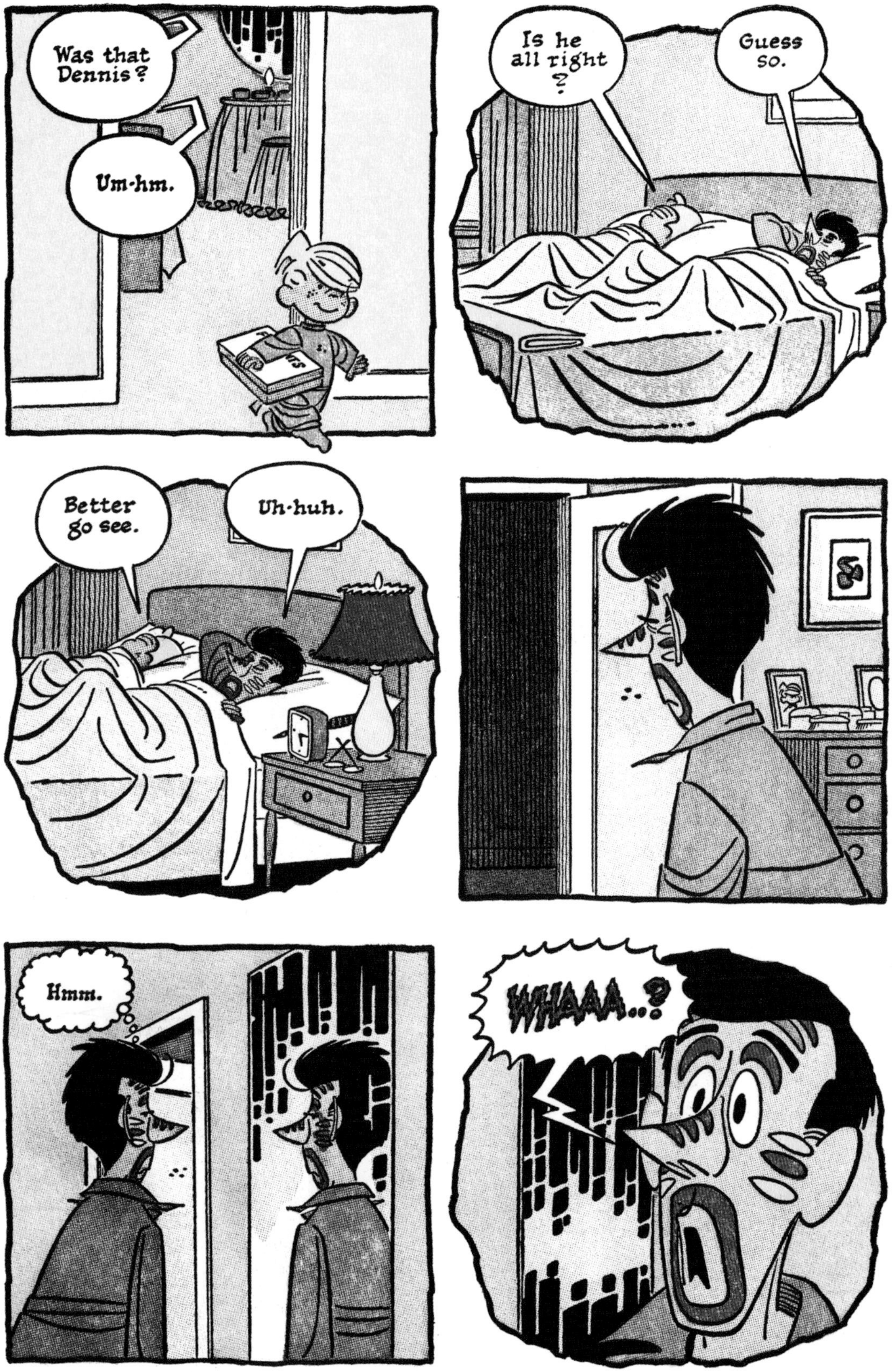
Was that Dennis?
Um-hm.
Is he all right?
Guess so.
Better go see.
Uh-huh.
Hmm.
WHAAA..?

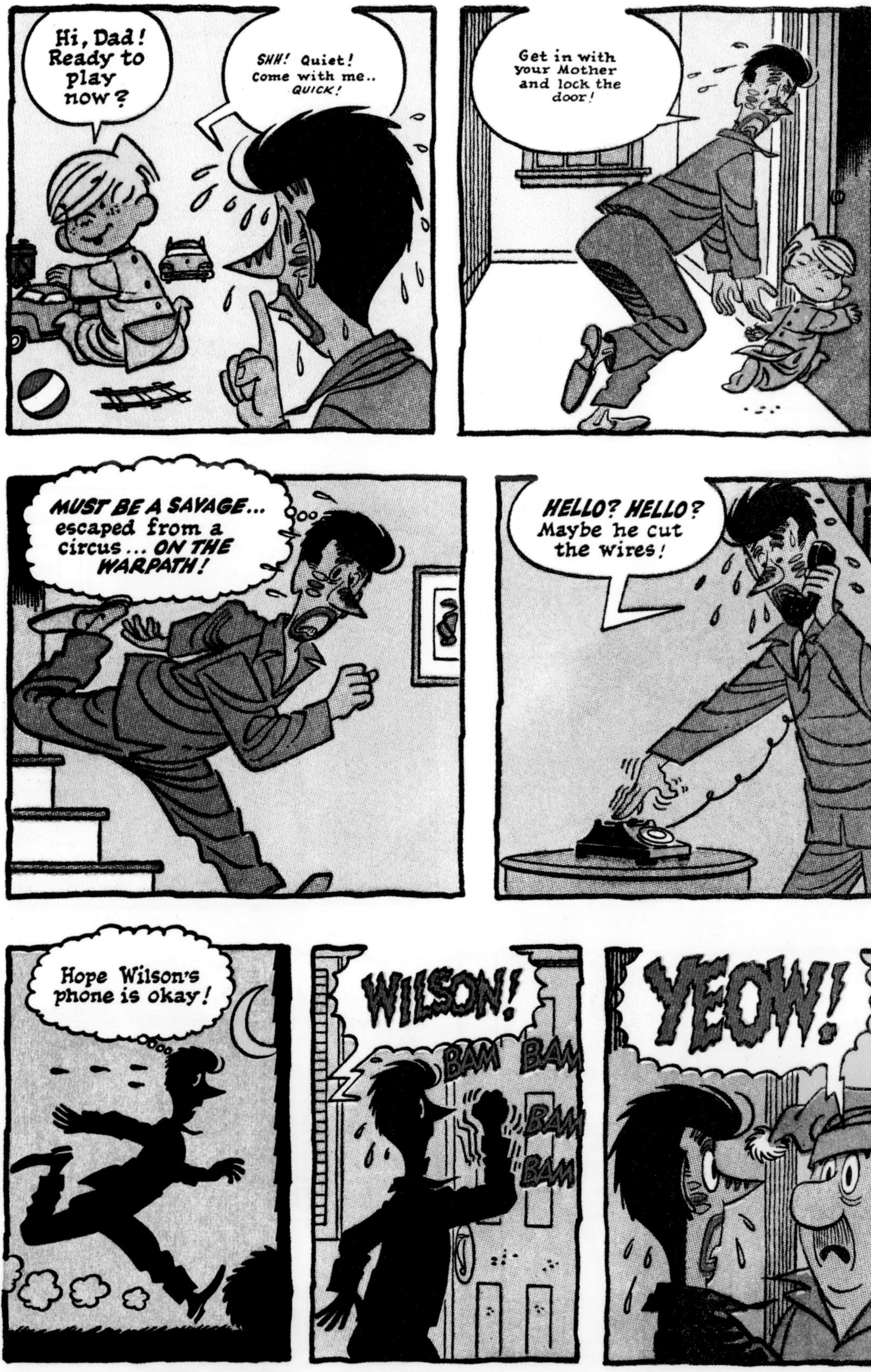
Hi, Dad! Ready to play now?
SHH! Quiet! Come with me.. QUICK!
Get in with your Mother and lock the door!
MUST BE A SAVAGE... escaped from a circus... ON THE WARPATH!
HELLO? HELLO? Maybe he cut the wires!
Hope Wilson's phone is okay!
WILSON!
BAM BAM BAM BAM
YEOW!

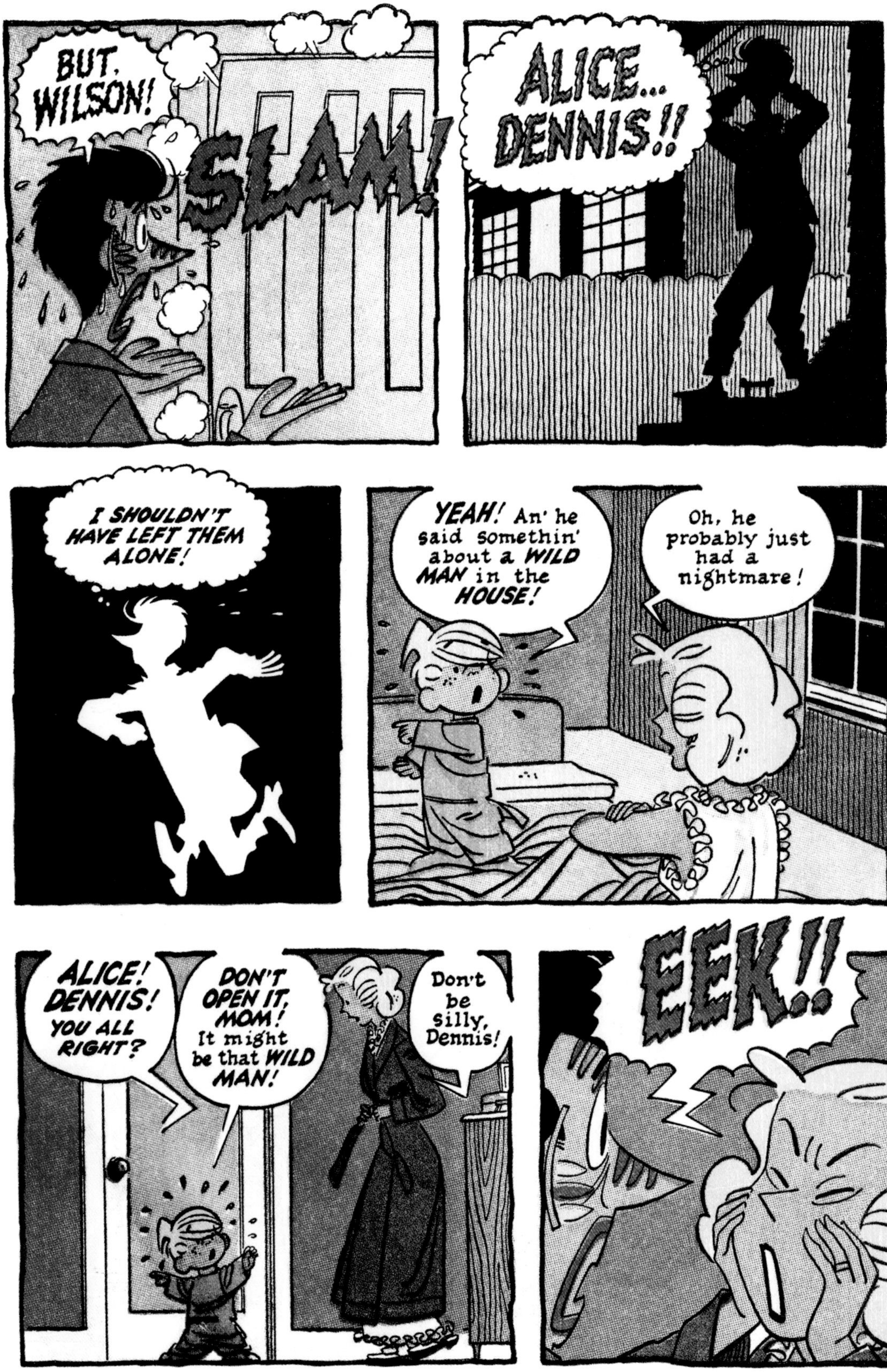
BUT, WILSON!
SLAM!
ALICE... DENNIS!!
I SHOULDN'T HAVE LEFT THEM ALONE!
YEAH! An' he said somethin' about a WILD MAN in the HOUSE!
Oh, he probably just had a nightmare!
ALICE! DENNIS! YOU ALL RIGHT?
DON'T OPEN IT, MOM! It might be that WILD MAN!
Don't be silly, Dennis!
EEK!!

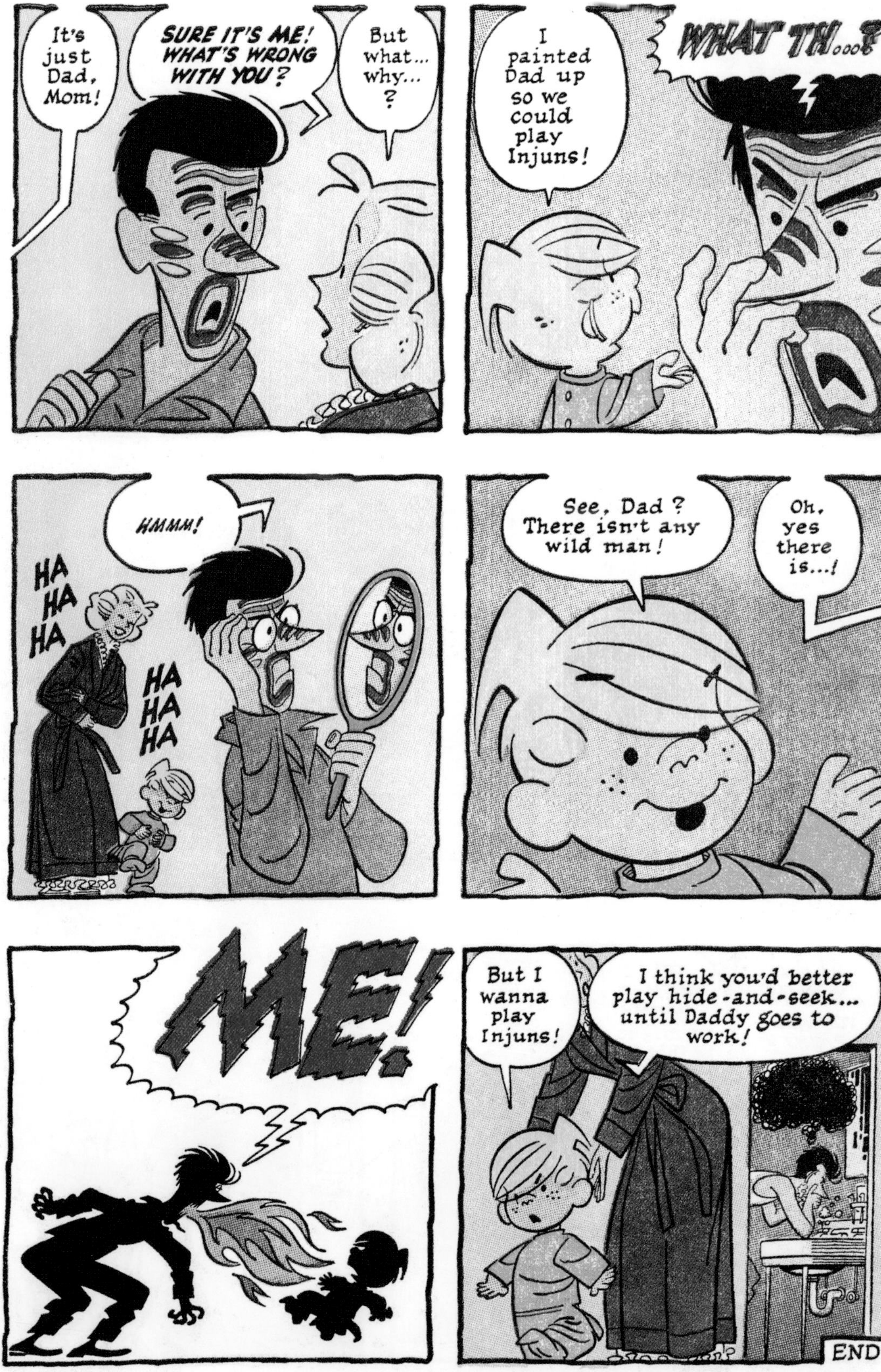
It's just Dad, Mom!
SURE IT'S ME! WHAT'S WRONG WITH YOU?
But what... why... ?
I painted Dad up so we could play Injuns!
WHAT TH...?
HMMM!
HA HA HA
HA HA HA
See, Dad? There isn't any wild man!
Oh, yes there is...!
ME!
But I wanna play Injuns!
I think you'd better play hide-and-seek... until Daddy goes to work!
END

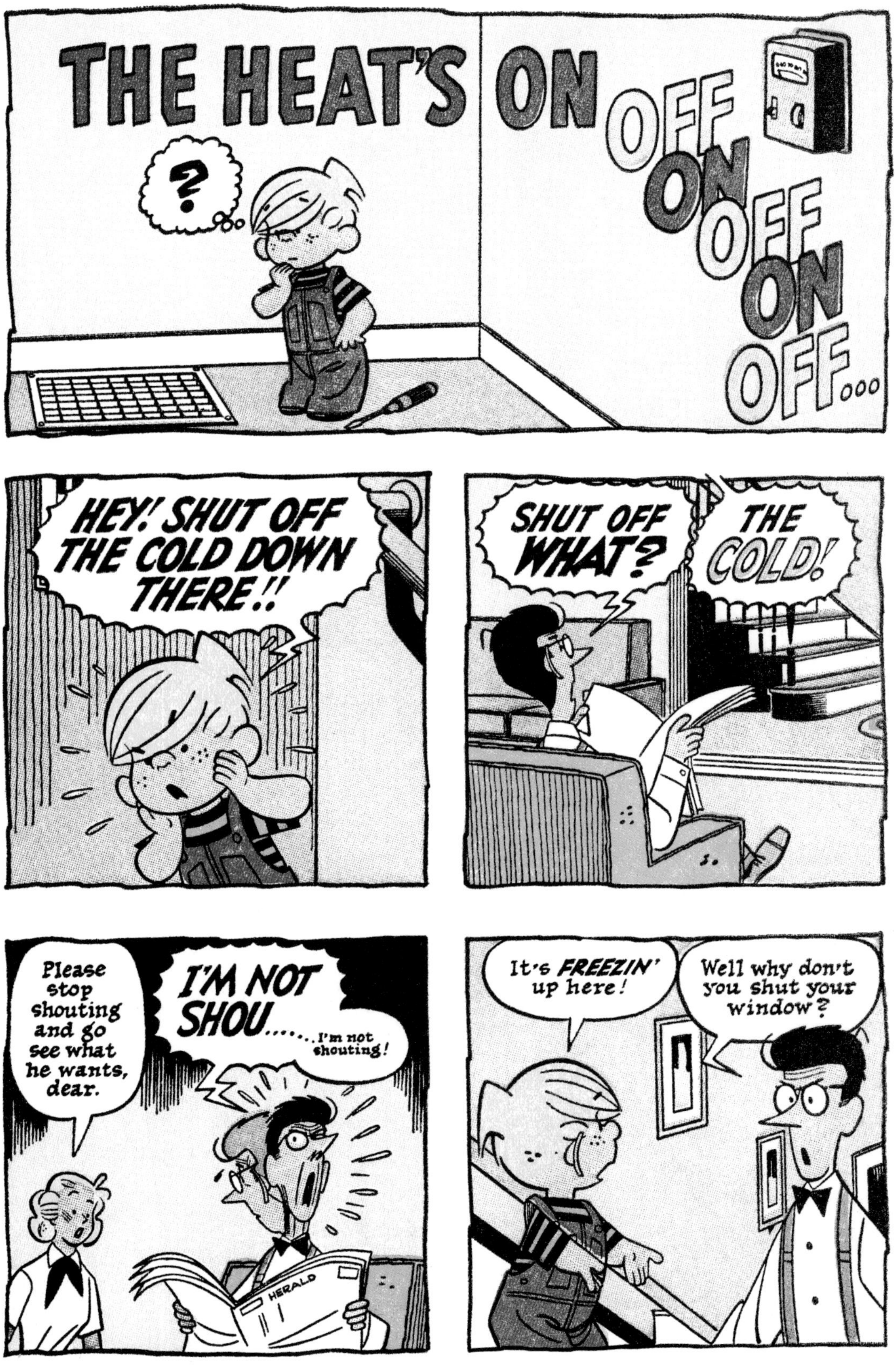
THE HEAT'S ON
OFF ON OFF ON OFF...
?
HEY! SHUT OFF THE COLD DOWN THERE!!
SHUT OFF WHAT?
THE COLD!
Please stop shouting and go see what he wants, dear.
I'M NOT SHOU......
I'm not shouting!
HERALD
It's FREEZIN' up here!
Well why don't you shut your window?

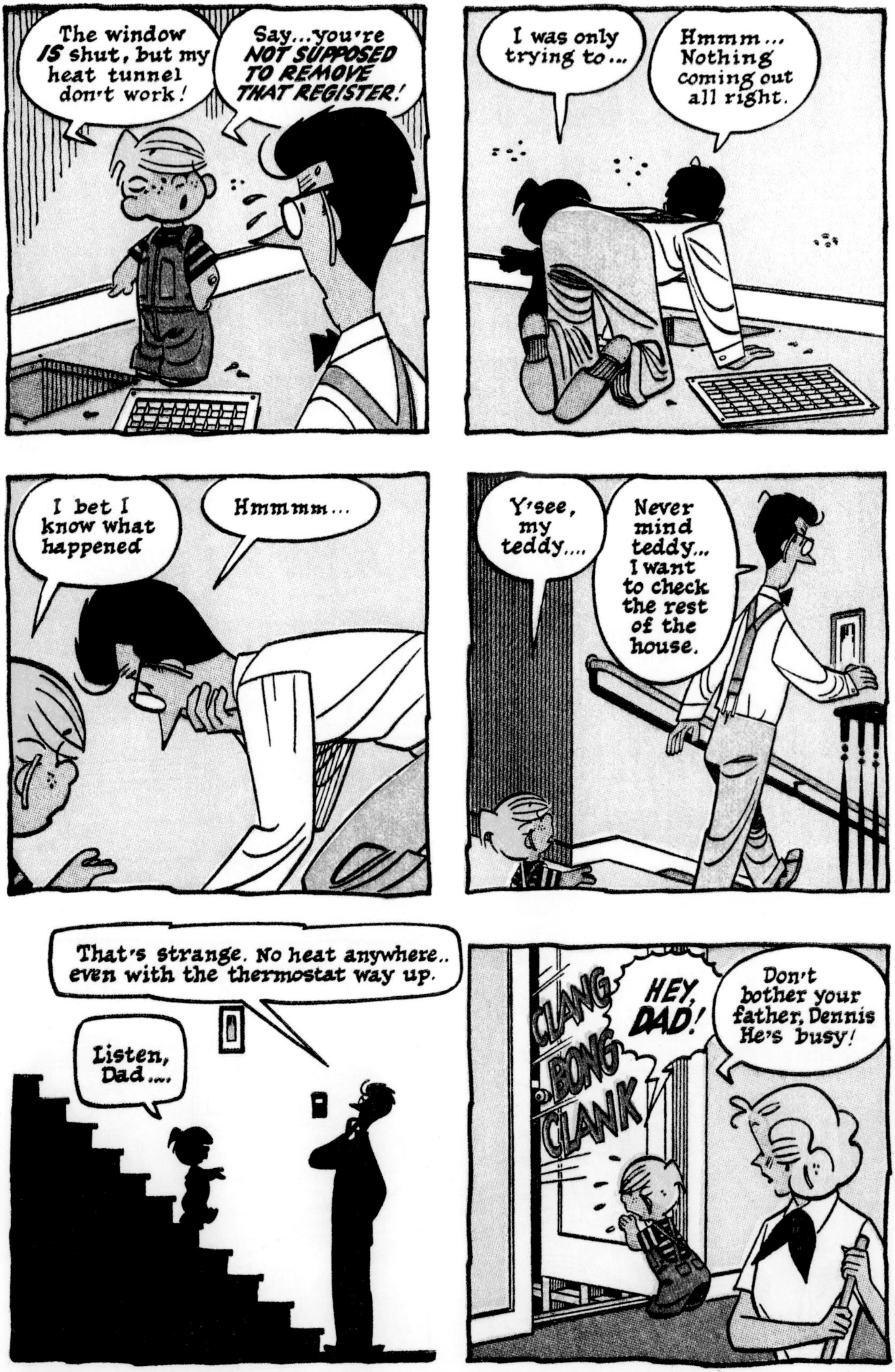
The window IS shut, but my heat tunnel don't work!
Say...you're NOT SUPPOSED TO REMOVE THAT REGISTER!
I was only trying to...
Hmmm... Nothing coming out all right.
I bet I know what happened
Hmmmm...
Y'see, my teddy....
Never mind teddy... I want to check the rest of the house.
That's strange. No heat anywhere.. even with the thermostat way up.
Listen, Dad....
CLANG
BONG
CLANK
HEY, DAD!
Don't bother your father, Dennis He's busy!

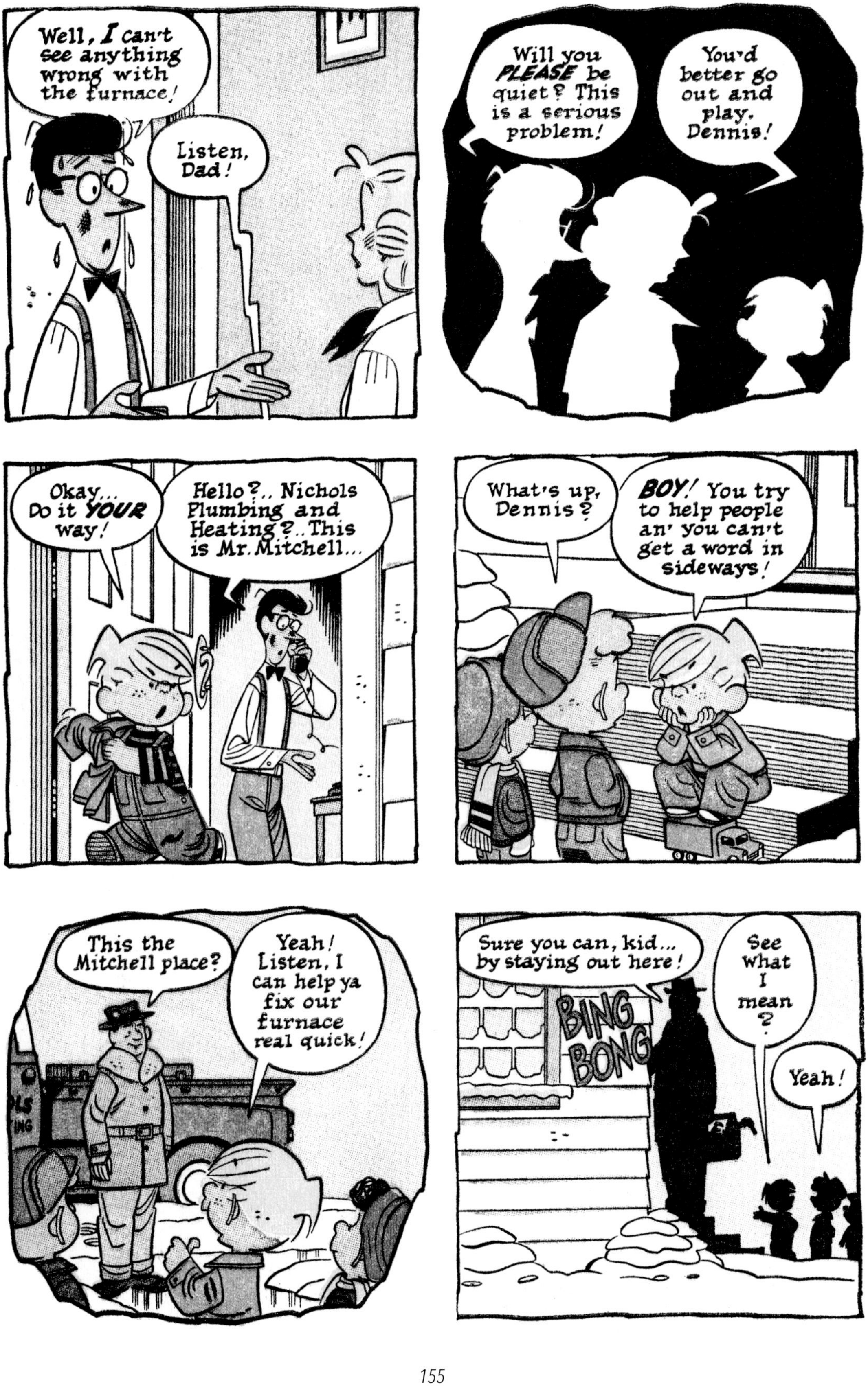
Well, I can't see anything wrong with the furnace!
Listen, Dad!
Will you PLEASE be quiet? This is a serious problem!
You'd better go out and play, Dennis!
Okay... Do it YOUR way!
Hello?.. Nichols Plumbing and Heating?..This is Mr. Mitchell...
What's up, Dennis?
BOY! You try to help people an' you can't get a word in sideways!
This the Mitchell place?
Yeah! Listen, I can help ya fix our furnace real quick!
Sure you can, kid... by staying out here!
BING BONG
See what I mean?
Yeah!

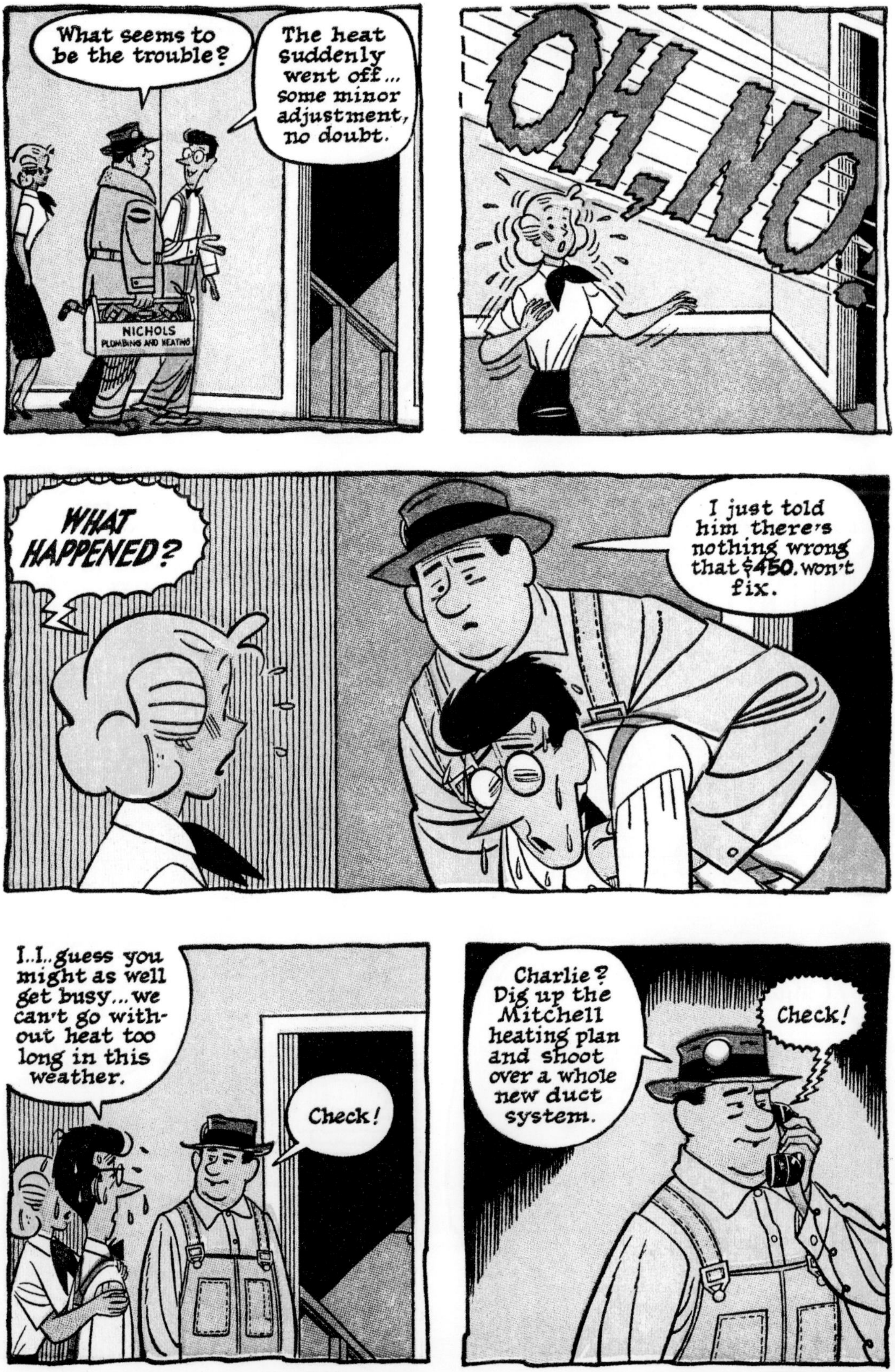
What seems to be the trouble?
The heat suddenly went off... some minor adjustment, no doubt.
NICHOLS PLUMBING AND HEATING
OH, NO
WHAT HAPPENED?
I just told him there's nothing wrong that $450. won't fix.
I..I..guess you might as well get busy... we can't go without heat too long in this weather.
Check!
Charlie? Dig up the Mitchell heating plan and shoot over a whole new duct system.
Check!

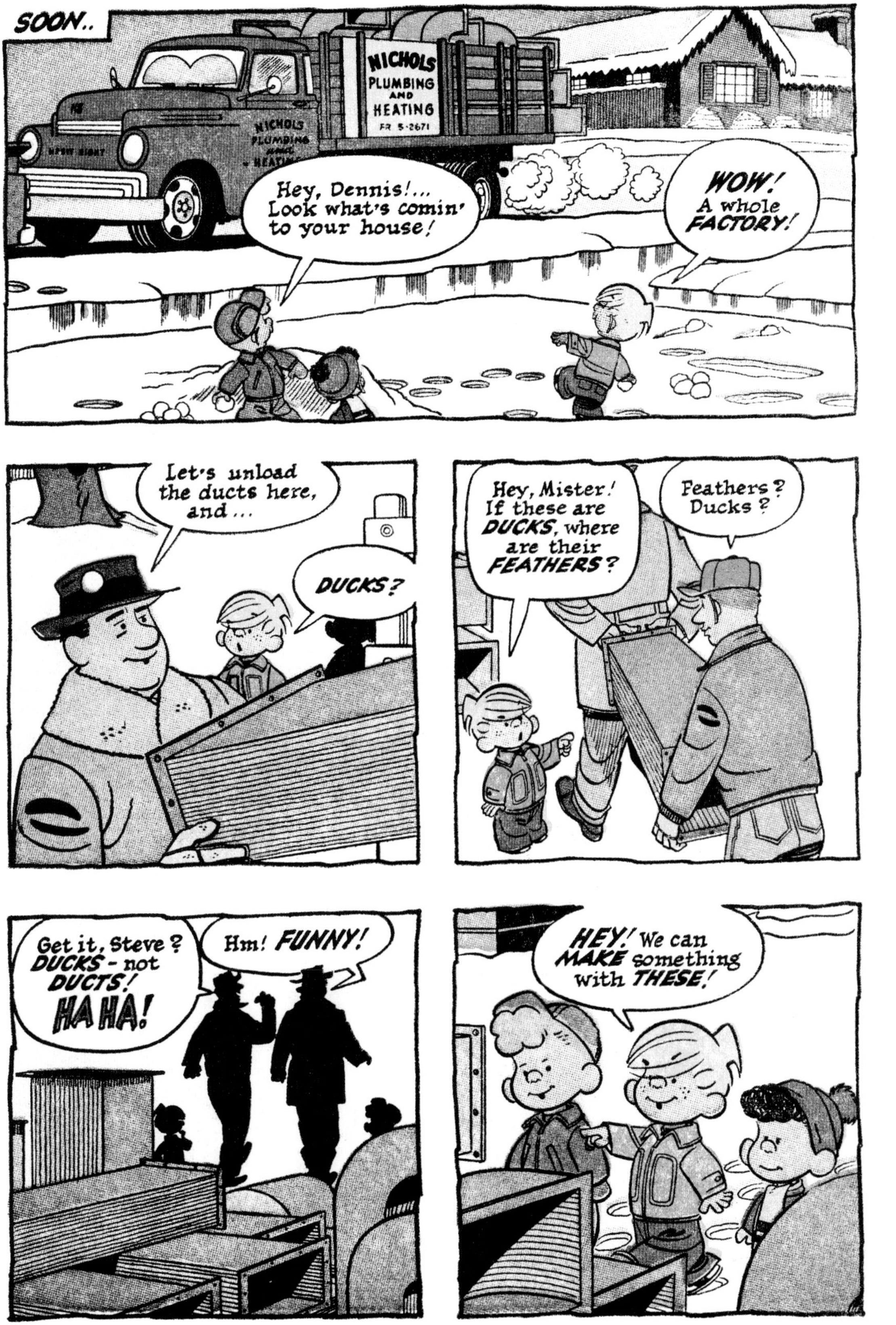
SOON..
NICHOLS PLUMBING AND HEATING FR 5-2671
Hey, Dennis!... Look what's comin' to your house!
WOW! A whole FACTORY!
Let's unload the ducts here, and ...
DUCKS?
Hey, Mister! If these are DUCKS, where are their FEATHERS?
Feathers? Ducks?
Get it, Steve? DUCKS - not DUCTS! HA HA!
Hm! FUNNY!
HEY! We can MAKE something with THESE!

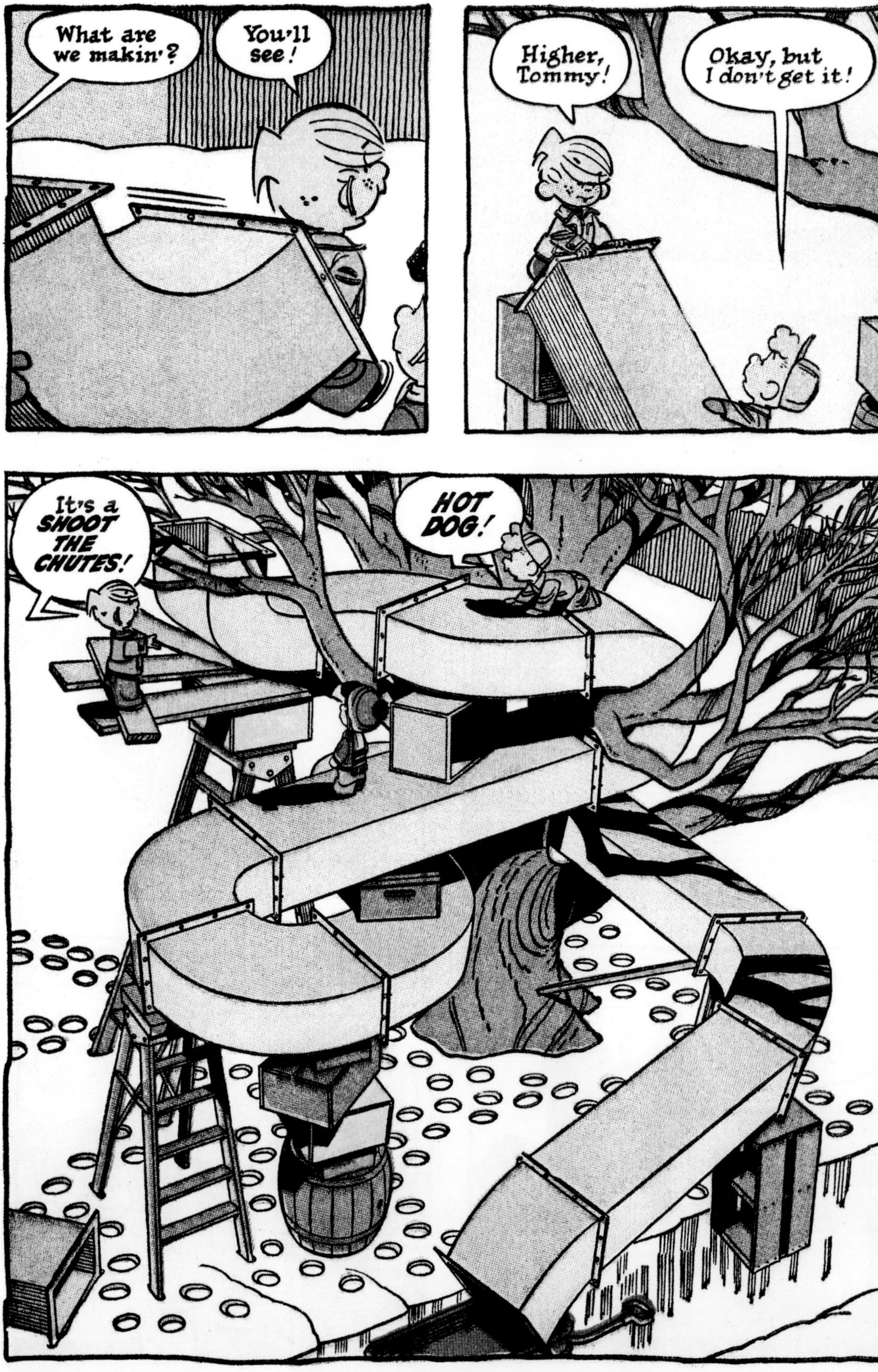

What are we makin'?
You'll see!
Higher, Tommy!
Okay, but I don't get it!
It's a SHOOT THE CHUTES!
HOT DOG!

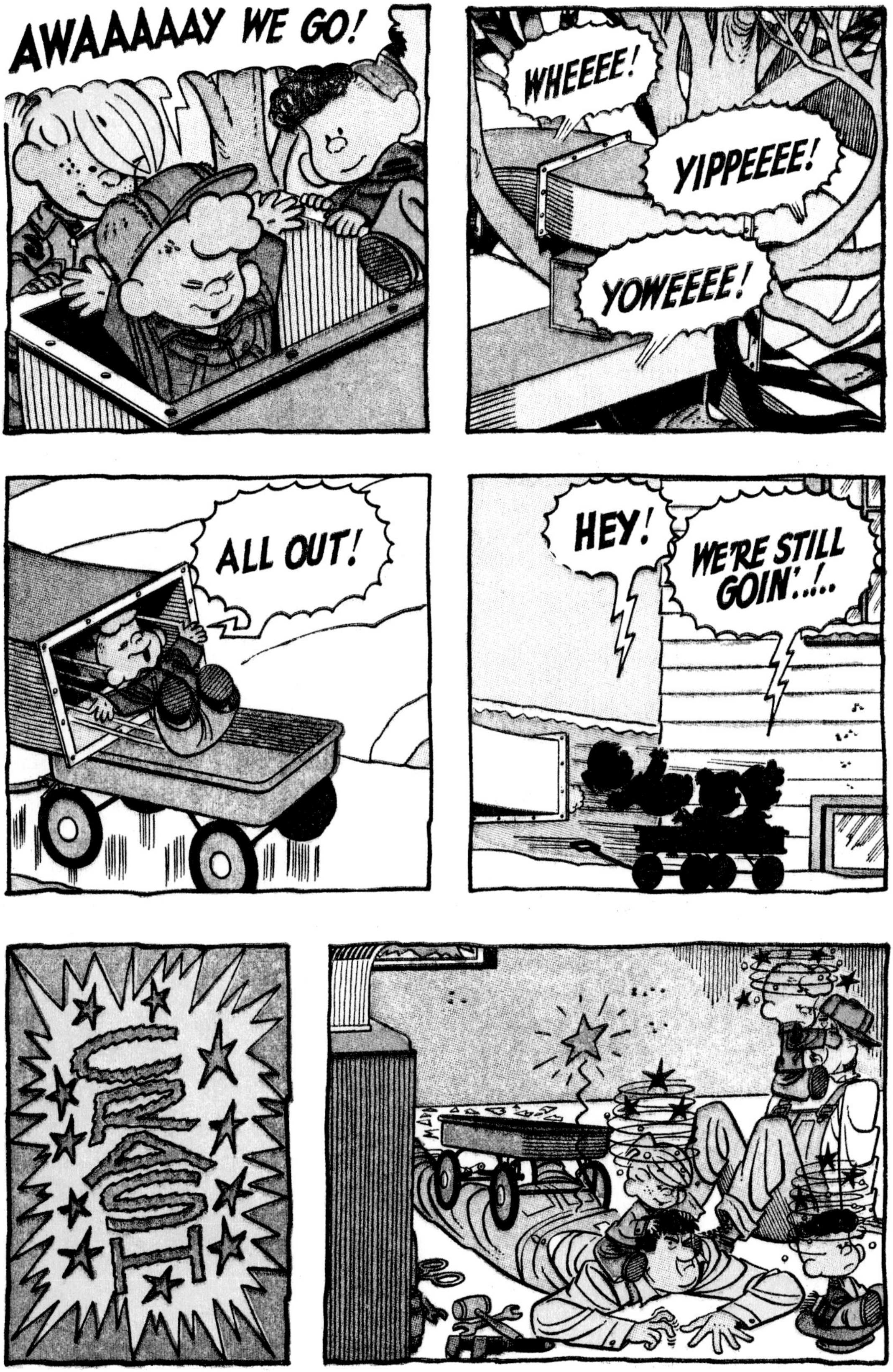
AWAAAAAY WE GO!
WHEEEE!
YIPPEEEE!
YOWEEEE!
ALL OUT!
HEY!
WE'RE STILL GOIN'..!..
CRASH

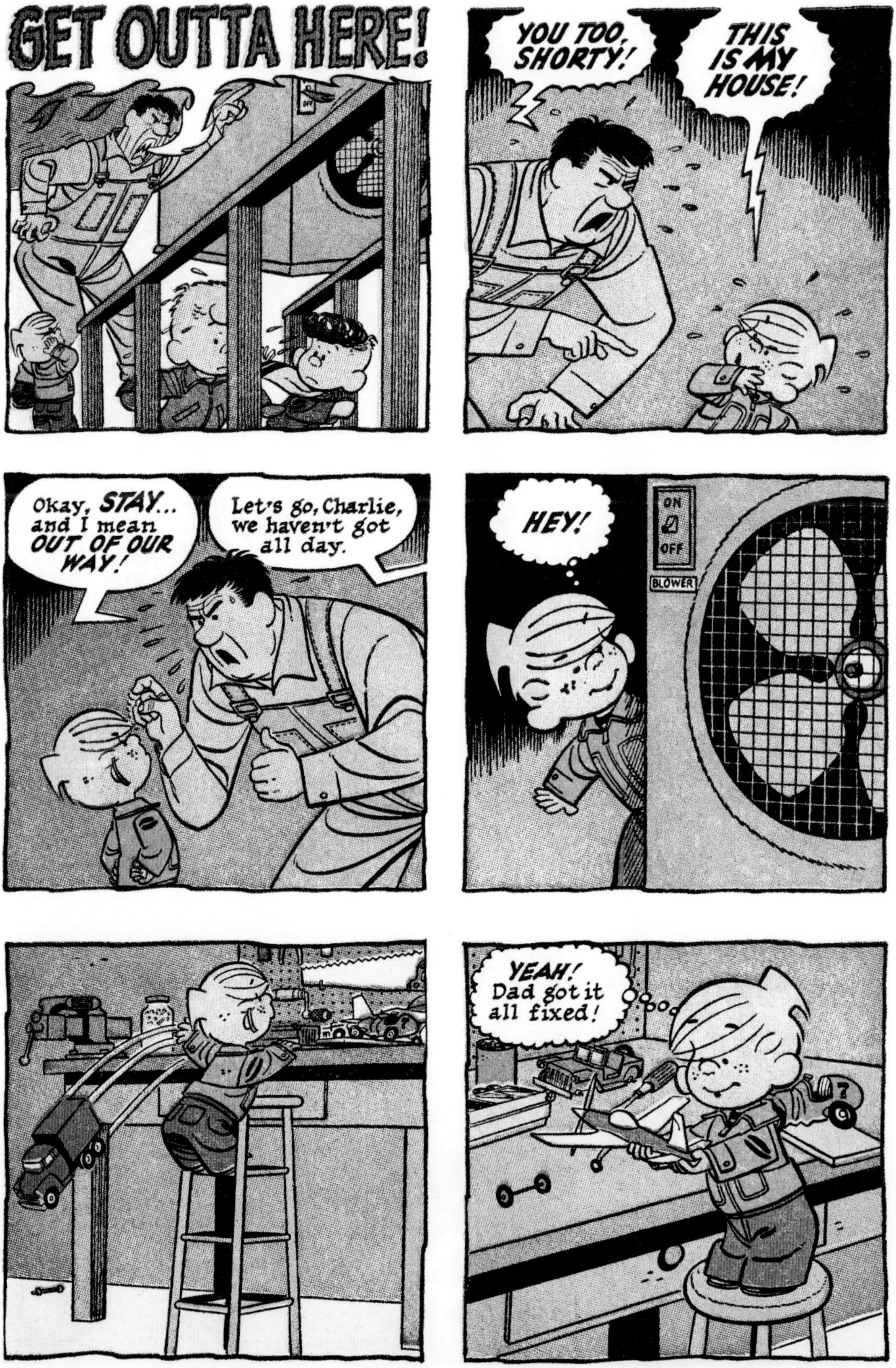
GET OUTTA HERE!
OFF
YOU TOO, SHORTY!
THIS IS MY HOUSE!
Okay, STAY... and I mean OUT OF OUR WAY!
Let's go, Charlie, we haven't got all day.
HEY!
ON
OFF
BLOWER
YEAH! Dad got it all fixed!

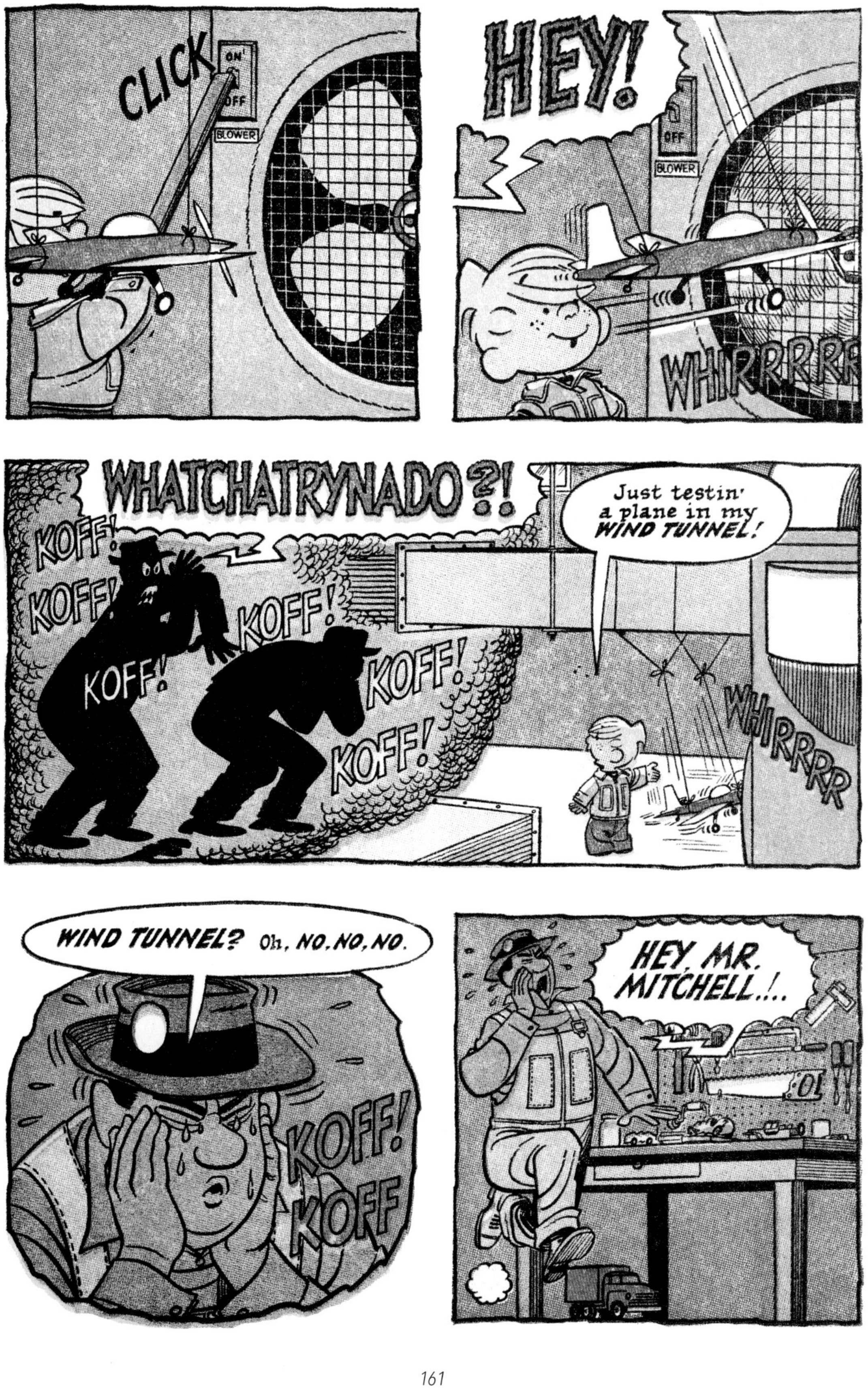
CLICK
ON
OFF
BLOWER
HEY!
OFF
BLOWER
WHIRRRRR
WHATCHATRYNADO?!
KOFF!
KOFF!
KOFF!
KOFF!
KOFF!
KOFF!
Just testin' a plane in my WIND TUNNEL!
WHIRRRRR
WIND TUNNEL? Oh, NO, NO, NO.
KOFF!
KOFF
HEY, MR. MITCHELL..!..

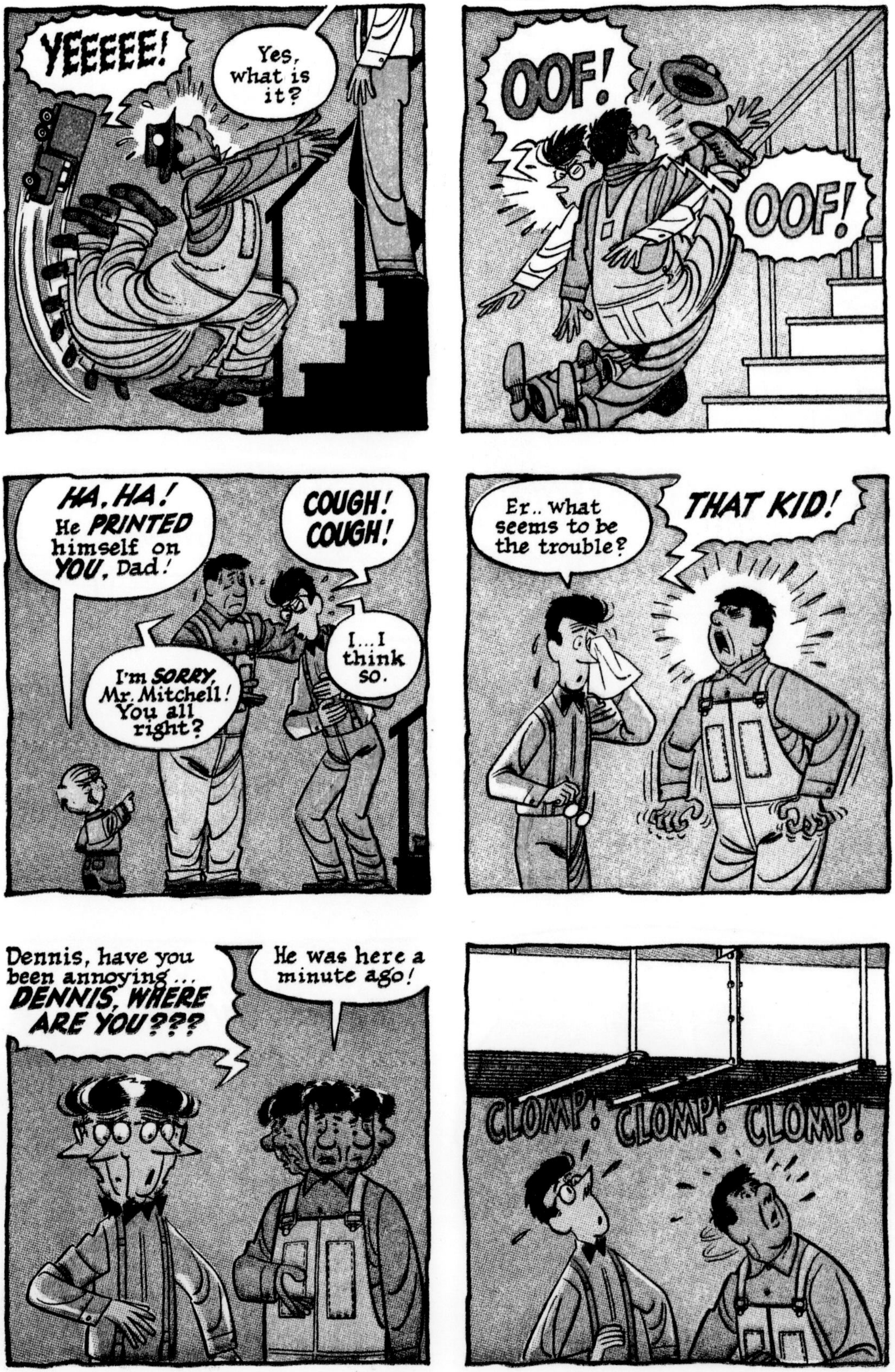
YEEEEE!
Yes, what is it?
OOF!
OOF!
HA, HA! He PRINTED himself on YOU, Dad!
COUGH! COUGH!
I'm SORRY, Mr. Mitchell! You all right?
I...I think so.
Er.. what seems to be the trouble?
THAT KID!
Dennis, have you been annoying ... DENNIS, WHERE ARE YOU???
He was here a minute ago!
CLOMP! CLOMP! CLOMP!

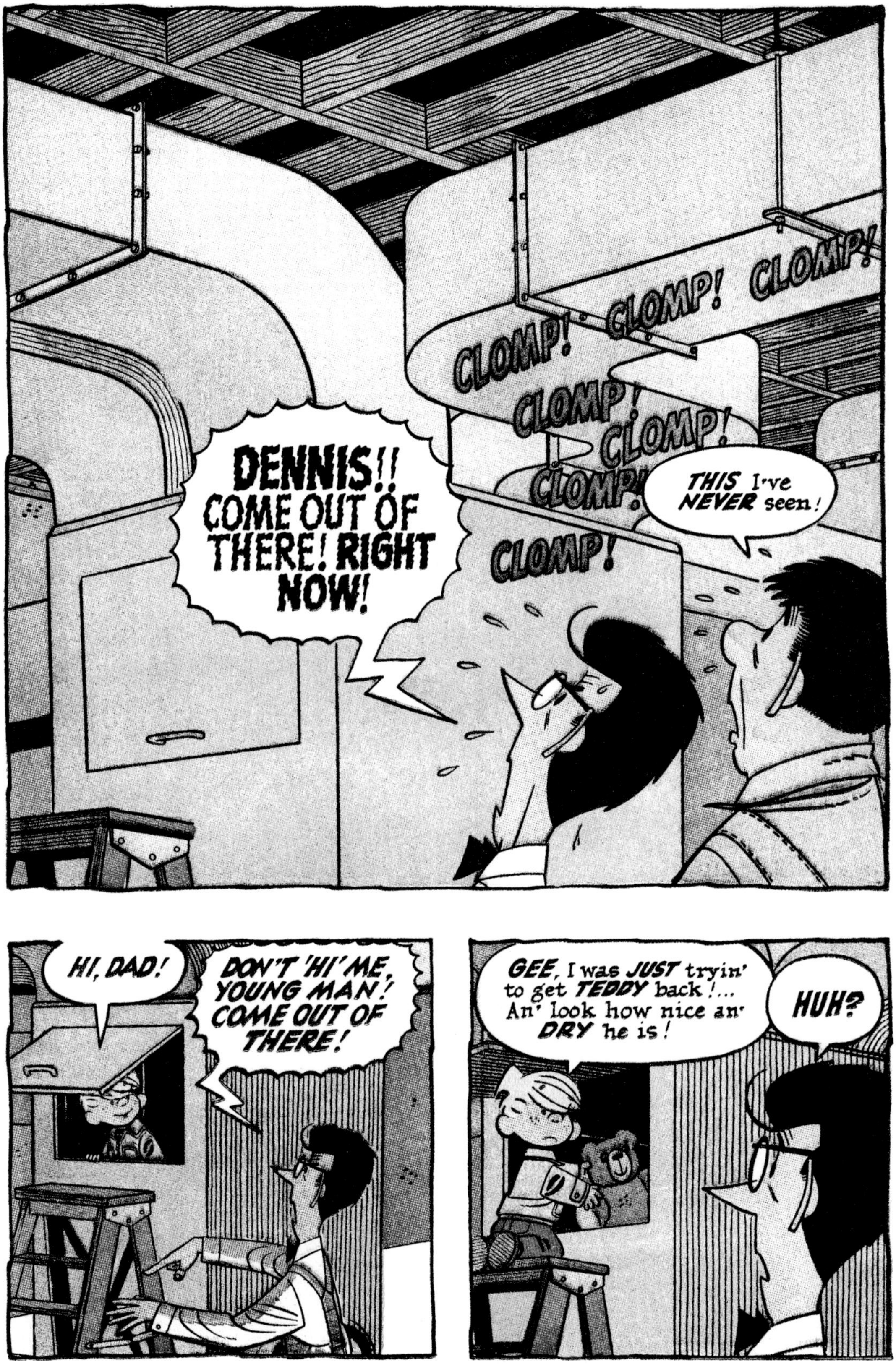

CLOMP! CLOMP! CLOMP!
CLOMP!
CLOMP!
CLOMP!
CLOMP!
DENNIS!! COME OUT OF THERE! RIGHT NOW!
THIS I've NEVER seen!
HI, DAD!
DON'T 'HI' ME, YOUNG MAN! COME OUT OF THERE!
GEE, I was JUST tryin' to get TEDDY back!... An' look how nice an' DRY he is!
HUH?

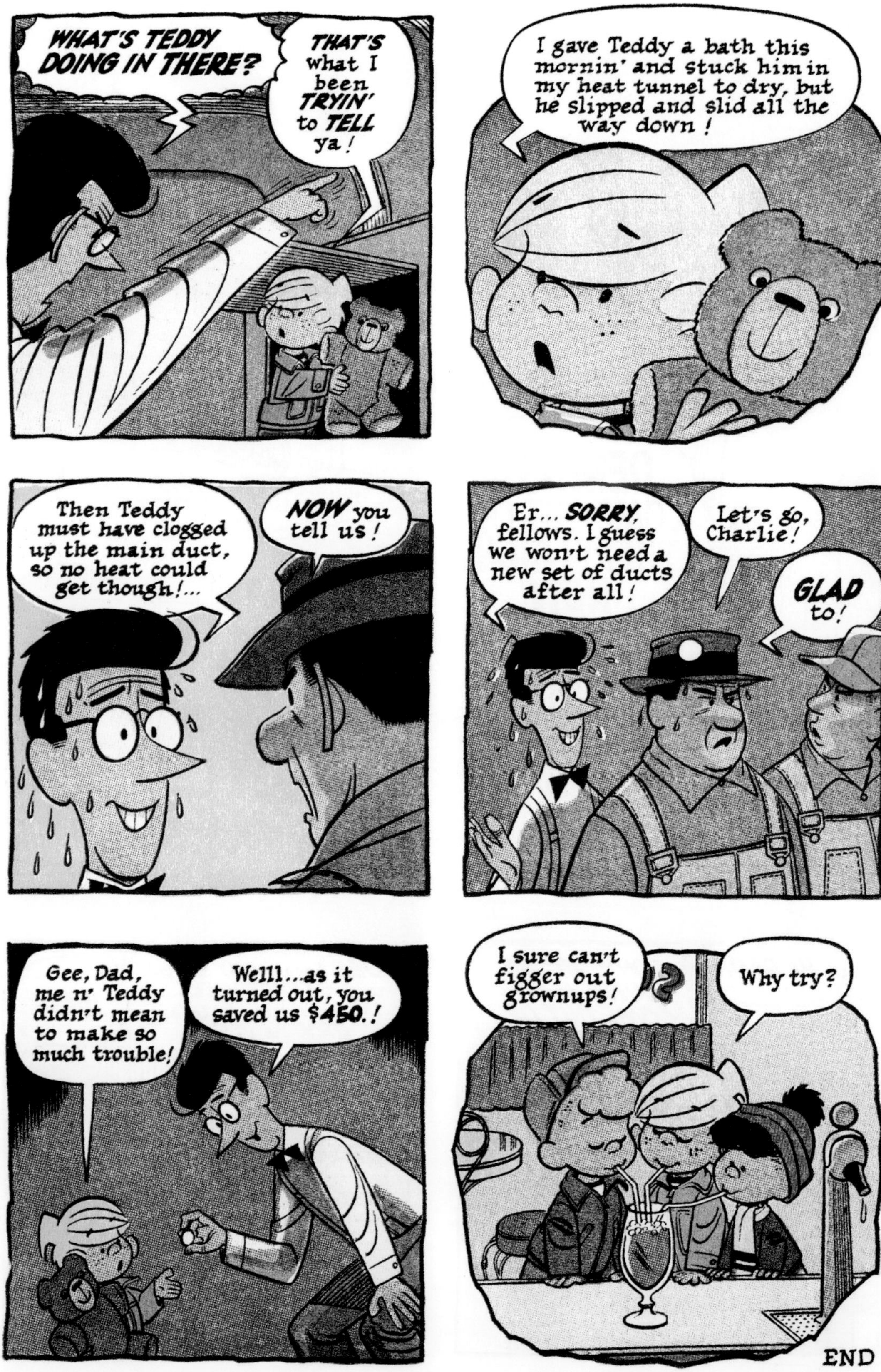
WHAT'S TEDDY DOING IN THERE?
THAT'S what I been TRYIN' to TELL ya!
I gave Teddy a bath this mornin' and stuck him in my heat tunnel to dry, but he slipped and slid all the way down!
Then Teddy must have clogged up the main duct, so no heat could get though!...
NOW you tell us!
Er... SORRY, fellows. I guess we won't need a new set of ducts after all!
Let's go, Charlie!
GLAD to!
Gee, Dad, me n' Teddy didn't mean to make so much trouble!
Welll...as it turned out, you saved us $450.!
I sure can't figger out grownups!
?
Why try?
END

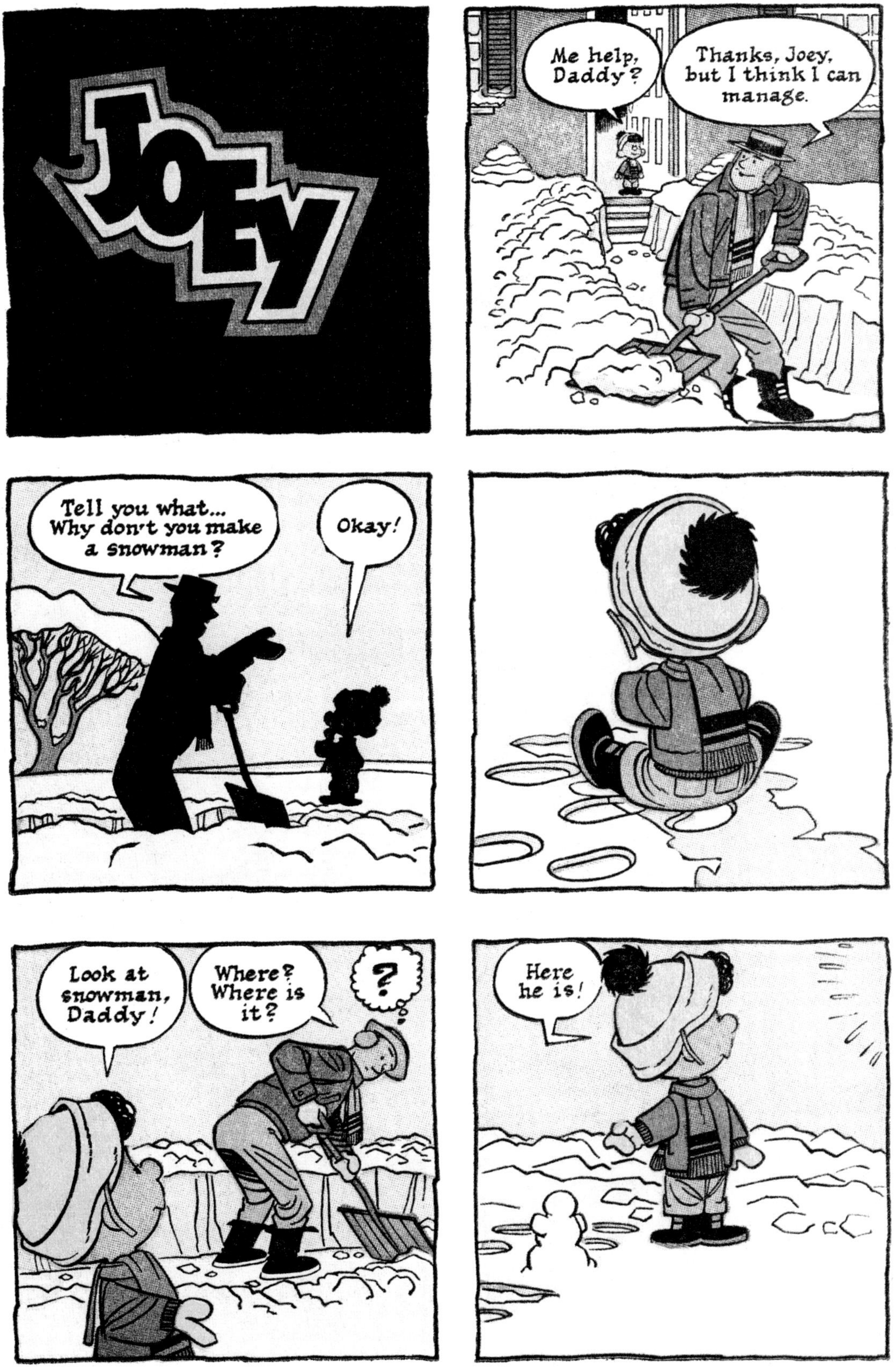
JOEY
Me help, Daddy?
Thanks, Joey, but I think I can manage.
Tell you what... Why don't you make a snowman?
Okay!
Look at snowman, Daddy!
Where? Where is it?
?
Here he is!

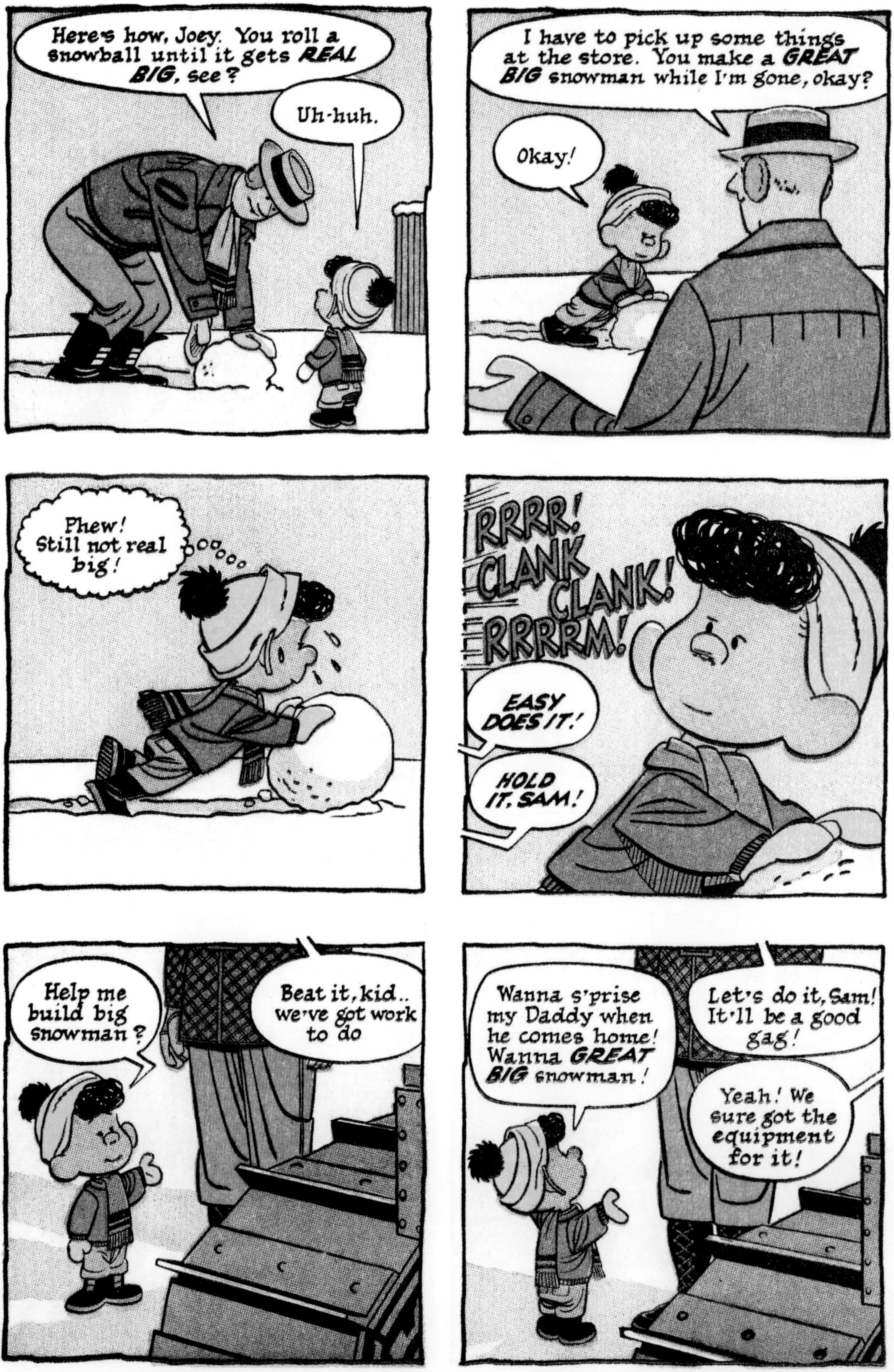
Here's how, Joey. You roll a snowball until it gets REAL BIG, see?
Uh-huh.
I have to pick up some things at the store. You make a GREAT BIG snowman while I'm gone, okay?
Okay!
Phew! Still not real big!
RRRR! CLANK CLANK! RRRRM!
EASY DOES IT!
HOLD IT, SAM!
Help me build big snowman?
Beat it, kid.. we've got work to do
Wanna s'prise my Daddy when he comes home! Wanna GREAT BIG snowman!
Let's do it, Sam! It'll be a good gag!
Yeah! We sure got the equipment for it!

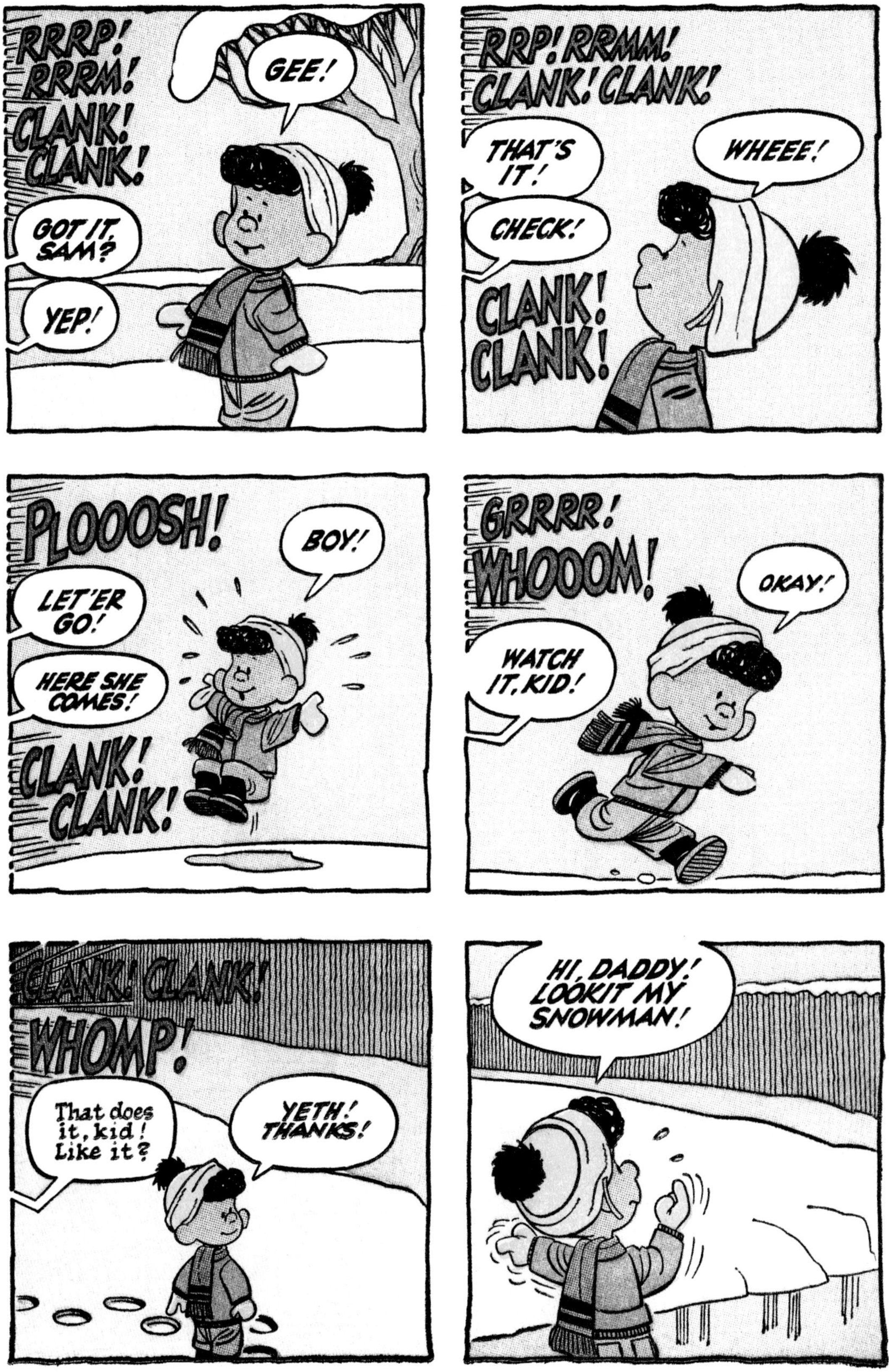
RRRP! RRRM! CLANK! CLANK!
GEE!
GOT IT, SAM?
YEP!
RRP! RRMM! CLANK! CLANK!
THAT'S IT!
WHEEE!
CHECK!
CLANK! CLANK!
PLOOOSH!
BOY!
LET'ER GO!
HERE SHE COMES!
CLANK! CLANK!
GRRRR! WHOOOM!
OKAY!
WATCH IT, KID!
CLANK! CLANK! WHOMP!
That does it, kid! Like it?
YETH! THANKS!
HI, DADDY! LOOKIT MY SNOWMAN!

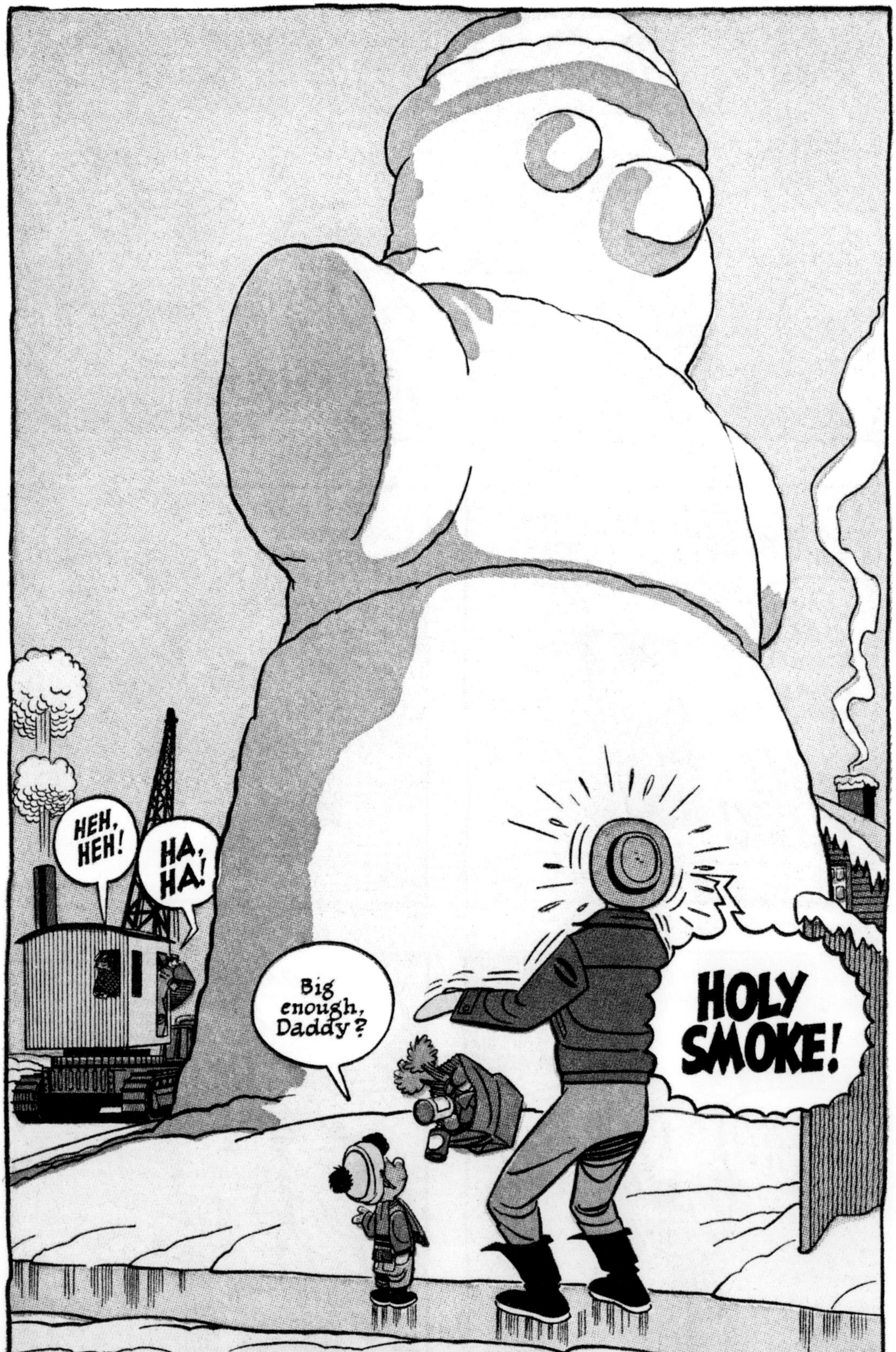
HEH, HEH!
HA, HA!
Big enough, Daddy?
HOLY SMOKE!
END

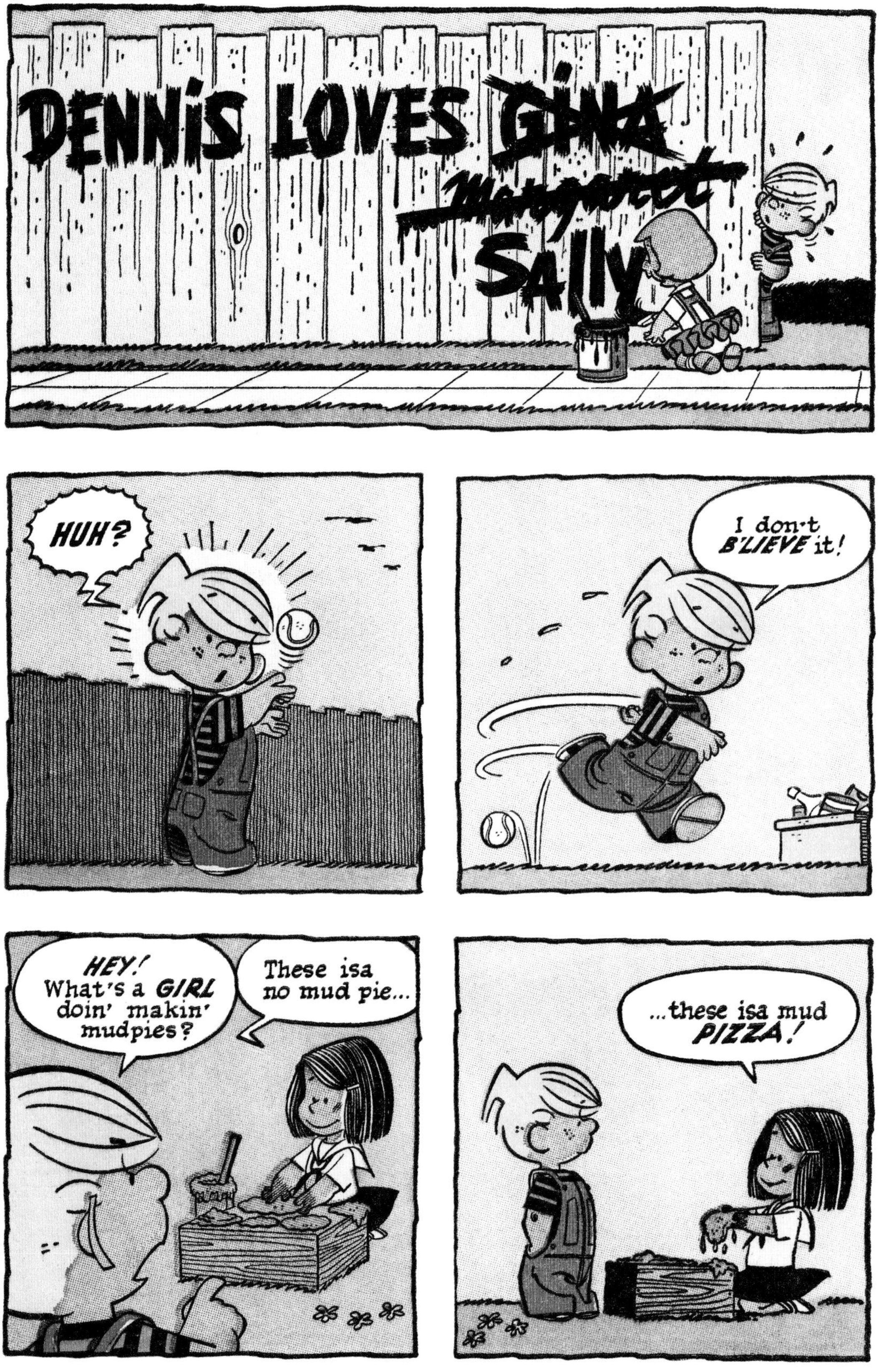
DENNIS LOVES GINA
Margaret
SALLY
HUH?
I don't B'LIEVE it!
HEY! What's a GIRL doin' makin' mudpies?
These isa no mud pie...
...these isa mud PIZZA!

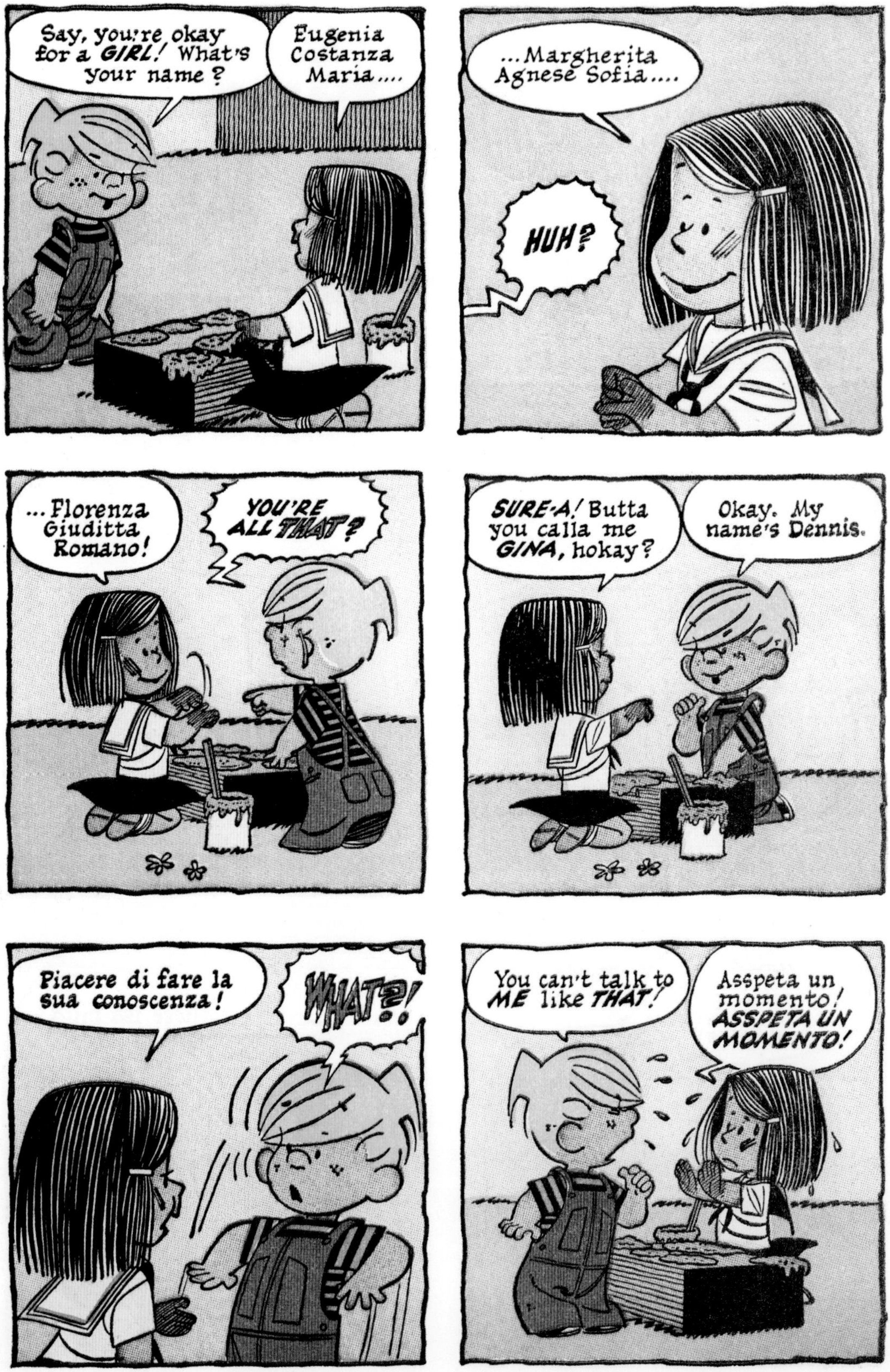

Say, you're okay for a GIRL! What's your name?
Eugenia Costanza Maria....
...Margherita Agnese Sofia....
HUH?
...Florenza Giuditta Romano!
YOU'RE ALL THAT?
SURE-A! Butta you calla me GINA, hokay?
Okay. My name's Dennis.
Piacere di fare la sua conoscenza!
WHAT?!
You can't talk to ME like THAT!
Asspeta un momento! ASSPETA UN MOMENTO!

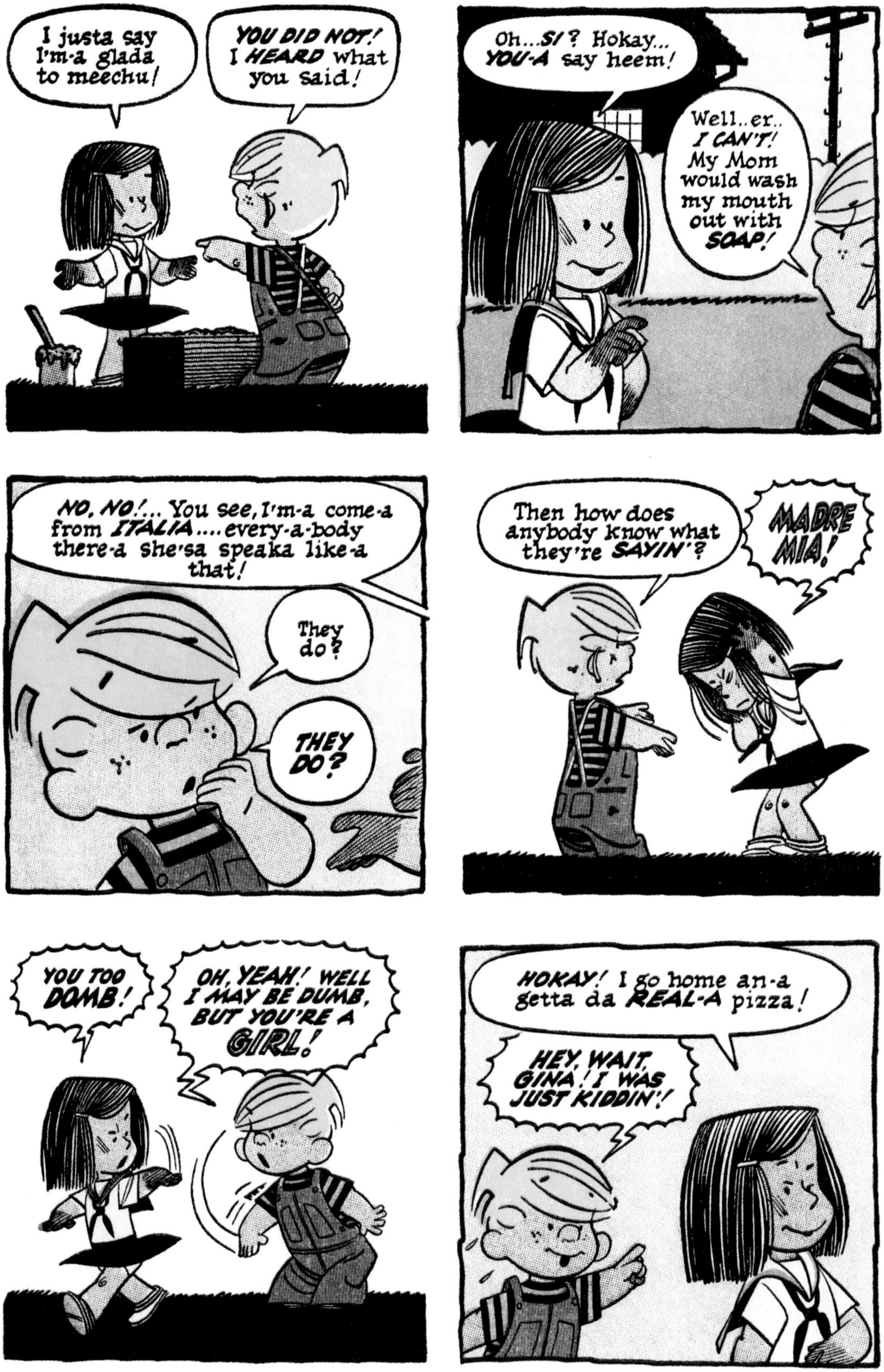
I justa say I'm-a glada to meechu!
YOU DID NOT! I HEARD what you said!
Oh...SI? Hokay... YOU-A say heem!
Well..er.. I CAN'T! My Mom would wash my mouth out with SOAP!
NO, NO!... You see, I'm-a come-a from ITALIA....every-a-body there-a she'sa speaka like-a that!
They do?
THEY DO?
Then how does anybody know what they're SAYIN'?
MADRE MIA!
YOU TOO DOMB!
OH, YEAH! WELL I MAY BE DUMB, BUT YOU'RE A GIRL!
HOKAY! I go home an-a getta da REAL-A pizza!
HEY, WAIT, GINA! I WAS JUST KIDDIN'!

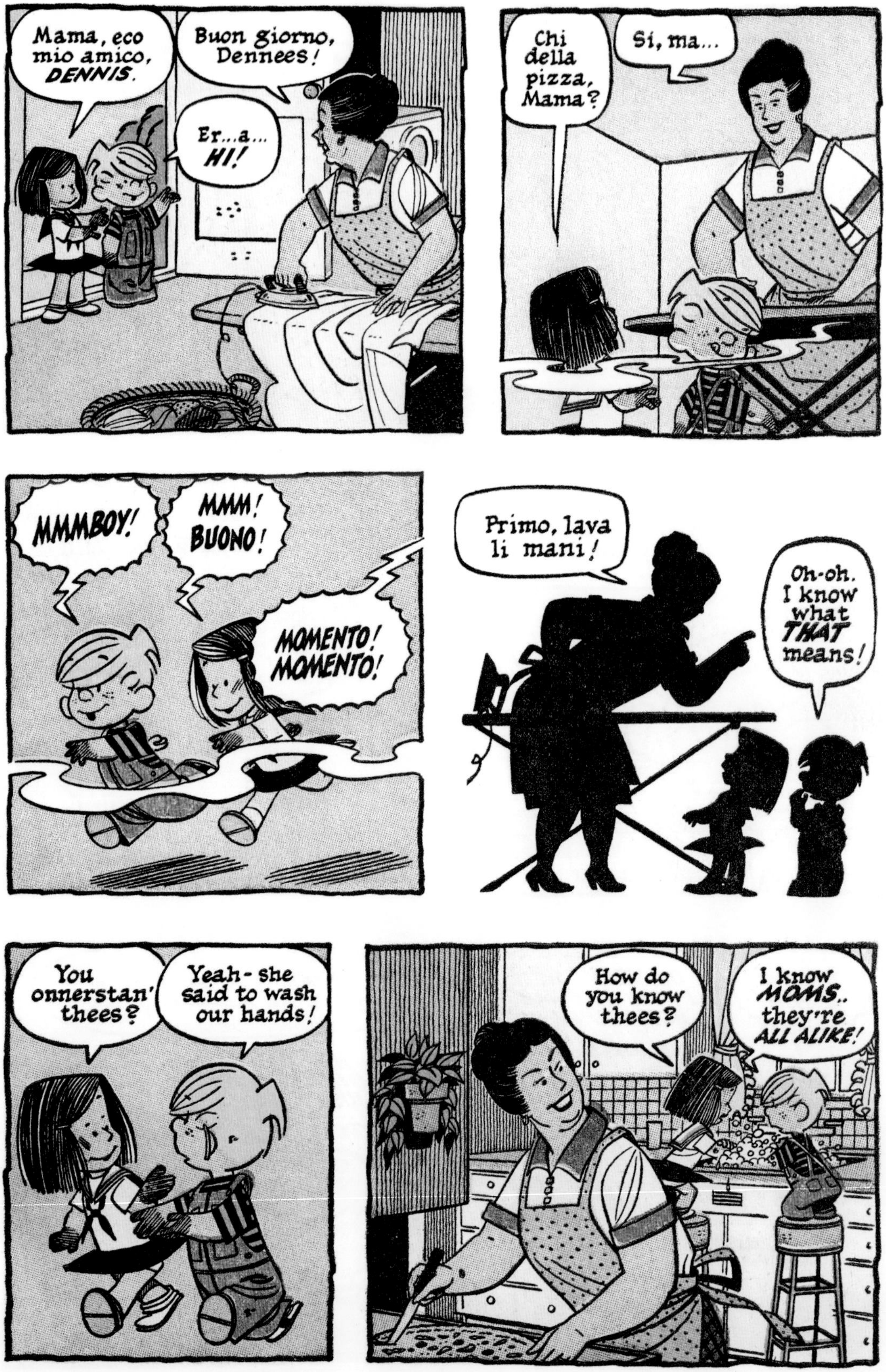

Mama, eco mio amico, DENNIS.
Buon giorno, Dennees!
Er...a... HI!
Chi della pizza, Mama?
Si, ma...
MMMBOY!
MMM! BUONO!
MOMENTO! MOMENTO!
Primo, lava li mani!
Oh-oh. I know what THAT means!
You onnerstan' thees?
Yeah - she said to wash our hands!
How do you know thees?
I know MOMS.. they're ALL ALIKE!

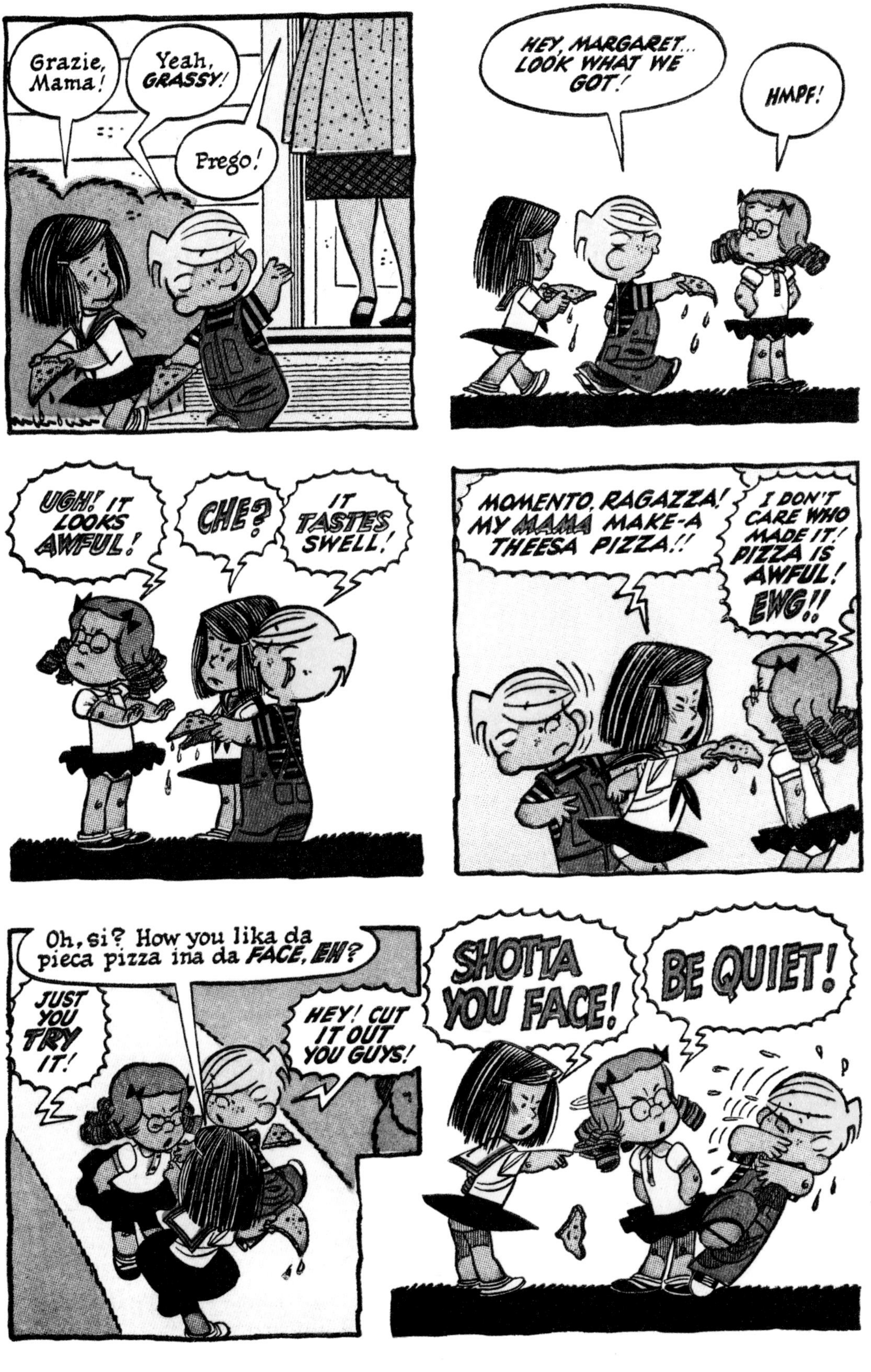
Grazie, Mama!
Yeah, GRASSY!
Prego!
HEY, MARGARET... LOOK WHAT WE GOT!
HMPF!
UGH! IT LOOKS AWFUL!
CHE?
IT TASTES SWELL!
MOMENTO, RAGAZZA! MY MAMA MAKE-A THEESA PIZZA!!
I DON'T CARE WHO MADE IT! PIZZA IS AWFUL! EWG!!
Oh, si? How you lika da pieca pizza ina da FACE, EH?
JUST YOU TRY IT!
HEY! CUT IT OUT YOU GUYS!
SHOTTA YOU FACE!
BE QUIET!

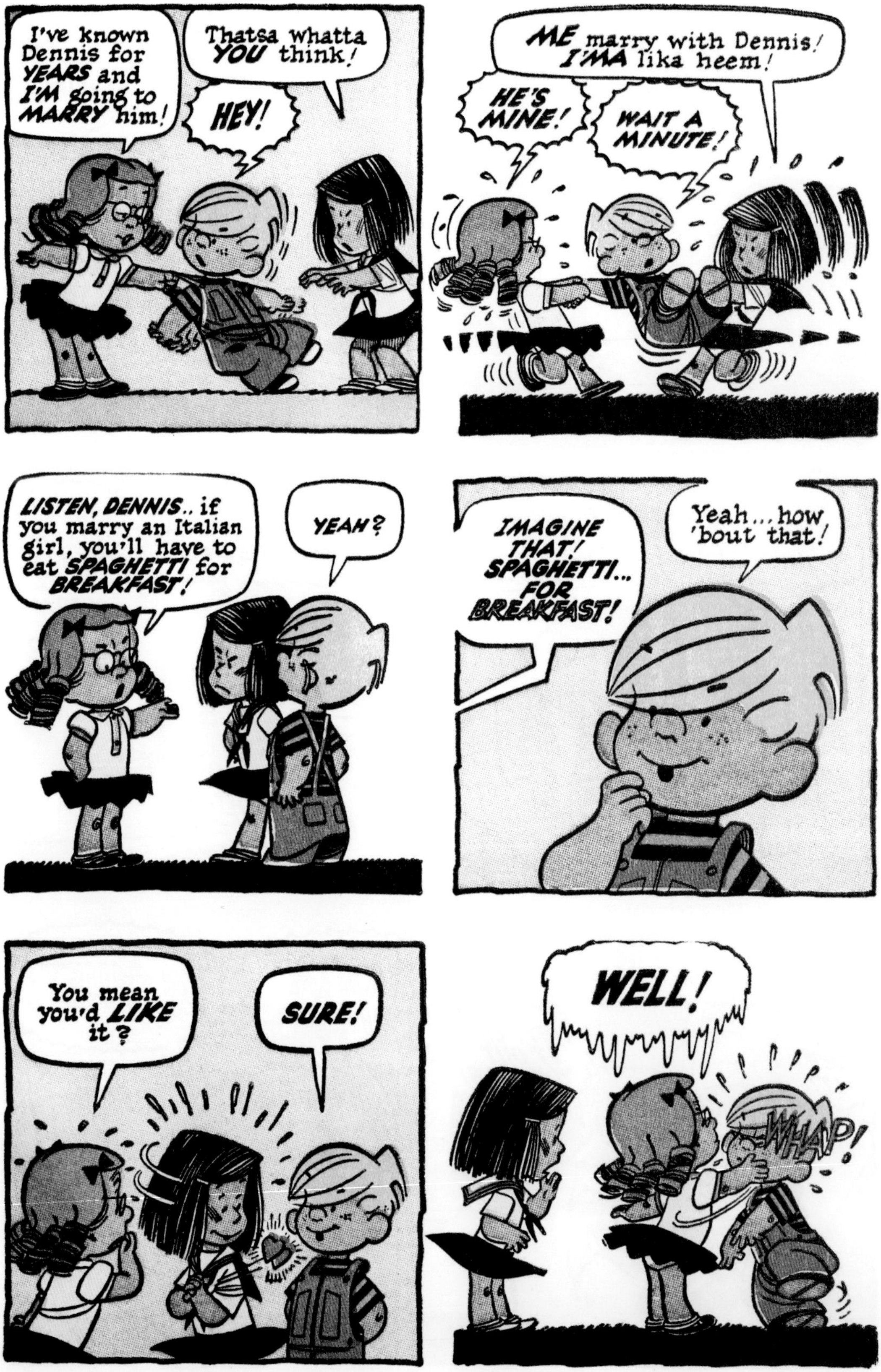
I've known Dennis for YEARS and I'M going to MARRY him!
HEY!
Thatsa whatta YOU think!
ME marry with Dennis! I'MA lika heem!
HE'S MINE!
WAIT A MINUTE!
LISTEN, DENNIS.. if you marry an Italian girl, you'll have to eat SPAGHETTI for BREAKFAST!
YEAH?
IMAGINE THAT! SPAGHETTI... FOR BREAKFAST!
Yeah... how 'bout that!
You mean you'd LIKE it?
SURE!
WELL!
WHAP!

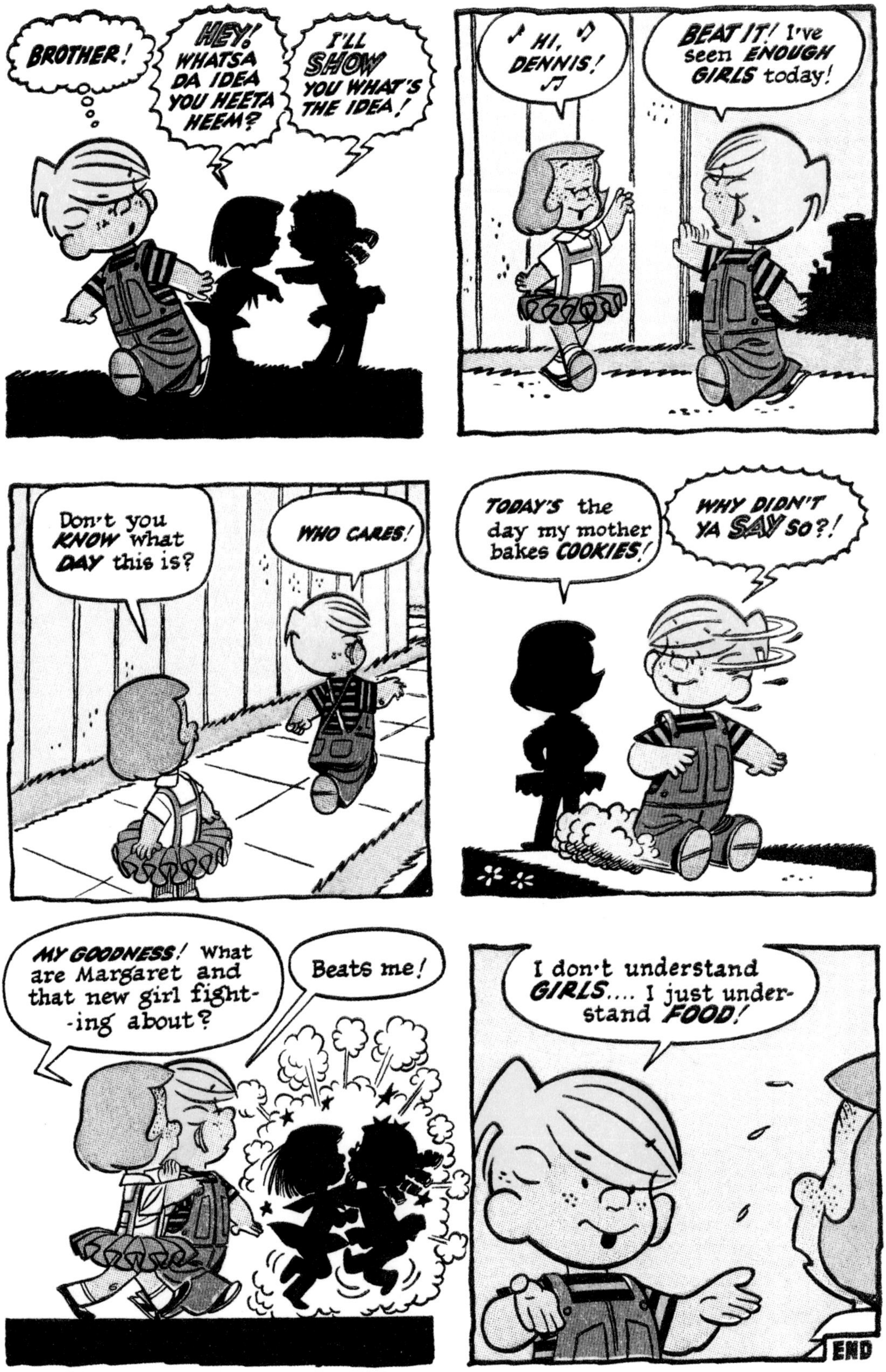
BROTHER!
HEY! WHATSA DA IDEA YOU HEETA HEEM?
I'LL SHOW YOU WHAT'S THE IDEA!
HI, DENNIS!
BEAT IT! I've seen ENOUGH GIRLS today!
Don't you KNOW what DAY this is?
WHO CARES!
TODAY'S the day my mother bakes COOKIES!
WHY DIDN'T YA SAY SO?!
MY GOODNESS! What are Margaret and that new girl fight- -ing about?
Beats me!
I don't understand GIRLS.... I just under- stand FOOD!
END

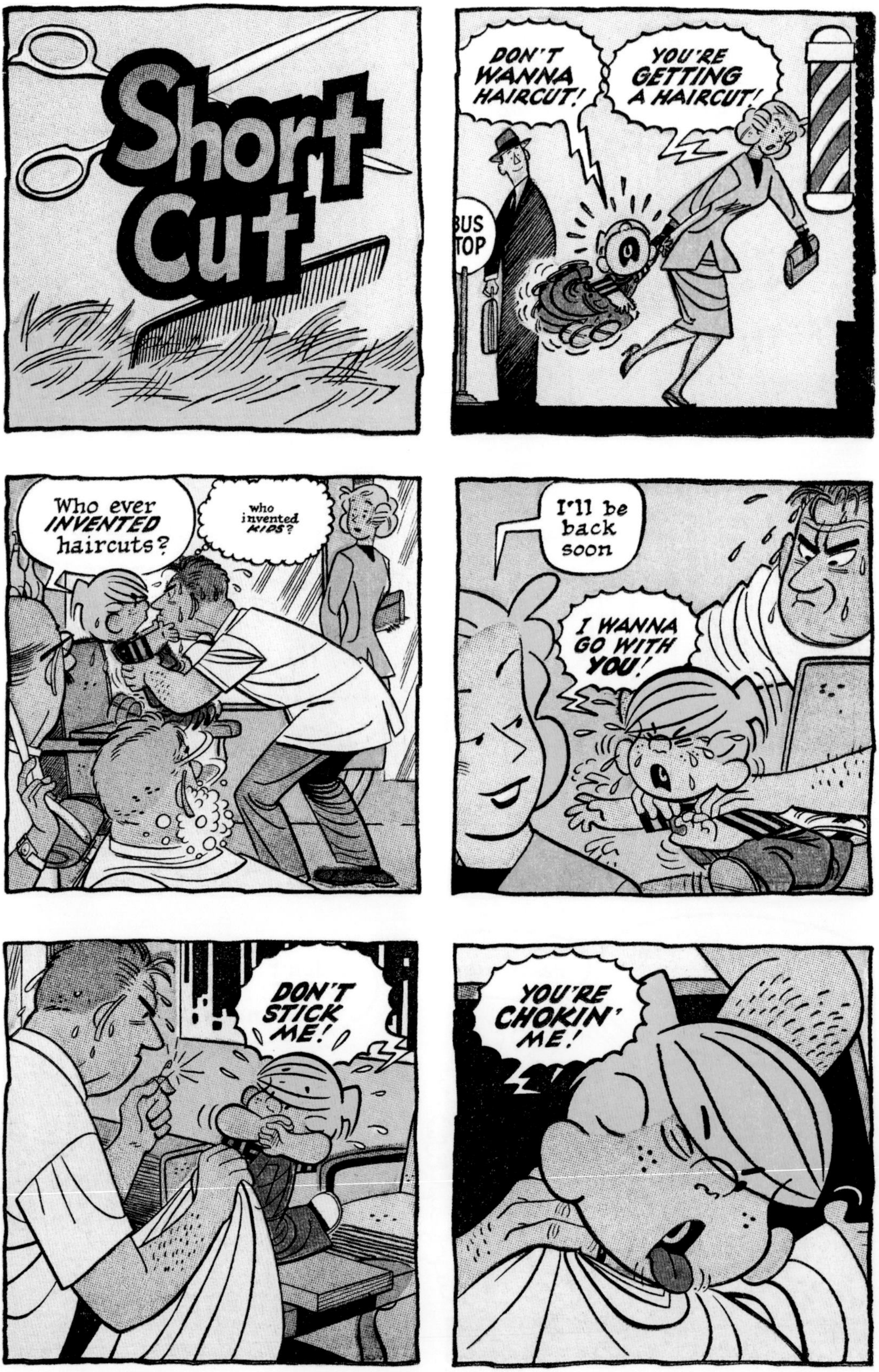
Short Cut
DON'T WANNA HAIRCUT!
YOU'RE GETTING A HAIRCUT!
BUS
TOP
Who ever INVENTED haircuts?
who invented KIDS?
I'll be back soon
I WANNA GO WITH YOU!
DON'T STICK ME!
YOU'RE CHOKIN' ME!

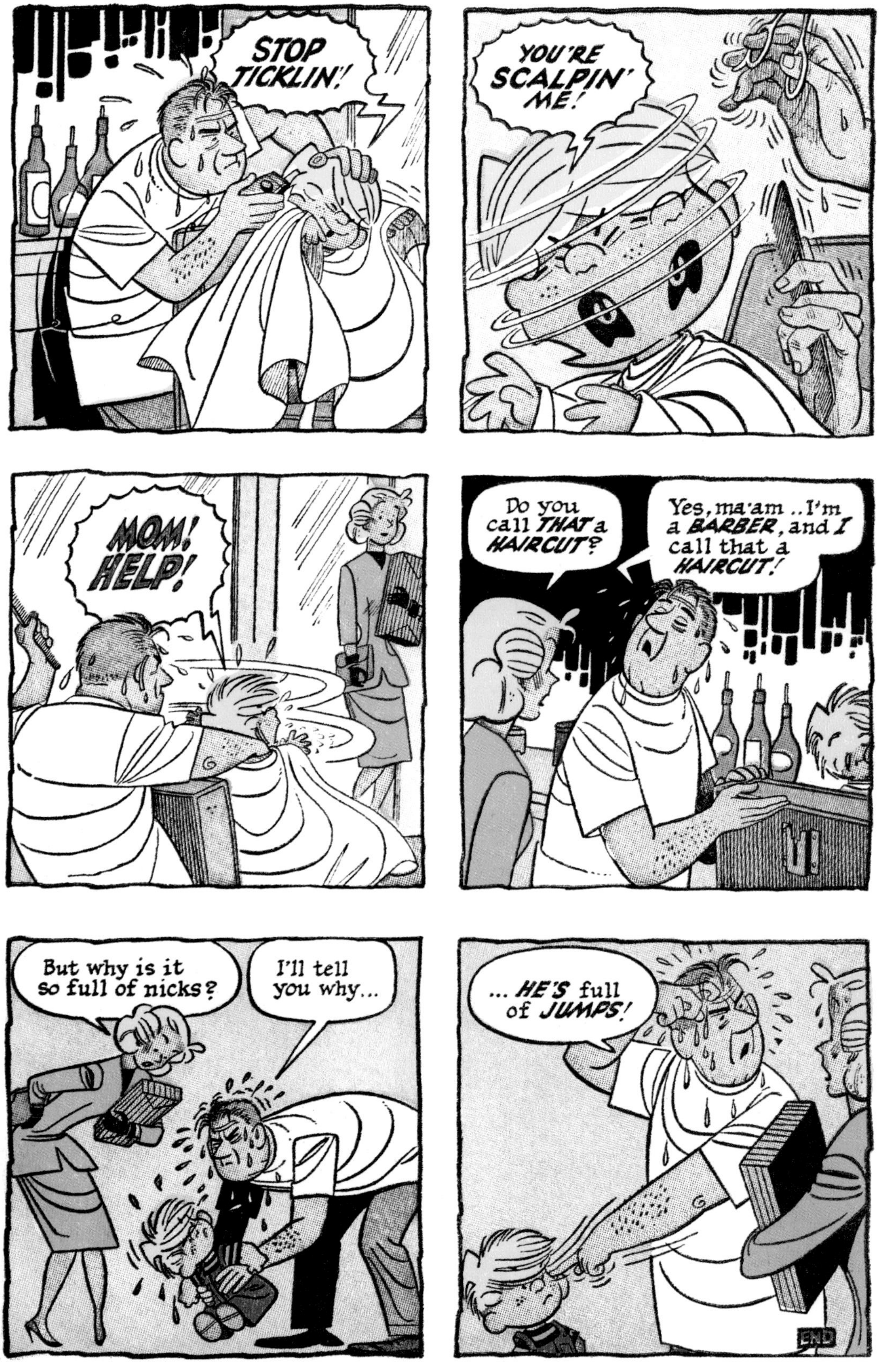
STOP TICKLIN'!
YOU'RE SCALPIN' ME!
MOM! HELP!
Do you call THAT a HAIRCUT?
Yes, ma'am ..I'm a BARBER, and I call that a HAIRCUT!
But why is it so full of nicks?
I'll tell you why...
... HE'S full of JUMPS!
END

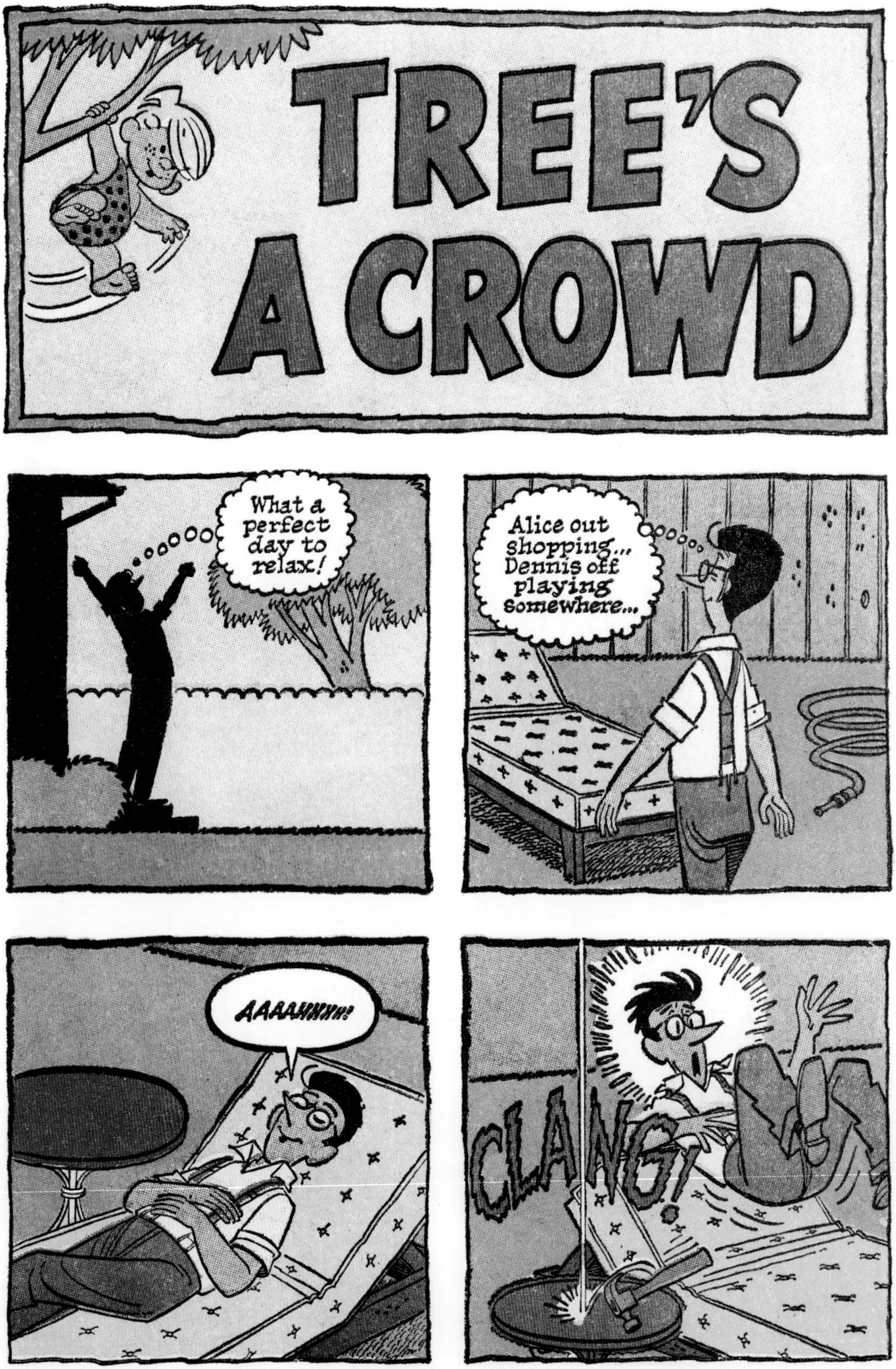
TREE'S A CROWD
What a perfect day to relax!
Alice out shopping... Dennis off playing somewhere...
AAAAHHH!
CLANG!

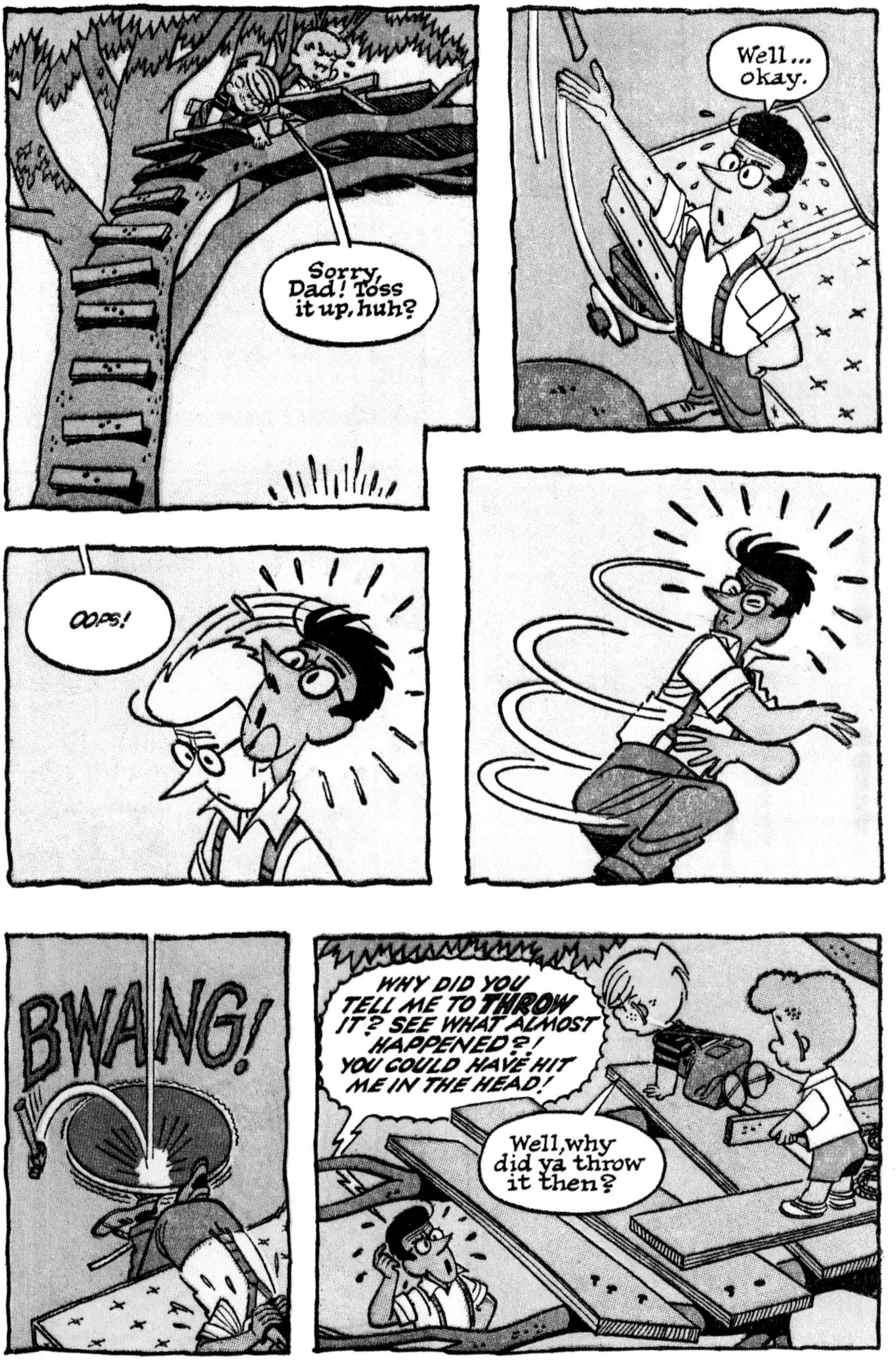
Sorry, Dad! Toss it up, huh?
Well... okay.
OOPS!
BWANG!
WHY DID YOU TELL ME TO THROW IT? SEE WHAT ALMOST HAPPENED?! YOU COULD HAVE HIT ME IN THE HEAD!
Well, why did ya throw it then?

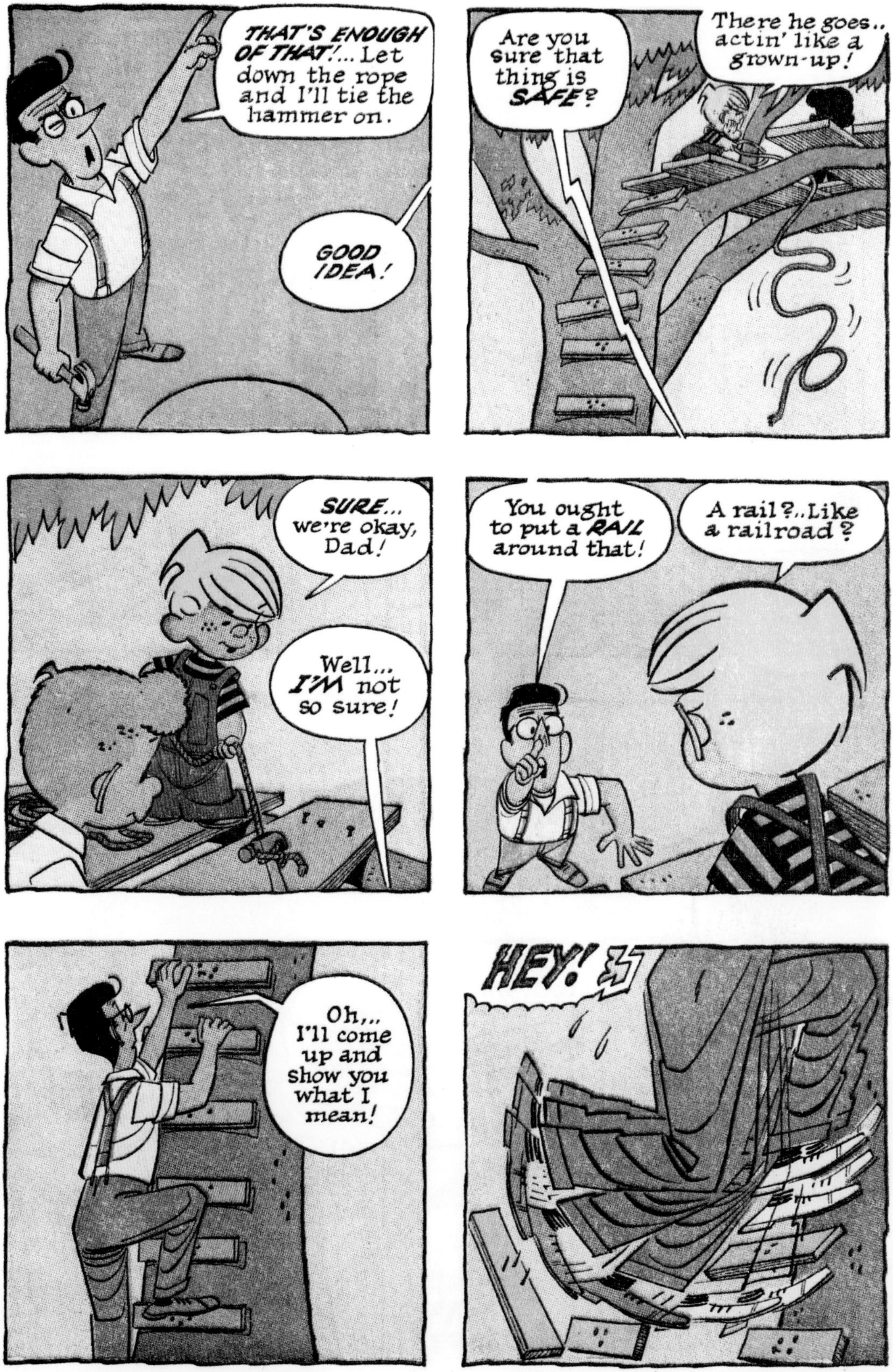
THAT'S ENOUGH OF THAT!... Let down the rope and I'll tie the hammer on.
GOOD IDEA!
Are you sure that thing is SAFE?
There he goes.. actin' like a grown-up!
SURE... we're okay, Dad!
Well... I'M not so sure!
You ought to put a RAIL around that!
A rail?..Like a railroad?
Oh,.. I'll come up and show you what I mean!
HEY!

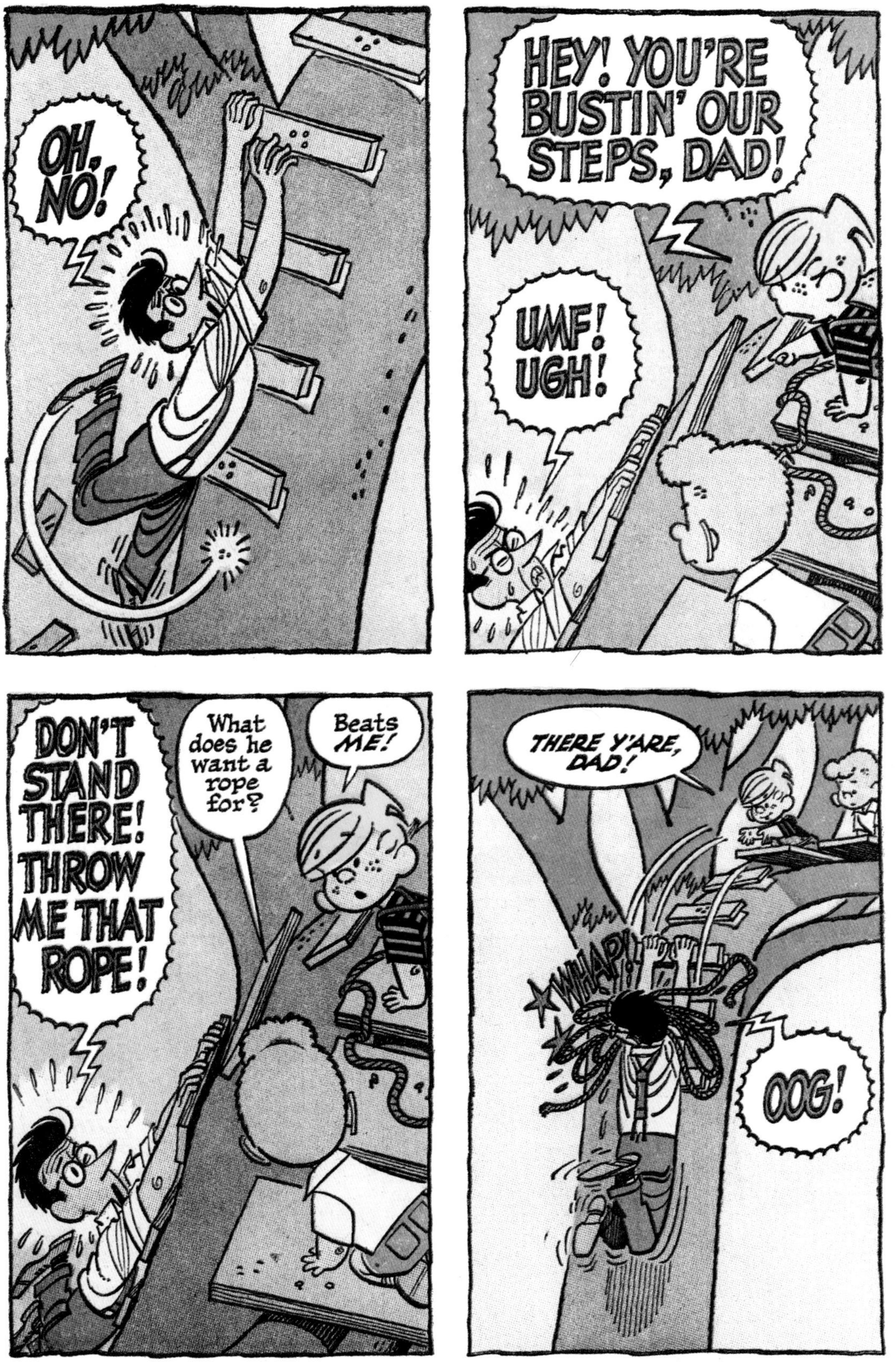
OH, NO!
HEY! YOU'RE BUSTIN' OUR STEPS, DAD!
UMF! UGH!
DON'T STAND THERE! THROW ME THAT ROPE!
What does he want a rope for?
Beats ME!
THERE Y'ARE, DAD!
WHAP!
OOG!

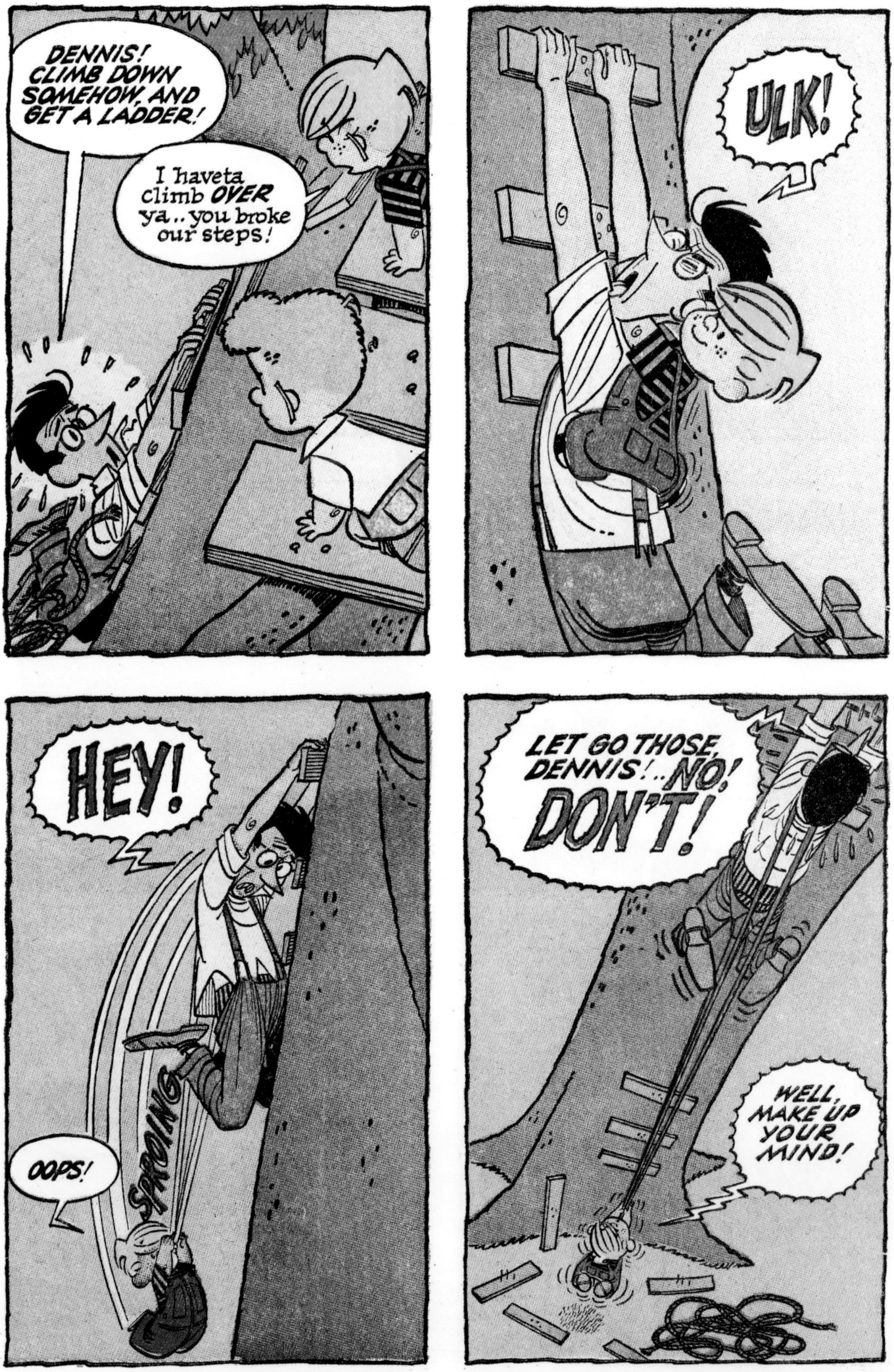
DENNIS! CLIMB DOWN SOMEHOW, AND GET A LADDER!
I haveta climb OVER ya.. you broke our steps!
ULK!
HEY!
OOPS!
SPROING
LET GO THOSE, DENNIS!.. NO! DON'T!
WELL, MAKE UP YOUR MIND!

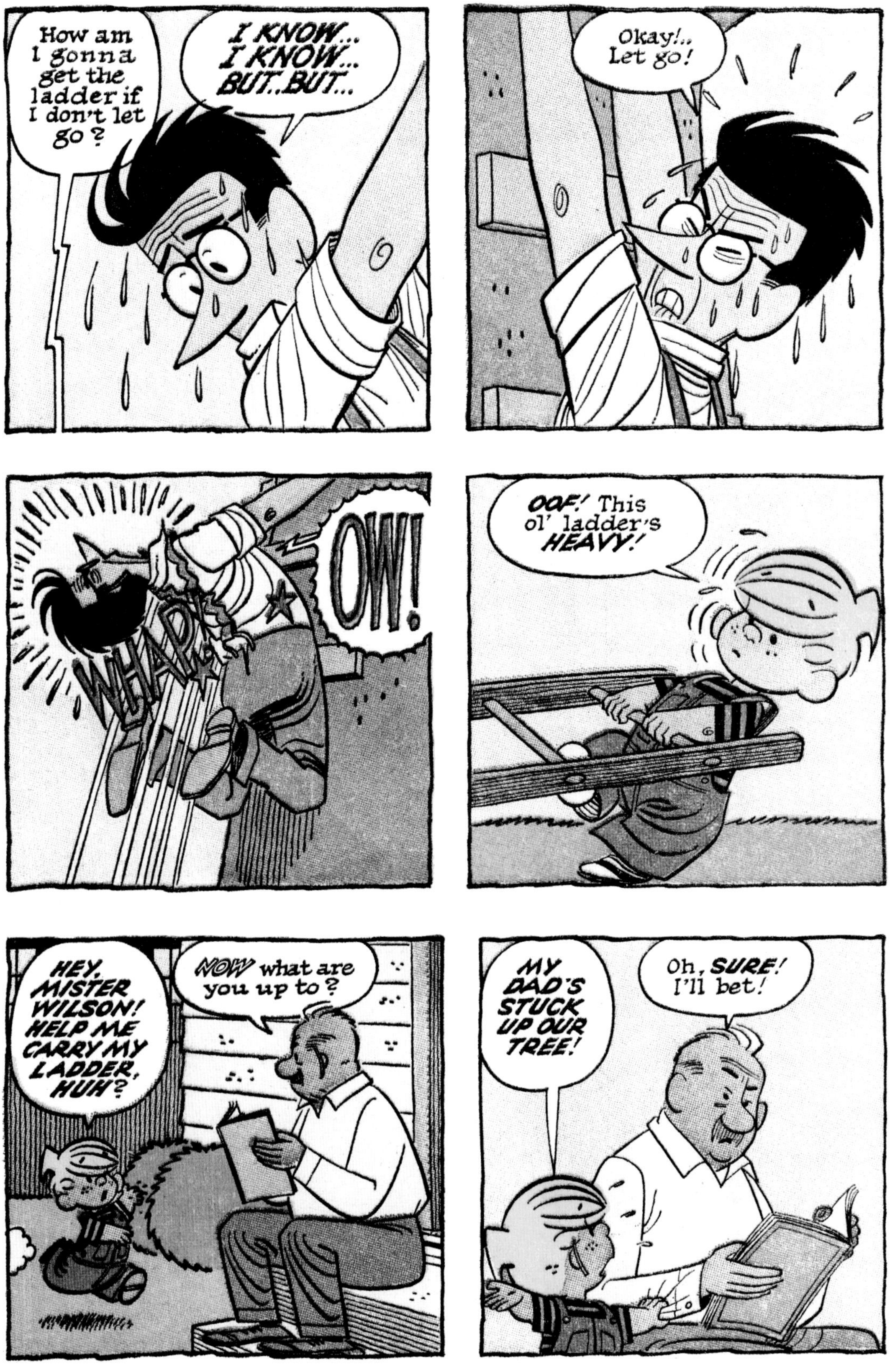
How am I gonna get the ladder if I don't let go?
I KNOW... I KNOW... BUT..BUT...
Okay!.. Let go!
WHAP!
OW!
OOF! This ol' ladder's HEAVY!
HEY, MISTER WILSON! HELP ME CARRY MY LADDER, HUH?
NOW what are you up to?
MY DAD'S STUCK UP OUR TREE!
Oh, SURE! I'll bet!

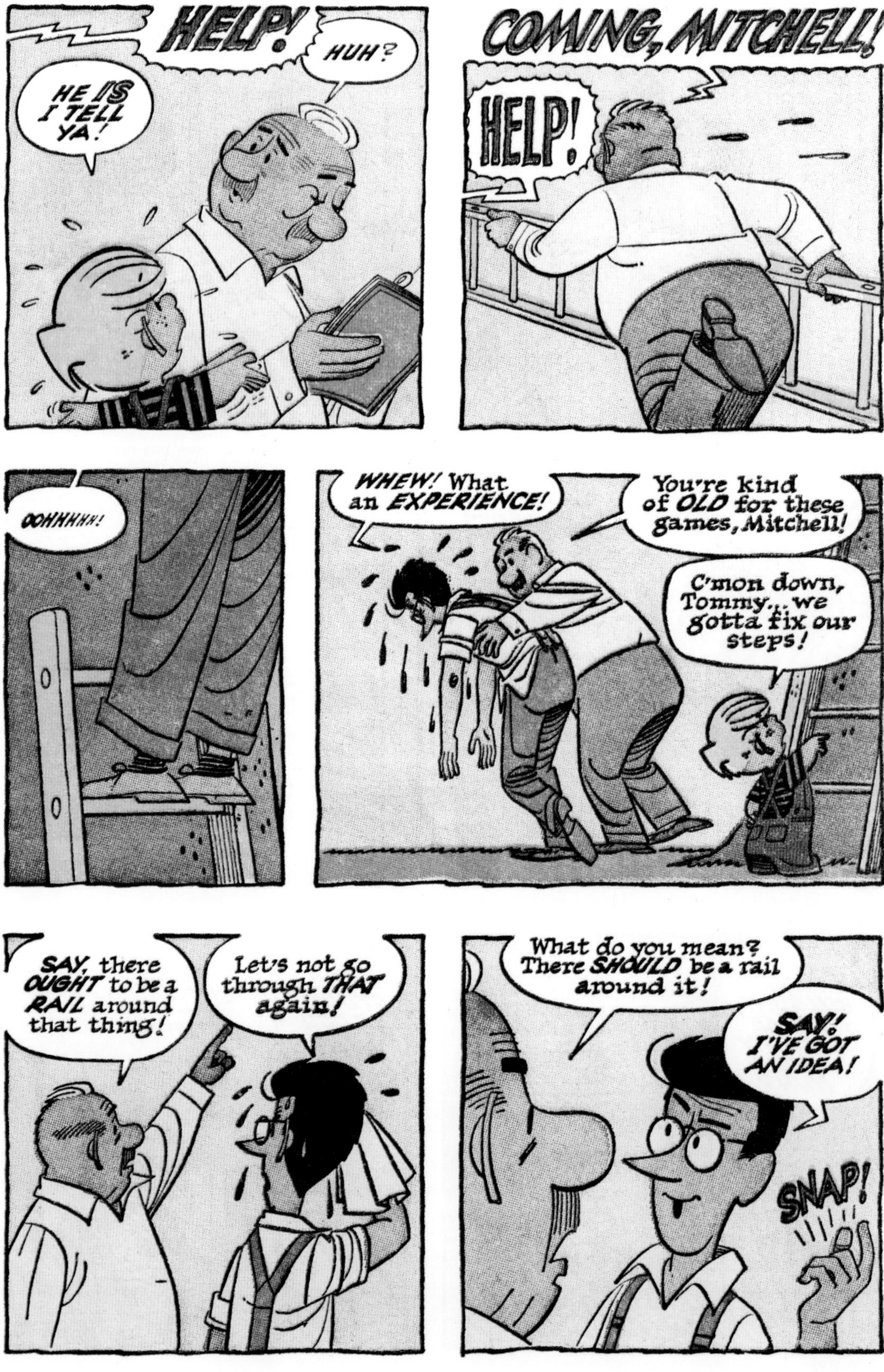
HELP!
HUH?
HE IS I TELL YA!
COMING, MITCHELL!
HELP!
OOHHHHH!
WHEW! What an EXPERIENCE!
You're kind of OLD for these games, Mitchell!
C'mon down, Tommy... we gotta fix our steps!
SAY, there OUGHT to be a RAIL around that thing!
Let's not go through THAT again!
What do you mean? There SHOULD be a rail around it!
SAY! I'VE GOT AN IDEA!
SNAP!

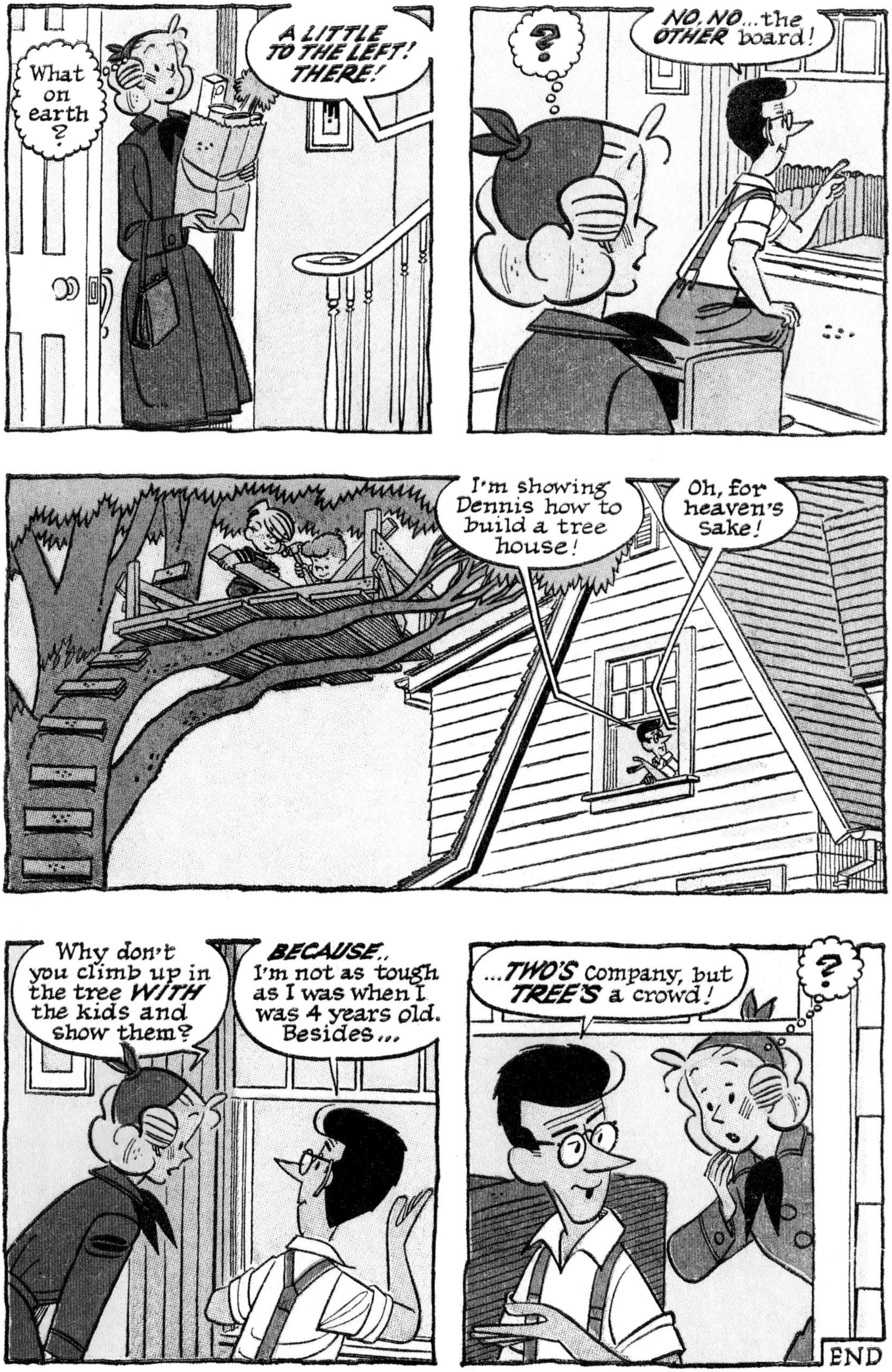
What on earth?
A LITTLE TO THE LEFT! THERE!
?
NO, NO... the OTHER board!
I'm showing Dennis how to build a tree house!
Oh, for heaven's sake!
Why don't you climb up in the tree WITH the kids and show them?
BECAUSE.. I'm not as tough as I was when I was 4 years old. Besides...
...TWO'S company, but TREE'S a crowd!
?
END

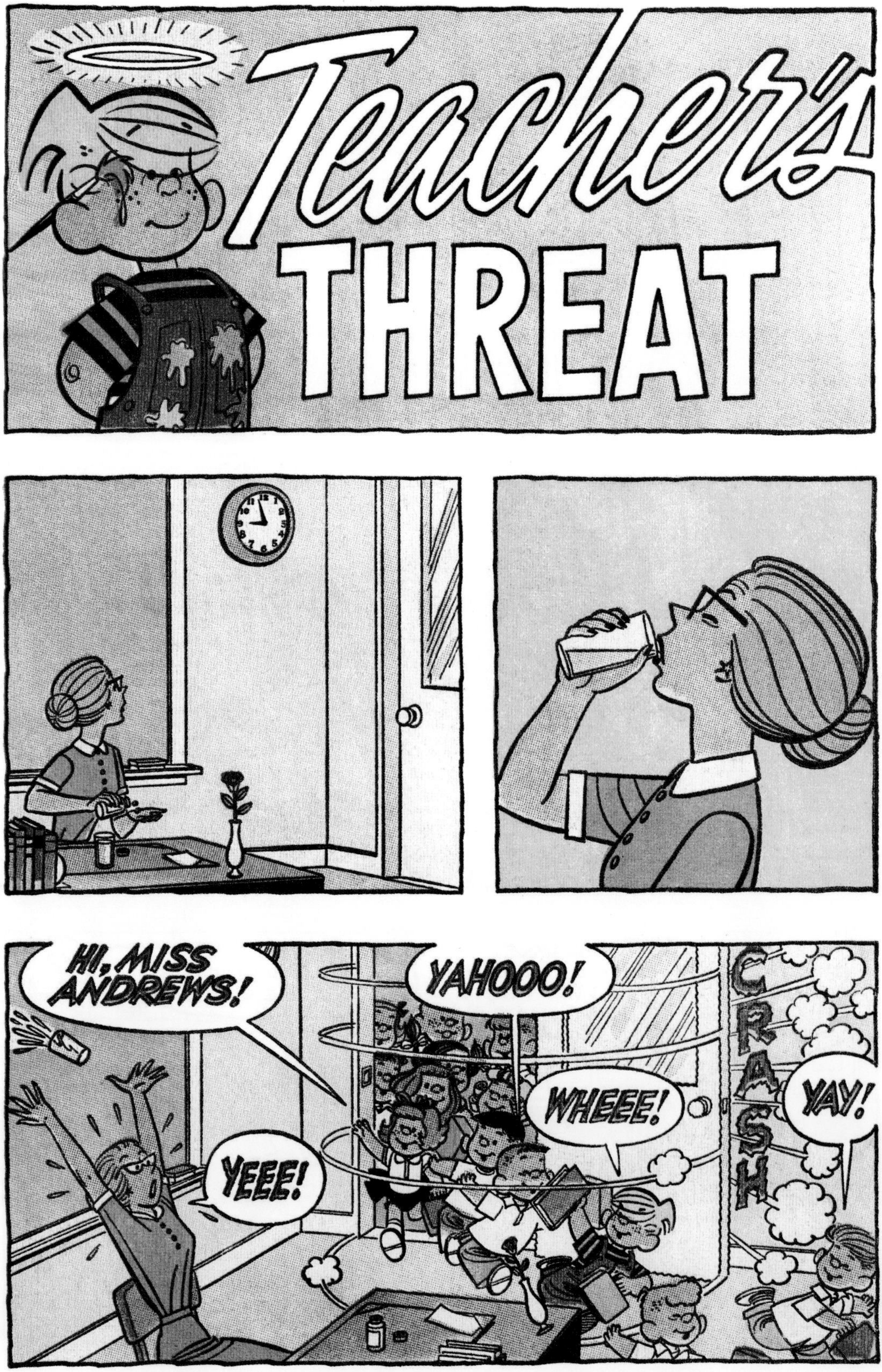
Teacher's
THREAT
HI, MISS ANDREWS!
YAHOOO!
WHEEE!
YAY!
YEEE!
CRASH

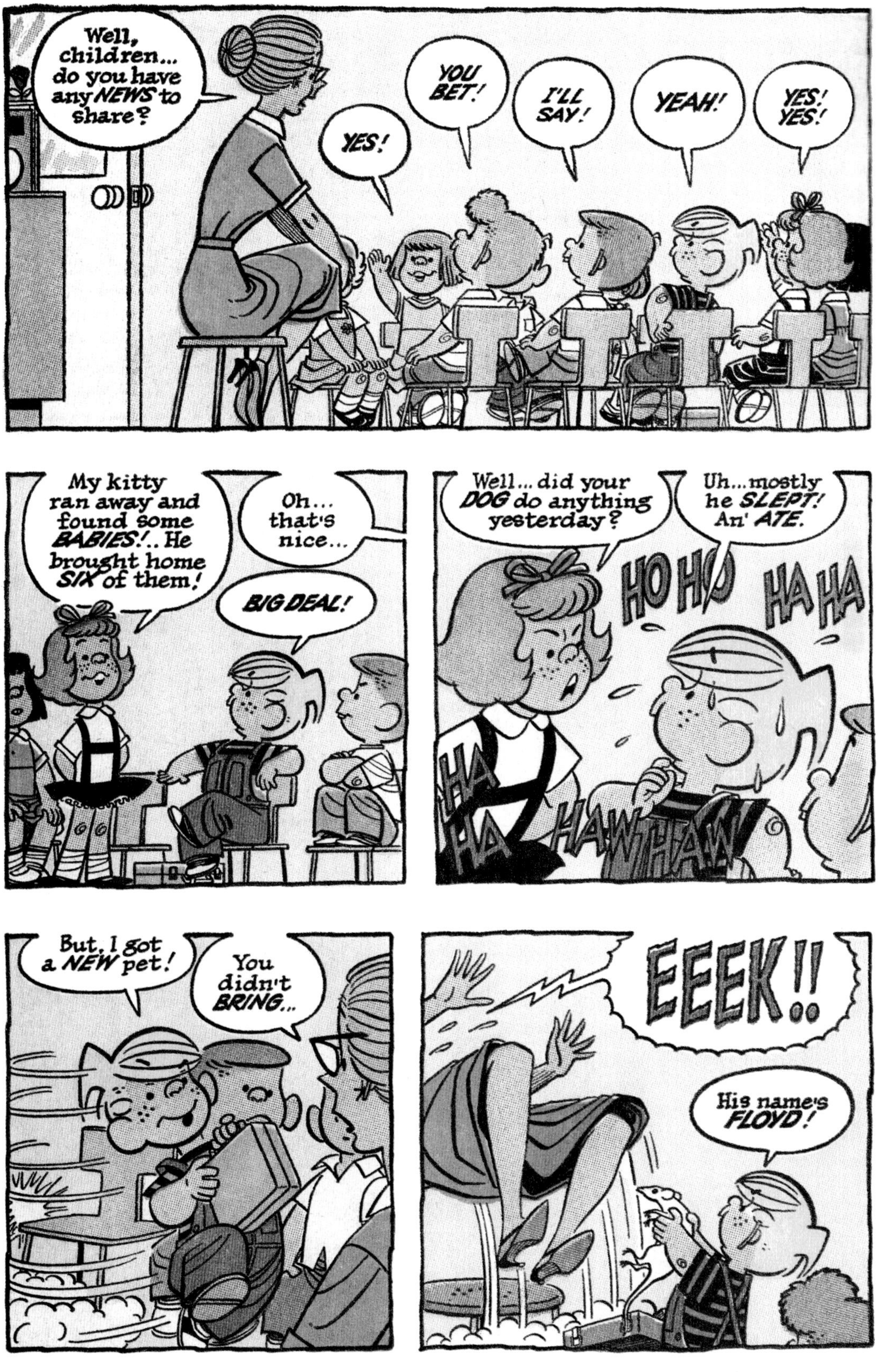
Well, children... do you have any NEWS to share?
YES!
YOU BET!
I'LL SAY!
YEAH!
YES! YES!
My kitty ran away and found some BABIES!.. He brought home SIX of them!
Oh... that's nice...
BIG DEAL!
Well... did your DOG do anything yesterday?
Uh...mostly he SLEPT! An' ATE.
HO HO
HA HA
HA HA
HAW HAW
But, I got a NEW pet!
You didn't BRING...
EEEK!!
His name's FLOYD!

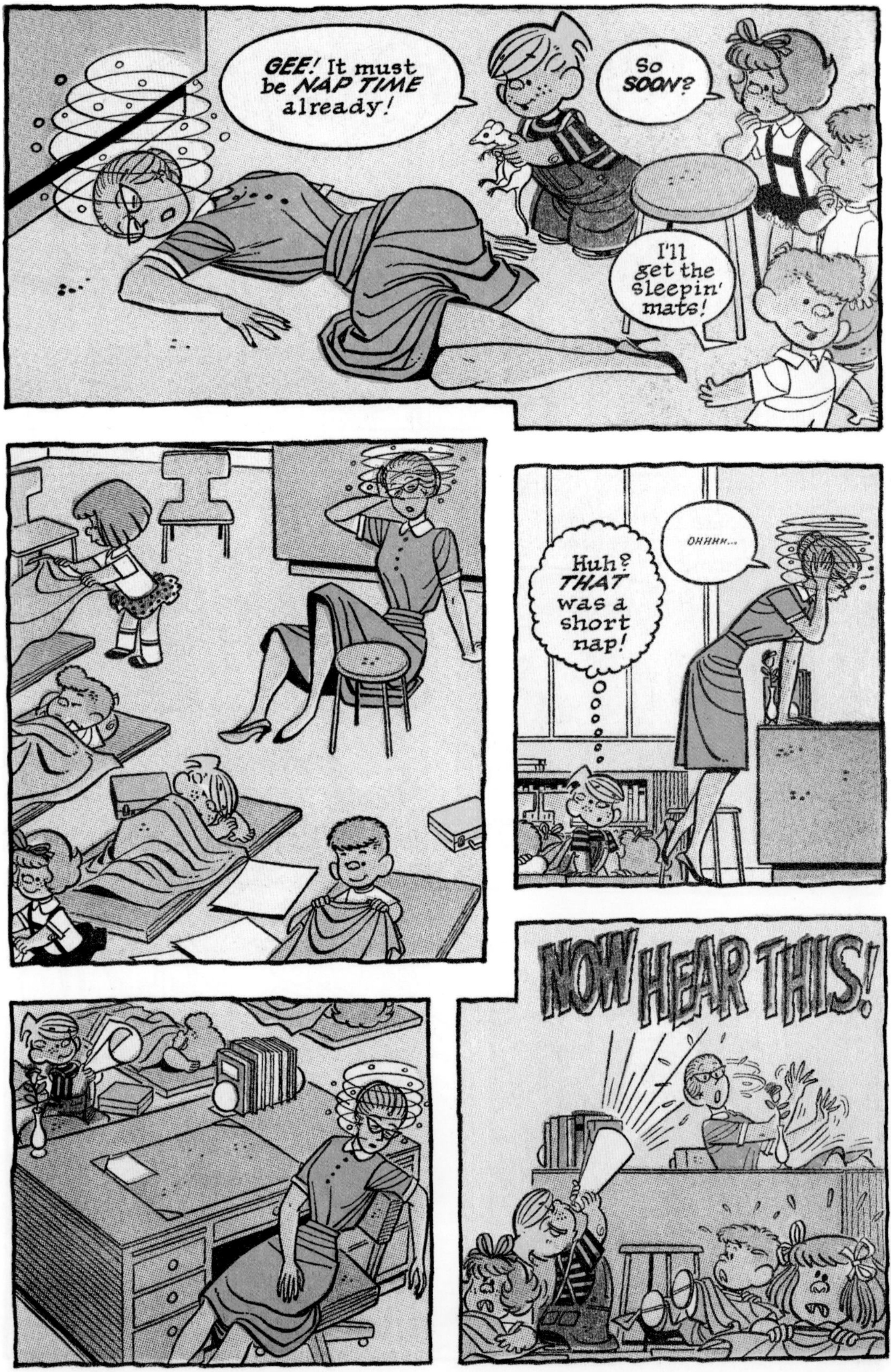

GEE! It must be NAP TIME already!
So SOON?
I'll get the sleepin' mats!
OHHHH...
Huh? THAT was a short nap!
NOW HEAR THIS!

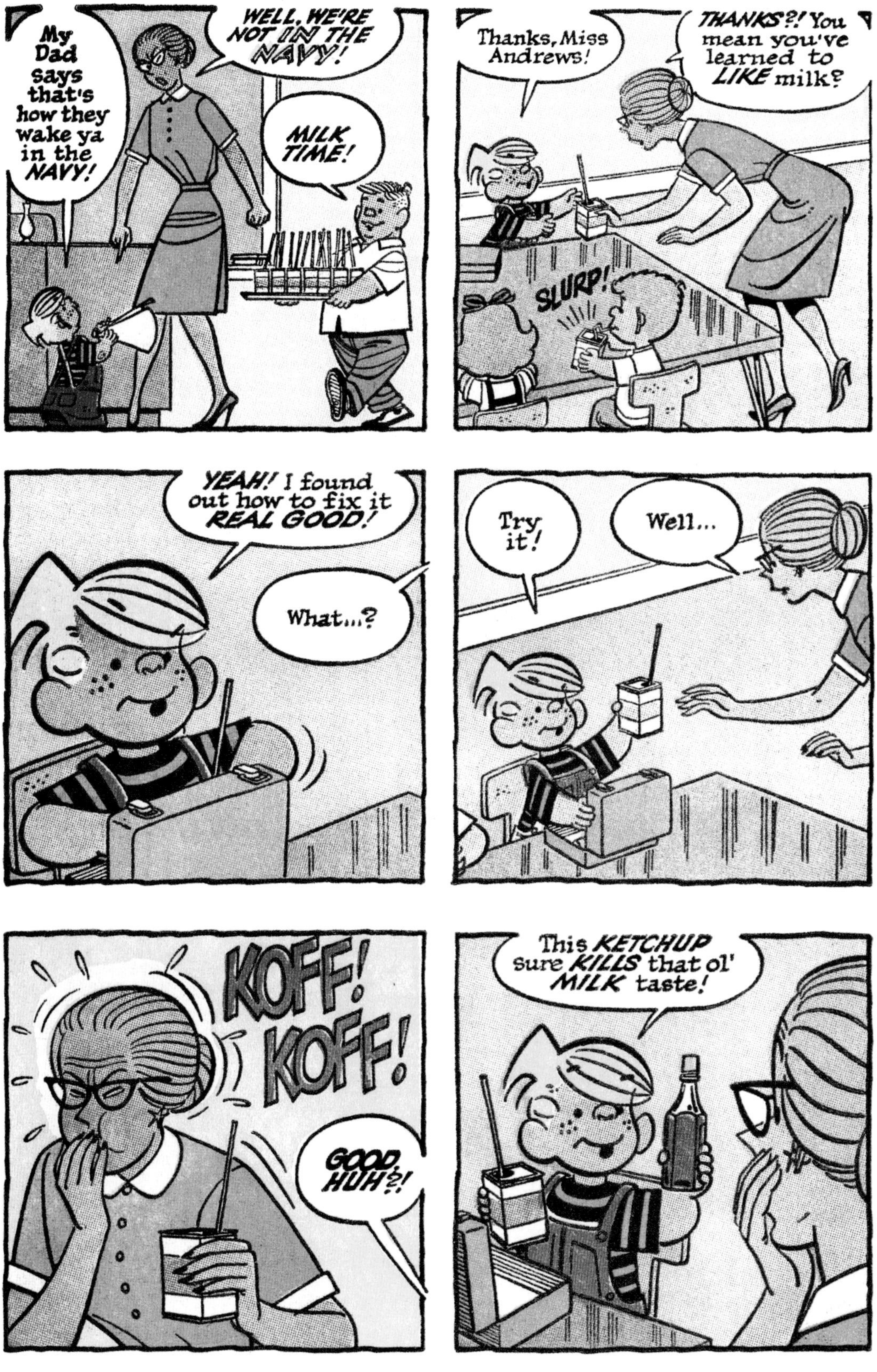
My Dad says that's how they wake ya in the NAVY!
WELL, WE'RE NOT IN THE NAVY!
MILK TIME!
Thanks, Miss Andrews!
THANKS?! You mean you've learned to LIKE milk?
SLURP!
YEAH! I found out how to fix it REAL GOOD!
What...?
Try it!
Well...
KOFF! KOFF!
GOOD, HUH?!
This KETCHUP sure KILLS that ol' MILK taste!

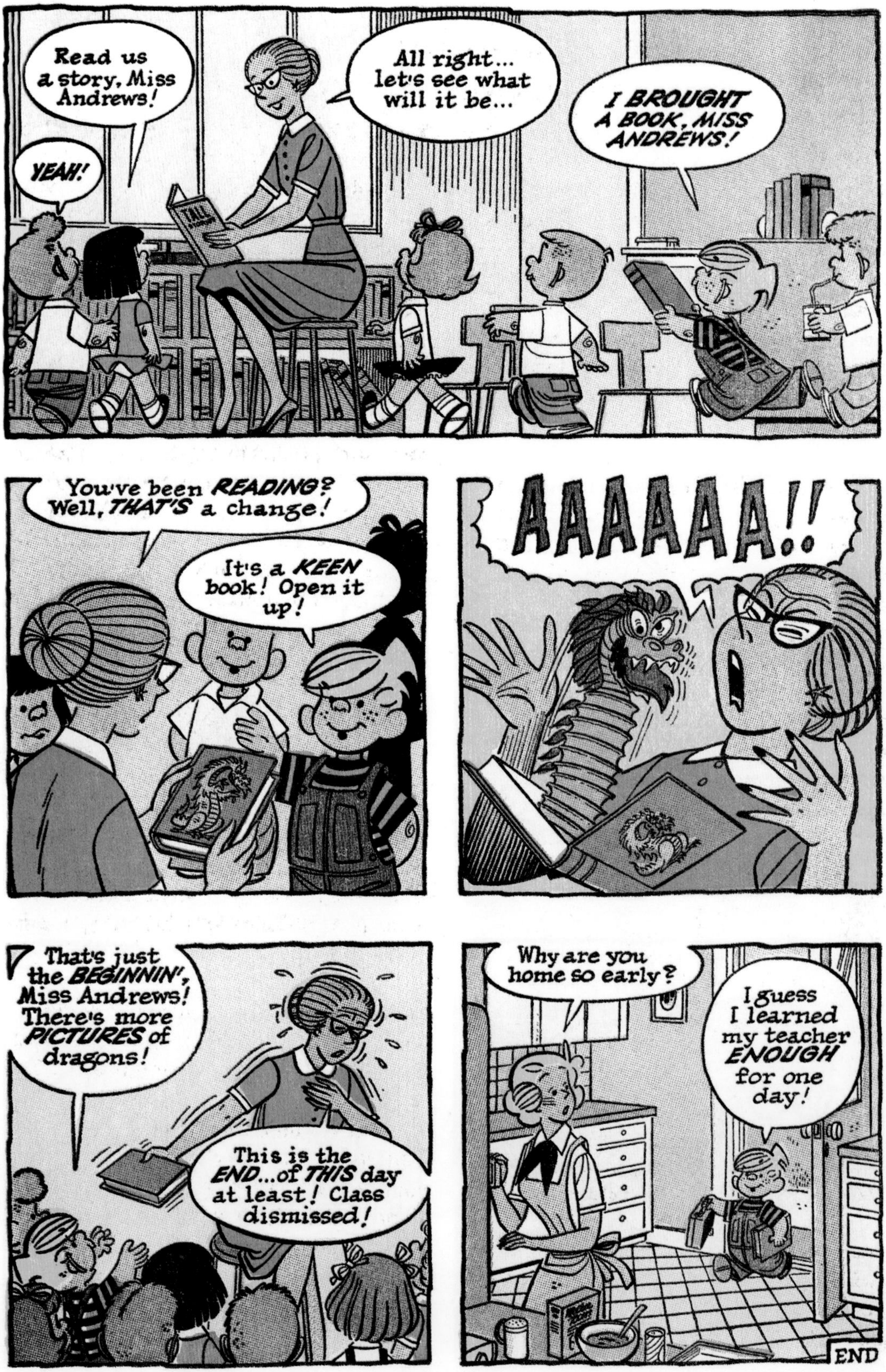
Read us a story, Miss Andrews!
YEAH!
All right... let's see what will it be...
I BROUGHT A BOOK, MISS ANDREWS!
You've been READING? Well, THAT'S a change!
It's a KEEN book! Open it up!
AAAAAA!!
That's just the BEGINNIN', Miss Andrews! There's more PICTURES of dragons!
This is the END...of THIS day at least! Class dismissed!
Why are you home so early?
I guess I learned my teacher ENOUGH for one day!
END

AFTERWORD

"Al Wiseman: making Ketcham great"
An Appreciation by Bill Wray

Legend has it that over the years, with the rise of the success of the *Dennis the Menace* comic strip, creator Hank Ketcham became what is politically referred to in any normal profession as a controlling person. Strong-willed, demanding the best work from himself and his assistants and figuratively married to his drawing table as much as his wife and family. A successful comic strip is enough to keep anyone busy, but a hugely successful one takes over your life.

It's no surprise that the early Dennis character was a holy terror in the days before the concept formed that humorous entertainment needed to be a good influence on children, brought about by arguably well-meaning crusaders. These unrestrained early *Dennis* panels are my favorites, where guns, animal abuse and cigarettes were still comedy staples to be mined for the funny cartoonist. Even MAD magazine had to work hard at being meaner then the real strips produced by Ketcham and Wiseman by making Dennis a psychotic arsonist.

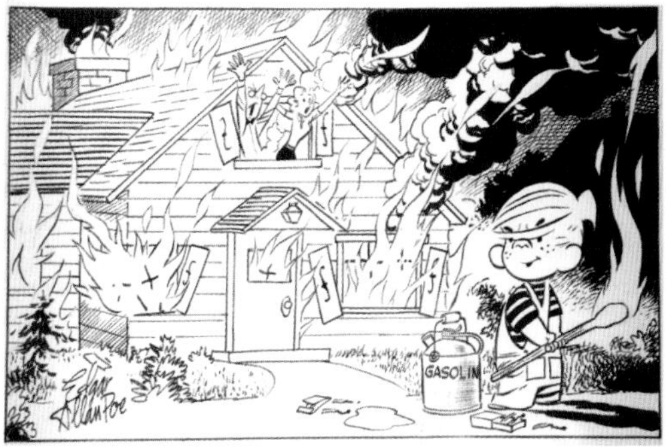
GASOLIN

Above: 1959 Mad Magazine Parody of Dennis The Menace by Wally Wood. ©E.C. Publications, Inc.

Many of the great cartoons and comics of that era had an unrestrained humor that often projected the cartoonists own personality and insecurities. Charlie Brown's personality made it clear that Schulz felt like a bullied looser in life. Dennis felt like a self-assured little bully. Did that mean Hank was a controlling bully? I never knew him so I cannot say, but I have heard stories he was pretty demanding on his assistants.

With the success of the daily strip, Hank needed to do a Sunday strip and furnish art for the burgeoning merchandising empire he was building. Ketcham was going to need some strong artists to help him out to maintain his high standards and to control all of the art needed. Al Wiseman was hired away from the advertising cartooning world and, in a move as important to Ketcham's legend as Jack Kirby was to Stan Lee's, a great team was formed.

Arguably, Al could even technically draw "better" than Hank early on, or at least more realistically. It's said that Al tried to work from life for his backgrounds and would use live figure reference too. I have to say I think these early DENNIS comics were some of the best humor comics ever done. The writing by Fred Toole being perfectly balanced between cartoony plots and situations that were possible in real life.

In regards to the evolution of style when drawing DENNIS, I think there was a subtle competition where Hank was influenced by Al, drawing the cartoony daily strip more realistically himself in answer to Al's more solid style in the comicbook. As Hank's work got less wacky cartoony, Al's DENNIS comicbooks (right down to the charmingly great word balloon lettering) kept raising the bar higher in that direction to the point where his backgrounds looked like stylized photos in comic drawing form. Personally, I love the earlier period where Al was forced to "dumb down" his style to match with Ketcham's Kurtzmanish cartooning. The synthesis of the two cartoonists was a new Dennis style that was the best of both worlds. This balance lasted for about 20 issues of the DENNIS comics, then slowly became more entirely Al's personal style.

This is pure conjecture, but one had to assume that this subtle form of the boss trying to catch up to the "assistant" could be a source of resentment for Al along with feeling the large parts of the characters development of Dennis and his cast were Al's (and Toole's) contributions, all credited to Ketcham down to Hank's signature, who (like a Walt Disney ghost artist), Al would flawlessly sign. When Al finally couldn't take working for Ketcham anymore and left, the comicbook and Hank's work soon slipped to a competent formula and later to a breezy under-structured work in the strip, epitomized by his other long-time assistant Owen Fitzgerald or just about any other cartoonist who worked for Ketcham.

Imagine Al having to watch Ketcham make millions while he got fairly paid (I assume),

Above: Bill Wray's tribute to Wally Wood's MAD MAGAZINE parody of Dennis the Menace.

but never wealthy. Doing all that work in another man's style he helped create had to be a soul killer. A boss who had respect enough to compete with you, but rarely gave you credit and you had to sign his name to "your" art.

This book is long overdo and will give Al some of the credit he deserved for doing so many great Al Wiseman DENNIS comics.

-Bill Wray

Above: A faded 1946 photo of pre-DENNIS THE MENACE friends Hank Ketcham, Al Wiseman, Alice Ketcham (then pregnant with Dennis) and Al's wife Vadis. Both families were living in Conneticut at the time, which allowed Hank and Al to venture into New York City and sell gag cartoons to Manhattan-based magazines. The Ketchams and the Wisemans later moved to California to further Hank's and Al's cartooning careers.

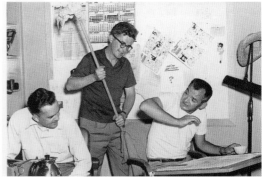

Above: "Toole, Ketcham, and Wiseman ham it up for another PR photo session." 1950s Ketcham studio photo printed in Hank's 1990 autobiography THE MECHANT OF DENNIS THE MENACE.

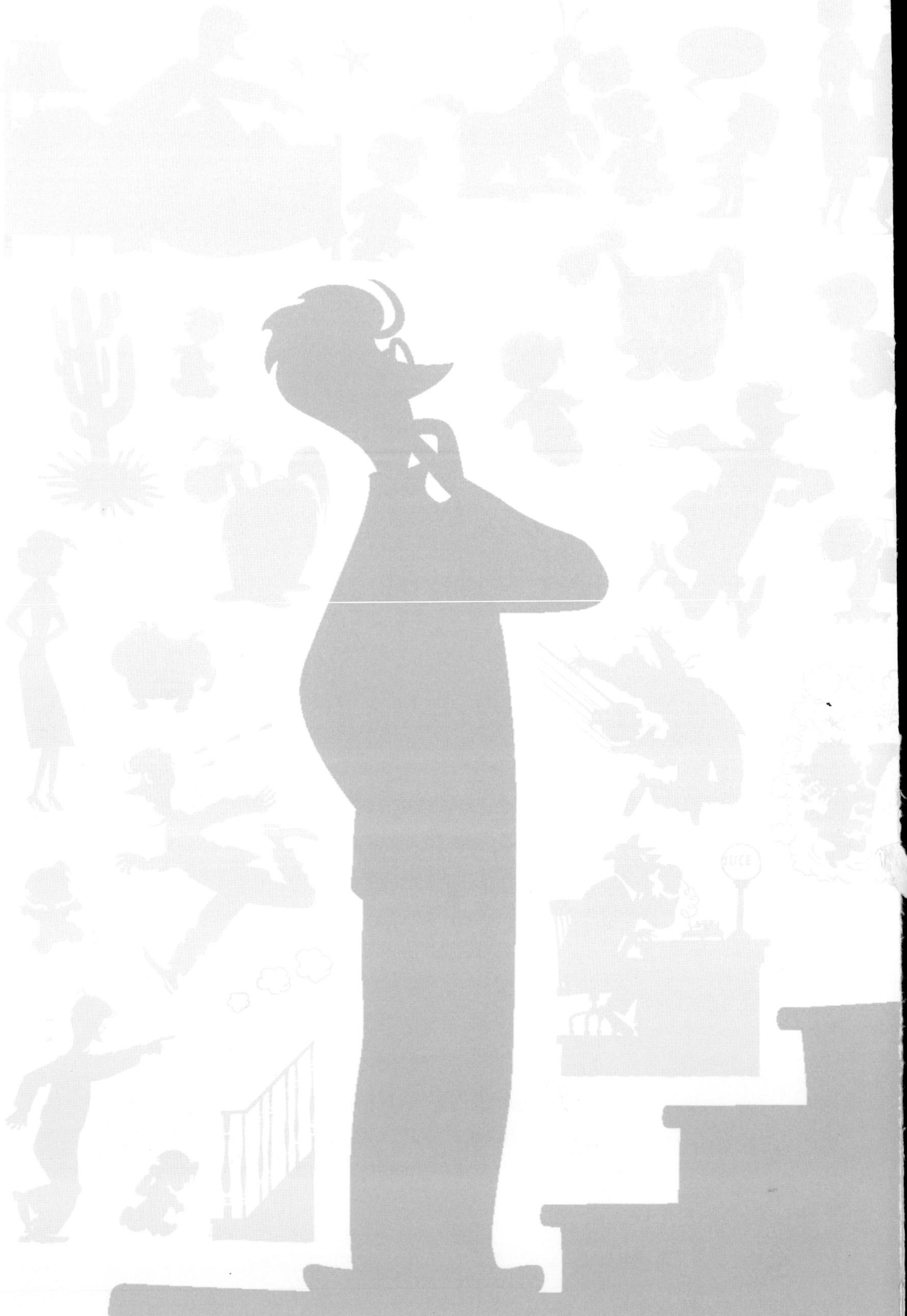

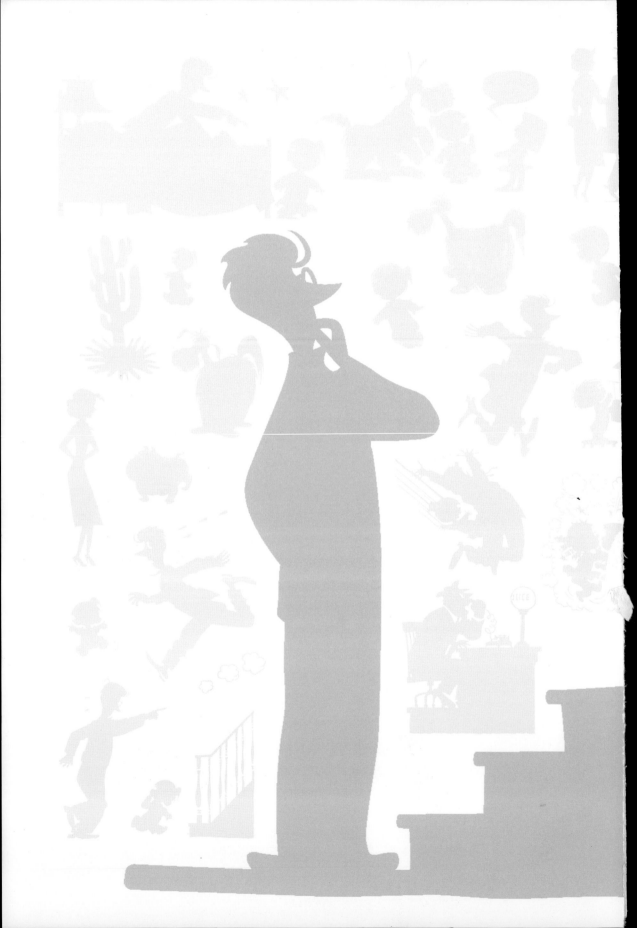